Publication No. F.50/7R

SERVICE MANUAL
FOR
MAC (RIGID FRAME) MODEL
(including MOV and RIGID FRAME MSS MODELS)

VELOCE LIMITED
(P.O. Box No. 275)
HALL GREEN WORKS
YORK ROAD, HALL GREEN
BIRMINGHAM 28

TELEphone: SPRingfield 1145/6/7.
TELEgrams: "Veloce, Birmingham."

October 1955

PAGE NUMBERS

The total number of pages in this manual is 196. However, the Service Manual and the Parts Manual have their own individual page numbers. The Parts Manual begins immediately after page 126 of the Service Manual.

INTRODUCTION

Welcome to the world of digital publishing ~ the book you now hold in your hand was printed using the latest state of the art digital technology. The advent of print-on-demand has forever changed the publishing process, never has information been so accessible and it is our hope that this book serves your informational needs for years to come. If this is your first exposure to digital publishing, we hope that you are pleased with the results. Many more titles of interest to the classic automobile and motorcycle enthusiast, collector and restorer are available via our website at www.VelocePress.com. We hope that you find this title as interesting as we do.

NOTE FROM THE PUBLISHER

The information presented is true and complete to the best of our knowledge. All recommendations are made without any guarantees on the part of the author or the publisher, who also disclaim all liability incurred with the use of this information.

TRADEMARKS

We recognize that some words, model names and designations, for example, mentioned herein are the property of the trademark holder. We use them for identification purposes only. This is not an official publication.

INFORMATION ON THE USE OF THIS PUBLICATION

This manual is an invaluable resource for those interested in performing their own maintenance. However, in today's information age we are constantly subject to changes in common practice, new technology, availability of improved materials and increased awareness of chemical toxicity. As such, it is advised that the user consult with an experienced professional prior to undertaking any procedure described herein. While every care has been taken to ensure correctness of information, it is obviously not possible to guarantee complete freedom from errors or omissions or to accept liability arising from such errors or omissions. Therefore, any individual that uses the information contained within, or elects to perform or participate in do-it-yourself repairs or modifications acknowledges that there is a risk factor involved and that the publisher or its associates cannot be held responsible for personal injury or property damage resulting from the use of the information or the outcome of such procedures.

WARNING!

One final word of advice, this publication is intended to be used as a reference guide, and when in doubt the reader should consult with a qualified technician.

www.VelocePress.com

FOREWORD

This Service Manual is issued as a guide to the complete maintenance and repair of the rigid frame MAC Model, and includes the information usually given in an Owners' Handbook.

Special tools and equipment essential for the completion of certain jobs are described and it is earnestly hoped that Agents and Repairers will equip their workshops with any of this equipment that they do not already have. By using the correct tools for the job in hand much time is saved and there is less risk of damage to components.

Private owners who like to do their own repairs are advised to entrust to the nearest Velocette Agent or Repairer any work for which they lack the correct tools, and not to undertake anything likely to prove beyond their capabilities to complete satisfactorily.

In order to cover the MOV and rigid frame MSS models which are no longer in production special references are made to these machines where necessary. Where the text does not apply in strict detail to some old machines still in commission the reader should ask for our advice upon any point that is not quite clear. Any such enquiries will be promptly and fully answered.

F50/7R/2M/10/55.

Oct., 1955.

SERVICE DEPARTMENT.
Veloce Limited,
P.O. Box 275, Hall Green,
Birmingham 28.

INDEX

A.
	Page
Ammeter	4, 103
Automatic Timing Unit (Illustration)	57

B.
Big-End Bearing	60
Brakes, Adjustment of	34
Brake (Rear). Removal of	83

C.
Carburetter, Adjustment of	90
Carburetter. Working of	80
Chains, Adjustment of	34
Charging System	97
Check Valve	40 & 41
Check Valve (Illustration)	40
Clutch Adjustment	69 & 70
Clutch. Working of	67
Clutch (Diagram)	69
Clutch-cable. Fitting new	72
Clutch. Dismantling and Re-assembling	72
Crankshaft Pinion. Removal of	59
Crankshaft Pinion. (Illustration)	59
Cut-out. Working of	102
Cylinder. Removal of	55
Cylinder. Inspection of	56
Cylinder head. Removal of	46
Cylinder head joint	50
Cylinder Oil Feed	13

D.
Dynamo	97
Dynamo belt, Adjustment of	42

E.
Electrical System	97
Engine. Dismantling and re-assembling	54 &c.
Engine. Decarbonising	45 &c.

F.
Flywheels. Lining up	61
Flywheels. Refitting to crankcase	63
Footstarter. Dismantling and assembling	81
Fork. Adjustment of	23
Fork. Dismantling	27 &c.

G.
Gearbox. Dismantling	74 &c.
Gearbox. (Illustration)	78

I.
Ignition-timing. Checking and Setting	66
Intermediate Timing-gear Adjustment	63

L.
	Page
Lighting System	97
Lubrication System. Engine	37
Lubrication System. (Illustration)	37

M.
Magneto, Removal of	57
Magneto, Dismantling, etc.	109-114
Mainbearings	59-61

O.
Oil Pump. Removal of	58
Oil Pump. (Illustration)	59
Oil Tank. Removal of	41

P.
Piston. Removing and Refitting	55
Piston Rings	56

R.
Rocker Box. Removal of	46

S.
Shock Absorber (Engine Shaft). Removal of	53
Sparking Plug	93
Suction Filter	39
Suction Filter (Illustrations)	39-40
Steering head. Dismantling and Assembling	26-30, &c.
Switch-Lighting and Charging	4

T.
Tappets, Adjustment	52
Tappet-Exhaust (Illustration)	53
Timing Gears. Removal of	57
Timing Unit. Removal of	56
Timing, Checking and Setting of	65

V.
Valves. Removing and refitting	48-49
Valve Timing. Checking and resetting	65
Valve Seats. Recutting	48
Voltage Control Unit. Working of	102

W.
Wheel (Rear). Removal of	84
Wheel (Front). Removal of	15-18

TAKING DELIVERY.

As new motor cycles are not usually delivered to the Agents' Showrooms by road it is necessary to make certain before starting up the engine, or taking the machine over, that the fuel and oil tanks are filled and that there is the correct amount of oil in the gearbox. Also as the accumulator may not have been filled with electrolite (or charged) these details should be checked over and attended to as required.

The oil tank should be filled to about 1-in. of the top (*i.e.*, about 2½-in. below the top face of the filler cap neck).

<u>Do not start the engine of a new machine or one on which the oil feed pipe has been disturbed before priming the oil pump. See page 13.</u>

The gearbox is filled with ordinary engine oil through the opening in the end cover from which the plug marked "Oil" has first been removed. Also remove the level plug from the end cover (see Figs. 15 and 36) and pour in oil until it is seen to drain out of the level plug hole with the machine held upright. Capacity about 2/3rd. pint.

When the flow ceases replace and tighten both plugs. Be very careful not to over-tighten the level plug or the cover may be damaged or the plug broken off.

Do not in any circumstances use anything except engine oil for gearbox lubrication. Grease or heavy gear oil may cause the bearings to run dry.

THE CONTROLS (HAND).

Clutch Lever. The larger of the two levers on the left side of the handlebar; when pulled right back until it touches the grip disengages (or frees) the clutch, disconnecting the drive between the engine and the gearbox.

It must not be operated to ease the engine by slipping the clutch instead of changing to a lower gear, or be held up in order to " free wheel." Keep the hand off it when driving normally and do not hold it up with the machine stationary, and the engine running. If stopped in a traffic block select neutral position for the gears and release the lever.

The control cable attached to this lever should move freely for at least $\frac{3}{16}$-in. before the pressure of the clutch springs is felt. This freedom will be likely to decrease with use, particularly on a new machine, or on one in which the clutch has been relined, particularly during the first few hundred miles' running.

Readjust *as soon as* this is noticed—as described on page 69.

Exhaust Valve Lifter. The smaller of the two levers on the left side of the handlebar. When pulled towards the rubber grip holds the exhaust valve off its seating and relieves compression in the cylinder. Its use (as described fully later) is for starting up. In certain conditions it may be used when the machine is being ridden slowly with low gear engaged down exceptionally steep or difficult gradients in order to prevent the rear wheel locking on a loose surface. It is not used in normal driving on main or secondary roads.

The Air Control Lever. A small lever clipped to the top of the handlebar on the right. Pull back towards the saddle to open the air valve. For details of use see pages 7 and 90.

The Front Brake Lever. Similar in appearance to the clutch lever, but fitted on the right-hand side. When pulled towards the grip applies the brake in the front hub.

The Horn Button. Fitted to the left of the brake lever. Press to sound the horn.

The Throttle. Operated by turning the right-hand grip. Movement back towards the rider opens the throttle valve in the carburetter and in most conditions increases the speed of the engine (and, when the gears and clutch are engaged) the speed of the machine. Keep closed when starting up. Movement of the twist grip when starting (familiarly known as " shaking the bottle ") will nearly always cause difficulty in starting.

Ignition Control.

Except on some early models there is no control for the ignition as on some other makes. The spark is advanced and retarded entirely automatically. On machines fitted with manual ignition control the lever is moved towards the rider to retard the spark.

FOOT CONTROLS.

Brake Pedal. Slightly ahead of the left footrest. Press down to apply the rear brake.

† **Gear Pedal.** Ahead of the right footrest. Press down to engage a higher gear. Raise to get a lower gear. After each movement the lever must be allowed to regain its central position. Keep the foot off the pedal when driving and do not kick or " stamp down " the pedal. See also " Driving Instructions."

Footstarter. Behind right footrest. Footpiece swivels out of the way when not in use.

FUEL TAPS.

Situated underneath the fuel tank (one at each side) at the rear end. Must be shut off when the machine is left standing for more than a minute or so. The plungers work horizontally. To open, the hexagon knob (marked PUSH-ON) is pushed towards the body of the tap (Fig. 3). To close, press the round milled knob (marked PUSH-OFF). Use only one tap and the other side will then act as a small reserve supply which is usually sufficient to run the machine about 3 to 4 miles. Either side may be used as the main supply. Always refuel as soon as possible after being forced to call upon the reserve and at once close the " reserve " tap again.

LIGHTING SWITCH.

Fitted to the top of the head lamp behind the Ammeter. The lever has four positions, indicated on the black moulding below the switch lever as follows :—OFF—CH.—The position for daylight running. H.—Headlamp bulb and tail lamp on. L.—Parking (dim) bulb on in headlamp and rear lamp on. The dipper switch for the headlamp bulb is at the right of the clutch lever.

INSTRUMENTS.

Ammeter. In the top of headlamp. Indicates the flow of current into or out of the battery. Discharge (outflow) indicated on left of dial. Charge (inflow) indicated on the right.

Speedometer. On the top of the fork, Registers total mileage run and indicates speed.

† *This control is arranged to work the reverse way to that described on all pre-war models and on some machines produced for the War Office.*

CONTROL LEVERS.

These are all capable of being set on the handlebar in the best positions to suit any individual rider. A few moments spent in arranging their positions as desired are very well spent.

The levers are also adjustable for freedom of working. The Air lever should be adjusted so that whilst free enough to operate without difficulty it does not shut back of its own accord when machine is in use. The centre screw or hexagon head controls this setting. Turn clockwise to tighten.

The adjustment of the other levers is by tightening or loosening the fulcrum pin after slacking off the small fulcrum pin lock nut. Set the fulcrum pins so that freedom without slackness is obtained, otherwise levers tend to vibrate and wear the fulcrum pins excessively.

Oil all pivots and working parts from time to time.

FIG. 1. ARRANGEMENT OF CONTROLS (Girder Fork).

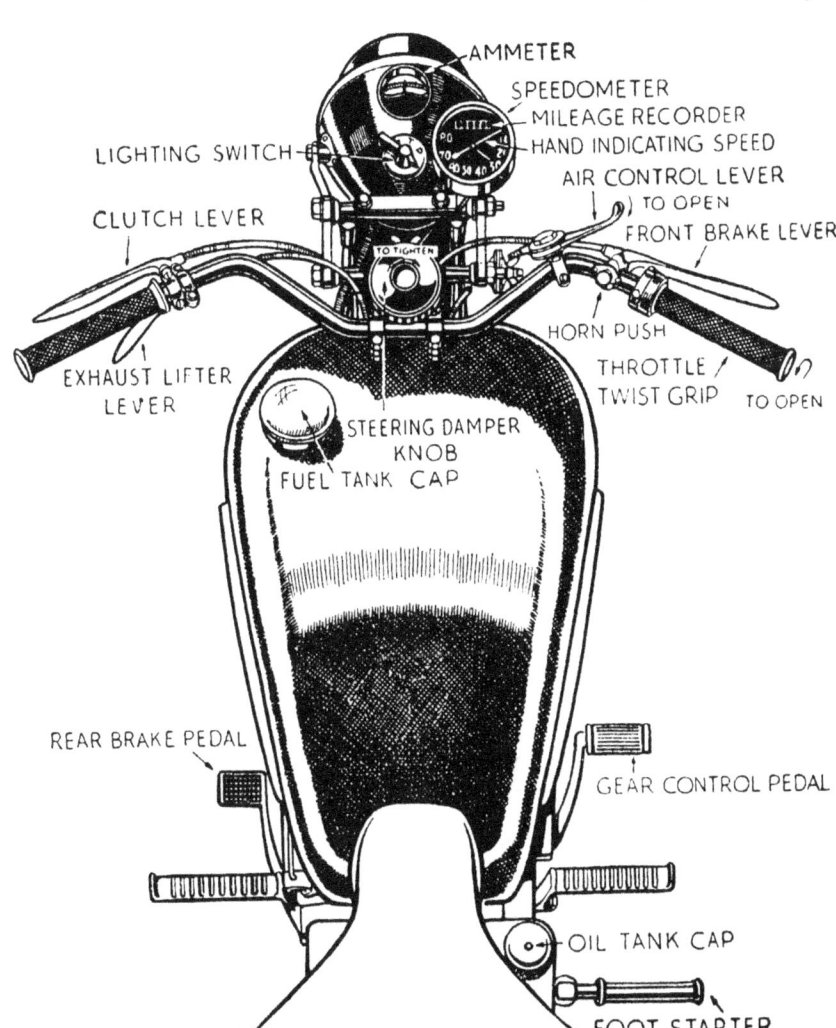

DRIVING INSTRUCTIONS.

Always, before taking out the machine, or even starting the engine, make sure that it is ready for the road. See that there is a sufficient amount of fuel for the journey, and that there is enough oil in the oil tank and gearbox.

FIG. 2. ARRANGEMENT OF CONTROLS (Telescopic Type Fork).

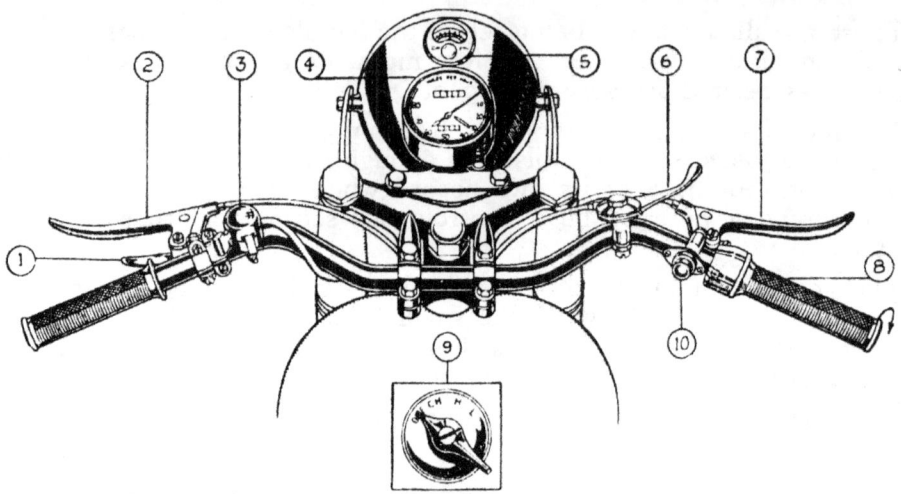

(1) Exhaust Lifter Lever.
(2) Clutch Lever.
(3) Diplite Switch.
(4) Speedometer.
(5) Ammeter.
(6) Air Lever.
(7) Front Brake Lever.
(8) Twist Grip Throttle Control.
(9) (Inset enlarged) View of Lighting Switch.
(10) Horn Push-button.

Driving Instructions (*continued*).

Before attempting to start up the engine make sure that the gears are in neutral ("free engine") position. This can be found out by raising the clutch lever and pressing down on the foot-starter. If a gear is engaged the foot-starter will not go down freely but will cause the machine to run forward. To select neutral move gear pedal as required. The number of movements needed will depend on which gear is engaged, as the following explanation will show.

The gear control pedal operates a spring loaded spindle (in the gearbox) carrying a pawl that moves the cam plate one position at a time, and after each movement either up or down returns to its central position. If 1st(low) gear is in engagement and the pedal is pressed down as far as it will go, 2nd gear will be selected. A second pressure downwards on the pedal will give 3rd gear, and a third movement down will give 4th (top) gear. From 4th gear position three successive lifts of the pedal (moving it to its limit and releasing it each time) will select 1st speed. The neutral position is between 1st and 2nd gears. From 1st speed a half movement of the pedal downwards will be needed or from 2nd gear a **half** movement upwards.†

It must be remembered that in trying to select the gears one after another with the engine and machine at rest it is exceedingly unlikely that all four speeds will engage straight away without moving the gears by turning the engine or the rear wheel because, as often happens, the driving dogs which have to interlock will probably be opposite one another. In such a position forcing the lever will only cause damage. A slight movement of the machine either backwards or forwards will, however, alter the position of the dogs and allow engagement to take place.

A rider will very soon become accustomed to detecting whether engagement has taken place as a distinct "click" will be heard (just before the lever reaches the end of its travel) as the spring loaded indexing pawl snaps into the gear location notch in the edge of the cam plate. A novice is advised to select neutral from 1st gear position rather than from 2nd gear.

NOTE SPECIALLY. The pedal must be moved to the full extent of its travel when selecting a gear either up or down—**half** a movement only for neutral.

† *See footnote on page 4.*

The pedal must not be stamped upon or forced. At the same time hesitant or half-hearted movement may not give engagement.

Therefore always move the pedal firmly and decisively till it stops. Keep the foot away from the pedal except when changing gear. Unless the lever can return freely the next gear will not engage.

To Start the Engine. First open one of the fuel taps (preferably the right-hand one) by pressing in the hexagon knob. Lean the machine sharply over to the right side for about 20 seconds to flood the carburetter or depress the "Tickler." The "Tickler" is a small spring loaded button on the lid of the float chamber (Fig. 45). After a few seconds, whichever method is used fuel will be seen to seep out through a small hole in the side of the mixing chamber body. As soon as this occurs release the "tickler" or return the machine to the vertical. Do not flood excessively when cold. **Do not flood at all when the engine is hot.**

Turn the small throttle stop screw clockwise till the lug on the screw touches the side of the mixing chamber body (Fig. 45). This screw is fitted obliquely upwards in the side of the mixing chamber and has a small crossbar in the head to provide a convenient grip for the fingers. It holds the throttle valve slightly open in the best position for starting. Shut off the twist grip fully and if engine is cold close the air control lever.* Now raise the exhaust valve by operating the small control lever on the handlebar. While holding this lever up press the footpiece of the starter slowly down. After a short distance the ratchet will be felt to engage the ratchet gear in the gear box when pressure should be continued to rotate the engine. When fully depressed release the footpiece, which will be returned to the top by its return spring. Repeat this operation a few times to fill the cylinder with combustible mixture, and to free the engine.

When this has been done release the exhaust lifter lever and press the footstarter down slowly as before. Resistance will now be encountered due to the compression of gas in the cylinder. When this is felt, raise the exhaust lifter lever and press the footpiece down slowly to the bottom. Allow the footpiece to return to the top once more, move down to engage the ratchets and give it a sharp downward thrust without raising the exhaust lifter lever. This should rotate the engine fast enough for it to start. If it does not do so at the first attempt—Try again.

Notes on using the Footstarter. It is very important not to kick sharply before the ratchet has engaged properly. It will be noticed that as the footpiece moves down, the ratchet is allowed to slide into the ratchet housing on the end cover due to the lug running off the disengaging cam formed at the end of the housing. It must be allowed to slide in properly, otherwise the ratchet will not engage properly, and damage will be caused to the teeth on the ratchet and ratchet gear. Do not hurry the operation— by being careful and deliberate time will be saved in the long run. Always release the footpiece as soon as the engine starts.

When the engine is running open the air control lever gradually. After a few moments the engine will accept the full air supply. Should the air not be opened soon enough the engine will fire irregularly, usually missing every other beat (eight stroking) and black smoke will issue from the silencer. Open the air fully immediately either of these symptoms is noticed.

When the engine is running regularly with full air supply turn the throttle stop screw as far as it will go anti-clockwise (stop lug to the rear) to the correct setting for slow running and for starting when the engine is hot. Generally speaking, the "fast" position of the stop screw (that is with the lug forward) is only necessary for starting a cold engine.

* *Set ignition lever about one-third advanced if old machine with manual control.*

Notes on Obstinacy in Starting. During cold and damp weather the cause may be a damp or dirty high tension cable from the magneto to the sparking plug or the outside insulation of the plug may be coated with mud. This provides a path for the high tension current which " leaks " to " earth," diminishing the intensity of the spark at the plug points. Clean the affected parts with dry rag.

Over-rich Mixture caused by excessive flooding of the carburetter or of flooding when hot. Rectify by opening throttle and air controls fully and rotate engine sharply several times with the footstarter to clear the over-rich mixture. Turn off the fuel. Close throttle, leave air control full open and try again. If still unsuccessful take out sparking plug and clean internal insulation and firing points; they will probably be " wet " with excess unvapourized fuel. Before replacing the sparking plug check the cap between the firing points (this should be .018" to .023") and reset if needed. Also rotate engine several times to clear out the rich mixture from the combustion chamber.

Provided the trouble is not of a more serious nature, necessitating workshop attention, the engine should start after this. Turn on the fuel after the engine starts.

When the Engine is Cold always allow a few minutes to elapse after starting for the oil to circulate before running it up to high speed. A fairly fast tick-over is about right. The circulation of the oil can be checked by taking off the cap from the oil tank, when oil will be observed running back into the tank from the pipe inside the neck of the tank. See also page 13.

Starting Away. Having got the engine running, **push up the prop stand** on the left side of the machine. If folds backwards and upwards below the frame tube. This is very important. If left down it can be very dangerous.

Free the clutch by gripping the clutch lever and pulling it back into contact with the handlebar grip. Raise the gear pedal to engage first speed.† The dogs should be felt or heard to engage. Release the pedal. If the dogs do not engage do not force the pedal but move the machine slightly backwards or forwards to alter the position of the dogs and try again. Alternatively, momentarily release the clutch lever with the gears in neutral and then make another attempt. **Never in any circumstances** move the gear pedal unless the clutch is freed first if the engine is running. Note specially that no amount of force will engage the dogs unless they are in such a position that they can interlock or mesh with one another. Having engaged first speed (low gear) by the upward movement of the control pedal release the clutch lever very gradually and at the same time open the throttle slightly when the drive will gradually be taken up and the machine will begin to move forward. When this occurs do not be in a hurry to release the clutch lever suddenly or the engine may stall. Continue to let it out slowly and at the same time increase the amount of throttle opening. Conversely, do not " race " the engine up to high speed without releasing the clutch lever. It cannot drive the machine at all until the clutch commences to grip. A good driver can always be picked out by his clutch work as he always gets away with the minimum amount of fuss and noise and does not race the engine excessively.

When well under way and at about 15 m.p.h. on the level free the clutch again and slightly close the throttle, pause about a second and then press down the gear pedal firmly until it stops, release the clutch again as this is done and open the throttle gradually. Take the foot off the gear pedal allowing it to return to mid position. Change up to third speed at about 25 m.p.h. by repeating the process, and when a speed of 35 m.p.h. is reached, change into top.

† *See footnote page 4.*

To change to a lower gear the procedure is similar except that the throttle should be left open and the pedal moved upwards **as far as it will go.** Three upward movements in succession from top will bring the gears back to first speed.

Bear in mind that a little practice is required in order to become proficient. Remember that the throttle should be closed when changing to a higher gear and the change made slowly, whilst a change to a lower gear should be made quickly with the throttle open. Never look down when changing gear. Keep looking at the road ahead. Never change gear with the heel.

The road speeds quoted are for a fully run in engine and are right for all general riding. Special conditions, as when starting on a gradient, may make it necessary to reach a higher road speed before changing up as of necessity some speed is lost as a change is made and if made too early the machine may be running too slowly for the engine to pull away properly by the time the higher gear is engaged.

To stop, close the throttle, and as the machine slows to about 15 m.p.h. free the clutch. Raise the gear pedal fully and release it twice in succession, and then raise it half way slowly until the pawl is felt to click into the neutral notch. Apply the brakes and release the clutch lever gradually. Never release it suddenly before it is certain that neutral has been found. When the machine is stationary close the fuel tap if the machine is not to be driven away at once, and raise the exhaust lifter lever to stop the engine.

Running in a New Engine. A new machine requires to be driven with restraint until all working parts become thoroughly free or " bedded down " and will not give of its best until this has occurred and it is, as it is termed, " run in." It is a mistake to drive a new machine hard and give it too much " collar work " to do. Hard pulling (" slogging ") on a large throttle opening uphill must be avoided, and liberal use should be made of the gearbox so as to ease the load on the engine and allow it to run as lightly loaded as possible. A high road speed is not injurious and can in fact be beneficial if the speed is reached without opening the throttle wide and as this condition will often arise going down hill, we do not necessarily advise that the speed in top gear should be limited to any set speed. It has been found by experience that to run in a new engine at a fixed and regular speed is sometimes very unsatisfactory. Vary the speed as much as possible, but **always run the engine lightly loaded,** indulging in short, sharp bursts of speed occasionally. The speed and duration of these may be increased as the mileage reaches the 500 figure and after about 1,000 miles the engine should be properly run in.

GENERAL HINTS ON DRIVING.

Do not forget to raise the prop stand before driving away, and always use this stand whenever possible in preference to leaning the machine against walls or kerbstones.

See that the stand works freely. Lubricate the pivot if the stand is stiff.

Do not forget to open the air lever fully when running.

Do not race the engine unnecessarily or let the clutch in suddenly. This causes increased wear on the tyres, chains and transmission generally. Try to obtain a neat and smooth get-way.

Keep the feet clear of the brake and gear pedals when not actually braking or changing gear, and keep the hand off the clutch lever when it is not in use.

Drive as much as possible on the throttle, making the minimum use of the brakes.

Use both brakes, not the rear only.

Do all hard braking when the machine is running straight and avoid braking when cornering.

Icy roads are often less slippery at the edges where grit collects. Try to pick a path which is rough. Shiny surfaces should be avoided.

Do not let the engine slog on a high gear. Change to a lower ratio in good time.

Do not kick or " stamp down " the gear pedal. Force is unnecessary.

Do not attempt to start with the throttle too far open, and keep the hand off the twist grip when starting.

Operate the gear pedal with the front of the foot—never with the heel.

Do not neglect essential adjustments, particularly the clutch adjustment.

Feel the footstarter ratchet engage before putting the full weight on the footpiece.

Do not in any circumstances tamper with the silencer. More noise may make the machine seem faster, but experience has shewn that alterations usually reduce the performance.

Keep the elbows close to the body when riding.

Always close fuel taps when leaving the machine for any length of time.

Tighten any loose nuts or bolts as soon as they are seen to need attention.

MAINTENANCE.
(Based on an assumed weekly mileage of 500.)

Control Cables. — Lubricate all exposed ends of cables from oil can. Check all controls for freedom and see that nipples work freely in control levers. Remove any tight nipples from levers, ease, lubricate and refit.

Any cables showing signs of sticking within the outer casing must be detached from the levers and oil worked down into outer casing by feeding in oil from can and working casing up and down on inner cable whilst cable is held as upright as possible.

Control Levers. — Lubricate all moving parts of levers.

Brake Controls. — Lubricate felt washers behind front and rear cam levers, trunnions at front and rear ends of rear brake rod, felts and exposed portion of brake cable on front brake cam lever.

Stands. — Lubricate pivots of prop stand and rear stand.

Footrests. — Lubricate pillion footrest pivots.

Girder Fork Spindles.* — Grease five nipples.

Footstarter. — Lubricate footpiece pivot.

* Only on early models.

PERIODIC MAINTENANCE :—

Oil Tank. — Drain, clean feed filter, and re-fill to within 1-in. from top of tank (*i.e.*, 2½-ins. from top face of Filler neck) after every 2,000 miles running. On new or reconditioned engines this must be done after the first 500 miles and at 2,000 miles. At the same time clean suction filter plug. Remove crankcase drain plug, drain, and re-fit. Renew oil filter element at 10,000 miles.

Gearbox. — Every 5,000 miles drain completely. Remove level plug, re-fill with oil. When surplus oil is drained out re-fit level plug. On new or reconditioned gearboxes this must be done after the first 1,000 miles.

Clutch.	Check adjustment for free movement.
Wheel Bearings.	These are packed with high melting-point grease during manufacture. Dismantle bearings and re-pack with grease every 20,000 miles.
Speedometer Reduction Gearbox.	Grease every 1,000 miles. (Do not over-lubricate as excess grease may get on to the brake linings and reduce the efficiency of the brake if front wheel drive).
Gear Lever Pivot.	Grease every 1,000 miles. (MOV & MAC Models only.)
Brake Cam Bearing, Rear.	Grease every 1,000 miles. (Do not over-lubricate as excess grease may get on the brake linings and reduce the efficiency of the brake).
Chains.	Every 2,000 miles test tension of front and rear driving chains, re-adjust if required.

PERIODICAL ATTENTION. LUBRICATION.

The importance of efficient lubrication cannot be over-estimated. The use of cheap oils is false economy, and we only recommend the employment of those oils and greases which we have found from our own experience to be the most suitable for the machine.

<u>Do not use additives in the oil or fuel</u>—they are unnecessary.

It is specially recommended that towards the end of September in Great Britain the oil tank should be drained and should be refilled with one of the grades recommended for Winter use, the use of such a grade being continued throughout the Winter months. At the beginning of May the tank should again be drained out and one of the grades recommended for Summer lubrication employed.

The oil should not at any time be kept in use for longer than 2,000 miles running. All old oil should be discarded after this distance has been run and the tank refilled with fresh oil. Instructions for changing the oil and cleaning the filters, etc., appear on other pages.

The identifying letters used by most oil firms denoting the different grades under which their oils are supplied are often imitated, and it is essential when ordering oil to specify the Brand as well as the Grade. As an additional precaution see that the oil is taken from branded cabinets or from sealed packages. See also that if oil is bought loose it is brought in a clean container.

The following high-grade lubricants are recommended :—

ENGINE LUBRICATION — SUMMER

Ambient Temperatures above 60°F. (Viscosity S.A.E.50).

Shell "X100" S.A.E.50
Essolube "50"
B.P. Energol S.A.E.50
Mobiloil B.B.

Castrol XXL
Duckham's NOL Fifty

ENGINE LUBRICATION—WINTER

Ambient Temperatures below 60°F. (Viscosity S.A.E. 30.)

Duckham's NOL Thirty
Castrol XL
Mobiloil A
B.P. Energol S.A.E.30.
Essolube " 30 "
Shell " X100 " S.A.E.30.

GEARBOX LUBRICATION—SUMMER AND WINTER.

(Viscosity S.A.E.50).

Use Summer Grade Oil.

HUB LUBRICATION.

B.P. Energrease C3
Mobil Hub Grease
Castrolease Heavy
Shell Retinax "A"
Esso Grease.
Duckham's H.B.B. Grease

GREASE NIPPLES.

Shell Retinax "A"
Esso Grease
Duckham's H.P.G. Grease
B.P. Energrease C3
Mobilgrease No. 2
Castrolease Medium

REAR CHAIN LUBRICATION.

Duckham's Laminoid
Castrolease G
Mobilgrease No. 2
B.P. Energrease C3G
Esso Grease
Shell Retinax "A"

TELESCOPIC FORKS—ALL SEASONS (Viscosity S.A.E.20).

Duckham's NOL Twenty
Mobiloil Arctic
Essolube 20
Castrolite
B.P. Energol S.A.E.20
Shell X100 20/20W

IN THE OIL CAN—ALL SEASONS (Viscosity SAE.10).

Wakefield's Oilit
Mobil Handy Oil
Duckham's NOL Ten
B.P. Energol 10
Shell Donax A1
Essolube " 10 "

ENGINE LUBRICATION SYSTEM.

Engine Oil must be changed at intervals of 2,000 miles running. (After first 500 miles on new or overhauled engine.) To change proceed as follows :—

Drain oil tank by removing drain plug, below tank. Note that on MAC machines fitted with the fabric oil filter about half a pint of oil will be left in the filter chamber in the tank. Drain this oil off as described on page 43 and fill filter chamber with clean oil. Remove and clean suction filter plug (see later).

Loosen clip on top end of rubber hose between return union on crankcase and pipe on tank. Pull hose away from tank. Refill tank with fresh oil to within 1-in. from top of tank (i.e., 2½-in. from top face of filler neck). Start engine—catch dirty oil (which will be returned up return pipe hose) in small tin. When return begins to run clean stop engine and refit hose. Tighten hose clip.

Never carry out the job in dusty surroundings. Always see that oil is poured into tank from clean measures and containers.

(See also page 13).

PRIMING THE OIL PUMP.

Owing to the use of a spring-loaded ball valve between the oil tank and pump on all MAC models fitted with the fabric oil filter (that is all machines from Engine No. MAC15523 onwards), the pump will not feed oil into the engine if the main oil feed pipe has been disturbed and emptied of oil.

Before starting a new or overhauled engine, or if the oil pipe has been disturbed always fill the pipe with oil to prime the pump. This will be easier if the banjo union hollow bolt at the crankcase end of the pipe is first loosened to relieve air locks as the oil is injected at the top from a force feed oil can or a syringe. Tighten the bolt when the pipe is full and also tighten the union nut at the top.

Check the oil supply as described in the next section.

CHECKING THE OIL FEED.

Loosen the union nut securing the rocker oil feed pipe to the top of the timing cover.

Start the engine and run it slowly. After a few moments the oil should be forced out at the loose union in a steady stream showing that the pump is working. If the flow remains steady for not less than one full minute the union nut may be tightened and the machine put into commission.

If there is no flow stop the engine at once and reprime the oil pipe. The oil pump will not operate if there is any air leakage into the feed line between the ball valve and the pump. After long service the hose may be found to have swelled internally and the hose should therefore be checked for condition and renewed if it is in doubtful condition.

THE SUCTION FILTER.†

Remove filter plug every 2,000 miles by unscrewing from rear bottom corner of crankcase, using tubular sparking plug spanner. Clean plug in petrol. See that red fibre washer is in order. Refit plug and tighten up fully. (See Fig. 18.)

THE CYLINDER OIL FEED.†
(Not fitted after Engine No. MAC 15522.)

Every 2,000 miles remove bolt below cylinder base joint at rear on left side. Bolt is marked "jet" on head. Clean in petrol. See that small cross hole in the centre of bolt is clear. See that fibre washer below head is in order. Replace. Exercise great care in tightening so that bolt is not sheared off. (See Fig. 19.)

PERIODICAL ATTENTION. LUBRICATION (GEARBOX).

Every 2,000 miles top up to correct level.

The gearbox is lubricated with oil of the same grade as that which is used for Summer lubrication of engine.

To fill, remove the filler and level plugs, see Fig. 36. Pour in a small quantity of oil through the filler plug hole until it commences to run out of the level plug hole with the machine standing upright.

Allow the oil to run until the flow ceases and refit both plugs. If oil will run out of the level plug hole with the machine standing upright it is an indication that there is too much oil in the gearbox.

Too high a level will not prove detrimental, as the excess oil will only be likely to run into the primary chain cover, where it can of course do no harm. It cannot cause the clutch to slip if the clutch is adjusted correctly. After a new machine has covered 500 miles it is desirable to drain the gearbox. The drain plug is at the rear of the housing at the bottom. To remove any sediment that may have collected in the bottom of the gearbox it may be flushed out with clean petrol. This must all be allowed to drain away before refilling with oil.

† *These are not incorporated on early pre-war models*

Screw in the drain plug after the gearbox has been drained and re-fill with oil as described above.

In normal service the gearbox oil should be changed about every 5,000 miles. No other attention is necessary.

Heavy gear oil or grease will not find its way to the various bearings in a satisfactory manner, and may involve some part running dry with the consequent risk of seizure. For this reason therefore, such lubricants must not be used.

LUBRICATION OF GIRDER FORK SPINDLES, BRAKE CAMS, NIPPLES AND CYCLE PARTS, etc.

When using the grease gun bear in mind that it is better to lubricate a little and often rather than to neglect this attention for a considerable time and then over-lubricate. In very wet or dirty conditions, lubrication of the various points should be carried out more liberally. Should it be found that for some reason or another grease will not enter a bearing but escapes between the grease gun nozzle and the nipple, this can usually be prevented by inserting a piece of clean rag between the nipple and the grease gun nozzle. The rag forms an effective seal and will usually prevent all leakage but will allow grease to pass freely into the nipple. Do not use heavier grades of grease than are specified as there is a danger that the various bearings and bushes may not receive a proper supply due to the grease choking the passages, etc. When greasing girder fork spindles it is advantageous to support the machine with the front wheel off the ground to get the grease between surfaces normally in hard contact.

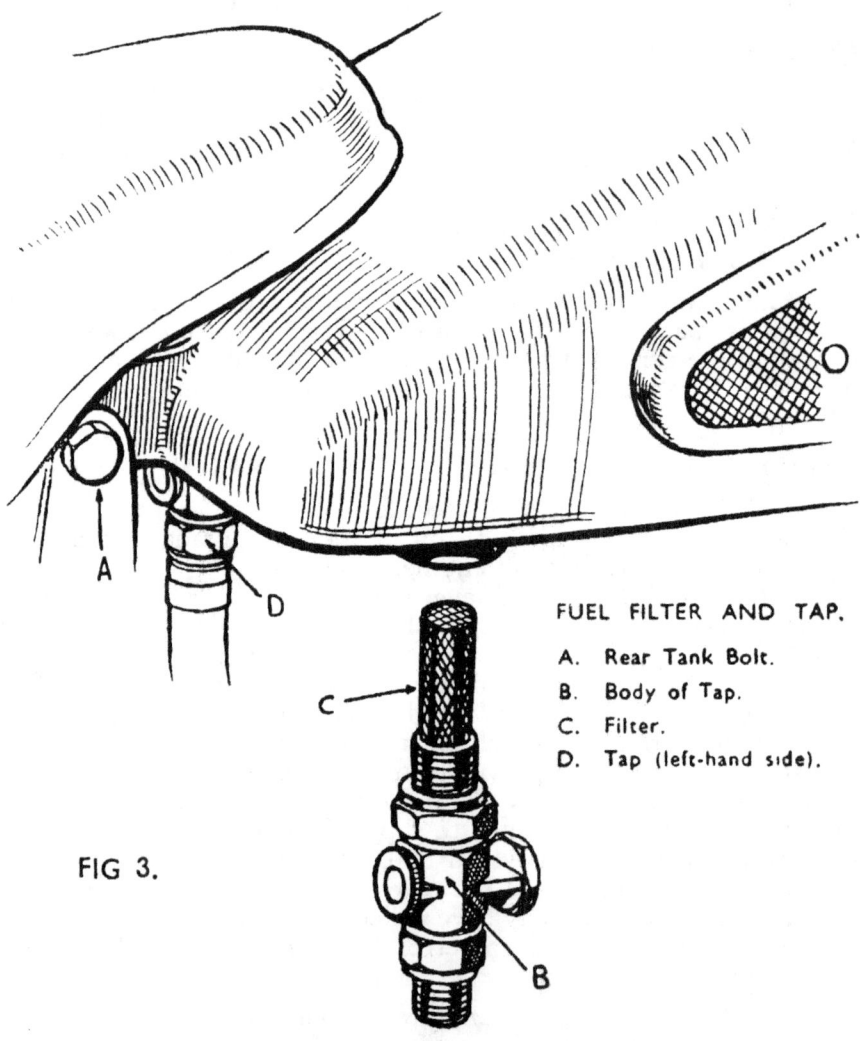

FIG 3.

FUEL FILTER AND TAP.

A. Rear Tank Bolt.
B. Body of Tap.
C. Filter.
D. Tap (left-hand side).

FUEL FILTERS.

Two filters are fitted as a part of the fuel taps. To clean—drain fuel from tank into clean container. Unscrew both taps from tank. When unscrewing the taps use a second spanner to hold the tap to prevent the petrol pipe twisting. Clean filters in petrol. See that fibre washers on taps are in good order. Replace taps.

TYRE MAINTENANCE.

Minimum Inflation Pressures.	NOMINAL TYRE SECTION.					
	2.375"	2.75"	3.00"	3.25"	3.50"	4.00"
Lbs. per □ inch.	LOAD PER WHEEL IN LBS.					
16	120	140	160	200	280	360
18	140	160	180	240	320	400
20	160	180	200	280	350	430
24	185	210	240	350	400	500
28	210	250	300	400	450	—
32	240	280	350	440	500	—

For all normal purposes the minimum pressures for the three types should be:—

    MOV & MAC. Front .. 16-lbs.   MSS. 16-lbs.
    ,,   ,,   Rear .. 18-lbs.   ,, 16-lbs.

Additional loading such as a heavy rider, pillion passenger, or the addition of a sidecar will require a higher pressure. Owing to the difference in the various sidecars available we do not quote pressures, but recommend that the loaded weight upon each wheel be checked on a public weighbridge. With this information the correct pressures can be found from the table.

Check the pressures weekly and inflate if loss of pressure is noticed.

NEVER RUN TYRES UNDER-INFLATED.

Occasionally examine the tyres for cuts, and in order to remove flints or nails which may be partly embedded in the treads. Partly deflate tyres to remove nails or flints.

REMOVING AND REPLACING FRONT WHEEL (On

Machines with Telescopic Forks. (See Figs. 4 and 7).

Place a suitable block under the crankcase so that the fork is fully extended and the wheel clear of the ground. Disconnect the brake cable from the cam lever and unscrew the adjuster removing the adjuster and cable from the brake plate. Loosen and take off the spindle nut and washer on the right-hand side. Slacken the clamping bolt in the left-hand fork end, tap out the spindles (which may bring the split collar with it) and the wheel will then come out. The fork sliders will spring over to the right about 20°.

To replace the wheel, push the wheel up into position, being careful to engage the slot in the brake plate over the brake anchor bolt on the fork. Push the spindle through the hollow spindle of the wheel, locating the split collar on the spindle in the split fork end on the left. Fit the spindle washer and nut and tighten the nut fully. Lift the machine off the block and when it is standing on its wheels bounce the fork a few times on the ground. Tighten the clamping bolt on the left-hand fork end and replace the brake cable and re-adjust.

The object of the bouncing explained in the preceding paragraph is to ensure that the sliders of the fork align themselves correctly so that they will work freely.

DISMANTLING FRONT WHEEL BEARINGS (Fig. 4). (**On Models fitted with Telescopic Forks**). (It is advisable to let a Velocette Service Depot do this job).

Before removing wheel test for ball-bearing wear, Slight freedom is usual. Remove wheel as described in preceding section. Remove brake plate assembly from end of hollow spindle. Obtain a punch made from brass or aluminium bar slightly less than $\frac{7}{8}$-in. diameter and about 9-in. long and turned down at one end to just under $\frac{5}{8}$-in. dia. for a distance of about $\frac{1}{2}$-in. This is necessary to protect the end of the hollow spindle from damage when driving it out. Fit the reduced end of the punch into the end of the hollow spindle on the left-hand side of the hub (remote from the brake drum) and drive out towards the drum. A 1-lb. hammer will usually be sufficiently large to move the hollow spindle satisfactorily. The hollow spindle will drive out of the dust cap on the left-hand side of the hub and carry with it the ballrace from the right and the inner dust cap. This bearing, which will still be in place on the spindle, must be thoroughly cleaned and tested for condition. If any undue slackness is noticed or if the bearing is felt to turn roughly, jerkily, or is stiff, it should be removed by pressing it off and a replacement fitted. If in order, it may be put aside with the spindle until it is needed to re-assemble the hub. The hub ballraces are not adjustable.

Now unscrew the ballrace retaining ring from the left-hand end of the hub, using the peg spanner from the kit. **This ring, unlike the corresponding part in the rear hub on machines with rear driven speedometers is a right-hand thread and unscrews anti-clockwise.**

The condition of the left-hand bearing can be checked without removal. If satisfactory, pack it with high melting point grease, and re-fit and tighten the retaining ring. Should it be necessary to replace with a new one it must be driven out from the opposite side of the hub and it may be convenient to use the hollow spindle to do it and thus avoid damage to the inner grease retainers. To remove, press the spindle out of the other ballrace and pass it through the hub from the right-hand end of the hub until it is pushed through into the ballrace which it is desired to remove. Fit the punch into the other end of the spindle and drive the ballrace out of the hub. It should be noted that behind each ballrace a steel washer is used to prevent grease working into the hollow barrel of the hub where it is of no use. Before re-fitting either ballrace therefore, always see that these are in place. (The concave surfaces are always towards the ballraces). Also observe carefully that the ends of the hollow spindle which are reduced to fit the ballraces are not of equal length. **The longer ground end must always be fitted into the ballrace on the left of the hub and enters the hub first on re-assembly.** This apparently trivial detail is emphasised as it is impossible to assemble the remainder of the hub parts if the spindle is placed the wrong way round. With the ballrace fitted to the shorter reduced end of the spindle and the inner grease retainer in place, push the spindle and bearing into the right-hand end of the hub and with the hammer and punch drive them home. Pack the right-hand ballrace with grease and re-fit the small dust cap. Press the dust cover on to the left-hand end of the hollow spindle, refit the brake assembly when the wheel is ready for re-fitting to machine.

See drawing Illustration 4.

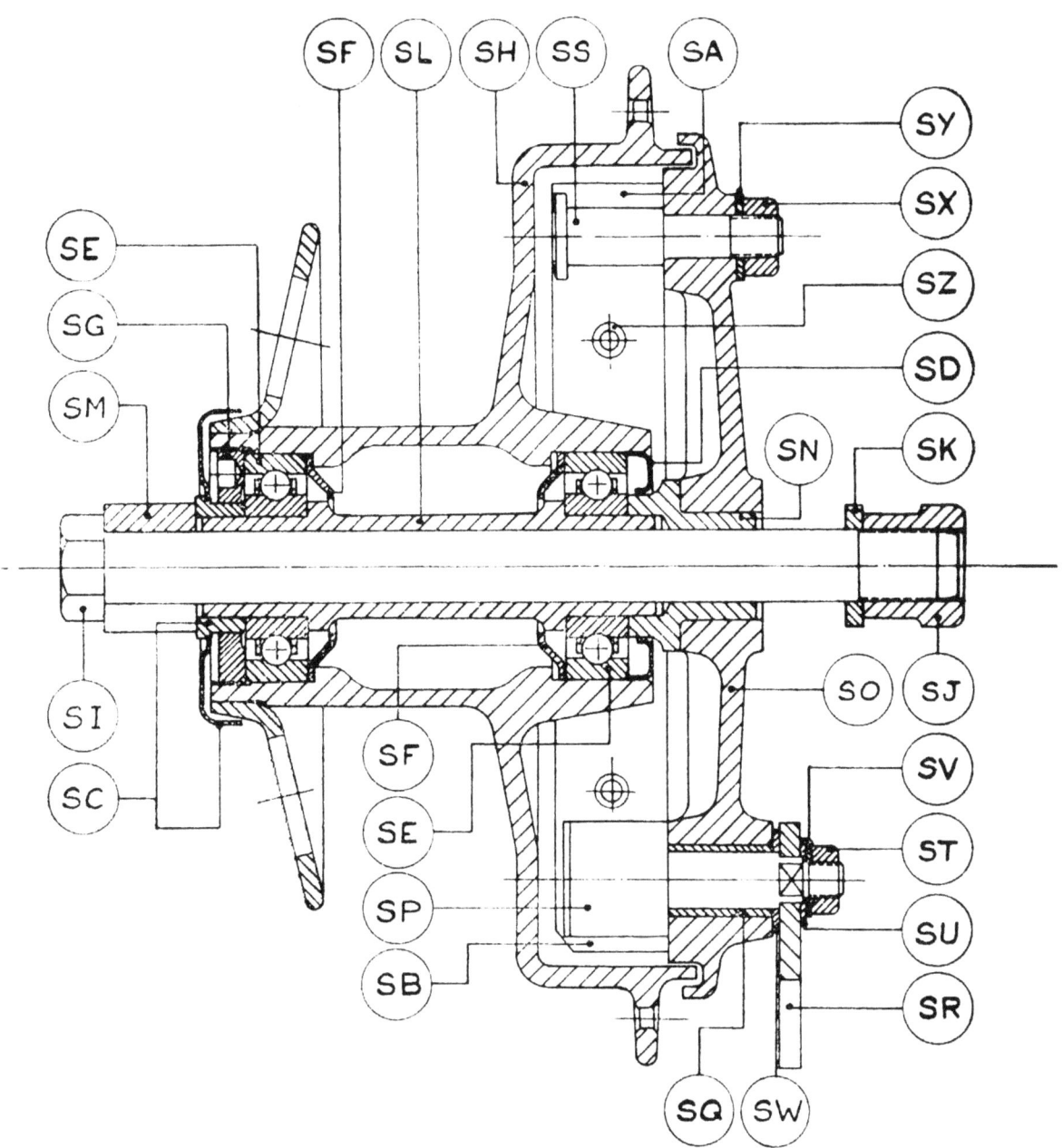

FIG. 4. SECTION THROUGH FRONT HUB ASSEMBLY—BALL BEARING TYPE.

- SA. Brake Shoes
- SB. Brake Shoe Slipper.
- SC. Outer Dust Cap and Sleeve.
- SD. Inner Dust Cap.
- SE. Ballraces.
- SF. Grease Retainers.
- SG. Ballrace Retaining Ring.
- SH. Front Hub Shell.
- SI. Detachable Spindle.
- SJ. Nut for Detachable Spindle.
- SK. Washer for Spindle Nut.
- SL. Hollow Spindle.
- SM. Split Sleeve for Spindle.
- SN. Bearing Clamping Sleeve
- SO. Brake Plate.
- SP. Brake Cam
- SQ. Bush for Brake Cam.
- SR. Lever for Brake Cam.
- SS. Fulcrum Pin.
- ST. Nut for Cam.
- SU. Square Hole Washer for Cam.
- SV. Lock Washer
- SW. Felt Washer for Cam
- SX. Nut for Fulcrum Pin
- SY. Plain Washer for Fulcrum Pin.
- SZ. Brake Shoe Spring.

REMOVAL OF FRONT WHEEL. (Figs. 5 and 6).
(From Webb Fork only).

Raise the machine on to the rear stand. Loosen the front stand from the mudguard and raise the machine on to the front stand. Pull the brake lever towards the handlebar, grasp the casing of the control cable close to the lever and slip it out of the recess whilst at the same time releasing the lever. Slide the nipple out of the lever, detach all cable clips. Unscrew the hexagon nut at the lower end of the flexible speedometer drive and slip the flex out of engagement with the reduction gearbox. Loosen both spindle nuts, prise the washers out of the recesses in the outside of the fork ends, when the wheel will drop out and can be removed.

DISMANTLING FRONT WHEEL BEARINGS (Models with Webb Fork Only). (See Fig. 5).

Take off both spindle nuts, and lift out the brake plate and shoes from the brake drum. By using two spanners working against each other, loosen the lock-nut on the left-hand end of the spindle and take this nut and the bearing adjustment nut off the spindle. Take off the dust cap. Using a punch made of brass, copper, or aluminium-alloy drive the spindle through the hub towards the brake drum. **In no circumstances must the spindle be driven out from the brake-drum side** towards the left. The centre of the roller bearing on the right-hand side will come out with the spindle. The dust cap from the left-hand side of the hub is easily prised out of place and the centre part of the bearing can be taken out. Both bearing cups in the hub can now be repacked with grease.

If the roller bearings have to be renewed due to wear or damage, the old outer bearing rings have to be driven out of the hub in which they are a fairly tight fit. When removing them it is almost impossible to avoid scrapping the grease retaining washers that are inserted between the outer bearing rings and the internal shoulders in the barrel of the hub. If a punch is to hand that will just fit through the barrel of the hub the retainer on one side may be saved, but as one ring and one washer must be taken out before such a punch could be used it is usual simply to drive both rings out of place with an ordinary bar about $\frac{3}{16}$-in. diameter and 10-in. long, replacing both grease retainers with new ones on assembly.

Reassembly. (Models with Webb Fork only).

When fitting new roller bearings (which are supplied comprising the centre race, rollers, cage, and outer ring) do not mix up the component parts—see that each centre race with rollers is fitted to run with the ring with which it was supplied.

Place one grease retainer in place—concave side outwards or towards the bearing, press the outer ring of the bearing firmly into the recess in the hub until it is hard up against the grease retainer, which it will then hold in position. Fit the two parts to the other side in a similar manner.

To re-assemble a vice is desirable but not essential. First slide the centre of the brake-side roller bearing up to the shoulder on the right-hand end of the spindle. A small collar or washer will be noticed at the shoulder between the ground part of the spindle and the larger unmachined centre part. The inner ring of the bearing presses against this. Slip the spindle into place from the brake drum side and see that the rollers fit into the bearing outer ring in the hub. The centre part of the bearing must of course be fitted so that the large ends of the taper rollers are outermost. Tap the inner dust cap back into the hub and wipe away any excess grease that may have squeezed out. Put on the flat inside distance washer. Follow up this with the brake plate and shoes, making sure that the small pinion on the reduction gearbox is meshed with the driving gear on the hub. Incidentally, this driving gear is a parallel press fit on to the shoulder of the hub. It is very seldom necessary to replace it, but it can be "prised" out of place using two large spanners packed up (with nuts of suitable thickness) from the back of the brake drum.

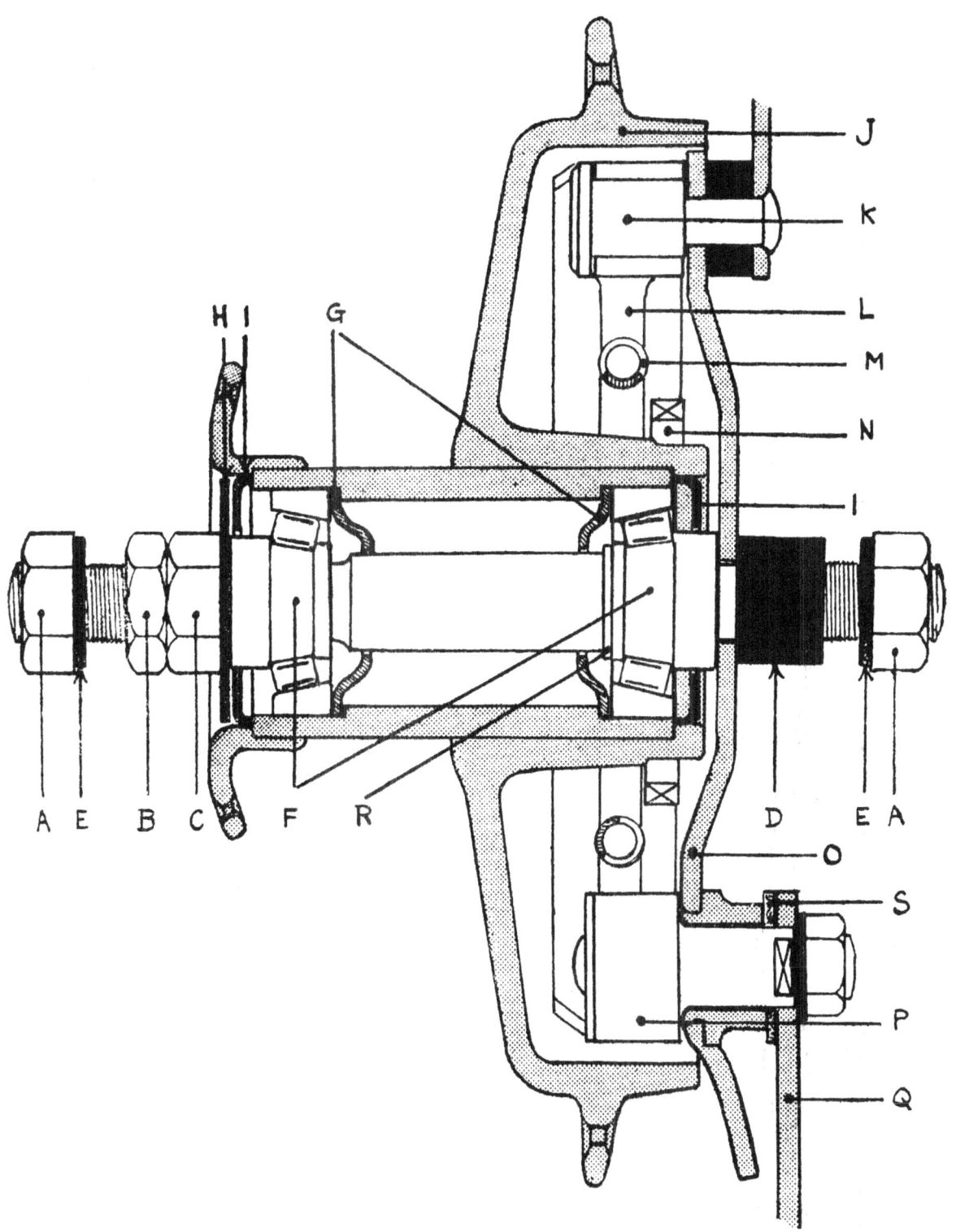

FIG. 5.

SECTION OF FRONT HUB AND BRAKE—ROLLER BEARING TYPE.

- A. Spindle Nuts.
- B. Lock Nut.
- C. Bearing Adjusting Nut.
- D. Brake Plate Distance Piece.
- E. Spindle Nut Washers.
- F. Wheel Bearings.
- G. Grease Retaining Washers.
- H. Outer Dust Washer.
- I. Inner Dust Caps.
- J. Brake Drum.
- K. Brake Shoe Fulcrum Pin.
- L. Brake Shoe.
- M. Brake Shoe Spring.
- N. Speedometer Drive Gear.
- O. Brake Plate.
- P. Brake Cam.
- Q. Brake Cam Lever.
- R. Bearing Seating Collar.
- S. Brake Cam Felt Washer.

Refit the tubular distance piece, spindle-nut and washer, and tighten down the nut to hold the brake plate lightly. Now hold the wheel (brake drum downwards) in a vice by gripping the spindle nut firmly between the jaws. Fit the roller bearing centre into the left-hand bearing ring and tap the inner dust cap into place. Place the flat dust washer in position and tighten down the adjusting nut **lightly** far enough to allow the wheel to turn freely with only a very slight amount of slackness (about $\frac{1}{64}$-in.) noticeable at the wheel rim in all positions. Fit the lock nut and screw it down lightly against the adjuster nut. The setting of the bearings is then near enough for the wheel to be re-fitted to the machine. To do this, slack off the spindle nut at the brake side enough to allow the spindle to slide up into the fork end and push the wheel up into place. See that the outside washers are snugly fitted into the recesses in the fork ends, the brake plate engaged with the lug on the fork girder, and tighten down both nuts. Check the adjustment. If incorrect, *i.e.*, wheel tight or excessivly slack, see next section.

When correctly adjusted connect up the brake cable and adjust the brake (Fig. 6).

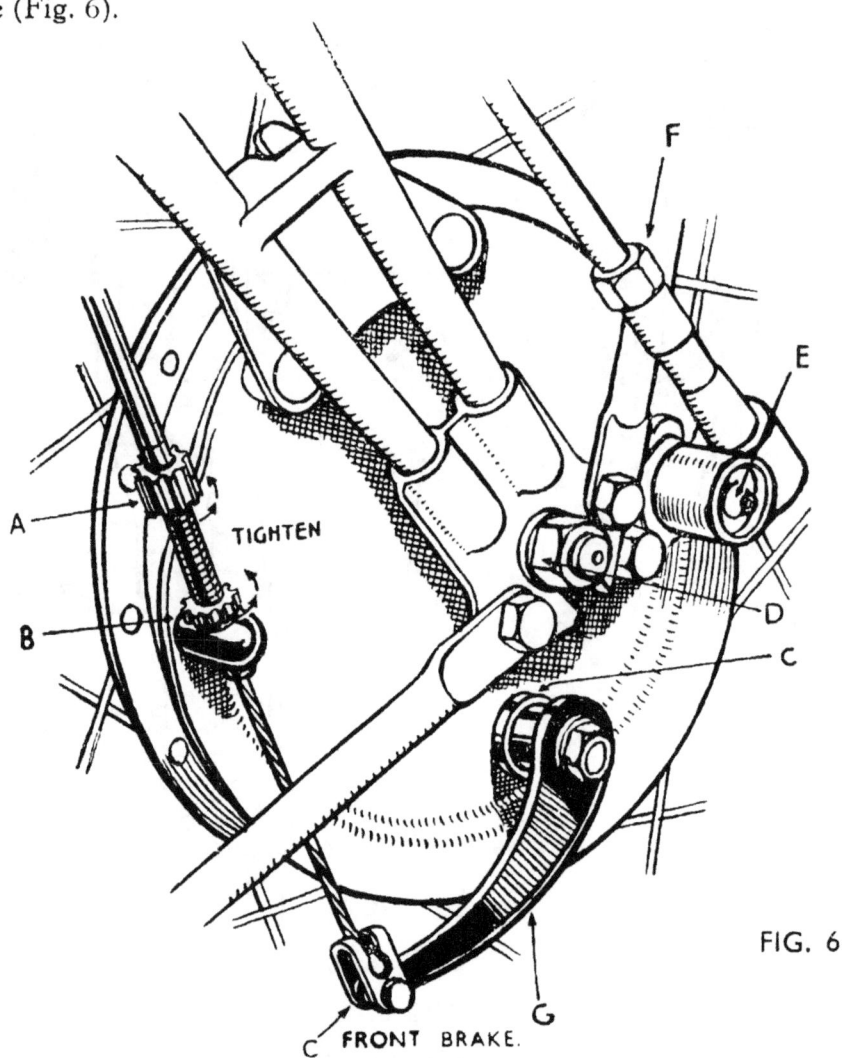

FIG. 6

FRONT BRAKE.

    A. Adjuster.
    B. Lock Nut.
    C. Felt Washers (keep oily).
    D. Spindle Nut.
    E. Greaser for Reduction Gearbox.
    F. Nut (securing flexible drive).
    G. Cam Lever.

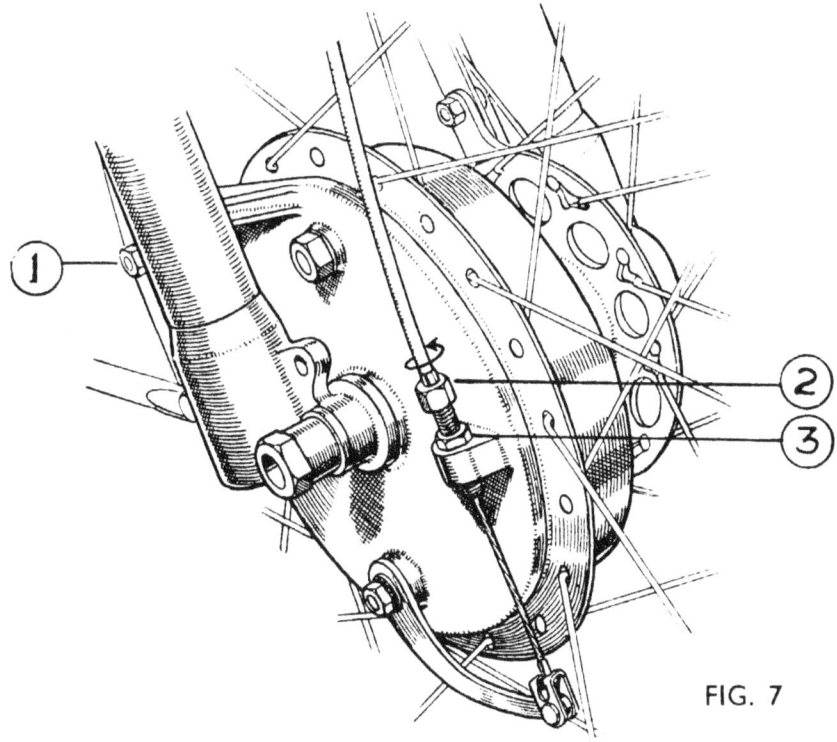

FIG. 7

We advise that when dismantling the hub, or in fact any part of the machine, a careful note be made of the positions that the various nuts, washers and other parts occupy before removal. If they are systematically placed in order as taken off and their positions memorised, much time and trouble would be saved and there will not be any of those odd and unaccounted for "left over" parts when the job is done.

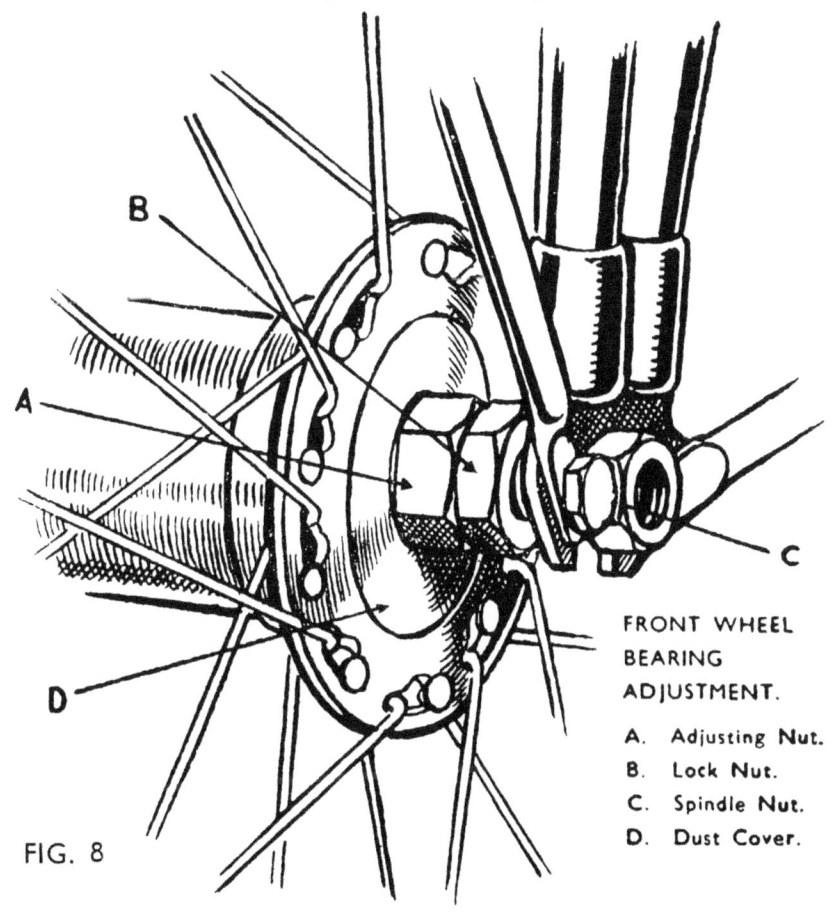

FRONT WHEEL BEARING ADJUSTMENT.

A. Adjusting Nut.
B. Lock Nut.
C. Spindle Nut.
D. Dust Cover.

FIG. 8

ADJUSTMENT OF FRONT WHEEL BEARINGS (See Fig. 8).
(On Machines with Webb Fork only).

Should the wheel be too slack loosen the nearside spindle nut, slack back the lock nut slightly and tighten the adjusting nut until the play is nearly all taken up. Check with the wheel in several positions allowing not more than $\frac{1}{64}$-in. play at the wheel rim. Tighten the lock nut, being careful not to shift the adjusting nut. Tighten the spindle nut again and check adjustment once more.

If the bearings are too tight, proceed as above, but slack back the adjuster nut away from the hub. Tap the brake drum over from the off-side, using a wood mallet or a block of wood until play is obtained. Then adjust as described previously.

MAINTENANCE INSTRUCTIONS FOR THE VELOCETTE-DOWTY OLEOMATIC FORK. See page 119 for Dowty factory manual.

Working.

The forks are air sprung and oil damped. Air springing has the advantage of allowing considerable deflection for normal surface irregularities, whilst maintaining the ability to absorb considerable shocks without excess fork movement.

The movement of the synthetic rubber cushions in oil provides approximately equal and constant damping in both directions. These cushions also absorb the shock should the forks extend fully, whilst the oil cushion between the pistons and internal top fittings prevents too rapid closing on compression.

Inflation and Adjustment to load.

A red dot is marked on the front of each lower sliding tube. When correctly inflated to the load, the bottom edges of the shrouds should coincide with the red dots with rider or riders in position.

To obtain the correct adjustment, over-inflate the fork slightly by removing the inflation valve dust cap and coupling an ordinary tyre pump to the valve. The rider should then sit on the machine, keeping his feet on the footrests and maintaining balance from some convenient support. Air should then be released in small quantities, by depressing the stem of the inflation valve, until the bottom of the shrouds line up with the red dots. Replace the dust cap on the inflation valve.

It will be seen from the above that the forks can be correctly adjusted for solo, sidecar or pillion riding.

Inflation Valve.

The inflation valve is fitted with a special core designed to open at low pressure and fitted with oil resisting rubber seatings. **In no circumstances** must a normal tyre valve core be used, as the action of the oil would rapidly destroy the natural rubber seatings. Dowty valve cores can be obtained from your Dealer or direct from us.

Topping Up.

Topping up becomes necessary only if "bottoming" occurs in spite of correct inflation. Scrupulous cleanliness is essential.

Remove inflation valve dust cap, depress valve stem and allow all air to escape. The forks will close. Rest the crankcase on a block so that the forks are approximately 1-in. from the fully closed position. Unscrew the filler plugs and fill each leg with one of the recommended oils. (See "Filling.") Replace and tighten filler plugs.

Remove the block from beneath the crank case and depress the inflation valve, thus allowing surplus oil to drain off and the forks to close completely.

Carry out air inflation procedure, adjust to the load and replace valve dust cap.

Filling.

Forks are supplied correctly filled and inflated. When filling, it is important that the recommended grade of oil be used, as its viscosity does not change appreciably over a wide range of temperatures. Consequently there is little or no alteration in its damping characteristics.

The recommended oils are listed on page 12.

The procedure for filling is exactly the same as described under "Topping-up," except that more oil will be required.

Unless dirt has been allowed to enter with the oil during filling or topping up, the oil need never be changed during the life of the machine.

Greasing.

The bottom bearings in each leg should be greased weekly. Six shots with the grease gun should be given to each greaser, situated at the back of the outer tubes, at the lower bearings. Only clean, high-grade grease should be used. Vent holes are provided in the sides of the outer tubes below the fork crown; these allow surplus grease to escape.

Nuts and Screws.

Periodically check the tightness of all nuts and screws to ensure completely efficient working. It is particularly important that the steering tube pad bolt is kept really tight, otherwise the fork may become mal-aligned.

ADJUSTING STEERING HEAD. (Dowty Fork).

Slacken both the clamp bolts on the fork crown fitting and the pad bolt on the handlebar clip lug. Adjust steering head nut as required. Re-tighten pad bolt hard and clamp bolts on completion of adjustment.

It is important that these two clamp bolts (in the lower head fitting) are not over-tightened, as it is comparatively easy to deform the outer tubes by excessive tightening.

If the outer tubes become deformed by this over-tightening it will be appreciated that the rubber seal will not be able to hold either air or oil and deflation of the forks will follow.

ADJUSTING THE FORK SPINDLES. (Webb Fork).

(See Fig. 9)

See that the adjustment of the shock absorber is slacked right off before checking or resetting the adjustment of the fork spindles.

The final adjustment of the spindles must a low perfect freedom of movement of the fork spindles with no noticeable end clearance between the inner faces of the links, the spacing washers, and the faces on the top-clip, column, and girder cross-members. If on checking the adjustment **one** spacing washer on each spindle can be turned with the finger and thumb and has no side tilt the adjustment of the particular spindle is correct. Adjustment is needed when the washers are loose **and** can tilt.

Reference to the illustration will show that the spindles are reduced in diameter on the nearside ends and fit into unthreaded holes in the nearside links into which they are secured by the nearside spindle nuts.

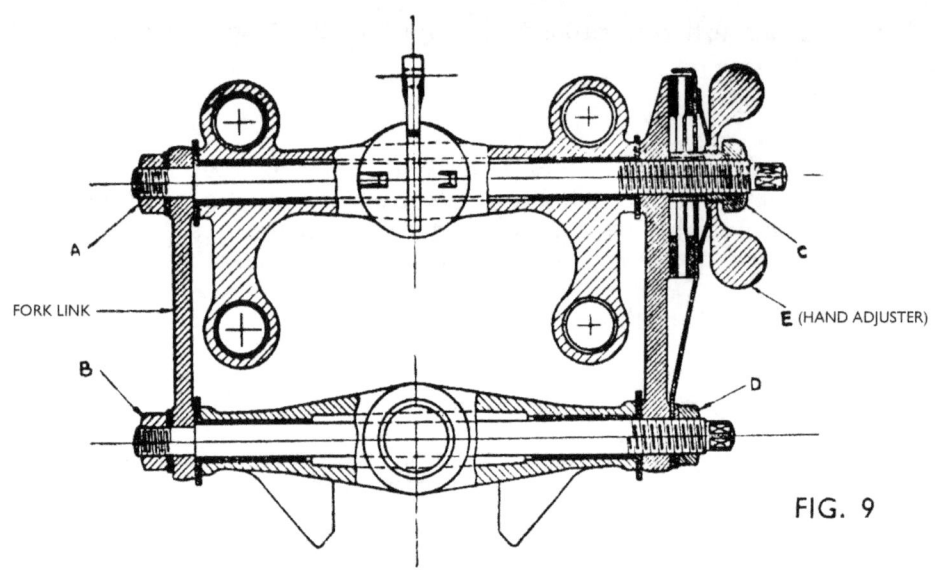

SECTION THROUGH BOTTOM SPINDLES OF FORK.
A, B, C and D. Spindle Nuts.   E. Adjuster for S Absorber.

The offside links and offside ends of the spindles are threaded so that the distance between the inner faces of the links is variable by turning a spindle in the links.

To take up play loosen the nut on the nearside of the spindle that needs adjustment, and then the nut on the offside. Grip the square offside end of the spindle with a moveable spanner and turn the spindle anti-clockwise slightly until the play is **nearly** all taken up. Tighten up both nuts fully and check as described above. If too tight loosen the nuts again and turn the spindle slightly clockwise. Tighten nuts and check again. All four spindles adjust in a similar manner.

Early pattern forks have shock-absorbers at both sides. The spindles on these are adjusted in just the same way.

ADJUSTMENT OF STEERING HEAD BEARINGS.
(Figs. 10 and 11.)

On machines with girder forks slacken the steering damper right off and tighten the shock absorber fully to prevent the fork extending when the wheel is clear of the ground, otherwise the extended spring will foul the head lug and it will be impossible to check the bearings.

Final adjustment must allow perfect freedom in the column without trace of play. Support the machine with a block beneath the crankcase to allow the tyre to clear the ground. To remove play slacken the clamping bolt nut and tighten down the column lock-nut until the column begins to bind when turned. Gradually slacken the column lock-nut until the column is found to be just free with no trace of play or roughness in working. When correctly adjusted tighten the clamp bolt nut.

Should the column turn jerkily or roughly suspect that the head race cups and cones are worn and pitted, and dismantle the column for inspection and if necessary the renewal of the worn parts.

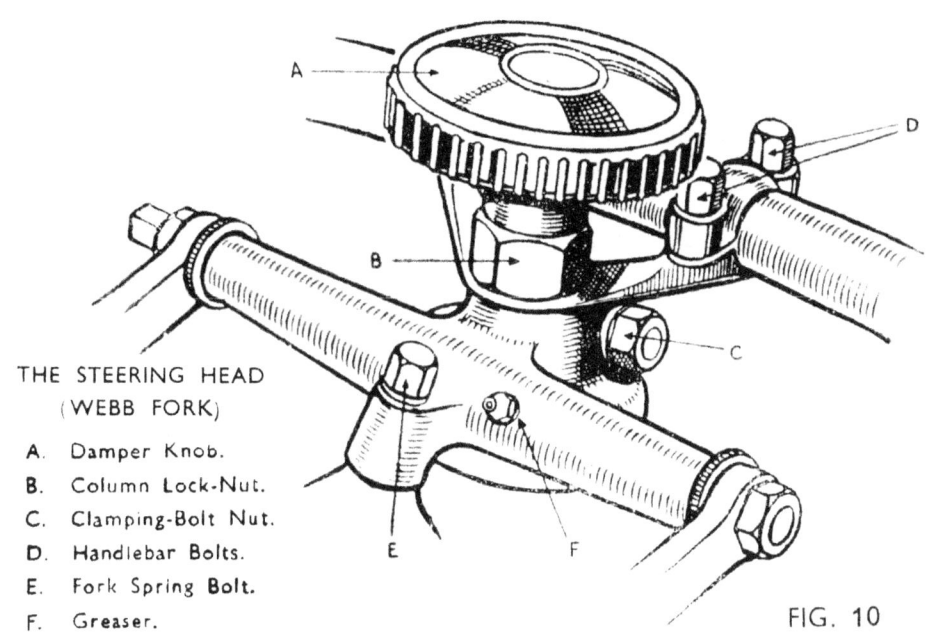

THE STEERING HEAD
(WEBB FORK)

A. Damper Knob.
B. Column Lock-Nut.
C. Clamping-Bolt Nut.
D. Handlebar Bolts.
E. Fork Spring Bolt.
F. Greaser.

FIG. 10

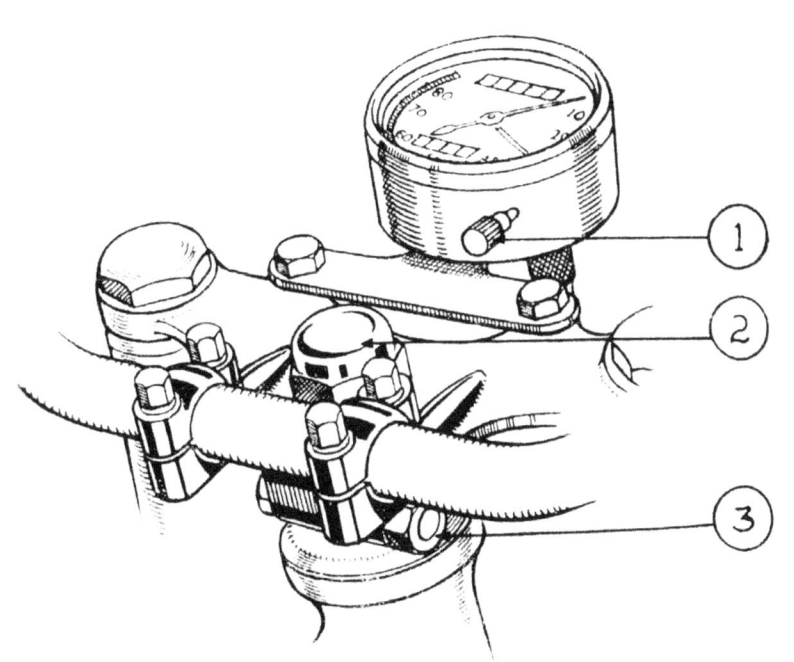

FIG. 11

ADJUSTMENT OF STEERING HEAD—VELOCETTE FORK.

(1) Speedometer Trip Mileage Resetting Knob.
(2) Steering Column Lock Nut.
(3) Top Cross Member Clamp Bolt Nut.

THE FRONT FORK. Velocette Telescopic Type.

Maintenance.

The only attention (and this is optional) is the draining of the oil from the struts every 10,000 miles, and refilling with clean oil. **The oil used must be absolutely clean and poured from a clean measure.**

Each strut has ⅛-pint of oil (Viscosity SAE20) put into it during manufacture.

To drain, remove the drain plugs from the fork ends. Do not confuse the drain plugs, which are set at an angle, with the hexagon nuts holding the fork damper assemblies into the centre of the fork ends at the bottom.

Having drained the struts refit and tighten the drain plugs, and unscrew the two hexagon head plugs from the centre tubes at the top. These plugs are screwed on to the damper rods and will not come away but can be raised far enough to allow the oil to be poured in. After refilling screw them in again and tighten up.

Removal of Fork from Machine.

If it is not intended to dismantle the fork, but only to renew the steering head bearings, the fork and wheel can be removed together and the headlamp can be left connected to the lighting cables and can be laid back over the tank after removing the fork top cross member. If the lamp is left attached to the cables it should be well protected by wrapping it in sacking or other suitable material, and secured so that it cannot fall.

The other course is to remove the lamp entirely after disconnecting all cables at the switch, but if this is to be done the first, and most important step, is to disconnect the positive lead and horn wire from the battery. **Do this first before beginning to remove the headlamp.**

Remove the headlamp front with glass and reflector and disconnect the three bulb leads. Disconnect all wires from the switch, marking them for easy and correct replacement. There is a wiring diagram on Page 105 (Fig. 57). Remove the dipper switch from the handlebar and unbolt and take off the headlamp.

Disconnect the flexible drive from underneath the speedometer and detach the speedometer from the top cross-member. Disconnect the brake cable from the handlebar lever.

Remove all four handlebar clamping bolts and lift off the handlebar, laying it back out of the way across the tank. Immediately replace the caps and bolts in their correct positions.

If the fork is to be dismantled the easier method is to remove the front wheel, front mudguard and stays before removing the fork.

Unscrew and lift up the two hexagon-headed adaptors from the fork centre tubes. If the fork is not to be dismantled wind a length of soft wire round each of the damper rods, which are screwed into the caps. Soft wire, about 22 gauge and about 36 inches long will do if cut into two equal lengths. The object of this is to provide a means of pulling up the damper rods so as to screw on the adaptors on refitting the fork. If the damper rods are not wired they will drop down inside the centre tubes when the adaptors are removed and will be difficult to retrieve.

Slacken the lock nuts on the damper rods and unscrew the adaptors off the rods.

Remove the hexagon steering column nut and loosen the clamping bolt nut in the top cross member. Support the front of the machine far enough just to take the weight but leaving the front wheel resting on the ground, and tap the cross member up off the column and the fork centre tubes.

If not previously removed take out the two headlamp bolts, and lay the lamp (wrapped up to preserve it from damage) on the tank.

Remove from each of the fork struts the two rubber buffer housing washers with the buffer between them, and the locating collar. One of each of these is fitted above each lamp bracket assembly.

Remove the head race dust cap.

Pull off both lamp bracket assemblies and the locating collars in which they are fitted at the lower end against the bottom cross member. Note that the lamp bracket assemblies are made left and right-hand, and must be refitted correctly.

Raise the machine higher by lifting by the front wheel or by grasping the two dust covers on the fork struts whilst an assistant places extra support below the machine to allow the wheel to clear the ground whilst the fork is removed.

When the machine is supported gradually lower the wheel and fork, so drawing the steering column out of the head lug on the frame, and be prepared to catch the nineteen $\frac{1}{4}$-in. bearing balls which will be released from the bottom bearing as the column comes away.

Keeping the fork as upright as possible to save the oil leaking out. Take it away with the wheel, and store upright.

Dismantling the Front Fork.

Remove the drain plugs and drain out the oil. Having removed the fork from the machine, support it in the vice by holding the column horizontally between the vice jaws—protected by clamps of brass, copper or aluminium over the jaws.

Except for the left and right-hand fork ends on the sliders the fork struts are identical, so that the directions for stripping and reassembling which follow apply equally to both.

To remove a strut from the column for dismantling, undo the clamping bolt nut on the bottom cross member, and pull the strut downwards through the hole. Pull off the cowl or dust cover, exposing the spring and the rubber buffer.

Take the column from the vice and hold the centre tube of the strut in its place. Tap the split sleeve round to unscrew it from the top of the spring. Remove the centre tube from the vice and slide the split sleeve up the tube and take it off. Hold the slider firmly and twist the spring out of the bottom spring mounting on the slider. Pull the spring off the tube.

Again hold the tube in the vice and push the slider up as far as possible. Grasp it firmly and pull it back sharply to dislodge the oil seal and bush from their housings in the upper end of the slider. As they come out the slider will pull right off the centre tube, leaving the bottom bush on the centre tube, but will bring away with it the damper assembly, which must be drawn out of the tube.

If it is required to fit a new bottom bush to the centre tube prise the circlip from the groove at the extreme end of the tube, and pull off the bush.

The damper assembly may now be removed from the slider. It is held by a nut into the centre of the fork end, and on removal of the nut and washer will tap out upwards.

It should be unnecessary to take it apart, but if it is desired to do so it is dismantled by first prising out the small circlip from the groove just inside the top of the damper tube assembly. Hold the damper tube assembly in one hand, and the damper rod in the other. Pull them apart smartly to drag out the damper rod bush from the top of the damper tube assembly.

The damper piston is fitted at the lower end of the damper rod and can be removed by taking off the nut and washer from the end of the rod. When refitting the piston, or renewing it, note that the shiny end face of the piston is facing the bottom and is next to the accurately ground face of the piston valve washer.

Note also that the damper rod bush has one end face radiused and this face must be uppermost in the damper tube assembly, otherwise the circlip which retains the bush will not seat properly in its groove.

Reassembling the Front Fork.

Insert the damper assembly into the slider so that the threaded end of the tube assembly goes through the central hole in the bottom of the slider. Make certain that the shoulder on the damper tube assembly spigots into the hole in the fork end, fit the washer and nut and tighten up.

Hold the central tube in the vice with the top bush slipped over it, and if it was removed when dismantling push the bottom bush on to the end of the tube up to the shoulder and refit the circlip.

Set the upper bush with the groove which is cut across its upper face underneath. Oil the bottom bush, and push the slider into position entering the damper rod and tube through the centre tube, and the bottom bush into the slider, which must be held with the front part which carries the wheel spindle uppermost. It will be noted that the upper bush must be set so that when the fork is assembled to the machine, and the wheel is fitted the groove in the top face of the bush will be at the rear of the strut.

Using the Split collar (Service Tool No. LET796) slipped over the central tube against the top face of the bush, tap the bush sharply into place up to the shoulder in the slider. Remove the tube from the vice and slip the oil seal into place, metal backing upwards, and tap the oil seal into place above the bush also using the Tool LET796.

Slide the spring over the tube and twist it firmly into its mounting on the slider. Pull the slider out to the limit.

Slide the split sleeve down the tube and set it so that the upper edge of the tapered section is exactly 7.187-in. ($7\frac{3}{16}$-in.) from the top of the central tube. Push the slider up once more and twist the spring into its fixing on the sleeve. Slip the rubber buffer over the split sleeve followed by the dust cover.

Replace the column in the vice and push the centre tube through the hole in the bottom cross member entering it from the side away from the column, and making sure that it is fitted on the correct side. (The right-hand slider is the one with the plain hole for the spindle. The left-hand one carries the spindle clamping bolt).

Set the slider and strut facing over to the brake side about 20° out of straight, and partly tighten the clamping bolt in the bottom cross member.

Fit the bottom locating collar flat side down against the upper side of the cross member, and follow it with the lamp bracket assembly, again noting that it is the correct "hand" bracket for the strut to which it is being fitted. Pull up the damper rods and wire them up.

The other strut is dealt with in the same manner.

Refitting the Fork to the Machine.

Stick into each steering head cup nineteen $\frac{1}{4}$-in. bearing balls and push the column up into the steering head. Fit the top cone and dust cap—flat side up. Fit the locating washers over the lamp bracket assemblies and fit the rubber buffers and washers.

If the headlamp was left attached to the wiring bring it forward, leading the wires down between the steering head of the frame and the fork strut, and place the top cross member in position, threading through the holes in it the wires attached to the damper rods, and locate it over the steering column and the centre tubes, seating these in the counterbores.

Fit the column locknut and tighten down finger tight.

Adjust the steering head races by means of the column lock nut and when correct tighten up the clamping bolt nut on the top cross member.

The remainder of the reassembling is quite straightforward, but it should be noted that when refitting the front wheel the two sliders will be pointing over slightly towards the brake (right-hand) side. They are intentionally set in this way when assembling the fork so as to keep the springs twisted into their mountings.

After fitting the wheel but before tightening the spindle clamping bolt bounce the front end up and down to line up the struts and get them working freely, and to tighten the dust covers on to their buffers.

Should the mudguards and stays have been removed, or more particularly should new or repaired stays have been fitted, it is essential to set the ends of the stays to the correct widths, otherwise in fitting them they may " spring " the struts and cause binding.

The correct widths are : Front stay $5\frac{5}{8}$-in., vertical stay $5\frac{1}{2}$-in., rear stay (fitted outside the vertical stay) $5\frac{3}{4}$-in.

This point is well worth attention, as the working of the fork can be seriously affected if the stays are sprung into place when being fitted.

Pour into each strut $\frac{1}{8}$-pint oil (Viscosity SAE20) and screw the hexagon adaptors on to the damper rods securing these by tightening the locknuts carefully. Remove the wires from the damper rods.

Tighten the clamping bolts in the bottom cross member, and fit the two adaptors into the centre tubes. Tighten adaptors.

It may still be possible to twist the dust covers round, but this is in order provided that they are tight enough to prevent rattle. See below.

With this type of fork it is most important that if the front wheel is taken out the sliders are not rotated anti-clockwise, as this will unscrew the springs from their fixings, and would entail removing the struts and partially dismantling to refix them.

Tightening Fork Spring Dust Covers (Velocette Telescopic Fork).

Should a slight rattle develop due to a loose dust cover this must be tightened at once, otherwise the rubber washer will become damaged and the whole strut assembly have to be dismantled to replace it.

To tighten a loose cover first drain all oil from both struts, and slightly slacken the bottom cross member clamping bolt in the side needing attention. Raise the front of the machine and bounce the front wheel sharply on the ground to shift the split sleeve up the centre tube and compress the rubber washer between the shoulder of the sleeve and the dust cover. It is essential to drain out the oil as otherwise a hydraulic lock forms preventing full closure of the springs and the split sleeve will not move. Also do not slacken the clamping bolt too much or the split sleeve will move back again down the tube when the springs extend. The dust covers will never be held so firmly that they cannot be turned by hand, but they must be secure enough not to rattle.

When correct tighten clamp bolt and refill fork with oil.

DISMANTLING THE STEERING HEAD & FRONT FORK.
(Girder Type).

Should it be required to attend to the spindles or links of the fork only, there is of course no need to remove the fork. It is, however, not possible to take out one spindle separately, and two should always be removed together as follows (the procedure is the same for top or bottom spindles except that to remove the bottom ones it will also be necessary to take out the bolt securing the shock absorber plate to the girder) :—

Raise the front of the machine and support the frame at the front end, preferably so as to leave the front tyre just lightly resting on the ground. Take off both nuts from the nearside ends of the spindles which are to be removed. Tap the link off the spindles. Tap the offside link away from the machine towards the right, and it will pull both spindles out of position with it. Provided that these spindles are not turned in the link they should need very little re-adjustment after re-assembly.

Each spindle bears in two bushes. There are no left-hand threads used in the construction of the fork assembly.

Disconnect the positive wire and horn cable from the rear terminal on the battery. Remove the headlamp front and disconnect all wires from the switch (Figs. 56 and 57). Take off the lamp by taking out the bolts securing the brackets to the fork. Disconnect the flexible speedometer drive from the reduction gearbox on the brake-plate (Fig. 6), and remove the speedometer.

As described on page 18, disconnect the front brake-cable from the lever on the handlebar.

Completely unscrew the steering damper knob and pull it up with the rod, star spring, and locating-plate. Remove the four bolts securing the handlebar to the top-clip of the fork, raise the handlebar out of position and pull back and rest it on the top of the fuel tank. At once refit the two half-clips and four bolts to the top-clip in the positions they occupied originally.

Should any work be being undertaken to the fork take out the front wheel, after supporting the machine with a box or block of wood placed under the front end of the frame. Loosen the clamping bolt in the top clip and remove the steering-column lock-nut. Take out the bolt securing the top lug of the spring to the top-clip and tap the lug out of the taper. Tap the top-clip clear of the column and pull out the column from the steering head. Care must be taken to catch the balls from the lower head bearing. There should be nineteen in each race.

Before refitting the steering column and fork to the frame check the condition of the cups in the frame and the cones which are fitted to the column. Should there be the slightest signs of pitting, new cups, cones and balls must be fitted. To refit the fork to the machine, first smear stiff grease into the bearing cups in the frame and stick the balls (19 ¼-in. diameter in each) into place. Push the steering column up from below and whilst supporting it firmly in place put on the cone at the top and tap it down into position. Fit the dust-cap and then slip the top-clip into place and fit and screw down the lock-nut. This should be tightened down just far enough to leave the column free in its bearings without any trace of play. When checking the adjustment see that the fork spring is not catching the head-lug of the frame. Refit and tighten the clamping pin in the top-clip. The remainder of the work is just a reversal of operations described previously and does not call for special mention.

INSTRUCTIONS FOR DISMANTLING VELOCETTE DOWTY "OLEOMATIC" FORK.

(see page 119 for Dowty factory manual)

1. Lift front of machine and place a suitable block under crankcase so that fork can extend fully with the wheel just clear of the ground.

2. Remove inflation valve dust cap and slightly depress valve stem, allowing all air pressure to release. (Do not depress the valve stem too far, as this may damage the spring and impair the sealing qualities of the valve.)

3. Disconnect brake cable, remove wheel and mudguard with stays complete.

4. Slacken off $\frac{5}{16}$-in. B.S.F. bolts on fork crown fitting.

5. Grasp outer tube PD 1701-4A or PD 1701-4B with both hands, and by careful twisting and pulling slide down off the top static seal PP 17-22. This operation is to be performed carefully, otherwise the seal may stick to the tube and tend to jump out of its groove. If this does occur, the ring should be carefully replaced, making sure that it is not twisted.

At this stage, it is advisable to place a piece of stout, greased paper around the top portion of the outer tube, to prevent the paint from being scratched on withdrawal of the outer tube through the holes in the fork crown fitting PD 1701-19.

6. With a special spanner engaged in piston PD 1676, unscrew same by holding spanner and twisting axle fitting (right-hand thread). Inner and outer tubes may now be lowered and removed. The inner tube should not be withdrawn from the outer tube unless it is intended to examine the shroud and scraper ring as it is impossible to re-insert the scraper ring over the inner tube without damage unless the former together with the shroud is dismantled from the outer tube. If this is the case, slide the outer tube off the inner and remove the greaser P. 6B and screws PD 1811. The shroud PD 1682 will now slide off, together with the packing seal PP 16-15 and scraper PP 16-14, leaving the bearing exposed.

7. Unscrew nut from centre tube and remove flat washer and buffer PD 1701-30. The piston complete may now be withdrawn.

8. Remove split bearing PD 1677, spacer ring PD 1685 and gland ring PP 12-23M.

To Reassemble Forks reverse the above procedure.

It will be noted that all the above operations may be carried out without disturbing the fork crown fitting PD 1701-19 or the handlebar clip lug PC 1701-5. If it is necessary to remove these items, proceed as follows :—

1. Remove handlebars, speedometer, and drive, etc.

2. Unscrew steering damper knob PD 1502-10, and withdraw complete with rod.

3. Remove damper nut PD 1701-26.

4. Unscrew nut and slacken off cotter bolt PD 1701-23. The handlebar clip lug may now be lifted off and the fork crown fitting withdrawn through the headstem of the machine. Care is to be taken not to lose the balls from the steering races.

When re-assembling the fork, precautions should be taken so that all parts are scrupulously clean. It is advisable to smear glands and sealing rings with a little high-grade lubricating grease before reassembly.

To avoid the lengthy process of pouring oil through filler plug holes, the forks may be refilled in the following manner :—

After the piston has been assembled to inner tube, extend inner tube until there is approximately one inch gap between bottom of piston and lower buffer. Then, with outer tube about one and a half inches below the bottom of the top internal fitting, attached to the handlebar clip lug, pour in oil until full. Push outer tube up over static seal and tighten the clamp bolts on the fork crown, taking care that the small air vents on the outer tube are in their correct relative positions. Assemble mudguard, wheel and brake cable and lower machine to the ground.

With a suitable can held beneath the inflation valve, unscrew the valve core by means of the Schrader cap and allow the fork to close fully, surplus oil being collected in the can. Use only one of the following recommended grades of oil: Mobiloil "Arctic," Single Shell or "Castrolite." Replace valve core and inflate with tyre pump. The fork is correctly inflated when, with the rider mounted and balancing against some convenient support, the red marking dots on the inner sliding tubes are in line with the bottom edges of the shrouds PD 1682. A fork which has been completely dismantled is prone to "settle" slightly in the first few miles. It should be re-inflated to the correct position. Thereafter, the fork should require even less attention than that given to the tyres. Apply six shots from the grease gun to the greaser on each leg before road test.

When Fitting a New Fork Complete, as Supplied by the Makers, it is not necessary to disturb any of the air seals, if the following procedure is adopted:—

Remove damper knob and nut, and slacken off cotter bolt PD 1701-23 Unscrew filler plugs PD 1678. The handlebar clip lug may now be withdrawn from the fork. Place balls (nineteen balls) in the lower race of steering head on machine, using grease to make them adhere. Push steering tube of fork up through centre of steering head and hold in position whilst the top ball bearings, ball race and dust cover are mounted. Replace handlebar clip lug in position, and screw damper nut PD 1701-26 up finger tight.

Slacken off clamp bolts on fork crown fitting. Replace filler plugs and screw up tight. Tighten damper nut PD 1701-26 until correct adjustment of ball races is obtained. Tighten cotter bolt PD 1701-23. Tighten clamp bolts on fork crown fitting. Replace damper knob and adjust.

Fault Finding.

Fault.	Cause.	Remedy.
Fork is stiff in action.	Lack of lubricant on bearings.	Apply grease gun (six shots).
Ditto	Wheel spindle incorrectly adjusted.	Slacken clamp on axle fitting. Bounce fork a few times, and re-tighten.
Ditto	Fork crown clamp bolts so tight that outer tube becomes distorted, and presses on piston.	Slacken bolts until fork moves freely.
Ditto	Split bearings PD 1677 have been assembled with foreign matter beneath them, causing tightness in bore.	Dismantle split bearings, and remove high spots.
Ditto	Mudguard stays distorted.	Reset stays. See page 29

Fault.	Cause.	Remedy.
Malalignment.		See instructions on Removing Front Wheel. (Re-aligning outer tubes). Pages 15 and 16.
Fork is stiff in action.	Outer or inner tubes damaged accidentally.	Replace.
Insufficient damping	Lack of oil.	Top up.
Ditto	Viscosity of oil too low in tropical climates.	Replace oil with Mobiloil BB or Castrol XL.
Damping too fierce.	Oil too viscous.	Replace oil with recommended grade. If this is already in use, excessively low temperatures will have the same effect, but this is not usually serious, as the additional damping improves the steering characteristics under icy road conditions.
Fork "bottoms" readily.	Lack of air.	Inflate to correct position.
Ditto (fork correctly inflated with air)	Lack of oil.	Top up.
Fork hammers on full extension.	Over inflation.	Deflate to correct position.
Fork loses air pressure (oil traces on lower sliding tubes)	Leaking gland ring.	Replace. Examine bores for scores. If these are too deep to be polished out, replace outer tubes.
Ditto	Leaking static seal on piston PP 17-1.	Replace faulty seal.
Ditto (oil traces around top of outer tube)	Leaking static seal PD 17-22 on top internal fitting.	Replace faulty seal.
Ditto (no oil leakage).	Leaking inflation valve core; or Leaking inflation valve washer PD 1561-43, or Leaking static seal PP 17-22; or Leaking static seal PP 17-17; or Leaking balance pipe	Replace faulty part.

ADJUSTMENT OF BRAKES.

Front Brake. (See Fig. 2). The hand lever should not come up too close to the grip when the brake is fully applied, and as the brake wears it will be found that the lever will move further before full braking power is obtained. Adjustment is then necessary, and is carried out as follows:—Loosen the lock nut below the knurled head of the brake adjuster on the front brake plate, screw up the adjuster until the correct adjustment is obtained. It is best to have the adjustment set so that the lever is about a full inch away from the grip when the brake is fully applied. When correctly set tighten the lock nut. After adjusting make sure that the brake shoes are not fouling the drum when the lever is released. (The adjuster is on the fork girder on early types).

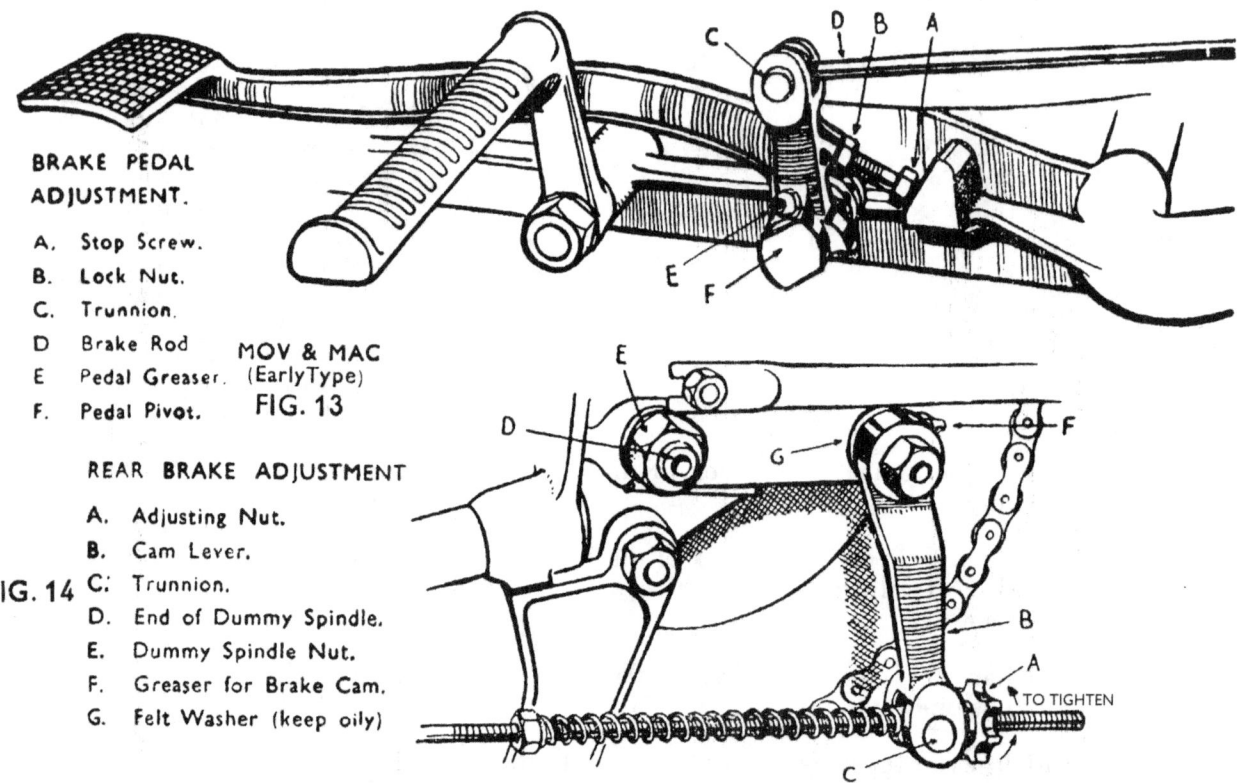

BRAKE PEDAL ADJUSTMENT.

- A. Stop Screw.
- B. Lock Nut.
- C. Trunnion.
- D. Brake Rod
- E. Pedal Greaser.
- F. Pedal Pivot.

MOV & MAC (Early Type) FIG. 13

REAR BRAKE ADJUSTMENT

FIG. 14
- A. Adjusting Nut.
- B. Cam Lever.
- C. Trunnion.
- D. End of Dummy Spindle.
- E. Dummy Spindle Nut.
- F. Greaser for Brake Cam.
- G. Felt Washer (keep oily)

Rear Brake. (See Fig. 14). To re-adjust screw the knurled nut further up the brake rod at the rear end until the correct adjustment is obtained. The brake pedal on some MOV and MAC machines can be adjusted for height to suit the rider's individual requirements by altering the setting of the brake pedal stop (see Fig. 13). See that it clears the footrest when the brake is fully applied. After adjusting brakes check wheels to see that brake shoes are not fouling.

ADJUSTMENT OF CHAINS.

Slack or incorrectly adjusted chains cause hard or snatchy running and excessive wear. The adjustment of both chains should be such that there is about $\frac{1}{2}$-in. free up and down movement midway between the sprockets. Check the adjustment of the front chain through the inspection hole in the chain cover—never attempt to check with chains in motion—an elementary point which if forgotten may result in the loss of, or injury to, the fingers. Always check the adjustment in several places and allow the specified amount of freedom in the tightest place. The tension is nearly always found to vary slightly in different places as the sprockets are turned.

The primary chain is adjusted by moving the gearbox which is pivotally mounted and which in the case of the MOV and MAC models is mounted on a cross tube of the frame to which it is held by two halfclips. On the

MSS model the gearbox is also pivotally mounted, but it is mounted on a bolt passing through the bottom of the housing, and the housing is held between the two rear engine plates. The driving load upon the rear chain always tends to pull back the gearbox and would tighten the front chain excessively if no positive means were provided to stop the gearbox "working" back. On the MOV and MAC models the top of the gearbox housing is provided with a shoulder through which passes a draw bolt secured to the left-hand rear engine plate, and on the MSS the draw bolt is fitted behind the rear of the two gearbox fixing bolts and passes through an "eye" bolt fixed to the engine plate (see Fig. 15). In each case two nuts are fitted on to the draw bolts by means of which it is possible to move the gearbox forward or backward on its mounting after the fixing clips, in the case of the models MOV and MAC are loosened.

Primary Chain Adjustment—MOV and MAC. (Fig. 36.)

Loosen the four nuts securing the half clips underneath, and loosen the rear nut on the draw bolt or gearbox adjuster. Screw this back about two turns. Now screw the front nut back in the same direction until it is tight and tighten up the nuts underneath to hold the half clips. Check the chain adjustment. Should the chain be too tight, loosen the nuts underneath again and turn the front nut forward a little and follow it up with the rear nut. Re-tighten the nuts underneath and re-check the chain. Finally check the adjuster nuts for tightness. Always make sure that the bolt which holds the adjuster or draw bolt to the rear engine plate is kept fully tightened up.

Primary Chain Adjustment—MSS. (Fig. 15.)

The adjusting nuts are on the right-hand side of the machine just alongside the rear engine plate. To tighten the chain, screw the front nut forward along the draw bolt a little and then turn the rear nut forward until it is tight. Check the chain adjustment. If too tight, screw the rear adjuster nut slightly to the rear and follow it up with the front nut. Check the adjustment and finally check the adjuster nuts for tightness.

Rear Chain Adjustment—All Models.

If slackness in the front chain is taken up it will be necessary to re-adjust the rear chain to compensate for the amount that it will have been slackened by the rearward movement of the gearbox.

To re-adjust the rear chain slacken the nut on the dummy spindle at the left-hand side frame fork end and slightly unscrew the detachable spindle which passes through the fork end of the frame on the right-hand side. On early models of the MOV and MAC types it is also necessary to slacken the rear brake plate anchor bolt (Fig. 43). On machines fitted with the early type integral hub and brake drum (non-detachable), slacken the nuts on both sides.

The wheel can be pushed to the rear to take up excess slackness in the chain by turning the chain adjusting screws each a little at a time clockwise after loosening the lock nuts which keep them secured in the frame fork ends. The heads of the adjusters and lock nuts are situated in the angle made between the saddle stay tubes (from fork end lugs to below saddle) and the chain stays (between fork end lugs and lower part of frame) (see Fig. 42.) A convenient way to keep the rear wheel in correct alignment is to count the number of turns given to each screw and turn them an equal amount. Push the wheel forward so as to contact the dummy spindle and detachable spindle with the ends of the adjusters and hold it in this position when tightening the spindle and the nut on the opposite side.

Check the adjustment of the chain, and if correct tighten the anchor bolt and the lock nuts on the adjusters and check the spindle and nut for tightness.

FIG. 15

The Gearbox (MSS Type) (The Gear Lever shown is an early type.)

LUBRICATION OF CHAINS.

The front chain is enclosed in a sheet metal cover and a small quantity of oil is put into the chain case before the machine is tested. The oil should be replenished at intervals of approximately 1,000 miles, more oil being poured in through the inspection plug hole in the front part of the primary cover. This inspection cap is approximately above the left-hand footrest. It is usually convenient to squirt oil over the chain from an oil can while the chain is moved forward by the starter.

The rear chain should be lubricated from an oil can from time to time, and occasionally should be removed and put into a bath of paraffin to allow the paraffin to penetrate into the interior of the chain joints and also brushed well to remove all external dirt. It should then be given another bath in fresh, clean paraffin, and after being well shaken should be hung up to drain. The chain is then ready to be lubricated before being refitted to the machine. This can be done by soaking it in a bath of warm, but not boiling, graphite grease or tallow. The grease or tallow must be warm enough to be quite fluid. After allowing the chain to remain in the bath from about 15 to 20 minutes, allow the bath to cool down until the contents almost set, and then remove the chain, wipe off excess grease and refit it.

When re-fitting the rear chain, make sure that the spring clip on the connecting link is fitted so that the closed end of the link faces forward in the direction of movement of the chain. This is important.

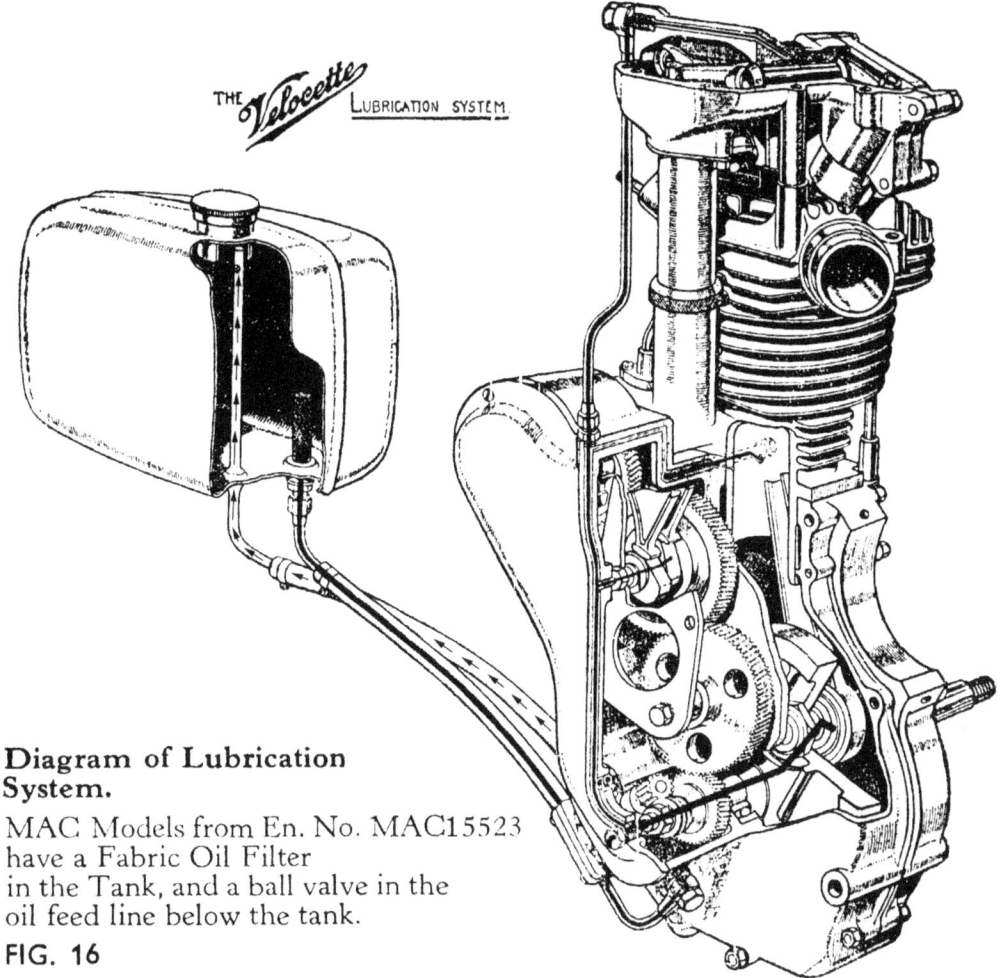

Diagram of Lubrication System.

MAC Models from En. No. MAC15523 have a Fabric Oil Filter in the Tank, and a ball valve in the oil feed line below the tank.

FIG. 16

THE ENGINE LUBRICATION SYSTEM. (Fig. 16.)

From the oil tank oil feeds by gravity through the gauze filter in the tank and the feed pipe to the oil pump situated in the lower part of the rear of the timing side crankcase. This pump is divided into two distinct parts—the upper pair of gears acting as the feed pump and the lower pair as the return pump. Both sets of gears are fitted in the one pump-body and are driven from the crankshaft by a worm on the main-shaft which meshes with a skew gear on the spindle of the pump. In order that it shall never be possible for more oil to be fed into the engine than the return side of the pump would be capable of clearing from the sump, the return gears are almost double the width of the feed gears. Thus the return side is able to handle nearly double the amount that can be supplied to the engine.

The illustration shows clearly the general arrangement of the lubrication system and should be referred to in conjunction with this explanation.

From the feed gears oil is fed out of the top of the pump into the passage drilled in the crankcase that leads obliquely upwards to the face of the timing-chest. On all models up to MAC engine No. MAC 15522 the oil has to pass a $\frac{1}{4}$-in. diameter steel ball which, when the pump is not working, is held against a seating in the oil passage by a light spring. The spring is held in position by a plug screwed down to a shoulder inside the mouth of the passage.† (See Fig. 18).

This arrangement is termed the check valve. Its purpose is to prevent any oil flowing into and thus flooding the engine when the machine is left standing. Engines from MAC 15523 have the check valve under the oil tank.

† *A small steel plate pressed into the oil passage was used instead of the screwed plug up to 1940.*

The timing cover which is secured to the face of the timing-chest acts as a distributor for the oil supply. A passage cored in the cover during casting registers with the mouth of the oil-passage in the crankcase and oil is thus fed into the passage in the cover.

By means of the passage in the cover oil is taken to an oil-jet (screwed into the cover) through which a supply passes into the hollow mainshaft and through a drilling to the crankpin, from which it issues from a hole in the centre of the roller track in the big-end. The revolving big-end dissipates the oil over the interior of the crankcase, lubricating the cylinder and piston and small end bearing. This oil ultimately drains to the bottom of the crankcase to be picked up by the return pump.

A second opening in the oil passage in the timing cover is arranged to fit over the end of the spindle carrying the cam-wheel and cams. The oil feeds along the hollow spindle on Engines up to MAC 15522 and passes out through two holes in the spindle to oil holes in the cam-wheel bush and through holes in the cam faces. Lubrication is thus provided directly for the bearing and the cams and cam-followers. From MAC 15523 the working faces of the cams are no longer drilled to provide an oil feed to the cams and followers, and the opening from the oil passage in the timing cover leads only to the cam wheel bush by means of the drilled cam spindle. An extra opening slightly above permits a supply of oil to be fed to the cam oil jet, the outer end of which locates in the cover. Oil from this is directed against the faces of the cams. Engines having this system can be identified by the later type smooth rounded timing cover.

* From the upper end of the passage oil is diverted through a drilling in the face of the timing cover into a drilled passage in the crankcase and to the rear of the cylinder wall. This supply has first to pass through a hollow bolt screwed into the crank case from the nearside. The head of this bolt is marked "jet." A small radial hole in the bolt allows sufficient oil to pass to the oil holes in the cylinder. (See Fig. 19.)

The remainder of the supply is taken by a pipe from the top of the timing cover to the rocker box. The rocker box cover is drilled to lead oil to the large oil grooves in the top bearing surfaces above the rockers.

From the bearings, the oil is free to run away down the push-rod cover into the timing-chest, where it lubricates the timing gears, etc. The crankshaft pinion dips into oil collected in the bottom of the timing-chest. The excess drains through a hole to the sump.

Lubrication of the intermediate-timing-gear bearing is provided from the spindle carrying the gear. The flange of this spindle (inside the crankcase) is drilled to communicate with a groove running the full length of the top of the spindle and a constant supply of oil runs into the oil hole and along the groove from the interior of the engine.

In addition to those parts which are lubricated directly from the pump, the valves and valve-guides receive adequate lubrication.

On engines with separate rocker boxes quite a lot of oil accumulates in the valve spring covers. The supply is restricted to some extent by the provision of two washers, one in each rocker, which are held in place by light springs attached to the tappet covers.

An addition to the system is a fabric filter carried in a cylindrical chamber in the oil tank.

All oil that drains back to the sump is drawn away past a filter plug† (Fig. 17) by the return side of the pump which delivers it to the oil tank.

The correct working of the system can be checked by starting the engine and removing the cap from the oil tank. Oil will be noticed returning in an intermittent stream from the top of the pipe just inside the filler neck.

The fact that the return is irregular sometimes give rise to enquiry, but it is quite in order. On starting the engine the return may be almost

† *Except on engines prior to M3472, MAC 5079 and MSS 3611.*

* *Not on engines after MAC 15522.*

constant for a few moments due to the amount of oil which has drained to the bottom of the crankcase whilst the engine was stationary, and until this surplus is cleared the return flow will exceed normal. During normal running, however, the return is somewhat intermittent, and mixed with bubbles of air due, partly to the fact that the return side of the pump has practically double the capacity of the feed side, and partly to variations in the amount of oil suspended in the crankcase due to engine speed. For example, upon sudden acceleration the return flow may cease for a time, but will of course resume at a greater rate upon the engine being slowed down.

The Suction Filter.† (Fig. 17.)

All oil has to pass this filter before reaching the return pump.

The head of the filter plug is situated at the bottom rear corner of the crankcase on the " off " or right-hand side of the machine, just below the rear engine bolt. It has a right-hand thread.

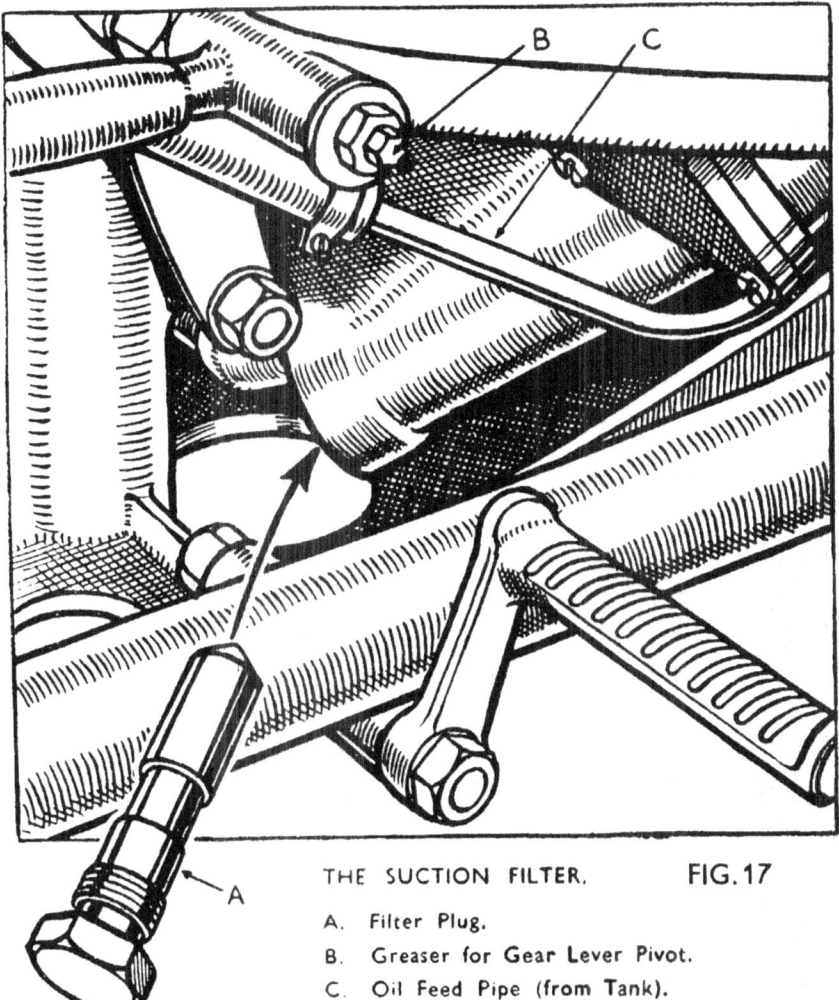

THE SUCTION FILTER.　　　　FIG. 17

A. Filter Plug.
B. Greaser for Gear Lever Pivot.
C. Oil Feed Pipe (from Tank).

The body of the plug is machined to fit with a very small diametric clearance from the bore in the crankcase in which it is fitted. The space whilst being ample to pass the oil will not permit anything to pass which could damage or lock the oil pump.

The plug may be unscrewed with the sparking plug spanner and should be removed occasionally for cleaning purposes, usually at intervals of approximately 2,000 miles running. If restricted or choked, excessive

† *Except on engines prior to M3472, MAC 5079 and MSS 3611.*

smoking at the exhaust will occur due to the return of oil to the tank being prevented, with consequent flooding of the crankcase.

When refitting see that the fibre washer is in place and the plug fully tightened. An air leak at this point will make impossible the proper working of the return side of the system.

The Check Valve (To Engine MAC15522.) (Fig. 18.)

Occasionally trouble is encountered with excessive smoking from the exhaust on starting, due to oil from the tank draining through into the crankcase when the engine is stationary owing to the check valve failing to close properly. The remedy is to remove the timing cover and reseat the ball. The valve consists of ¼-in. dia. steel ball held on a seating in the main oil passage above the oil pump by a light spring. The spring is held by a plug, screwed into the mouth of the oil passage. It can be unscrewed with a screwdriver and should bring the spring with it. Engines built prior to 1940 have a small plate pressed into the oil-way instead of the screwed plug illustrated. This plate can be pulled out by using a small pair of pliers with narrow jaws.

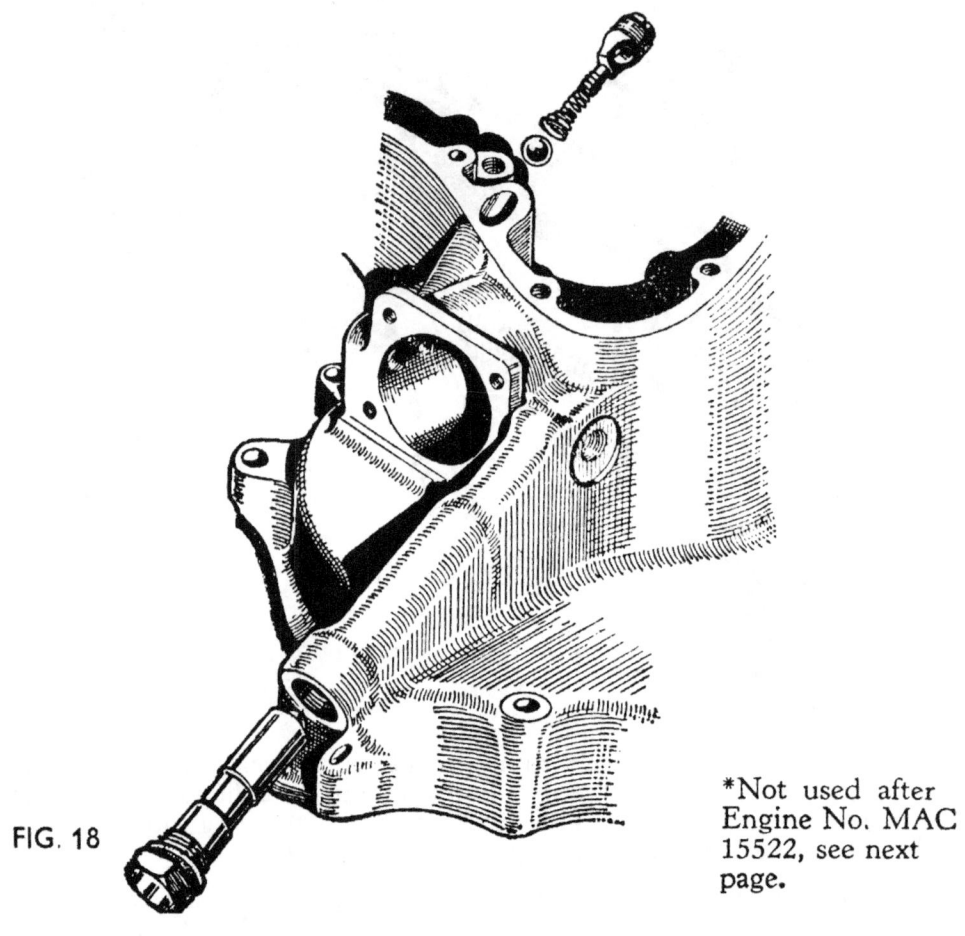

FIG. 18

*Not used after Engine No. MAC 15522, see next page.

THE SUCTION FILTER AND CHECK VALVE*

(Shown removed from the crankcase)

The passage into which the plug is fitted is readily visible as soon as the timing cover is taken off. The mouth is oval in shape, and its position is well shown in Fig. 40.

As a temporary measure the ball can sometimes be reseated by tapping it *lightly* against the seat using a suitable punch inserted through the oil feed hole against the ball. As the seat tends to widen under such treatment thus decreasing the unit pressure of the ball upon it the tapping must be carefully done.

As soon as possible the seat should be recut using the special cutter Service Tool No. X2958.

Make sure that the spring is in good order and if necessary renew it:

When re-fitting the check valve plug, screw it down as far as it will go against the shoulder in the oil passage.

After re-fitting the check valve plug and the timing cover, start the engine before attaching the rocker box oil feed pipe to the union on the cover. Oil should be forced out of the union in a steady flow. If satisfactory, stop the engine and connect up the pipe. If no oil comes out see that the check valve spring is not jammed. Slightly ease back the check valve plug and test again.

N.B.—The use of an engine oil of "heavier" grade than recommended, *i.e.*, a Summer Grade during the Winter, may also cause smoking on starting from cold in addition to making starting more difficult, and give rise to symptoms resembling those caused by the check valve leaking.

The Check Valve (from Engine No. MAC 15523.)

The check valve body carrying the $\frac{3}{8}$-in. diameter check valve ball and the spring is screwed on to the strainer gauze assembly in the bottom of the oil tank, and the oil feed pipe union nut screws on to its lower end.

To remove the check valve it is necessary first to drain the oil tank. Next unscrew the oil pipe union nut and disconnect the pipe. Unscrew the strainer gauze assembly from the tank.

To take the check valve apart for cleaning hold the check valve body in the vice between aluminium or copper "clamps" to avoid damage to the hexagon, and unscrew the strainer assembly from it, disclosing the ball and spring. The ball, spring and seating may be cleaned and examined.

Should the spring be removed make certain that it is correctly refitted into the ball-valve body and is fully home otherwise the pressure of the spring upon the ball will be too great and will prevent the ball opening when the engine starts. Cases have been known of owners putting back the spring above the ball and effectively cutting off all oil from the engine, so that the above warning should not be disregarded.

After refitting the check valve make certain that the oil feed pipe is full of oil, so that the oil pump is primed, and if the pipe has been removed or the oil in it has run out, pour oil into the open end until the pipe is full and connect it at once to the check valve body.

Refit the tank drain plug, and refill the tank. Start the engine and check the feed (see page 13). If no return is obtained after a few moments running take off the oil pipe once more and prime the pump again.

The Cylinder Oil Feed. On engines from M3472, MAC5079 and MSS 3611, not after MAC 15522.

Remove bolt below cylinder base joint at rear on left side. Bolt is marked "jet" on head. Clean in petrol. See that small radial hole in the centre of bolt is clear. See that fibre washer below head is in order. Replace. **Exercise great care in tightening so that bolt is not sheared off.**

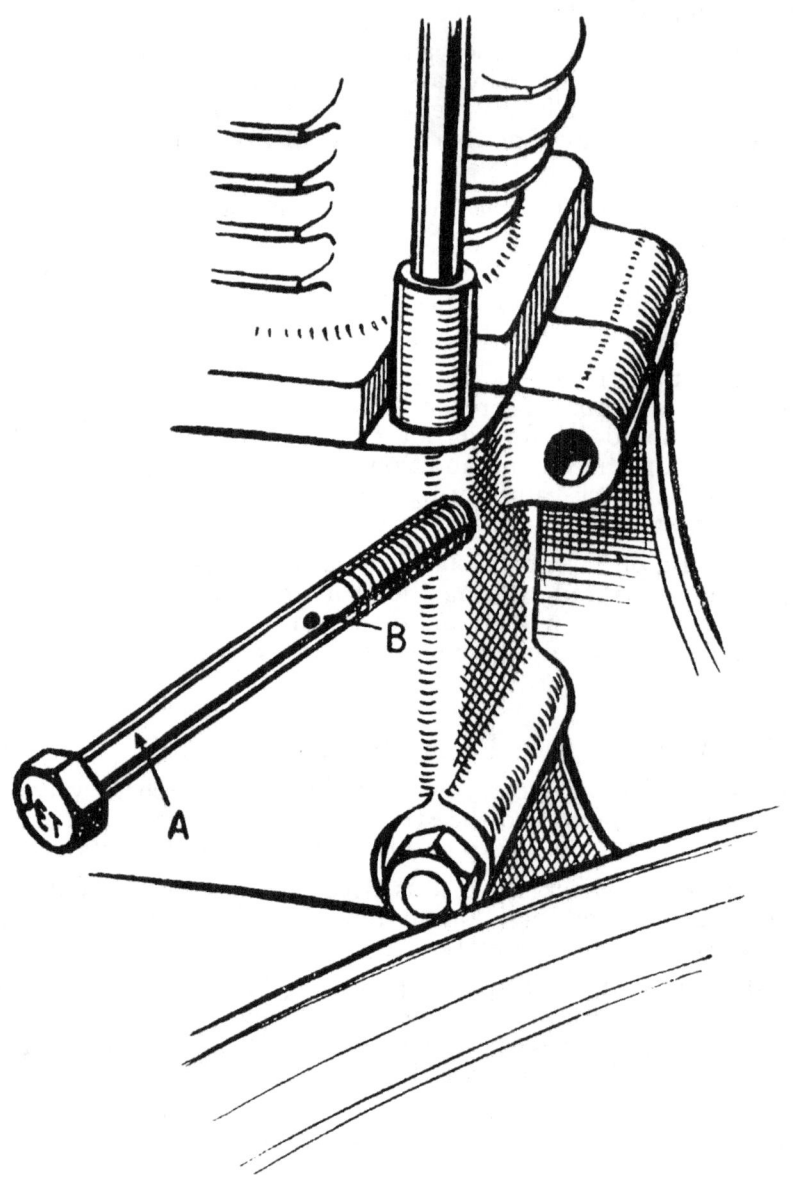

FIG. 19

CYLINDER OIL FEED (on nearside of Engine).
A. Hollow Bolt.   B. Oil Hole.
Not fitted after Engine No. MAC 15522.

ADJUSTMENT OF DYNAMO DRIVE BELT (Fig. 20.)

Take off belt cover by taking out bolt from centre of cover and nut securing cover to primary chain case. Loosen clamping bolt securing dynamo strap to crankcase in front of cylinder base. Turn dynamo slowly on crankcase being careful not to move it sideways and put pulleys out of line. The armature is eccentric to the body of the dynamo, so that rotation of the body varies the distance of the armature spindle from the crankshaft. When belt is just taut tighten clamping bolt.

Check alignment of belt. Replace cover.

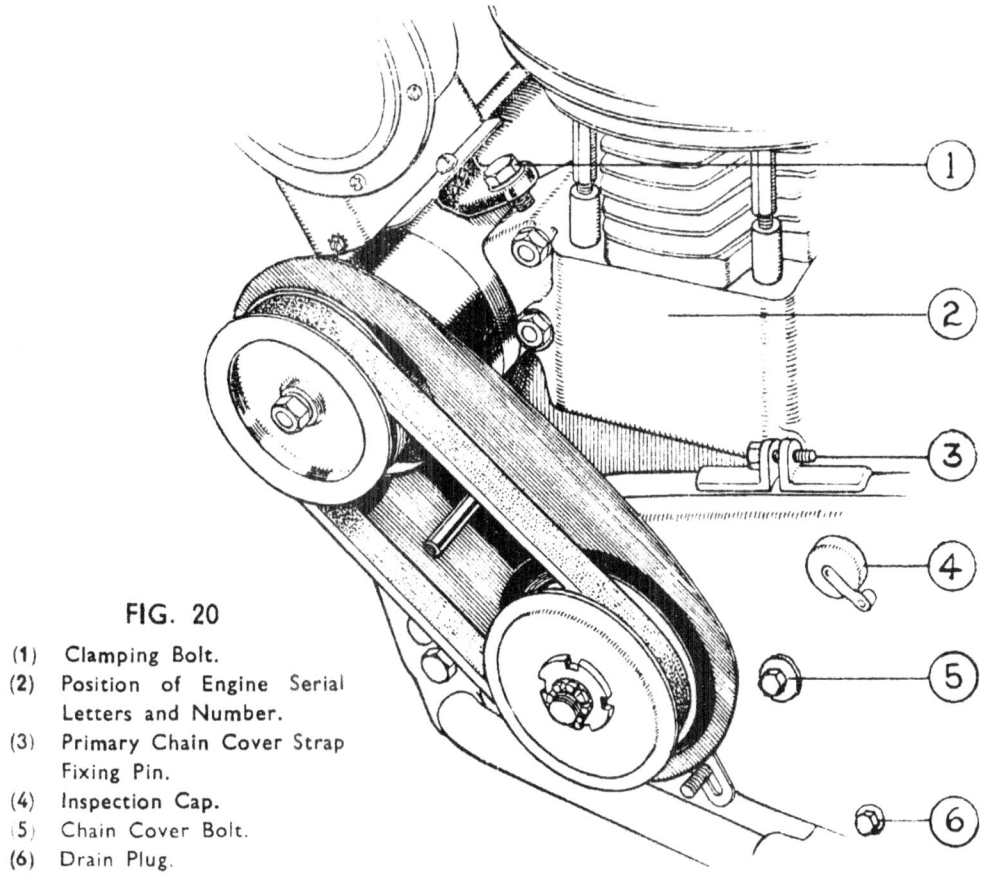

FIG. 20

(1) Clamping Bolt.
(2) Position of Engine Serial Letters and Number.
(3) Primary Chain Cover Strap Fixing Pin.
(4) Inspection Cap.
(5) Chain Cover Bolt.
(6) Drain Plug.

THE FABRIC OIL FILTER (On MAC only from Eng. No. MAC 15523.)

The fabric element needs no attention, but should be discarded and replaced by a new one after every 10,000 miles service.

The element is carried in a cylindrical chamber of the oil tank and all oil returned from the engine has to pass through it before going back into the tank.

To remove the element it is unnecessary to drain the tank, but as it is always advisable when fitting a new element to start with clean oil we recommend not **only** draining the tank but removing it entirely and washing it out thoroughly in clean petrol and allowing it to dry off before refitting.

In order to remove the filter element the return hose must be disconnected from the union nipple below the tank. (This will be disconnected in any case if the tank is being taken off).

Loosen the nut at the top end of the filter centre stud—in the centre of the filter top cap on the tank top and with a metal pan or dish held below the bottom filter cap prise the bottom cap away from the tank to allow the half-pint or so of oil trapped in the filter chamber to drain away. The complete removal of the nut and top cap will allow the bottom cap with centre stud to be pulled out. Retain the joint washers used between the two caps and the tank. The filter element can now be pulled out.

Wash out the tank as described above.

When dry fit the new filter element and replace the joint washer and the bottom cap. passing the centre stud up through the filter chamber. Have the top cap with joint washer and nut handy for refitting. Hold the bottom cap and oil union firmly against the tank to prevent leakage and pour clean oil of the correct grade into the oil filter chamber from the top. When up to the level of the opening leading into the tank put back the top joint washer, the cap and the nut and tighten this securely. Hold the tank upright and refit to the machine. Refit the drain plug, see that the check valve is in place and refill the tank.

Connect up the oil pipes, being careful to see that the feed pipe is full of oil (see page 13.)

The object of filling the filter chamber is two-fold. Firstly, if it is not filled when the filter is replaced the level of oil in the main tank will be reduced soon after starting by the amount of oil required to fill the filter chamber to the level of the outlet pipe. Secondly, no return of oil would be visible entering the tank after the engine was started until the chamber had filled.

REMOVAL OF OIL TANK. MOV and MAC Models only.

To remove the oil tank for cleaning purposes it is necessary first of all to disconnect the clutch cable, and this is done in the following manner :—

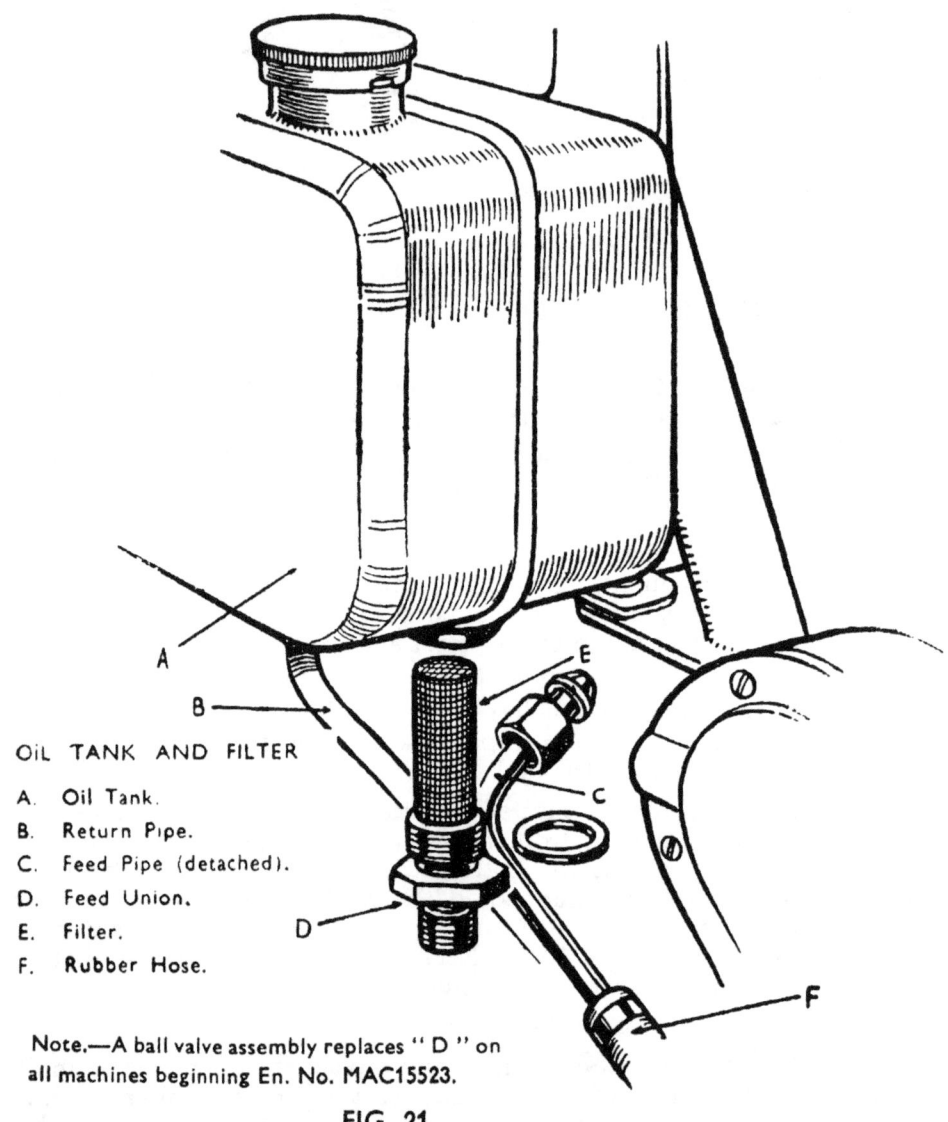

OIL TANK AND FILTER

A. Oil Tank.
B. Return Pipe.
C. Feed Pipe (detached).
D. Feed Union.
E. Filter.
F. Rubber Hose.

Note.—A ball valve assembly replaces "D" on all machines beginning En. No. MAC15523.

FIG. 21

Raise the handlebar clutch lever as when declutching when driving the machine ; grasp the outer casing of the clutch cable and release the handlebar lever, at the same time pull forward the outer casing so that it comes away from the socket of the lever.

The nipple can then be slipped out of the lever and the outer casing will slide up, enabling the cable stop to be taken out of the cable stop holder on the gearbox. (See Fig. 31).

Screw out the cable holder, and slip this up out of place, and then disconnect the small cable nipple from the slotted connecting piece just inside the gearbox by sliding the cable sideways. The cable and casing will then easily draw upwards through the tube in the oil tank. Drain the tank by removing the drain plug or oil feed union.

The oil pipes should then be disconnected and finally the tank can be unbolted and removed.

It is held by one bolt at the top to the saddle lug of the frame and at the bottom is secured to the battery platform by a nut which is screwed over a threaded boss surrounding the tube through which the clutch cable passes.

Note particularly before removing the oil pipes the position in which they are fitted so that they may be re-fitted in the correct way. (See Fig. 16).

The copper oil pipe which is attached to the oil tank by means of a union nut must be connected to the oil pipe which is secured to the crankcase by the hollow bolt.

The oil return hose is connected to an adapter under the bottom filter chamber cap (on earlier machines direct to a pipe welded to the tank).

Warning. Except on machines which do not have the ball valve underneath the oil tank (MOV and MSS rigid frame models and MAC models previous to engine MAC15523) the oil pump must be primed before starting the engine (see page 13).

In order to clear as much as possible of the dirty oil out of the engine it is best, after refilling the oil tank, to leave the return pipe hose disconnected and start up the engine. The dirty oil will be pumped up through the rubber hose and can be caught in a suitable container and ultimately discarded.

After a few moments' running, clean oil will be seen to issue from the rubber hose, and the engine should then be stopped and the hose connected up again to the tank. This is an easier and better method than attempting to flush out the engine. **Never flush out the engine with paraffin.**

If possible, always avoid disturbing the hollow bolt which secures the copper oil feed pipe to the crankcase below the pump, as it may be difficult to get the pipe oil-tight again if this is taken off.

Be careful when tightening this hollow bolt not to use excessive force or it may be broken.

REMOVAL OF OIL TANK MSS.

Proceed as described for the Models MOV and MAC except that the clutch cable can be left in place. The fixings of the tank at the top and bottom differ in detail only. At the bottom an ear on the tank is bolted to the rear engine plate. See also preceding section.

DECARBONISING AND GRINDING-IN VALVES.

Although basically similar to previous MAC engines, the modifications made when the aluminium alloy cylinder head and aluminium alloy jacketed cylinder were introduced make slightly different procedure necessary when dismantling the cylinder head.

The cylinder head now contains the overhead rockers, valve springs, and rocker bearings and the earlier pattern separate rocker box is deleted.

It is generally desirable to decarbonise the engine and to grind in the valves lightly on a new machine after it has covered the first 2,000 miles. It is not, however, necessary to repeat the process at anything like such frequent intervals and often a very considerable mileage can be covered before it is necessary to decarbonise again.

The usual indications that this work is required are—a falling off of power and tendency for the engine to pink excessively.

To dismantle the engine for decarbonising it is necessary first to remove the fuel tank. To do so loosen the front saddle bolt and slip the frame of the saddle away from the bolt. On Models MOV and MAC the saddle frame is slotted to allow it to be lifted out of position, and this will allow the front of the saddle to be lifted to make the rear tank bolt accessible.

Turn off the supply of fuel at both taps, undo the union nuts holding the fuel pipe to the taps. Do not allow the fuel pipe to twist. If a tap is not tight, prevent it from turning with a spanner on the hexagon section. Take out the two fixing bolts at the front of the tank with their steel washers. On Models MOV and MAC take off the nuts holding the small strap across the bottom of the tank at the front and remove the washers and strap. Loosen the nut from the rear bolt, push out the bolt to free tank. The tank is then free to come away.

Unscrew the ring holding the mixing chamber top to the mixing chamber of the carburetter, and pull out the throttle and air valves by the cables and tie them up out of the way to the top tube of the frame.

Take off the two nuts and remove the plain washers from the studs attaching the carburetter to the cylinder head and take off the carburetter and fuel pipe.

Removing Rocker Box. (Engines with Iron heads only.)

This is done by unscrewing and removing the bolts securing the tappet covers to the side of the rocker box and top cover. Take off both covers, being careful not to drop and lose the small oil control washers which are fitted in the centres of the rockers and which are held in place there by the rocker thrust springs fixed to the covers.

It will usually be found that there is an accumulation of oil in the spring covers and this oil may overflow on removal of the covers. This is quite normal and in order.

Take off the rocker box oil feed pipe.

Next take off the nuts and washers from the studs securing the top flange of the pushrod tube to the rocker box.

Slide the top part of the pushrod cover down off the studs into the lower part.

It will be noticed that between the two paper packing washers that are used on the top flange joint there is a steel pushrod guide plate.

When the rocker box is taken off be sure that this plate is not lost.

Finally, take out the three long bolts that hold the rocker box to the cylinder head. This will free the rocker box and it can then be lifted off.

Do not take apart the top and bottom halves of the rocker box as it is very unlikely that this will ever have to be done in the course of normal maintenance. The rocker bearings give almost indefinite service.

Removing the Cylinder Head. (Alum-Alloy type.)

After removing the fuel tank and the usual items, disconnect and remove the oil feed pipe from the timing case to the rocker cover. Take out the eight cover bolts and remove the cover. Occasionally the rocker cover may foul the inlet rocker and be prevented from coming off. If this occurs rotate the crankshaft until the inlet valve is full open. This will give clearance for the cover to slide off towards the front end first. Remove the sparking plug. Rotate the crankshaft with the kick starter until both valves are closed and the piston at top dead centre or thereabouts.

Take out three bolts securing the rocker bearing block to the cylinder head—the two end ones and the centre one—but leave the other two in place.

Remove the bearing block and the rockers, and lift out the two push rods, which should be marked "inlet" and "exhaust" respectively. They must be put back into their own places on refitting. The inlet is the nearer to the centre of the machine. Indelible pencil, if wetted, is a suitable marking medium. Take off the gasket from the rocker bearing block platform.

Take off the nuts and washers from the studs which hold the upper push rod flange to the head, and telescope the upper section of tube into the lower half, at the same time taking off the push rod guide plate and the two joint washers from the flange face. This guide plate is an important and vital part of the engine, and must be preserved for refitting.

Unscrew and take off the four cylinder head nuts and washers—two accessible outside the rocker box on the left-hand side of the head—and the other two down inside the holes or openings in the bearing block platform.

Unscrew and take out the four long cylinder studs.

Lift off the cylinder head, retaining the cylinder head gasket for use when reassembling. Do not remove the cylinder.

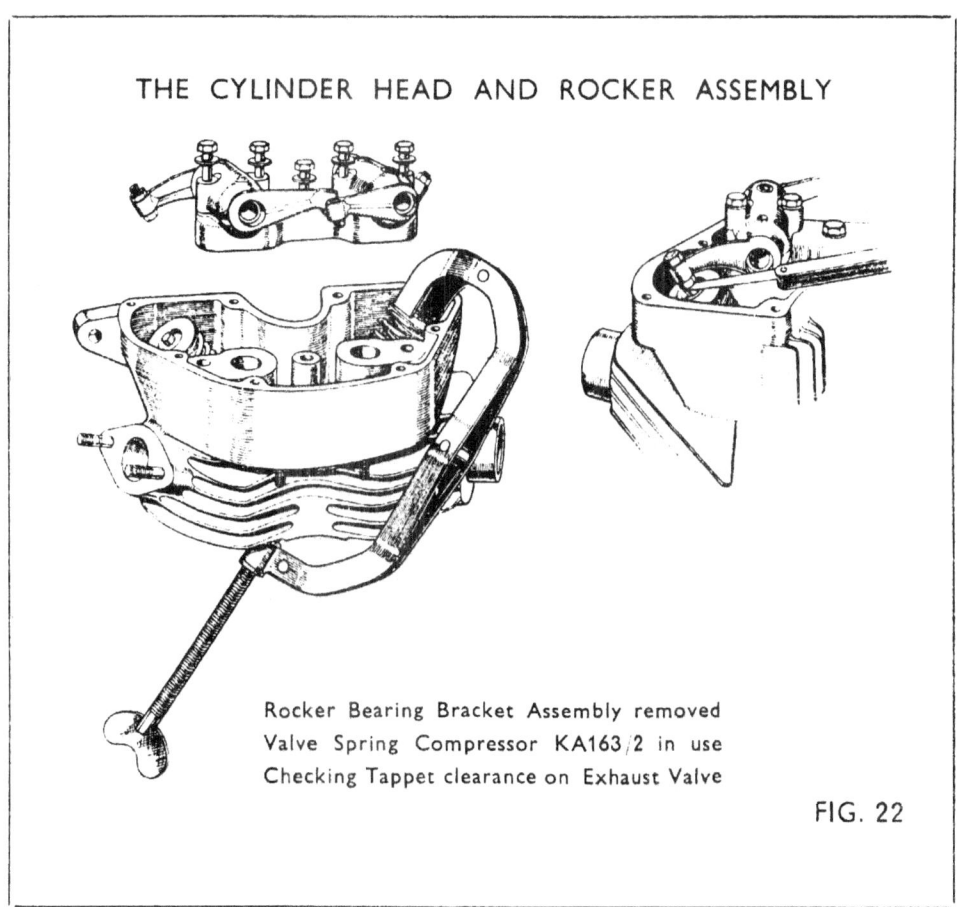

THE CYLINDER HEAD AND ROCKER ASSEMBLY

Rocker Bearing Bracket Assembly removed
Valve Spring Compressor KA163/2 in use
Checking Tappet clearance on Exhaust Valve

FIG. 22

Removing Cylinder Head. (Iron type only.)

Unscrew and remove the four cylinder head nuts—this will allow the cylinder head to be lifted off the barrel. No cylinder head gasket is fitted.†
It is unnecessary to remove the cylinder barrel, and we do not recom-

† *A gasket was only used on engines prior to M3472, MAC 5079 and MSS 3611, and on engines with alloy heads.*

mend it unless it has to be taken off for attention to the piston or piston rings, which is unlikely to be needed except after a considerable mileage has been run. The piston and piston rings should be disturbed as little as possible. Frequent removal and re-assembly sometimes causes heavy oil consumption.

Removing Valves and Springs (Alloy Head Model).

This is done in exactly the same manner as on the other models, but the Valve Spring Compressor Tool No. KA163/2 is required to clear the sides of the rocker chamber. The smaller size used on the previous types is unsuitable.

The valve top washers, cotters and springs are identical to the corresponding parts on earlier models, but there are loose bottom washers which fit over the valve guides and these come away when the springs are taken off.

Removing Valves and Springs. (Iron Head Models.)

The valves are removed by compressing the valve springs whilst holding the valve head on to the seating so as to allow the split cotter to be lifted out of the hollow in the valve-spring-washer. A (KA 163) compressor will suit. After removing keep the two halves of each cotter together. The odd halves are not interchangeable. The valve springs, valve-spring-covers and washers, etc., are interchangeable, but it is best to refit them in the same positions from which they were removed. The valves are also interchangeable on MOV and MAC Models. The best plan is to get two small boxes, marking them respectively " inlet " and " exhaust." and place the parts into the appropriate boxes as they are taken off. The inner valve springs are a tight fit within the outers. Do not separate them.

Having removed the valve-cotters the springs can be released, which will permit them to be taken out and the valve spring covers to be removed from the guides.

It should be noted that inside each cover there is a plain steel washer which provides a seating for the bottom of the valve springs, and underneath each cover and between the cover and the guide there are two packing washers which should be renewed when re-assembling the engine.

The valves will pull out of the guides and should be thoroughly cleaned.

Refacing and Grinding in Valves, etc.

Reface the seatings on a valve grinding machine equipped with a collett if such a machine is available. The seat angle is 45°.

An alternative method is to hold the stem carefully and as close to the head as possible in the chuck of a lathe or drilling machine, being careful not to mark the stem or otherwise damage it.

The valve head can then be cleaned and polished up with ordinary emery cloth, a fine grade being used for finishing purposes. It is desirable to true up the valve seats, before grinding in the valves because although a valve is a comparatively cheap replacement it is necessary to avoid wearing the seats in the cylinder head by prolonged grinding as the head or seats are expensive to replace.

To remove the carbon from the cylinder head it is best to use a scraper made from some soft metal such as brass. This will avoid scratching the surface of the head or damaging the valve seats. Scrape the carbon from the combustion space and from the exhaust port and finish off by cleaning up the ports with emery cloth.

Avoid scratching the valve seats when doing so.

It is unlikely that the seatings in the cylinder head will require truing up unless the machine has covered a considerable distance.

If recutting is needed see Page 55.

If the seats appear to be in reasonably good order, the valves should be lightly ground in. To grind in the valves, use a very fine emery powder mixed with oil or paraffin, or one of the numerous brands of valve grinding compounds. These compounds are sometimes put up in a double-ended tin, the coarse compound in one end and fine compound in the other. It is very seldom necessary to use the coarse variety on the valves. Use as little compound as possible smeared over the seating on the valve. Avoid getting any compound on to the stem or into the valve guide.

Slip the valve into position and hold the end of the stem near the cotter groove with a suitable holder (KA164/2) which should be tightened on to the valve carefully to avoid damaging the stem or the edges of the cotter groove.

Rotate the valve backwards and forwards, maintaining the valve head in contact with the seating by pulling lightly on the stem. Lift the valve frequently from the seating to prevent the formation of concentric rings and bring it down into another position, recommencing the back and forward movement for a further period.

A light coil spring can be used under the valve head to lift the valve off the seat when the pressure on the valve is removed.

After a few minutes light grinding the holder should be removed and the valve taken out. The compound should be wiped off the valve and off the seating in the head. The seatings should be a light grey in appearance, free from marks or black pits. As soon as a light grey seating is obtained all round the seat of the valve and all round the seat in the head, the grinding-in operation is complete, and the other valve should then be tackled.

Refitting Valves and Springs. (Iron Head Models.)

Before re-assembling, wash the valves and cylinder head very carefully in clean paraffin and wipe dry. Be particularly careful to see that there are no traces of valve grinding compound on the valves, and particularly in the guides.

Obtain four new packings and fit two in place over one of the valve guides. Place the valve spring cover in position and then fit the valve spring bottom washer in place over the valve guide inside the cover.

Put the valve springs into place, followed by the top washer, and after smearing the valve stem with lubricating oil, push the valve up into place, making sure that the stem comes through the top washer. The valve springs now have to be compressed again so that the two halves of the cotter may be refixed. If the insides of the cotters are lightly smeared with grease this will help to hold them to the stem whilst the valve springs are released again.

When compressing the valve springs either to remove or replace the valves be very careful to avoid damaging the spring-covers. If these are "burred" or set out of round it will not be possible to make the joints oil tight.

When fixing the cotters, make sure that the small lip on the cotter registers correctly with the groove in the stem of the valve.

If desired, a small quantity of jointing compound may be used on the asbestos washers, but this is not actually necessary. Jointing compound, however, is necessary for remaking the other joints on the engine (except the cylinder head joint, which will be dealt with later) and for this purpose we recommend Gasket Goo, which, after long experience we have found to be very satisfactory.

As an alternative jointing compound if Gasket Goo is not available, Seccotine is satisfactory.

Refitting Valves and Springs. (Alloy Head.)

The procedure is similar to that detailed above, but no gaskets need attention at this stage.

Cleaning Piston Top.

To clean the carbon from the top of the piston, bring the piston to the top of the stroke. A soft metal scraper as previously recommended for the cylinder head is necessary to avoid scratching the piston crown.

Scrape the carbon away and clean the top of the piston as much as possible with rag. **Do not use emery cloth to clean the piston crown.** Should this be used small abrasive particles of emery would be sure to **get** down between the piston and the cylinder and would rapidly prove disastrous to the engine. To remove all traces of carbon which have worked down between the top of the piston and the barrel push the piston slightly down into the bore and wipe away the carbon. Should the cylinder barrel have been taken off, the piston can best be cleaned after removal from the engine, as there is then no risk of pieces of carbon dropping into the crankcase.

The Cylinder Head Joint. (Iron Head Models.)†

The joint is made between the cylinder head and the barrel, these two parts being lapped together during original assembly, so that the surfaces are quite flat. **Do not attempt to prevent a leakage** by tightening the cylinder head nuts. In the unlikely event of this joint leaking, remove the head. It can be re-ground to the barrel without the slightest difficulty. It is better to take the cylinder off the engine, but the work can be carried out with the cylinder in position if the four long cylinder studs have previously been taken out.

If the work is done in this way, however, great care must be taken to make sure that no trace of the grinding compound which is used for lapping the head to the barrel is allowed to get down between the cylinder bore and piston, as owing to its abrasive nature it would naturally cause damage very quickly. To carry out the actual grinding-in operation, a small quantity of fine grinding compound mixed with oil should be smeared on the two lower faces on the top of the cylinder, and the head slipped into position on to the barrel and then rotated backwards and forwards in order to grind the surfaces together.

It is desirable to raise the head slightly from time to time, and bring it down into another position in much the same manner as described previously to be adopted when grinding in the valves. Having completed the grinding, which should leave a smooth, grey surface on the cylinder and cylinder head, it is necessary to clean the faces carefully of all traces of compound. Fit the sparking plug to the head.

> **Where " Tighten " is stated, remember that overtightening may cause serious damage through stripped threads or broken bolts and studs.**

Refitting the Cylinder Head, etc., after decarbonising.
(Alum. Alloy type.)

Refit the cylinder head gasket, and the head. Fit the four long cylinder studs, the four cylinder head nuts and washers and tighten down evenly. **Be careful not to overtighten, as the tension on the studs increases as the engine heats up, and if the nuts are strained down there is a grave risk of damage occurring.**

Place the push rod guide plate with a joint washer on each side of it over the push rod flange studs in the head, and push the upper flange up and over the studs. Fit and tighten the two nuts.

Check that the piston is at top dead centre of compression stroke and reset to this position if necessary, and thread the two push rods down through the pushrod guide plate and engage their ball ends in the cups formed in the cam followers.

† *See footnote, page 47.*

The object of setting the crankshaft so that the piston is at top of compression stroke is to allow the rockers and bearing block to be fitted without the valve springs having to be compressed. If the crankshaft has been moved from the position in which it was set before removing the bearing block and has to be reset, the fingers may be rested on the tops of the push rods and their up and down movements observed as the crankshaft is rotated. By turning until the inlet (inner) push rod lifts and then drops and then turning the crankshaft very slowly whilst observing the piston through the sparking plug hole the correct setting is easily found.

Place the bearing block gasket in position, fit the bearing block, entering the tips of the rockers in the cups on the push rods, and refit and tighten the three bearing block bolts. Spin the push rods with the fingers to check that they are seated properly in the cups at the bottom.

Refitting the Cylinder Head (Iron type only.)

When re-assembling the cylinder head do not use any jointing compound on the face joint.

The sparking plug should be fitted to the cylinder head and screwed down before the head is fitted to the barrel, otherwise any small pieces of dirt which may have collected in the sparking plug threads will be forced out of the plug hole into the combustion chamber and cause damage to the cylinder bore or the piston.

Screw down the four cylinder head nuts on the long studs until they are each in contact with the head, and then begin to tighten them down further, evenly, and in turn, that is to say, do not tighten one nut fully without touching the others DO NOT IN ANY CIRCUMSTANCES TIGHTEN THESE NUTS EXCESSIVELY. A good gastight joint is obtainable without forcing the nuts. The tension on the cylinder studs tends to increase as the engine heats up, and excessive tightening of the nuts in the first place may quite possibly involve serious damage to the engine.

Refitting the Rocker Cover. (Alloy Head Model.)

After resetting tappet clearances, fit a new gasket, replace the cover and tighten the eight bolts carefully and evenly. See Fig. 23. Refit the oil pipe.

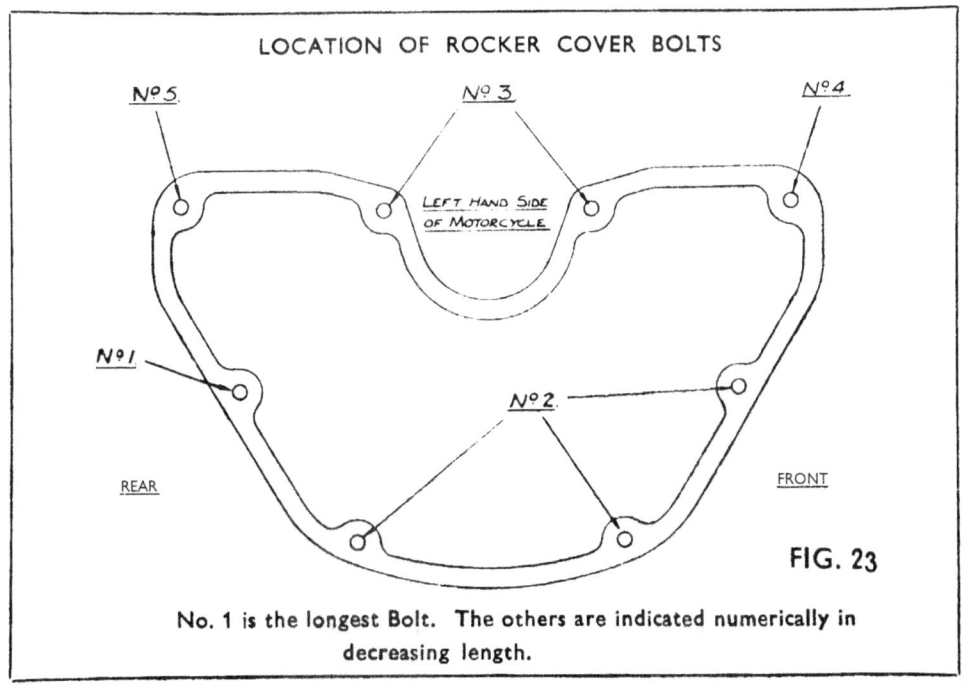

FIG. 23

No. 1 is the longest Bolt. The others are indicated numerically in decreasing length.

Refitting the Rocker Box. (Iron Head Models.)

Assuming that the rocker box has not been taken apart, it is necessary only to scrape off carefully any traces of the old jointing compound from the surfaces to which the tappet covers are attached and around the inside of the recesses which fit against the steel valve spring covers.

The latter surfaces should then be smeared lightly with good jointing compound (Gasket Goo, Seccotine or Gold Size). The tops of the platforms on the cylinder head and the underside of the rocker box bosses which fit on to them should be cleaned, and the rocker box fitted into place. The centre bolt must be in place in its hole before the rocker box is placed in position, as it cannot be put in afterwards on account of the top frame tube.

Make sure before fitting the rocker box, however, that the pushrods are in position, together with the guide plate and paper packing washers (one on each side of the guide plate), and see that the pushrods are engaged properly with the top and bottom rockers. Tighten the three bolts evenly and firmly, but not excessively. The joint surfaces at the top of the pushrod cover can then be smeared with compound and re-assembled.

Next in order the tappet clearances should be dealt with. The method of re-setting and correct clearances are given later. Having adjusted the tappets correctly, which should be done with the engine cold, clean the faces of the tappet covers, both the flat surfaces and the curved joint surfaces being dealt with at the same time.

See that the oil control washers are in place in the centre bosses of the rockers, smear the joint surfaces of the tappet covers with compound as described above, and fit the covers into position carefully, slipping the bolts through the holes and tightening them up evenly and a little at a time.

Care is necessary when dealing with these bolts not to overtighten them—they can be snapped off if excessive force is used.

Finally, refit the oil pipe to the timing cover and the rocker box, being careful not to overtighten the hollow bolt which secures the pipe to the rocker box cover.

Two fibre washers are used on this pipe, and one of these should be on either side of the banjo union.

Resetting the Tappet Clearances.

The cams are ground with quietening ramps and the positions at which the cams are set when checking or adjusting the clearances is therefore rather critical. Check and set when engine is cold.

When setting the inlet clearance set the crankshaft so that the exhaust valve is on the point of opening and turn it until the inlet valve is on the point of closing before setting the exhaust clearance.

(Different clearances are employed when checking the valve timing. See page 66.)

One turn of the tappet gives .038-in. variation in clearance (approx.)

To make the adjustment, slacken off the locknut, which is screwed on to the tappet and is above the end of the rocker.

Then turn the hexagon tappet head, which is below the rocker, to the right, to increase the clearance, or to the left to reduce it.

Check the clearance with a clearance gauge and tighten the locknut whilst the tappet head is held with a second spanner. After tightening the locknuts check the clearances again to be sure that they have not been altered whilst tightening the locknut.

FIG. 24

EXHAUST TAPPET COVER REMOVED.

(Cast Iron Cylinder Head)

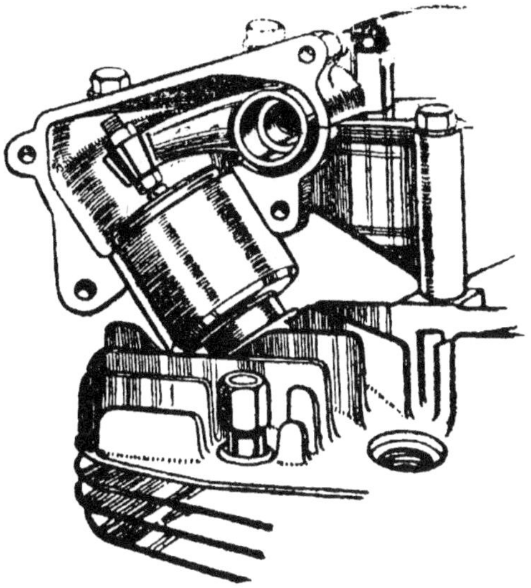

To find top dead centre of compression stroke, refer to paragraph " Checking the Valve Timing " (Page 66).

CHANGING A SHOCK ABSORBER SPRING.

Remove the front part of the dynamo belt cover and the dynamo belt as described in the next section, but do not loosen the gearshaft sprocket nut.

Take off the engine mainshaft nut with the dynamo driving pulley and flange which will permit the spring and splined shock absorber clutch to come away.

Before refitting the shock absorber clutch grease the face cams and splines liberally. Push the shock absorber clutch and spring into place and refit the pulley, pulley flange and nut. Fit a new split cotter and open out the ends.

DISMANTLING THE ENGINE SHAFT SHOCK ABSORBER AND PRIMARY CHAIN.

Take off the dynamo-belt cover, loosen the clamping bolt in the dynamo-strap, turn the dynamo in its mounting until the belt is loose, and remove the belt. Remove the cover from the front end of the rear chain—it is held at the front end by a nut to a stud on the primary-chain cover. Lift the ear on the cover off the stud, at the same time pull the cover forward out of the socket in the rear part of the chain-cover. Sometimes this is easier if the bolt holding the rear part of the cover to the mudguard valance is loosened first.

Remove the split cotters from the nut securing the rear driving sprocket and from the nut on the engine-shaft. Loosen the nut on the gearshaft **slightly.** This nut is usually very tight, and the spanner will need driving round with a hammer or mallet, and the rear brake should be held on firmly while doing so to prevent the sprocket turning.

Next engage top gear and remove the nut from the engine-shaft. This nut will also require to be driven round to start it and the engine-shaft prevented from turning by holding the rear brake on. Both nuts unscrew anti-clockwise. Special spanners are provided in the tool kit for both these nuts, the pegged spanner (closed end) and the " Ring " spanner respectively.

Unscrew the nut right off the engine-shaft with the belt pulley flange and spring. Do not lose the plain washer which is used between the nut and the shoulder of the shaft. Now unscrew and remove the nut from the gearshaft, take off the plain washer behind it. Pull the sprocket off the shaft, and unhook it out of the chain.

Remove the chain cover fixing screws or on later MAC machines take off the chain cover strap assembly from around the edge of the cover. On MOV and MAC machines remove the nut and washer from the stud below the inspection cap and half-way down the face of the cover. On MSS machines remove the single bolt securing the cover to the crankcase and take off the left-hand footrest and footrest square bar. Pull the outer half of the cover away from the inner part, being careful when separating them not to damage the joint-packing. A distance tube will be found between the two halves. This fits over the edges of the covers around the holes, through which the fixing stud or bolt passes. The purpose of the distance tube is to prevent oil leaking out, and to prevent the cover being crushed in when the fixing nut or bolt is tightened.

The sliding member or shock absorber clutch may now be pulled out off the engine shaft, but the sprocket and chain cannot be removed on account of the chain being of the "endless" type, this making it necessary to take off at the same time the chain wheel from the gearbox.

Remove the small grub screw and the locking plate from the flange of the sleeve-gear nut on the clutch.† It will be seen that the nut has four holes drilled in the flange and the peg-spanner is used to turn the nut.* Again it will almost certainly be necessary to start the nut (anti-clockwise) by driving round the spanner. Remove the nut and pull off the engine sprocket and whole of the clutch with the chain. To start the clutch out of position it may be necessary to lever the back plate away from the face of the gearbox. Be careful when the clutch is removed not to lose the three small thrust pins from the back plate.

After re-assembling note that the clutch will need re-adjustment. See page 70.

THE ENGINE—DISMANTLING AND RE-ASSEMBLING.
Preliminary Work—MOV and MAC Models only.

Before removing the engine from the frame remove the fuel tank, primary chain and clutch (see sections dealing with these points). Disconnect the cables from the positive battery terminal (the rear one).

Remove the dynamo with the inner half of the belt-cover after loosening the dynamo strap and pulling out the single pin plug from the dynamo. Take off the inner half of the primary chain cover—held by four screws. to the face of the gearbox. These screws are secured by locking wires. Cut these and use new wires when re-assembling.

Remove all bolts from the engine plates and disconnect the eye of the gearbox adjuster from the nearside rear engine-plate. Remove the engine from the frame.

THE ENGINE—DISMANTLING AND RE-ASSEMBLING—
Preliminary Work. (MSS.)

Proceed as in the previous section, but do not remove the bolts securing the crank case to the rear engine plates as the engine and gearbox have to be removed together with the rear engine plates attached. The gearbox adjuster can also be left in position. Loosen the bolts securing the engine plates to the crank case and lift the entire engine and gearbox out of the frame. Remove the front half of the primary chain cover, the clutch, engine sprocket, and chain.

† *Only on MAC and MSS Models after 1940.*
* *See page 76. Fig. 38.*

Cut the locking wire and take out the four shouldered screws securing the back half of the cover to the gearbox and take it off. Finally separate the gearbox from the engine on the bench.

Dismantling Cylinder and Piston.

Support the engine in a convenient position by gripping in a vice the front flange of the crankcase, supporting the rear of the engine from the bench by means of a steel bar bent to fit into one of the bolt holes and set to rest firmly on the bench. This takes a lot of the weight and prevents the engine sliding down in the vice.

Take off the rocker box and cylinder head as described on pages 46 and 47, remove the pushrods and guide plate and take off the pushrod tubes, top and bottom, by detaching from the crankcase. With the flat of the hands against the front and rear of the cylinder, push it sharply backwards and forwards alternately, exerting an upward pressure at the same time, to loosen the cylinder in the crankcase. When free, pull it up carefully off the piston. It is advisable to have an assistant to support the piston as it is freed from the cylinder, in order to avoid damage.

Make a note before removing the piston which side of the engine the slot for the removal of the circlip is situated, or mark the piston so that it is put back into the same position. On the MOV and MAC Models the larger of the two flat surfaces on the crown is below the exhaust valve.

Split-skirt pistons are always fitted with the split at the front.

Remove one of the circlips from the piston and drive out the gudgeon pin from the opposite side. A soft metal punch must be used against the end of the pin to prevent damage. An assistant is essential when driving out the pin, so that the piston is supported on the opposite side to avoid bending the connecting rod.

The pin is a light driving fit with the piston cold.

Removal of Piston Rings.

To remove the piston rings, gently expand the ends of the top piston ring away from the piston and insert three or four thin metal strips between the ring and the piston, sliding these round behind the ring until it is possible to slide the ring upwards over the piston crown. Take care not to spring the rings any more than is necessary to put the strips into place and to raise them out of the grooves as piston rings are rather brittle. This applies particularly to the slotted oil control ring. Some MSS engines have a "stepped" section scraper ring in the third groove from the top.

Re-cutting Valve Seats. (Iron Heads Only.)

The seatings in the head can then be cleaned up by using a 45° cutter with a pilot $\frac{5}{16}$-in. diameter, 4-in. long. A $\frac{3}{8}$-in. pilot will be needed for the MSS exhaust guide.

After prolonged service, and repeated cutting, the seatings may become sunk well below the surrounding surface of the combustion chamber, and this condition lowers the efficiency of the engine. The ridge of metal around the seat then needs cutting way and the surface blending into the hemisphere of the combustion chamber, otherwise the valves will be masked and loss of power will result.

Refacing Valve Seats. (Alloy Head.)

This can only be accomplished satisfactorily with a refacing stone and the work should be left to a Service Agent who will have the necessary 45° angle stone and tackle.

Replacing Valve Guides. (Alloy Head.)

The guides are bored to give a diametrical valve clearance of .0015-in. to .0025-in. and are fitted during manufacture when the cylinder head is heated.

When replacement is necessary the head must be heated before attempting to drive or press the old guides from the head or fit new ones. Note that the inlet guide is chamfered on the outside of the end fitting into the port.

After heating the head press in the guides until they stand $\frac{5}{8}$-in. above the machined faces surrounding the guide holes.

Replacing Valve Guides. (Iron Head Model.)

The valve guides are detachable, and can be removed and new ones fitted with a double diameter soft punch or drift. The small end should be $\frac{5}{16}$-in. diameter for about 2-in., and the remainder $\frac{1}{2}$-in. diameter approximately 4-in. long. Drive out the guides from inside the ports, but do not remove them unless they are worn or damaged so as to need replacement.

Inspection of Cylinder and Piston Rings.

The cylinder should now be inspected for condition of bore and piston rings. If the bore is worn badly or is scored, it will require re-boring and an oversize piston with rings. The original diameter of the bore is 2.677-in. in the case of MOV and MAC cylinders, and 3.189-in. on the MSS.

Re-boring is generally considered necessary when wear in excess of .008-in. has taken place, or the bore has become damaged or scored.

The rings when new, and when fitted to a new or re-bored cylinder have gap clearances as follows :—

MOV and MAC Compression rings	.. ..	.010-in.
,, ,, ,, Scraper ring	.. ..	.012-in.
MSS Compression rings	.. .. ..	.018-in.
,, Slotted scraper ring	.. .. ..	.016-in.
,, Stepped type scraper ring	.. .. ..	.016-in.

Oversize pistons and rings are made in only three oversizes :—
plus .020-in., plus .040-in., and .060-in. (not in .060-in. for MSS).

No intermediate sizes are used. It is not practicable to fit oversize rings to a worn cylinder unless the cylinder is re-bored and the appropriate larger piston fitted.

REMOVAL OF AUTOMATIC TIMING UNIT.
(See Fig. 25).

The removal of the timing cover should now be undertaken. It will come away easily when the screws have been taken out. Never attempt to remove the cover by inserting a screwdriver as a wedge between the faces. This damages the faces and will cause oil leakage after re-assembly. If the cover has stuck to the joint packing, tap it carefully at several points round the edge to free it.

The following procedure applies also to engines with hand controlled ignition, except that no sprag need be used when removing the magneto gear.

Having removed the cover, remove the automatic timing unit as follows : Loosen the hexagon nut in the centre. It will be found to tighten again shortly after becoming free. Continue turning it, when it will be found that the nut (which forms its own extractor) will withdraw the unit from the armature if the pressure on the spanner is maintained. The nut has a right-hand thread.

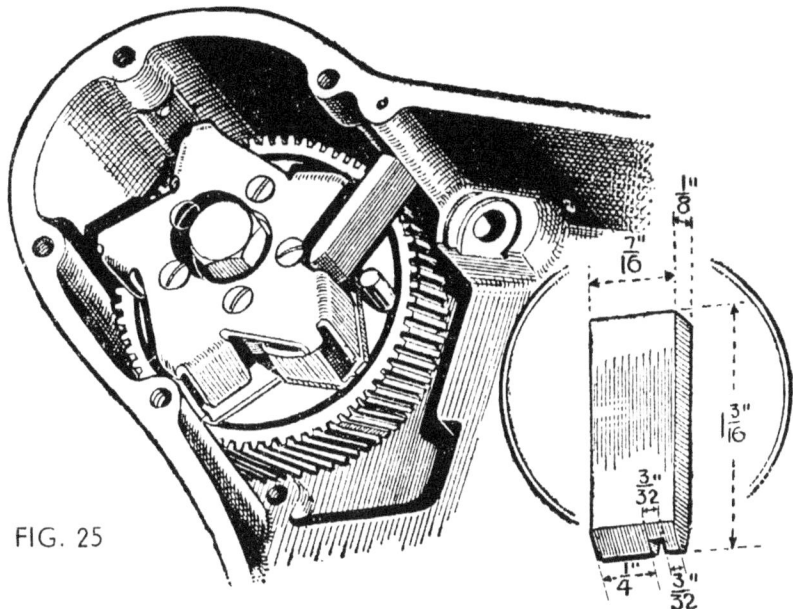

FIG. 25

The special sprag is shown in use.
(Inset—Sprag with dimensions).

The use of the sprag is essential when removing any B.T.H. timing unit fitted with a limiting stop as used up to 1946, otherwise one of the "ears" of the centre will foul the stop peg in the gear either bending the "ear" or loosening the peg. Either condition prevents proper working of the unit.

Take off the three fixing nuts securing the magneto flange to the crankcase and remove the magneto.

Access to the timing gears is obtained by taking off the strengthening plate, which is held by bolts and one nut on the end of the cam-wheel spindle. The cam-wheel, intermediate gear and cam-follows can be pulled off their spindles by hand. Behind the cam-followers is a "Belleville" washer. Take care not to lose this, and be sure to **replace** it when re-assembling.

Do Not Take the Unit Apart—It is seldom necessary

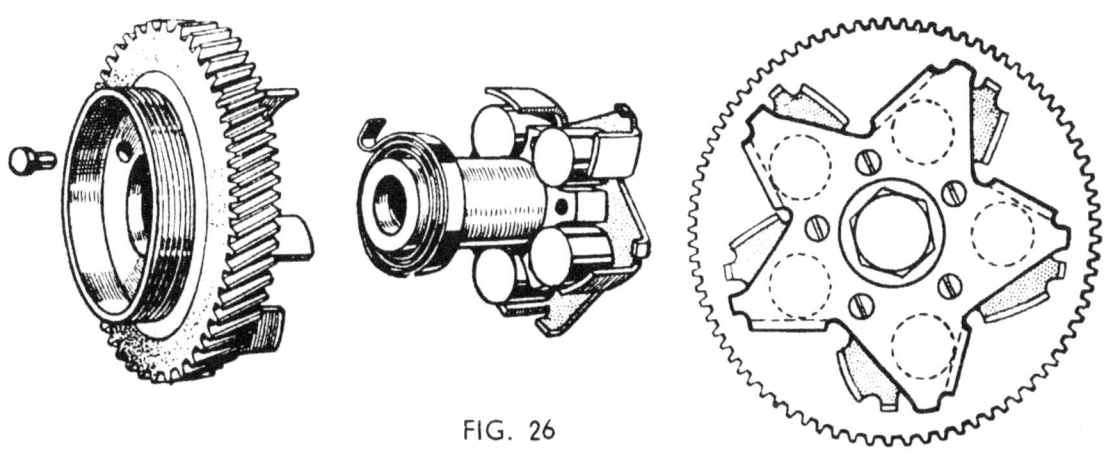

FIG. 26

The Automatic Timing Unit (B.T.H.)

Left : Showing return spring.   Right : In fully advanced position ("open")

57

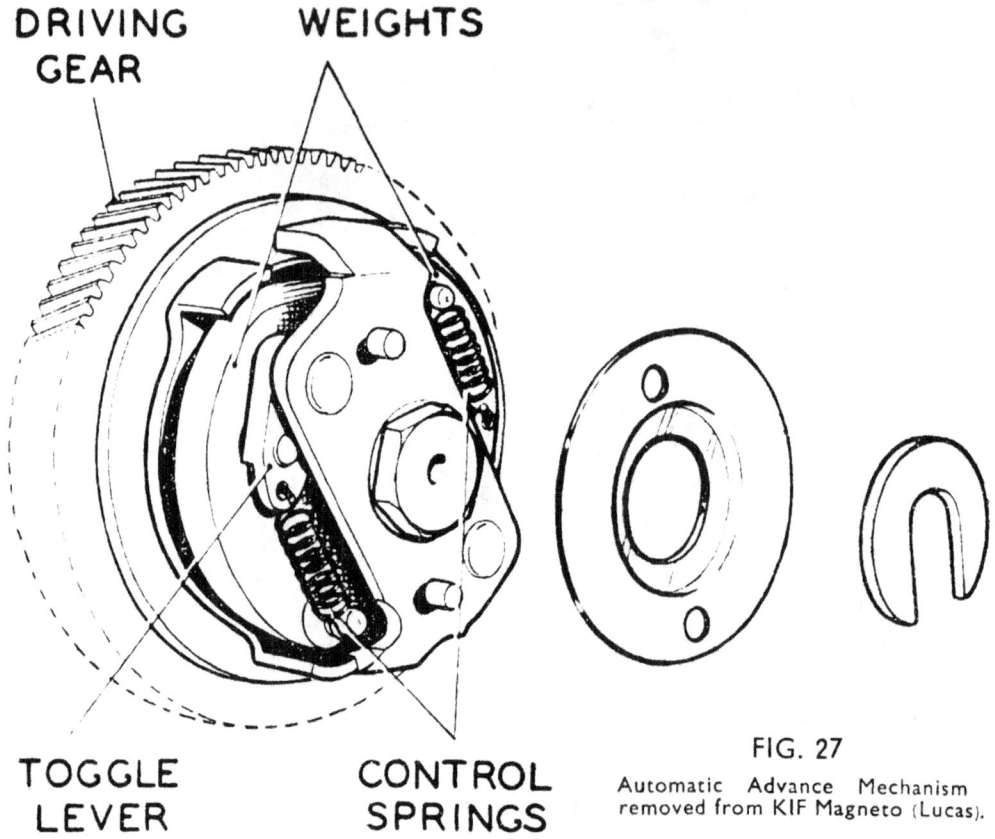

FIG. 27
Automatic Advance Mechanism removed from KIF Magneto (Lucas).

The Oil Pump. (See Fig. 28).

The oil pump has to be taken out before the worm gear and crankshaft pinion can be removed. **It is essential to heat the crankcase** surrounding the pump before any attempt is made to tap it out. Remove the four screws holding the base-plate of the pump to the crankcase—heat up the crankcase by means of a blowlamp, and when hot tap out the pump from inside the timing case, using a soft drift. Avoid applying the drift to the end of the spindle.

To take the pump apart for inspection of the gears, take out the four screws securing the pump body and cover to the base plate. Pull the cover and body apart and the gears will lift out of place. It will usually be found unnecessary to take the spindle from the pump-cover but to do so, take off the pinion which meshes with the driving worm by unscrewing it carefully from the spindle, it has a right-hand thread, and can be held most conveniently with a pair of pliers. The pump gears should be a close fit in the body without end float.

The pump cover must be accurately lined up with the body before attempting to refit it or lap in new gears and work should not be undertaken without the Pump Alignment Tool X2719.

Should new gears be fitted it may be necessary carefully to lap them in by rotating the spindle a few times with a small quantity of abrasive. For this purpose, fine Turkey-Stone Powder should be mixed with oil and should be run through the pump. In no circumstances should ordinary grinding compound or emery be used. After lapping it is of the

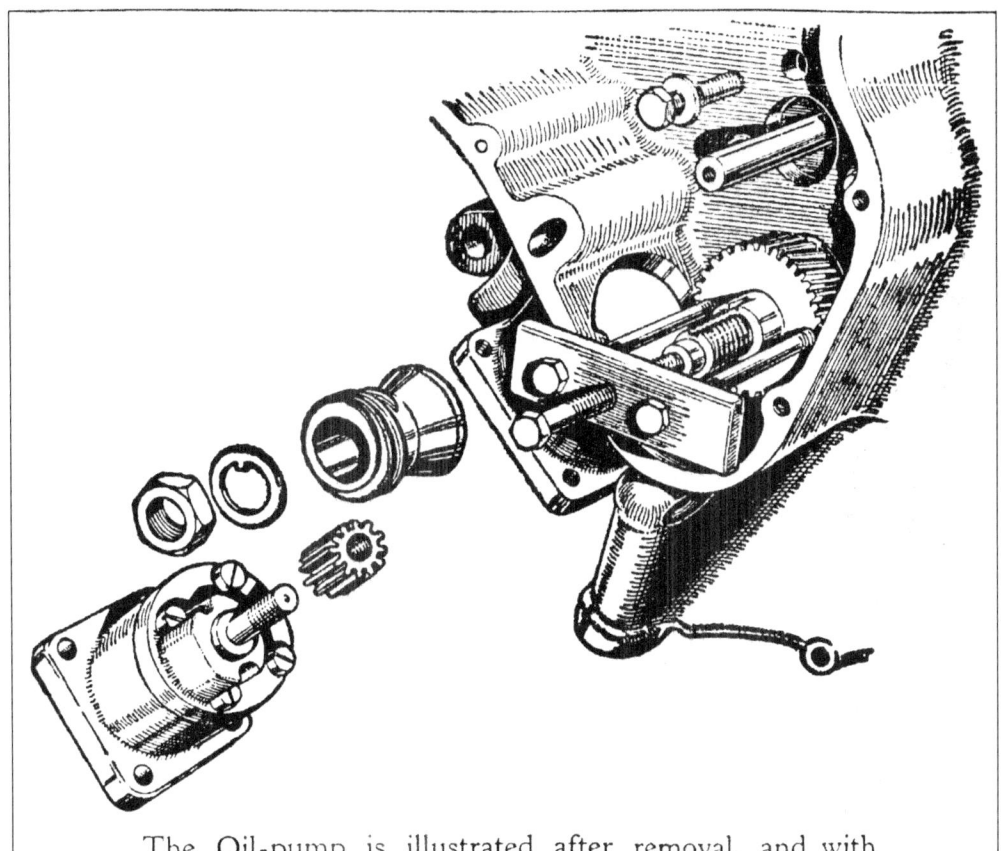

The Oil-pump is illustrated after removal, and with small driven pinion taken off. The Crankshaft Timing-pinion is about to be pulled off the shaft with the extractor. (Service Tool No. X2721.)

FIG. 28

utmost importance to take the pump apart again and to clean all parts thoroughly to remove even the smallest trace of abrasive. Re-assemble the pump with clean oil on the gears. Heat the crankcase before attempting to refit the pump, which must be replaced the same way round as originally fitted.

Extracting the Crankshaft Timing-Pinion.

(See Fig. 28.)

Removal of the pump permits the worm and crankshaft pinion to be taken off the mainshaft as follows : Remove the nut from the mainshaft —**left-hand thread**—and then the " tongued " washer. The worm can be prised off with two screwdrivers. A small puller will be needed for the removal of the pinion.

This is s simple tool, No. X2721, made from a steel plate 2-in. × 1-in. × $\frac{1}{4}$-in. with two $\frac{1}{4}$-in. clearance holes (17/64-in.) drilled at $1\frac{3}{32}$-in. centres. Midway between these holes drill and tap a hole $\frac{5}{16}$-in. B.S.F. thread. Two $\frac{1}{4}$-in. diameter × $2\frac{1}{2}$-in. long bolts should be reduced in diameter for $\frac{3}{8}$-in. at the ends and threaded 2 B.A. The extractor bolt for the centre hole should measure $\frac{5}{16}$ × 2-in. threaded up to the head. The finished puller and method of use can be clearly seen from the accompanying sketch.

Separating the Crankcase—Removal of Main-Bearings.

On all MOV and MAC models up to mid 1954 a ballrace on the timing side and a parallel roller race on the drive side support the flywheel assembly. Current MAC models employ parallel roller races on both sides.

MSS engines up to engine number MSS6300 are fitted with two parallel roller races—a double row type on the driving side and a single row the same as that now used on MAC models on the timing side. MSS engines from MSS6301 have two taper roller bearings—one on each side. See page 62.

Renew the bearings if there is any trace of roughness or if there has been up and down play on the shafts.

The separation of the crankcase halves is quite easy after taking out all the bolts and through studs which hold them together—including the cylinder oil feed bolt if an early model. The drive side case will lift off leaving the centre portion of the roller race on the main shaft. The bearing outer ring will come away in the crankcase. On engines fitted with a ball-race on the timing side the shaft will probably have to be lightly driven through the race leaving it in the case.

The ballrace and the outer rings of roller bearings are readily removable without special tools. Heat the half crankcase and when at about 100°C. jarr the bearings out of their housings by bringing down the crankcase smartly—joint face downwards—onto a solid wood surface such as the bench top. The centre portions of the parallel roller races can be prised off the mainshafts.

Whilst the crankcase is dismantled remove the suction filter plug and if previous to engine number MAC15523 the check valve plug, ball, and spring also. Carefully clean out all oil passages and drillings.

The Big-End Bearing.

The connecting rod should have no detectable vertical play with oil in the bearing. There will be about .008-in. in side play.

To dismantle the Flywheel assembly a heavy Box-Spanner will be needed. The crankpin nuts are invariably tight, and good leverage is required to shift them. The nuts are not locked.

For MOV big ends the spanner must be $\frac{5}{8}$-in. Whit. (1.101-in. across the flats) and the outside diameter around the hexagon must not exceed $1\frac{7}{16}$-in.

For the MAC and MSS a $\frac{3}{4}$-in. Whit. spanner (1.3-in. across the flats) and not exceeding $1\frac{5}{8}$-in. diameter around the hexagon will be needed, No. X2720.

The ends of the Crankpin are slightly taper and the pin will have to be driven out of the Flywheels. For inspection it is of course only necessary to take off one Flywheel, which will permit the connecting rod and the roller cage to be slid off the crankpin, making all parts accessible for close inspection.

The roller cage is supported on the crankpin and occasionally wears the outer edges. This is not important provided that the roller track in the centre is in good condition. Any pitting of the roller track calls for renewal of the affected part, and the Crankpin will have to be taken out of the other Flywheel.

The crankpin is made up of two parts*—a hardened steel sleeve being pressed on to a "soft" pin. Thus in the event of wear, the sleeve only can be renewed. These are made in the following diameters :—

	MOV.	MAC.	MSS.
Standard diameter ..	1.24292-in.	1.374-in.	1.4990-in.

* *Except before 1939 when the pins were made in one piece.*

Refitting the Crankpin.

See that the oil hole and oil passage in the crankpin assembly are clear also carefully clean the tapers and the faces of the pin and flywheels.

The crankpin assembly as distinct from the early one-piece type will fit either way round. Only on the very old type is it necessary to match up the oil hole through the radius of the crankpin shoulder with the oil hole in the timing side flywheel.

Set the crankpin assembly in the timing side flywheel so that the oil hole drilled through the roller track faces the centre, i.e., so that it points vertically downwards when the flywheels are at top dead centre position.

Push the pin into the taper as far as it will go and tighten up the nut just enough to draw the shoulder of the pin into contact with the flywheel face. **Do not tighten more than this or the pin will be drawn through the hardened sleeve.**

With a syringe or force feed oil can force oil into the end of the timing side mainshaft and make certain that it issues from the drilling in the roller track.

Place the roller cage in position on the crankpin and fit the rollers. These can be stuck in place with a little clean soft grease or vaseline.

Push the connecting rod into place over the rollers and check the fit. With grease or oil in the bearing the rod must turn on the rollers perfectly freely. If fitted up dry for checking purposes there should be just the very slightest perceptible vertical play in the bearing.

Oversize rollers are stocked and can be employed to eliminate play if the roller tracks of the sleeve and outer ring are not badly worn and are free of pitting. The outer ring in the rod can also be renewed separately.

The sleeve will often be found to have worn where it supports the roller cage. This wear can be disregarded if the roller track is in good order and if the wear is not so extensive as to leave the edges of the roller track unsupported.

Slight stiffness in the bearing can be eased by polishing the sleeve or lapping out the ring in the connecting rod.

When the bearing is correctly fitted place the driving side flywheel over the other end of the crankpin and press it down until the side faces are in contact and locating the rim of the wheel concentric with the rim of the timing side flywheel. Line up with a straight edge across the rims before finally trueing.

Lining up the Flywheels.

For lining up the Flywheels perfectly straightforward equipment is all that is required. The Flywheels should first be roughly lined up in the vice and then trued by placing the two Main-bearings on their shafts, resting these on V blocks 5-in. from the shaft centres to the base and $2\frac{3}{8}$-in. apart, and then checking with a Dial-gauge on the Mainshafts. The Shafts are allowed a maximum out of truth figure of .001-in.

When correctly lined up finally tighten both crankpin nuts and re-check the shafts for accuracy.

Refitting the Main Bearings.

MOV, MAC, and MSS, to Engine No. MSS 6300.

NOTE SPECIALLY that the inner rings of the main bearings taper .001-in. per inch and must therefore be fitted the correct way round to their respective shafts. The "large" ends of the inner rings are always fitted adjacent to the Flywheel bosses, i.e., they are placed on the shafts "large end first."

The " large " ends will be found on inspection to have a pronounced radius, but as an extra check, " Hoffman " bearings have the maker's name and identification serial numbers stamped on the opposite side of the races so that when correctly fitted these marks should be outside and remote from the Flywheels.

Should an attempt be made to fit the bearings the wrong way round it will be found that they will hardly go on to the mainshafts at all when pressed lightly into position with the fingers.

Heat the Crankcase halves before fitting the outer rings of the roller races by immersing each half in boiling water until it is hot enough to allow the outer ring to be dropped into the housing.

Usually the same quantity and thickness of shimming as originally used will be correct when reassembling.

Note that any packing shims used to control the end float on the flywheel assembly must be fitted into place before the bearings and see that the outer ring of the roller races are fitted with lip at the bottom of the housing, otherwise it will be impossible to slide the Crankcase into place owing to the rollers being unable to enter the outer rings.

Mainbearings—MSS Type. (From Engine No. MSS 6301).

Beginning at engine number MSS 6301, the use of parallel roller bearings was discontinued and this engine and those that follow are assembled with taper roller engine mainshaft bearings. This alteration involved modifications to the crankcase and the flywheels and to the timing pinion fitted to the crankshaft. The new catalogue numbers of the replacement parts concerned are as follows :—

M43/6	Crankcase driving side.	
M44/6	Crankcase timing side.	
M87/3	Crankshaft roller bearings. 2 off.	
M23/5AS	Flywheel assembly timing side.	
M25/5As	Flywheel assembly driving side.	
M245	Crankcase bearing shim .003-in. thick.	As required.
M245/2	,, ,, ,, .005-in. thick.	As required.
M245/3	,, ,, ,, .008-in. thick.	As required.
M234/4	,, ,, ,, .002-in. thick.	As required.

The modification to the timing pinion M32/4 consists of turning back a recess at the slotted end of the pinion to permit the end of the pinion to enter the end of the inner ring of the taper roller bearing on the mainshaft. In consequence the modified pinion must be used on an engine with taper roller bearings and an earlier type pinion will not be satisfactory, but the modified pinion may be used on all earlier engines of MOV, MAC and MSS type where 16 degree helix angle gears are fitted, and is supplied in replacement.

The fitting of these main bearings calls for a slightly different technique from that adopted with the previous types of mainbearings. Should it be necessary to replace a set of these bearings the crankcase is unbolted and dismantled in the usual way and the rings are removed from the crankcase in just the same manner as would be adopted for outer rings of the parallel roller races used previously. The inner portions of the bearings are however a tight fit on the mainshafts, and in order to remove the inner race it will be necessary to remove six of the rollers from the cage. (This work can be done with the aid of a sharpened spoke). The cage can easily be removed afterwards. The inner ring will then have to be ground and split to remove. Care should be taken not to grind the shaft of the flywheel. After pressing the new inner rings in position and fitting the outer rings, the crankcase must be fitted up with the flywheel assembly in place and bearing shims as required, should be fitted so that with the main bearings just binding there is a .004-in. gap (maximum) around the joint face of the crankcase.

The above instructions only apply to taper roller bearings.

Refitting Flywheels to Crankcase.

MOV, MAC, and MSS, prior to MSS 6301.

As to the re-assembly of the Crankcase, no particular difficulty is likely to occur, but care is necessary to see that the Flywheel Assembly is set so that with perfect freedom when cold, there is no detectable sideplay.

The best method of doing this part of the work is first to fit the main bearings into the Crankcase, bolt the two halves of the Crankcase together (there is no joint packing used between them) and measure carefully the distance between the faces of the two inner rings of the bearings. Use an internal micrometer for this. Next measure the width across between the main Bearing-bosses on the Flywheels. Any difference between the two dimensions may be made up by placing sims behind the outer rings of the bearings. As far as possible pack each side equally to keep the Flywheel Assembly central in the Crankcase. The shims are stocked in three thicknesses, .003-in., .005-in., and .012-in.

Re-Assembly of Crankcase.

Further assembly is then quite straightforward to anyone who has taken the engine apart. It may be an advantage to note that joint packings must be used on the Pump-Base-Plate, the Timing Cover, the push-rod tube flanges (2 at top, 1 at bottom), the Cylinder base and Carburetter. All other joints are metal to metal. Good jointing compound is necessary on all joints except the Cylinder head joint.

Adjustment of Intermediate Timing Gear.

When refitting the timing gears note that the spindle carrying the Intermediate gear is integral with a flange inside the Crankcase, to which the flange is secured by three $\frac{1}{4}$-in. $\times$ 26T Bolts.

These bolts pass through $\frac{11}{32}$-in. holes, and as the Spindle has considerable freedom in the hole through which it passes, a certain amount of movement is provided for adjusting the mesh of the Intermediate gear with the Crankshaft Pinion and Camshaft wheel. This adjustment is set correctly at the Factory, and generally no alteration to the setting is needed, but should the necessity arise, the Spindle should be set so that the three gears mesh without noticeable backlash, but run with perfect freedom of rotation.

When new the spindle for the Intermediate gear is .561-in. diameter, and a new bush should be bored out to .5625-in. The Camwheel spindle is .499-in. and the bush size should be .5-in. New bushes should be bored out in preference to reaming to ensure concentricity of the bearing with the gear teeth. These Timing gears should have end float not exceeding .0015-in. on their spindles. Check with feeler-gauge between end face of bush and strengthening plate.

Place the Crankshaft timing pinion in position on the mainshaft, engage it with the key and tap it up into place. Slide the pump driving worm into position, fit the tongued washer and screw up and tighten the left-hand thread retaining nut.

Re-Assembling the Piston and Cylinder.

(*Before re-assembling the cylinder, refer to paragraph re-cylinder head joint*).

If the magneto has been removed refit it before fitting the Cylinder.

Before refitting the Cylinder barrel, check the connecting rod for alignment if there is any indication from inspection of the Piston that it is not quite true or there is any reason to suspect that it may have been distorted. To check the Connecting Rod for accuracy, obtain a mandrel of the same diameter as the gudgeon pin and not less than 5-in. long. Pass this through the smallend bush, set the Flywheels with the big-end at T.D.C. and verify by means of a surface gauge that the mandrel is parallel with the top machined face of the Crankcase and in line with the Crankshaft centre line. Examine the piston bosses to make sure that the small-end eye of the rod has had sufficient side clearance from the Piston, and has not been thrusting up against one of the bosses.

If a split skirt piston is fitted, it must be refitted so that the split is at the front. Also on MOV or MAC see that the larger of the two flat machined surfaces on the piston crown faces forward.

Tap the gudgeon pin into one of the piston bosses, so that it protrudes very slightly beyond the inside face of the boss. Slip the piston over the top of the connecting rod engaging the protruding end of the gudgeon pin in the small-end bush which should previously have been smeared with clean oil, and drive the gudgeon pin back into place, obtaining assistance when doing so to support the piston on the opposite side, as described in a previous section for the removal of the piston.

Take care not to drive the gudgeon pin too far, and thus damage the piston boss on the other side by forcing it too hard against the circlip which is fitted. When the gudgeon pin is in position fit the other circlip into its groove, making sure that it is correctly seated.

Wipe the piston clean, fit the rings into position, space them so that the slots are approximately equidistant from one another around the circumference of the piston, and smear the skirt of the piston with clean oil.

If the packing washer on top of the crankcase has been taken off or broken, fit a new one into position over the spigot at the bottom of the cylinder.

Wipe the inside of the cylinder bore with clean rag, lightly smear it with clean engine oil and proceed to slide it over the piston, compressing the piston rings in turn with the fingers so as to enter them in the cylinder, which should then slide down easily into place.

It is an advantage if help is available, as an extra pair of hands are very useful during this part of the work. See that the cylinder is fitted the correct way round, the cutaway portion of the fins being of course behind the pushrod tubes. As the utmost cleanliness must be observed during the foregoing operations, it is advisable that the hands should be thoroughly wiped before carrying out this part of the work, as no dirt or foreign matter must be allowed to get on to the piston or cylinder bore, as this would be likely to cause damage. Also do not use " fluffy " rag.

Re-Fitting the Oil Pump.

The oil-pump may now be re-fitted. Heat the Crankcase with blow-lamp adjacent to the Pump housing. Do not concentrate the flame at one point but move it about to distribute the heat. Slip a new joint packing over the Pump on to the base plate and slide the Pump into place. Take care to engage the driving gear correctly with the worm and see that the screw holes in the base plate are exactly opposite the screw holes in the crankcase. Fit and tighten the four fixing screws. See Fig. 28 for correct position of pump for re-fitting. A longer screw is fitted into the inner front hole.

Re-Timing the Valves.

To re-time the valves, bring the mark on the Crankshaft pinion to the top (Fig. 29), by turning the Crankshaft. Fit the Camwheel and Intermediate wheel on their respective spindles so that the marks etched at the edges of the gears coincide. It should be noted that although there are two marks on the Intermediate gear, it is possible immediately to find out which mark should match with the Camwheel, and which with the Crankshaft gear, as the marks are not diametrically opposite, and the longer section between the marks is always facing the front of the machine.

Note specially that once the Crankshaft has been turned the marks will no longer coincide again until the shaft has turned 93 complete turns. This is because the Intermediate gear has an odd number of teeth (a "hunting" gear) to distribute the wear evenly on the teeth. The actual numbers of teeth are: Crankshaft Pinion, 46; Intermediate gear, 93; Camwheel and Automatic Timing Unit, 92.†

NOTE.—Because the timing marks on the Intermediate gear will not always register at once with those on the Camwheel and Crankshaft pinion when the mark on the latter is brought to the top on removing the Timing cover, it has sometimes been assumed that the engine has previously been timed incorrectly. From the information given above it will be clear that the chance of an engine stopping with the gears in the positions shown in Fig. 29, or thereabouts, is very remote.

When the Strengthening Plate has been refitted the Automatic Timing Unit can be replaced and the Ignition timing reset. Make sure that the Lockwashers have been refitted under the bolts securing the plate and that the bolts are properly tightened up.

POSITIONS OF TIMING MARKS.

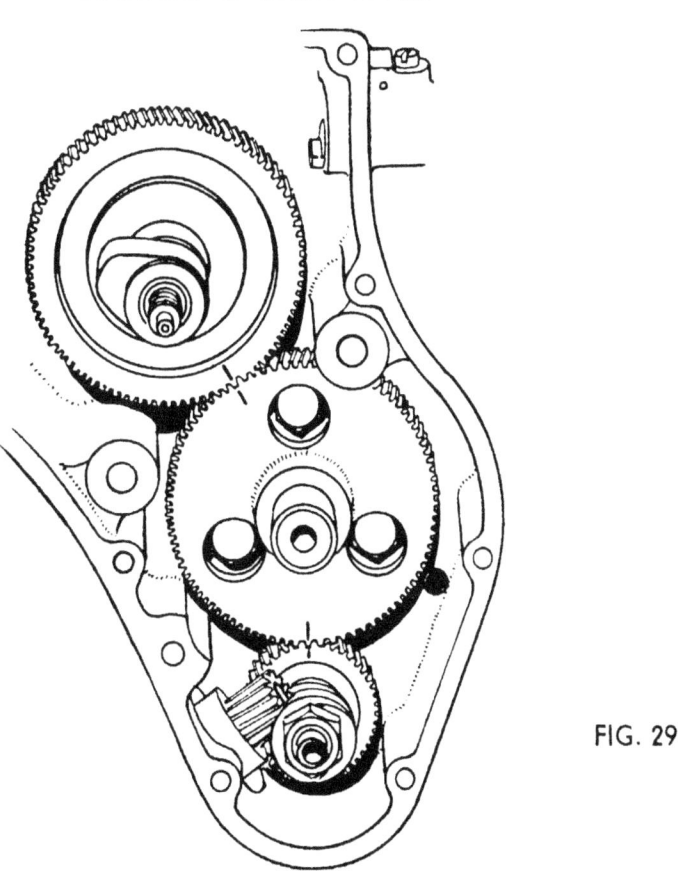

FIG. 29

The Intermediate Gear Spindle Bolt Heads are also visible through the holes in the gear.

The Valve Timing.

Before checking refer to Note above.

The following preliminary work is unnecessary if the engine is out of the machine.

Preliminary Work. On MAC and MSS Models remove the Fuel Tank. (See details, page 46).

† *Except on engines of pre-1936 make. Early types had 24 T. or 47 T. Crankshaft Pinions.*

Checking. Take out the sparking-plug and remove the cover from the dynamo belt. Fix a Timing Disc to the Crankshaft and a Pointer to some fixed part of the engine.

Rotate the Crankshaft slowly with the Footstarter until the Inlet-valve is seen to open and close.

Insert a spoke or a straight piece of stiff wire through the sparking-plug hole and then move the Crankshaft forward again VERY slowly until the piston is felt to reach its highest point in the Cylinder. By rocking the Crankshaft back and forward whilst holding the spoke or wire the top dead centre position is readily found.

DO NOT USE A SHORT PIECE OF WIRE—IT MAY BE DROPPED ACCIDENTALLY INTO THE CYLINDER.

Set the pointer to zero on the timing disc.

For checking the valve timing the tappet clearances used differ from those employed for running and the adjustment must be reset to the checking clearances before checking and reset to the running clearances afterwards. The cams are ground with quietening ramps and these take up the clearance gradually. A correct setting of the clearances can only be obtained when the bottom rocker pad of the valve being adjusted is resting on that part of the neutral of the cam which is opposite to the peak or point of highest lift.

To set the cam in the right place turn the crankshaft before setting the inlet clearance until the exhaust valve is just on the point of opening. Turn the crankshaft again before setting the exhaust clearance until the inlet valve is on the point of closing. **This is important.** All clearances are to be set cold.

Clearances for checking are :—

MAC (Alloy head type), Cam No. M17-5.	Both valves .030-in. to .035-in.	
MAC (Alloy head type), Cam No. M17-4.	Both valves .030-in. to .035-in.	
MAC and MOV (Iron head), Cam No. M17.	Inlet Valve .010-in.; Exhaust .015-in.	
MSS (Iron head), Cam No. M17-3*	Both Valves .025-in.	

With the clearances specified the timing for the respective cams is :—

Inlet opens :   Cams M17-5 & M17-3   30°   Cams M17-4 & M17
                                            50° Before top dead centre.
Inlet closes : Cams M17-5 & M17-3   60°   Cams M17-4 & M17
                                            60° After bottom dead centre.
Exhaust opens : Cams M17-5 & M17-3   60°   Cams M17-4 & M17
                                            70° Before bottom dead centre.
Exhaust closes : Cams M17-5 & M17-3 30°   Cams M17-4 & M17
                                            40° After top dead centre.

The inlet and exhaust cams are machined in one piece so that should there be a marked variation in the reading from one cam but the setting of the other be found correct the cams and followers should be inspected for wear.

With new cams and followers or those known to be in good condition it is sufficient to check only the inlet opening position. If this is right the remainder of the setting follows automatically.

After resetting and checking the timing readjust the tappet clearances for running, placing the crankshaft as instructed above.

Clearances for running are :

Both valves : .005" on MAC with cams M17/4 and M17/5.
Inlet .003" Exhaust .006" on MOV and MAC with cast iron heads.
Inlet .005" Exhaust .010" on MSS Models.
All clearances to be checked and set when engine is cold.

* Some ex Army 350 c.c. models have this cam.

The Ignition Timing (B.T.H. Magneto).

Important. Should it be necessary to alter the Ignition setting DO NOT ATTEMPT to loosen the nut securing the Automatic Timing-unit to the Magneto Armature before reading the instructions on page 57.

Preliminary Work. Remove the Contact-breaker Cover from the Magneto and rotate the Crankshaft with the Footstarter until the Contact-points are fully open.

Check the gap with the gauge on the Magneto Spanner, and if not correct reset the adjustable point to give the right clearance.

Fix a Timing Disc and Pointer (as described in the last section) after removing the Dynamo Belt-cover.

Open the Throttle and Air Controls fully.

Engage the Footstarter and rotate the Crankshaft until compression is felt in the Cylinder.

Release the Footstarter, and then remove the Sparking-plug.

Set the Piston to Top dead-centre and adjust the Pointer to zero on the Timing-disc (see previous section).

Move the Crankshaft BACK about 20°, and with the fingers separate the Contact-points. Place between the Points a small strip of Cigarette paper or paper of similar thickness (.001 to .0015-in.).

Release the Points on to the paper.

Checking. Rotate the Crankshaft forward very slowly whilst maintaining a light pull on the Cigarette paper.

If the timing is correct, the grip of the Points on the paper will cease when the Crankshaft is between 4° and zero, or 12° if Premium grade fuel is always used.

If not correct loosen the Automatic Timing-unit from the Armature (see page 57) and reset it.

Should no Timing Disc be available the timing can be set to Top Dead Centre by checking by the Piston, **but in no circumstances** must the timing be set so that the spark occurs AFTER Top Dead Centre.

A Timing Disc can be made quite easily by marking out a card or metal disc in degrees by means of a Protractor.

Note.—The apparent lateness of the timing is because the Automatic Timing-unit is holding the Magneto into full retard. When the Engine is running the timing is automatically advanced the correct amount to suit the Engine speed.

Checking the Ignition Timing (Lucas Magneto).

The procedure is as above except that the timing is set so that the points separate 38° before top dead centre with the timer unit fully advanced—i.e., fully open.

THE CLUTCH.

Description of Working. (Fig. 32).

The clutch is operated by a thrust cup carrying a thrust bearing instead of by the more usual single thrust rod operating through a hollow gear shaft as on the L.E. Model, and most other makes. The adjustment which becomes necessary periodically to allow for settling and wear on the friction linings is made by means of the screwed clutch spring holder threaded into the front plate of the clutch, and not by alteration to the cable adjustment. A cable adjuster is fitted, but this is used for controlling the cable adjustment only and must not be used as a " first aid " remedy for a slipping clutch.

CLUTCH CABLE AND STOP

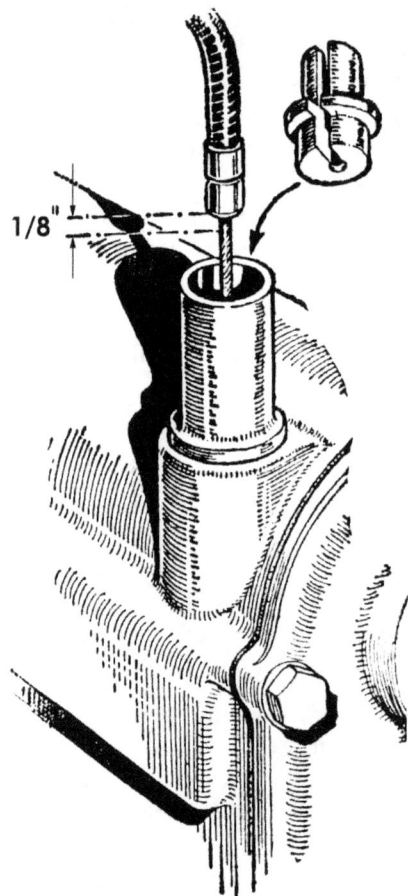

Sketch shows stop removed. Note that ⅛-in. freedom is absolute minimum permissible

FIG. 31

Before attempting any adjustment to the clutch it is important that the operation of the clutch is properly understood and the following explanation should be studied by anyone unfamiliar with the design.

The operating mechanism is shown diagrammatically (Fig. 32).

The movement of the handlebar lever (A) raises the operating lever (F) in the gearbox and the raised tip of the lever forces the large thrust pin (G) against the projecting lip of the thrust cup (J), causing the thrust cup to hinge outwards with the opposite side acting as the fulcrum.

If the outer clutch plate is observed whilst the handlebar lever is operated, with the clutch stationary, the plate will be seen to tilt outwards, as only that part of the plate nearest the thrust pin side of the clutch is freed from contact with the friction linings.

For the clutch to become fully disengaged the plates have to complete one revolution, after which the spherically seated, self-aligning ball thrust bearing (H) seated in the thrust cup levels the plates and frees them from the friction linings.

The disengagement of the front plate is arranged by the transmsision of the outward movement of the thrust through the bearing (H) and three thrust pins (I) against the adjustable clutch spring holder (M) screwed into the front plate (L).

The thrust pins (I) are fitted freely in holes in the back plate (K).

Because of the tilting of the front plate the plates are "peeled off" from contact with each other so that when correctly adjusted and maintained this type of clutch does not cause the unpleasant grating of the gears on starting away which is often noticeable with other makes.

68

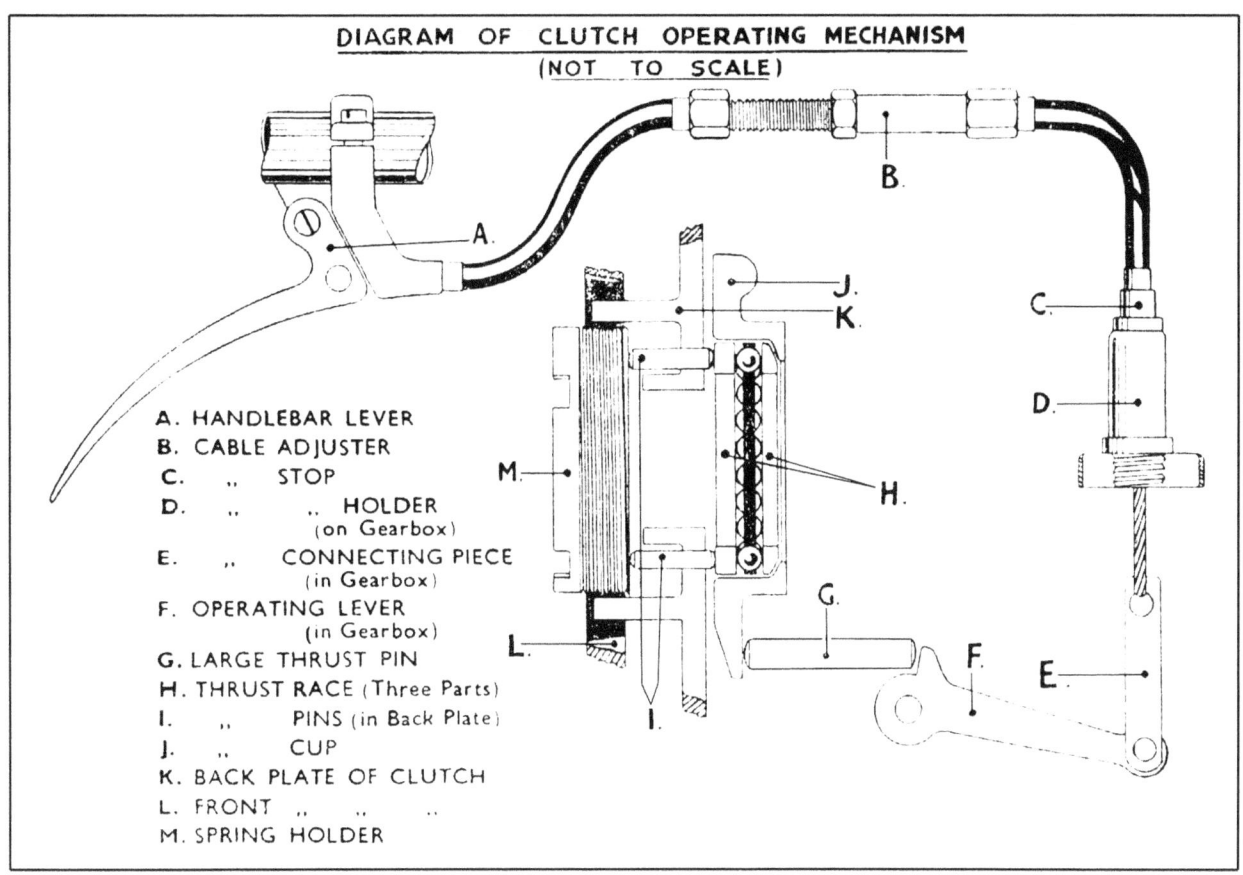

FIG 32.

It will be understood that in normal use and a condition of correct adjustment the thrust pins and thrust bearing are free of all thrust loading. It will also be noted that settling or wear of the friction linings will allow the outer plate (L) to close slightly towards the backplate (K) due to the reduction in friction lining thickness. As the thrust cup (J), when not in operation, is held against its seating and the face of the gearbox by a spring clip (not shown), it follows that the initial freedom in the thrust bearing and thrust pins will gradually be reduced, until a stage is reached in which, if adjustment is not carried out when needed the thrust pins and bearings will be carrying part of the pressure of the clutch springs. The result will be clutch slip and premature wearing of the thrust bearing.

In such circumstances adjustment has to be made to the clutch spring holder (M) which must be turned forward (anti-clockwise) in relation to the front plate (L) to restore free movement in the thrust mechanism.

Adjustment of Clutch. (Fig. 33.)

Only in special circumstances, as described later, is adjustment of the clutch cable midway adjuster required.

In the ordinary way the adjustment is made by turning the clutch spring holder in the clutch front plate by engaging the flat end of the adjusting tool KA62/2 with one of the notches in the edge of the clutch spring holder through the ¼-in. hole in the final drive sprocket and moving the rear wheel in the direction required (Fig. 33).

To use the adjusting peg in the sprocket the small cover on the rear chain guard has to be detached. The cover is marked to indicate the need for its removal.

The adjustment is made normally with the gears in neutral, and only in an exceptional case is it made when an indirect gear is engaged. Such contingencies will be dealt with later.

To prevent clutch slip, i.e., to increase free movement in the operation, pull the rear wheel forward so that the final drive sprocket and adjusting tool will move the clutch spring holder forward in relation to the clutch front plate.

Should the clutch fail to free properly after this adjustment, the clutch cable adjustment may need a little correction : see next section.

Adjustment of Clutch on New Machines or after fitting New Cable Assembly.

The adjustment of the clutch is correct when a new machine is despatched from the factory, but the friction linings (clutch inserts) may settle during the first few hundred miles running, and readjustment may be needed fairly soon.

FIG. 33. ADJUSTMENT OF CLUTCH.

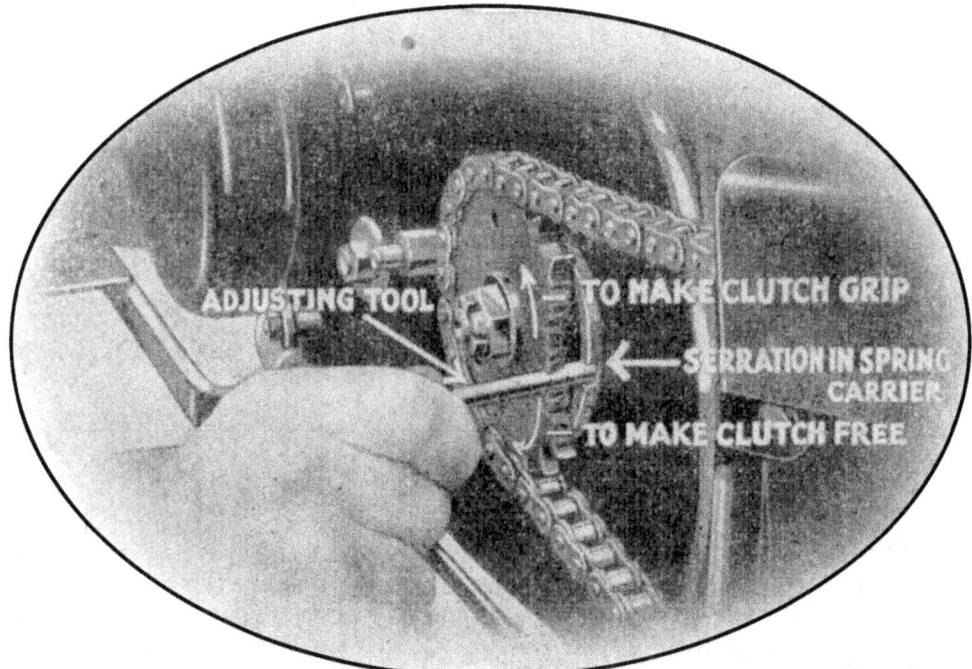

For clarity the sprocket is shown "broken away" to show the adjusting tool engaged in the clutch spring holder. Note that the movement is reversed if a gear is engaged whilst adjusting.—See page 72.

The clutch cable adjustment seldom needs attention after the initial compression and settling of the outer casings and ferrules of a new cable assembly has taken place. The control cable itself does not stretch, but very slight shortening of the total length of the casings may occur with new parts and has the same effect as a lengthened inner wire.

A careful watch should be kept on the clutch lever during the running in period of a new machine, if the clutch has been relined, or a new cable assembly has been fitted.

The settling down of the clutch inserts allows the clutch front plate to close in gradually towards the back plate and reduces the freedom allowed in the thrust bearing during assembly.

This in turn causes the control cable to lose some free movement. On the other hand any shortening of the control cable casings due to compression will tend to hide the fact that the inserts have settled and clutch slip is possible even whilst there is still some lost motion in the cable.

It is recommended, therefore, that during the service check normally carried out after the first 500 miles running, the clutch adjustment should be dealt with by carrying out a series of operations, each very simple, exactly as described later and in the order given.

With the clutch in correct adjustment it must be possible to pull back the clutch lever quite freely, and without operating the clutch at all, far enough to move the inner wire (or clutch cable) $\frac{1}{8}$-in to $\frac{3}{16}$-in. Should this free movement be seen to have decreased, re-adjustment must be made at once.

The sequence of operations for adjusting as mentioned previously is as follows :

Operation 1.—Slacken off the midway cable adjuster fully to allow the nipple to be detached from the handlebar lever and slip it out of the hole in the lever.

Operation 2.—Open both throttle and air controls fully. Select neutral position of the gears, and depress the kickstart against compression and test for clutch slip. If the clutch is felt to slip omit Operation 3 and carry on with Operation 4.

If no slip can be felt carry on with Operation 3.

Operation 3.—Using the clutch adjusting peg as already described, pull the rear wheel backward a quarter of a turn at a time checking for clutch slip after each movement. This will involve taking out the adjusting peg from engagement with the clutch spring holder before each test. As soon as the clutch can be felt to slip (and only just slip), proceed with Operation 4.

Operation 4.—Refit the cable nipple to the handlebar lever. Re-adjust the midway adjuster until all lost motion is taken out of the cable and the lever is just drawn up against the lever bracket on the handlebar. Do not force the adjuster but *only just* remove all play. When correct tighten the cable adjuster locknut.

Finally, refit the adjusting peg to the sprocket, engage it with the clutch spring holder, and pull the rear wheel forward a little at a time until free movement begins to appear on the cable when the handlebar lever is checked.

Adjust until there is free travel on the cable of $\frac{1}{8}$-in. to $\frac{3}{16}$-in.

The adjustment is now completed.

Although the foregoing may seem complicated at first sight the whole " drill " is both easily and quickly carried out, and after the initial settling of a new cable assembly has taken place is only likely to be needed in special circumstances, as for instance if it is not known whether adjustment is needed to the cable or the spring holder. The effect of the two adjustments is inter-related.

If in doubt as to whether the cable or spring holder should be adjusted the following should be referred to :—

Symptom : Clutch slipping. No lost motion on control cable.
Remedy : Readjust clutch spring holder forward.

Symptom : Clutch slipping. Lost motion present on control cable.*
Remedy : Carry out Operation 4 of Adjustment " drill."

Symptom : Clutch not freeing. Normal or excess lost motion on cable.
Remedy : Carry out full Adjustment " drill."

Symptom : Clutch slipping and also not freeing.*
Remedy : Carry out Operation 4 of Adjustment " drill."

It can be accepted that if clutch trouble is not eliminated by carrying out the " drill " exactly as described the clutch will have to be dismantled to attend to a mechanical fault, to rectify incorrect assembly, or to replace worn parts.

* See next section.

Adjusting a Tight Clutch Spring Holder.

If excessive slip through neglect of the adjustment, or a spring holder which is tight in the clutch front plate, causes the clutch front plate to turn with it when adjustment is attempted, the adjustment should be made in the following manner.

Engage either second or third gear, and after passing the adjusting peg through the sprocket, move the clutch by means of the kickstart until one of the notches in the spring holder is opposite the peg and engage the peg in the notch.

To make the clutch grip *move the rear wheel backwards.* This is the opposite direction to that used when adjusting with the gears in neutral.

By adjusting with an indirect gear engaged advantage is taken of the difference in the rates of movement of the clutch sleeve gear (to which the clutch driven plates are attached) and the final drive sprocket.

Oil in the Clutch.

The primary chain case is intended to carry enough oil to lubricate the chain, and the clutch will grip satisfactorily even if there is an excess of oil in the cover provided that from the outset the cover has had oil in it.

It has been found however, that a clutch which has been run completely free of oil over a period will be subject to slip if oil is subsequently introduced on to the friction surfaces. In such circumstances the clutch must be relined, and assembled with oil in the cover.

Fitting a New Clutch Cable.

In order to fit a new clutch cable or outer casing, it will be necessary to take off the fuel tank as the cable is clipped to the top tube of the frame below the tank. This is described in the section dealing with decarbonisation. Pull up the clutch control lever, grasp the outer casing firmly just ahead of the lever socket and pull sharply towards the centre of the machine as the lever is smartly released, slipping the casing at the same time out of the recess in the lever socket. Remove the cable stop from the cable stop holder on top of the gearbox and unscrew the stop holder right out. Hold this up out of the way under the Oil tank and disconnect the small cable nipple from the slotted connecting piece just inside the gearbox by sliding the cable sideways. The cable and casing will then easily be drawn up through the tube in the oil tank, after which the nipple can be slipped out of the handle-bar lever.*

Thread the new cable assembly down through the oil tank* and slip the cable stop holder over the end. Slide the nipple sideways into the connecting piece, screw the stop holder into place and put the cable stop into position.

Adjust the clutch spring holder clockwise until the clutch is in a slightly slipping condition when checked by pressing down the Footstarter. See that the cable adjuster is screwed up to its limit to make it as " short " as possible. Connect the nipple and outer casing to the handle-bar lever. Set the cable-adjuster so that there is JUST no free movement perceptible at the handle-bar end and tighten the lock-nut on the adjuster. Screw the clutch spring holder anti-clockwise until free movement is restored in the cable, and lastly refit the Fuel tank. See also page 70, dealing with clutch adjustment, etc.

† DISMANTLING AND RE-ASSEMBLING THE CLUTCH. MOV, MAC and MSS.

Begin as described on page 53 for dismantling the engine-shaft shock absorber and remove the whole clutch from the sleeve gear. Do not lose

* *On the MSS the cable passes behind the oil tank.*
† *All Model MOV (and MAC machines supplied before 1941) have single plate cork-lined clutches. The method of dismantling is similar.*

the three small thrust pins from the back plate. The front plate will now lift off, exposing a steel plate fitted with friction inserts; remove this and the steel "dished" plate below it. Slide the chain wheel and ballrace off the centre of the back plate. The ballrace should remain in the chain wheel and is intended to be a light push fit on the centre. Only one steel plate and an "inserted" plate remain to be lifted off. The clutch inserts, of which there are 66, will not need renewal unless they are worn down flush with the steel, or are very loose in the holes. The ball race should run freely, and should be fairly tight in the chain-wheel. The inserts are of Ferodo on the MAC and MSS and cork on the MOV.

The removal of the clutch will have exposed the thrust bearing. This consists of three parts. First, a flat thrust ring, followed by a caged ball thrust bearing, and finally a thrust washer having a flat face to provide a bearing for the balls, and a convex face on the other side which seats in a concave surface in the thrust cup. The thrust cup need not normally be removed. See that the flat bearing surfaces are free from pitting, and that the balls are in good order. If needed, fit new parts. The plain thrust may be reversed if worn on one side only, and will be quite satisfactory. The distance piece on the sleeve gear may be inspected, and if worn should be replaced. See that the brass cage of the ballrace is quite free upon it before assembling.

Refit the three parts of the thrust race in the following order : Spherical washer with convex face against the thrust cup, followed by the ball thrust, and finally the plain thrust ring. Coat all these parts with grease when fitting.

†To re-assemble the clutch lay the back plate, working surface upwards, on the bench, or obtain a used sleeve gear off any single cylinder Velocette, hold this by the driving dogs in a vice and mount the back plate upon it over the splines. Place one of the "insert" plates in position, followed by one of the steel "dished" plates. The projections on the inside of this plate must be engaged in the notches in the back plate. Take up the chain wheel and see that the ballrace is free. Press a little grease into the race and turn it round once or twice to distribute the grease. Slide the chain wheel and race over the centre of the back plate and turn the chain wheel until the notches on the outside engage the projections on the "insert" plate underneath.

The second "dished" plate is now fitted with its projections facing upwards.

Place the second "insert" plate in position, making sure that its outer projections fit into the recesses in the chain wheel. Finally place the front plate in position. It is occasionally difficult to fit this at the first attempt, as it is not possible always to locate its recesses over the projections on the "dished" plate, which, of course, cannot be seen when the front plate is lowered into position. By manoeuvring the chainwheel backwards and forwards, however, it will usually drop into place after one or two attempts. Screw the Spring-holder into place if it has previously been taken out. Lift the whole Clutch, being careful to hold the back and front plates together firmly, and smear a little grease into the holes for the three Thrust-pins. Put the Thrust-pins into place—the grease will hold them. Engage Top gear (to prevent the Sleeve-gear slipping back into the Gearbox) and slide the Clutch into position on to the splines of the Sleeve-gear.

Fit the Clutch-springs, setting them in position so that the ground edges of the Springs are on the outside of the Holder. The Spring-holder must be screwed in until it contacts the ends of the three Thrust-pins. Provided the Sleeve-gear is pushed well up into its Ballrace, i.e.,

† *All MOV Models (and MAC machines supplied before 1941) have single plate cork-lined clutches. The method of assembly is similar.*

has not been allowed to slip back into the Gearbox, the Sleeve-gear Nut can usually be started on the threads without having to compress the springs very much. There is a Service Tool X2959 for the job. See Fig. 34.

Should the sleeve gear nut fail to engage the threads on the sleeve gear due to the latter having slipped back through the ballrace, remove the clutch and screw up the sleeve gear nut against the distance tube to draw it back. When the end of the thread is reached remove the nut and carefully fit the clutch back plate. Fit and tighten the nut again to draw the sleeve gear further through the back plate. Remove the nut and finally assemble the clutch.

Tighten the Sleeve-gear Nut tightly with the Peg-spanner finishing by driving the Spanner round, and when tight refit, the Locking-plate and Set-screw.

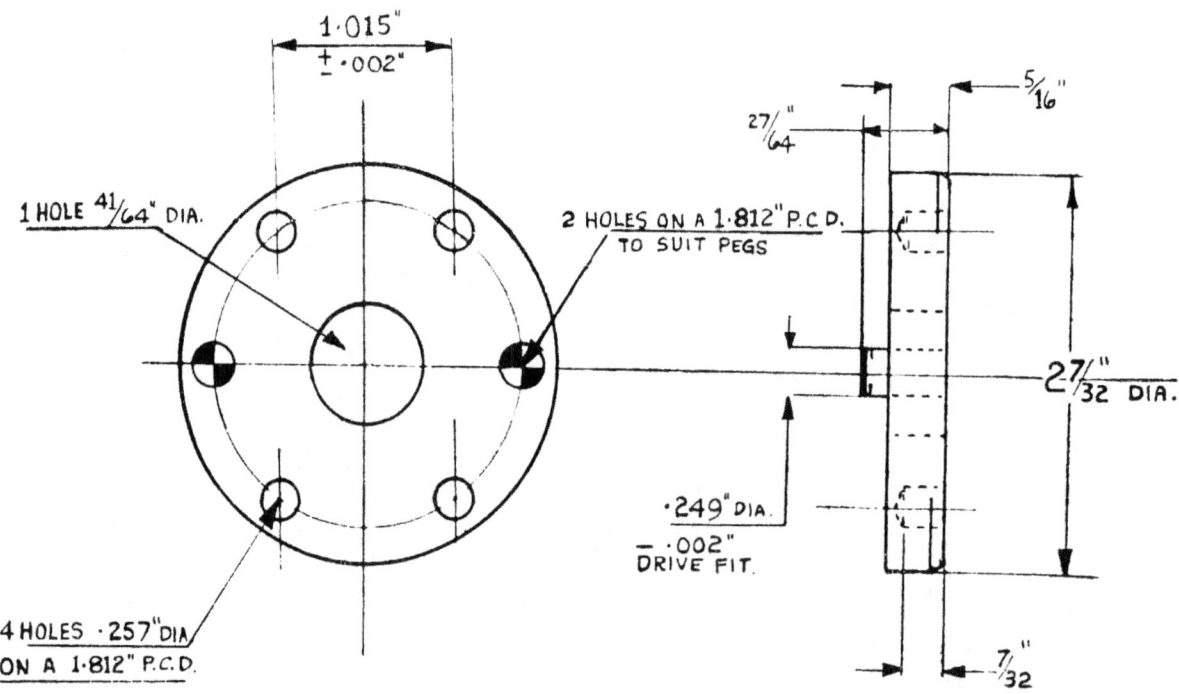

FIG. 34
X2959. SLEEVE GEAR NUT ADAPTOR.

Proceed to reset the adjustment as described on page 70.

THE GEARBOX—DISMANTLING AND RE-ASSEMBLING.

Unless a complete overhaul is needed there is no necessity to remove the Gearbox from the machine, as all internal parts are readily removable with the assembly still in the frame—if the work is undertaken in this way, however, the machine should be raised on to a trestle. The work is rendered much easier in this way.

Preliminary Work.

Disconnect the Clutch Control Cable from the Handlebar-lever first and then from the connecting-piece in the Gearbox.

Unscrew and remove the hexagon-headed Bearing Cap just above the Filler-plug in the Gearbox End-cover. Upon the standardisation of the rounded smooth outline gearbox end cover† a distance piece is fitted between the gearshaft ballrace outer ring and the cap. Loosen the large nut thus disclosed, holding the Gearshaft from turning meanwhile by having the Rear Brake applied by an assistant.

† At engine No. MAC15791.

On MOV and MAC to remove the gearbox from the machine, proceed as described on page 54 to remove the Primary Chain cover, the Chain and the Clutch. Remove the drain plug from the rear at the bottom of the Gearbox housing and drain out all oil. Take out the split-pin from and remove the bolt which secures the Adjuster-bolt at the top of the housing to the nearside rear engine-plate.

Take off the nut and washer from the Gear-control Pedal-pivot and pull the lever with the swivel and sleeve off the pivot. Unscrew the four nuts and remove the half-clips from the studs below the Gearbox. Raise the Gearbox off the cross tube of the frame and take it out of the machine.

On MSS Models remove engine and gearbox (see page 54).

Dismantling the End-Cover.

The pre-war MOV and MAC Models and all MSS Models have the gear control lever in a bushed lug at the top. (See Fig. 36). On these models the gear control lever and pivot with the control rod should be removed by taking off the nut from the pivot and disconnecting the gear rod swivel joint from the outside striking lever on the gearbox. The Footstarter ratchet is carried in a separate steel housing bolted to the cover. This housing can be removed before taking off the end cover or can be left attached as desired, but if attention is needed to the ratchet or return spring only, it is easier to take it off leaving the end cover in place.

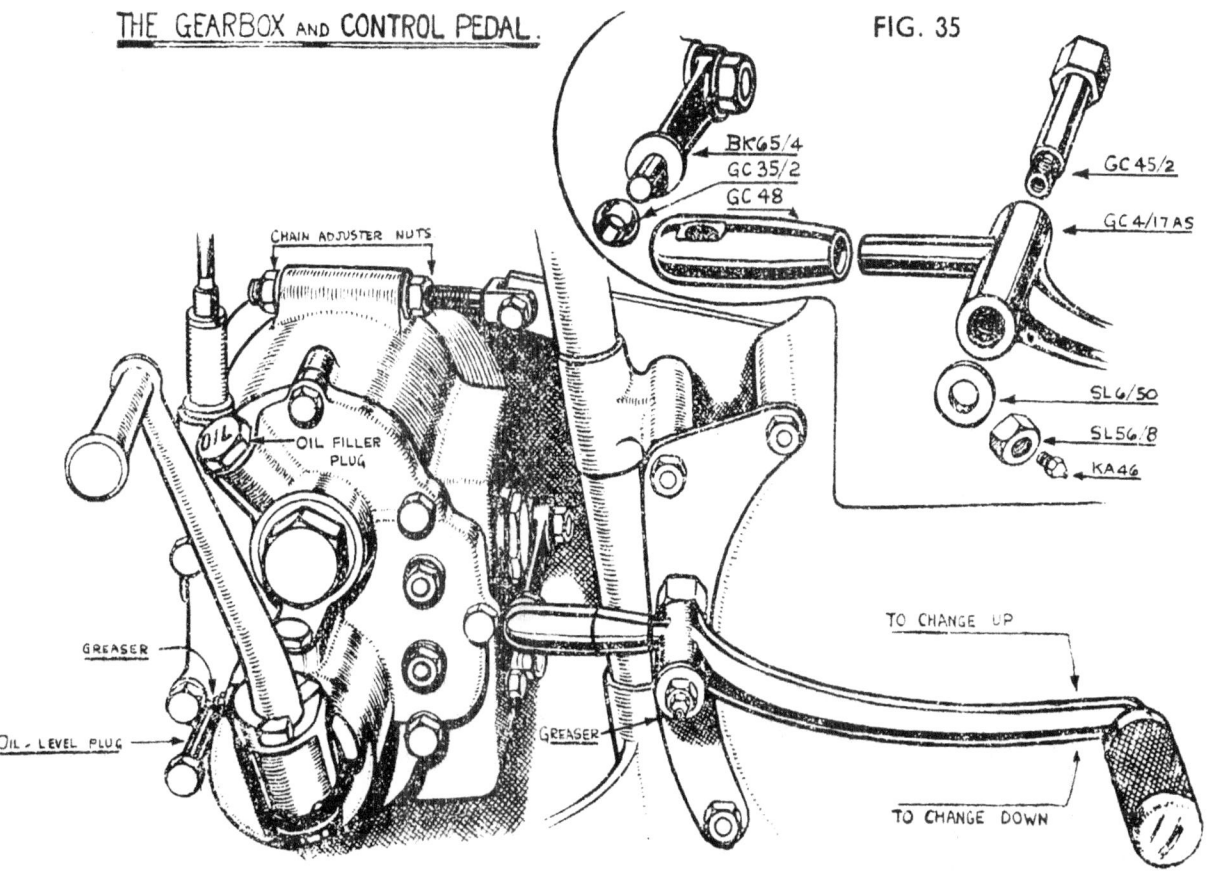

MOV and MAC MODEL GEAR CONTROL.
(Oil filler plug is in the position shown in Fig. 36.)

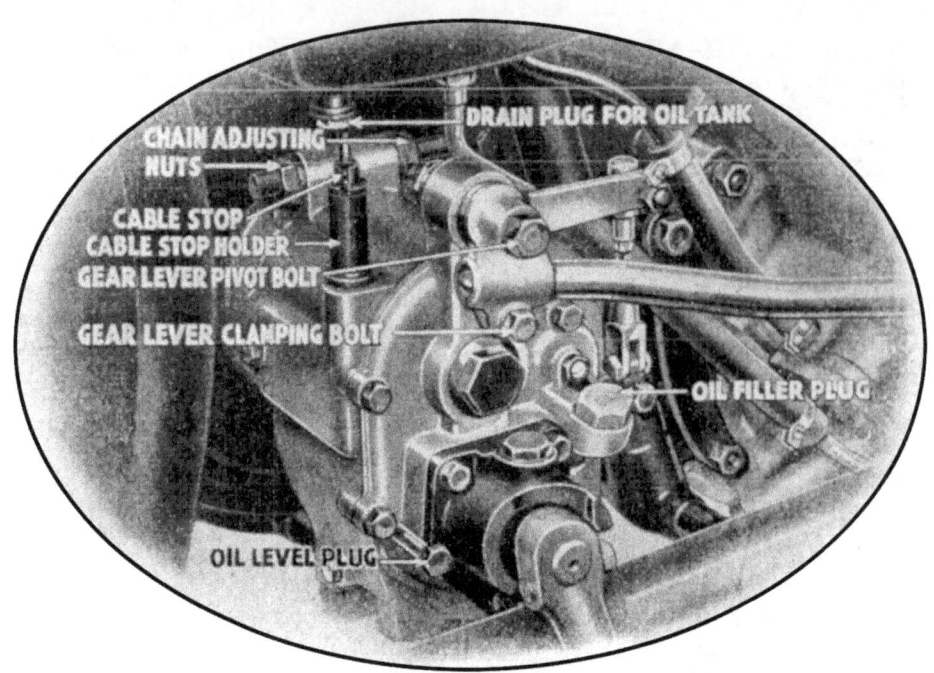

FIG. 36   PRE-WAR MAC MODEL GEAR CONTROL.

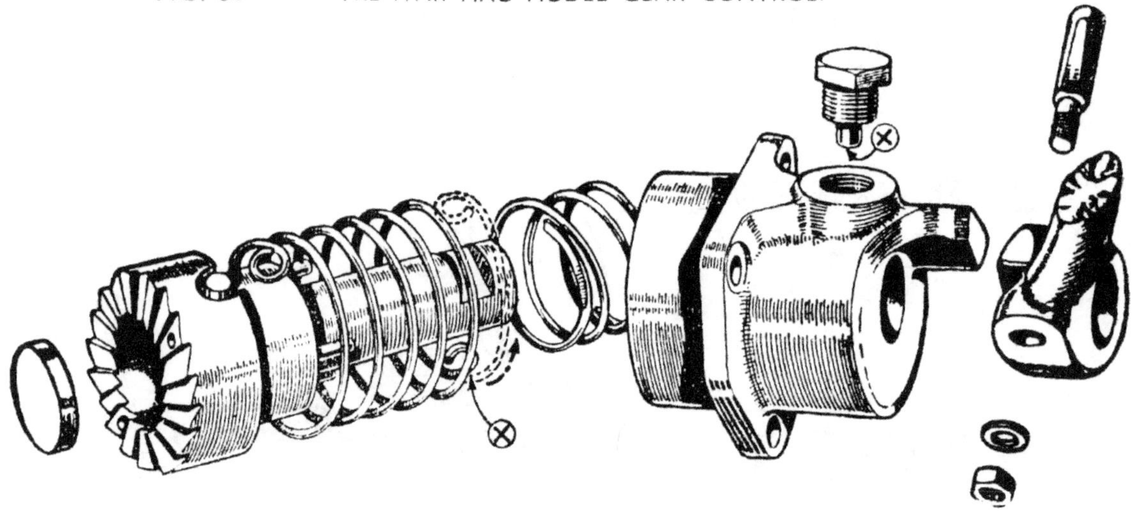

FIG. 37

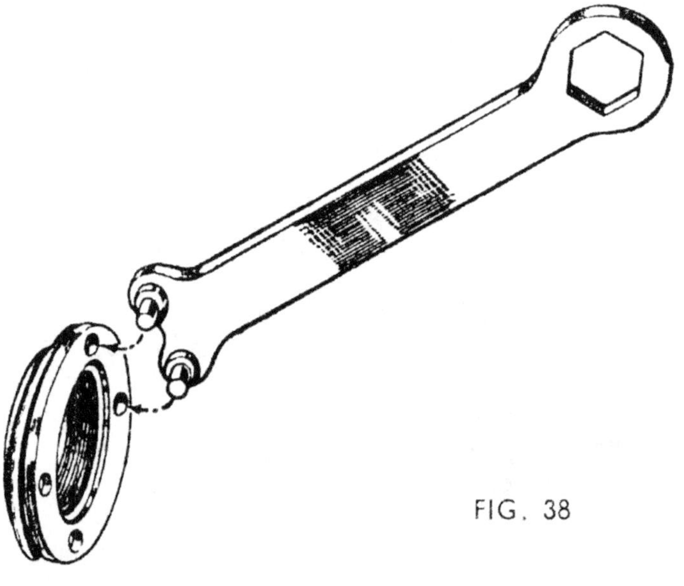

FIG. 38

If the Footstarter mechanism does not need attention, the housing can be left in place fixed to the cover and the dismantling carried out as described below.

If the Footstarter Ratchet or Return spring are to be renewed, loosen the Anchor pin for the Return spring in the top of the Ratchet Housing on the cover, and take off the nut and washer from the cotter securing the Footstarter crank to the Ratchet before taking off the housing or the cover.

Remove the Oil-level-plug from the end cover. Now remove the nut from the end of the Gearbox (previously loosened) and tap the shaft into the Gearbox about an inch.

Take out the bolts securing the End-cover to the housing, and the two nuts† off the ends of the Selector-fork Pins. Pull off the cover with the Footstarter mechanism all in one. Attention to the Footstarter is dealt with on page 81.

Note that the end of the Layshaft is supported in the Footstarter-ratchet in a floating bush.* This bush may remain on the end of the Layshaft or come out with the Ratchet. In either case, be careful not to lose it or the Thrust-washer inside the hollow end of the Ratchet behind the floating bush. The bush should be a free fit on the Layshaft and in the Ratchet.

Removal of Selector Fork Rods and Gears and Shafts.

Take off the loose low-gear wheel from the end of the Gearshaft. Engage either second or third speed and draw out the two Selector-fork Pins. They are now grooved at one end to provide a purchase for levering out. On earlier models thread the nuts back on to the ends of the Pins. The Pins can then be levered out with the end of a Screwdriver or Tyre-lever against a piece of material $\frac{3}{8}$-in. thick placed on the machined face of the Housing to act as a fulcrum. Pull out the Gearshaft from the Clutch side through the Sleeve-gear.

By twisting the upper Selector-fork so that the Operating-peg clears the cam track, the fork and the Double gear can be extracted. In a similar manner the Layshaft assembly and the lower Fork can be removed. This leaves only the Sleeve-gear, which can be tapped into the Housing through the large Ballrace.

SPECIAL NOTE.—On MSS Models with 17 T. Sleeve Gear and on other Models when close ratio (17-27) Gears are fitted, the Sleeve Gear has to be turned until a position is reached where the 16 T. Top Gear pick-up dogs do not mask the layshaft gear teeth, otherwise the layshaft gear cannot be withdrawn from mesh with the Sleeve Gear.

The Operating Mechanism. (Fig. 39).

It is exceedingly unlikely that any attention will be needed to this part of the Gearbox, as from experience over a period of many years we have found the parts comprising the internal Control-mechanism to be virtually non-wearing, and no case of a breakage occurring has ever been known.

Should the Cam plate have to be removed it may be taken out with the small centre piece on which it is fitted by first depressing the Indexing-pawl at the bottom. **Do not in any circumstances take the Cam-plate off the centre piece** before marking both parts, so that they can be re-assembled in the same relative positions and with the Cam plate facing the right way round (Fig. 39).

The remainder of the Mechanism is quite easily removed if need be, but should on no account be taken apart unnecessarily.

Early types have a roller bearing.

† *Not fitted on MAC Models after engine No. MAC 15790.*

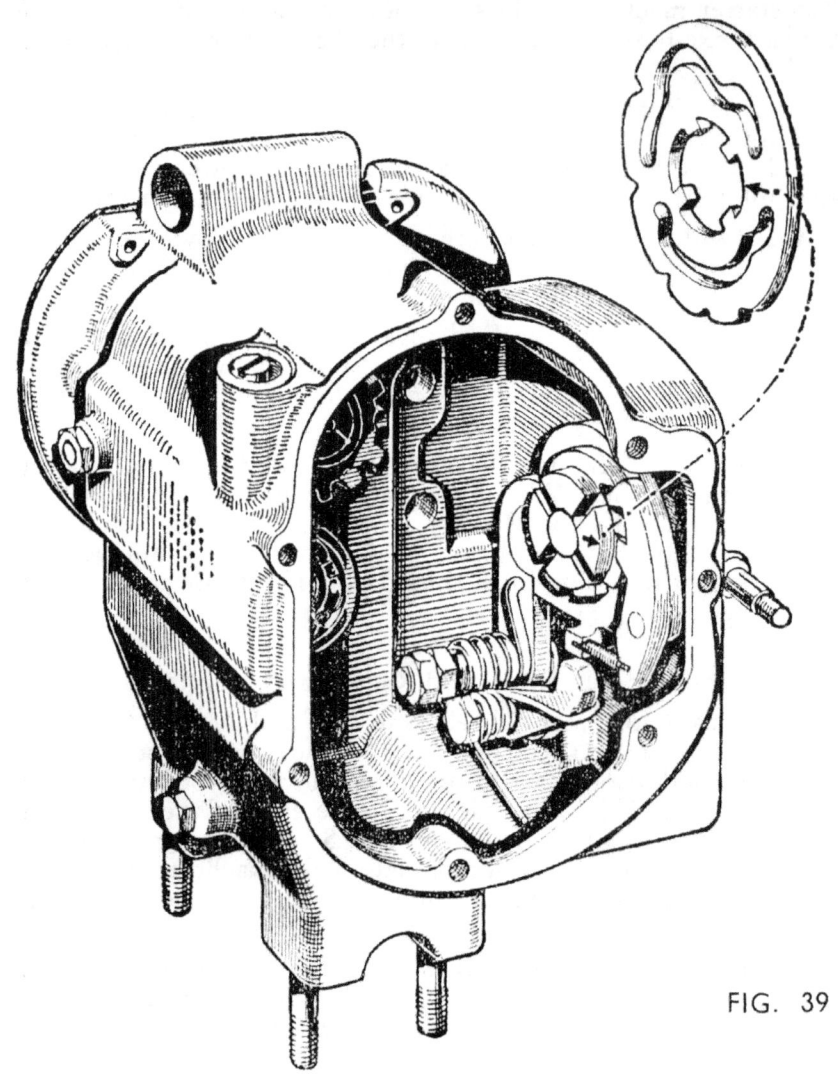

FIG. 39

THE OPERATING MECHANISM AND CAM PLATE (MOV and MAC).
(Showing cam plate removed and the markings for refitting.)

Removal of Chain Cover, Etc.

If the Sleeve-gear Ballrace or the Ballrace shims are to be replaced or removed for inspection, the inner half of the Primary chain cover must be removed. Remove it as follows:—Cut the locking wires from the securing screws. Remove the screws. Pull off the cover and joint packing behind it. Unscrew and remove two small screws securing the wire clip to the face of the housing. Take off the clip and lift out the Thrust cup. When re-assembling note that new locking wire must invariably be used.

The Bearings.

The condition of the large Sleeve-gear Ballrace and its Steel Shims can usually be verified without removal. Any sign of slackness or roughness in the bearing indicates that a replacement is needed. Inspect the shims (one at each side of the ballrace) to see that they are not worn or split. Pay particular attention to the inner one which may have been in contact with the Oil-thrower on the Sleeve-gear.

To remove the large Ballrace it is necessary to take out the Retaining ring by unscrewing it out of the housing. It is provided with three slots to facilitate removal. Use Service Tool X2725 (Fig. 40). If it is driven round with a punch it is essential to use one which is shaped properly to fit the slots, which will otherwise be damaged. Tap the bearing out when retaining ring and shim have been removed.

On refitting the Ballrace see that both shims are located as centrally as possible, so that the Distance piece for the Sleeve-gear does not foul when pulled up to the centre ring of the Ballrace. Also when the retaining ring has been screwed home fully the edge of the Housing must be "centre-popped" into the three notches around the outside.

The bearing for the Gearshaft in the end cover can be tapped out or into the cover with a drift $1\frac{1}{8}$-in. in diameter, 3-in. long, with a Pilot $\frac{1}{2}$-in. in diameter, $\frac{1}{2}$-in. long. The larger diameter should be recessed to a depth of $\frac{1}{16}$-in. round the pilot to a diameter of 1-in.

The Ballrace at the nearside end of the Layshaft can be driven out of its place into the Housing with a $\frac{7}{8}$-in. diameter drift 3-in. to 4-in. long, after knocking the Oil-retaining Cap outwards through the centre of the bearing with a $\frac{1}{2}$-in. diameter tommy bar. This Cap must be replaced and the housing "centre-popped" to secure it after the ballrace has been inserted. A drift $1\frac{1}{2}$-in. diameter, 5-in. long, with a $\frac{5}{8}$-in. diameter pilot $\frac{1}{2}$-in. long, recessed to a depth of $\frac{1}{16}$-in., and a diameter of $1\frac{1}{4}$in. round the pilot is suitable for refitting the bearing.

The low gear bush and those in the layshaft gears seldom need renewal. If new ones are fitted bore out the low gear bush to .625-in. and the others to .8125-in. The limits are $+.0007$-in.—$.0005$-in. in both cases. The sleeve gear bush which is pegged to the sleeve gear can be driven out with a $\frac{15}{16}$-in. diameter drift after the peg has been removed by drilling out with $\frac{3}{16}$-in. diameter drill.

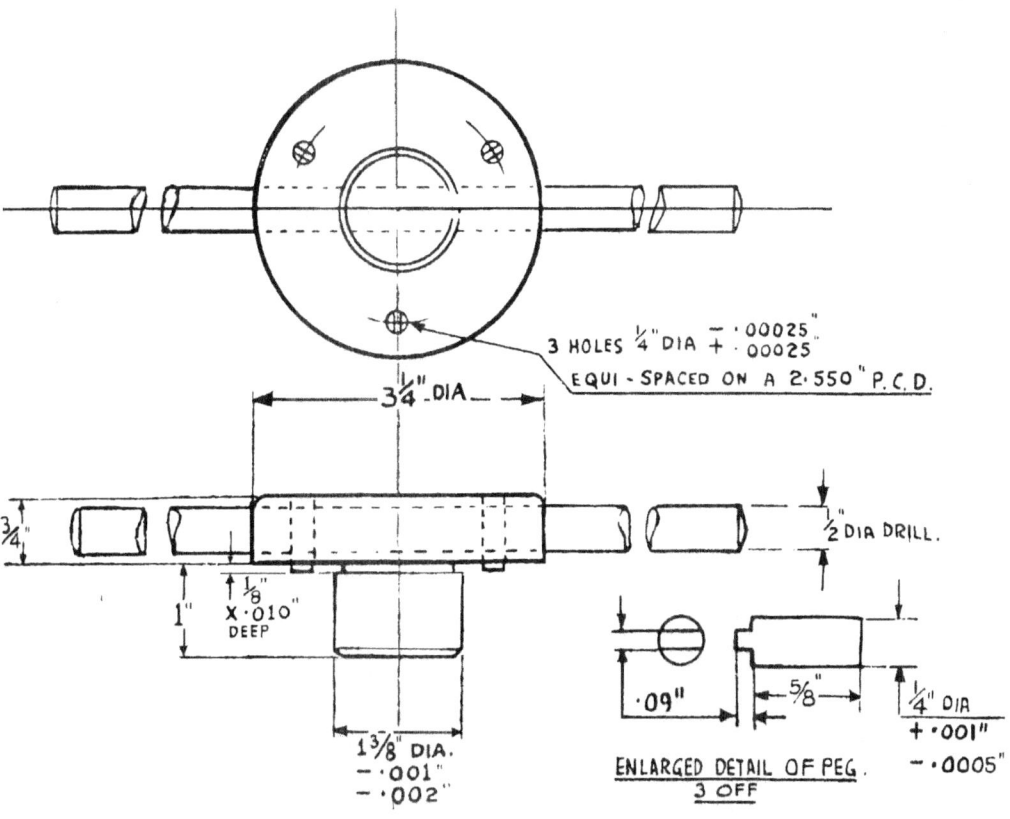

FIG. 40
X2725 BALLRACE RETAINING RING TOOL

When replaced, it should be bored to give a clearance of .001-in. above the shaft diameter. A good fit is essential to obviate any side loads on the main-bearing, and it is desirable to bore and not to ream the bush owing to the risk ,if reaming is resorted to, of the bearing being made bell-mouthed—a cause of oil leakage. When boring see that bore is concentric with the ground outside ballrace seating.

The Layshaft Assembly. (See Fig.) 41.

In order to remove the loose second and third speed gear wheels from the Layshaft it is necessary to remove the large Layshaft driven gear and the small ratchet gear respectively. The large Layshaft driven gear and the ratchet gear can be pressed or levered off the Layshaft. Note specially, however that a small thrust washer fits over the ends of the splines against the outside of the ratchet gear. Do not lose this. *Also note that on some ex-Army MAC machines a spring circlip retains the ratchet gear in position. It is important in such a case not to attempt to remove the ratchet gear before taking this circlip out of position.* It is however, necessary only to remove one of these gears, if only the sliding dog has to be replaced. The edges of the driving dogs on the second and third speed gears and upon the driving dog itself should be carefully inspected for wear as worn dogs may cause dis-engagement under load.

Assembly. (If MSS or close-ratio, see Special Note, Page 77.)

Re-assembly is the reverse procedure of dismantling. First the Sleeve gear is inserted from inside and pressed through the Ballrace, being careful first to slip the Oil thrower over the Sleeve gear with the concave face towards the gear teeth. Next the Cam-plate, etc., the Layshaft assembly and Gearshaft with its gears are refitted in that order. Care is, of course, necessary when replacing the Layshaft assembly and the Double gear to see that the pegs of the Selector forks are properly engaged with the track in the Cam.

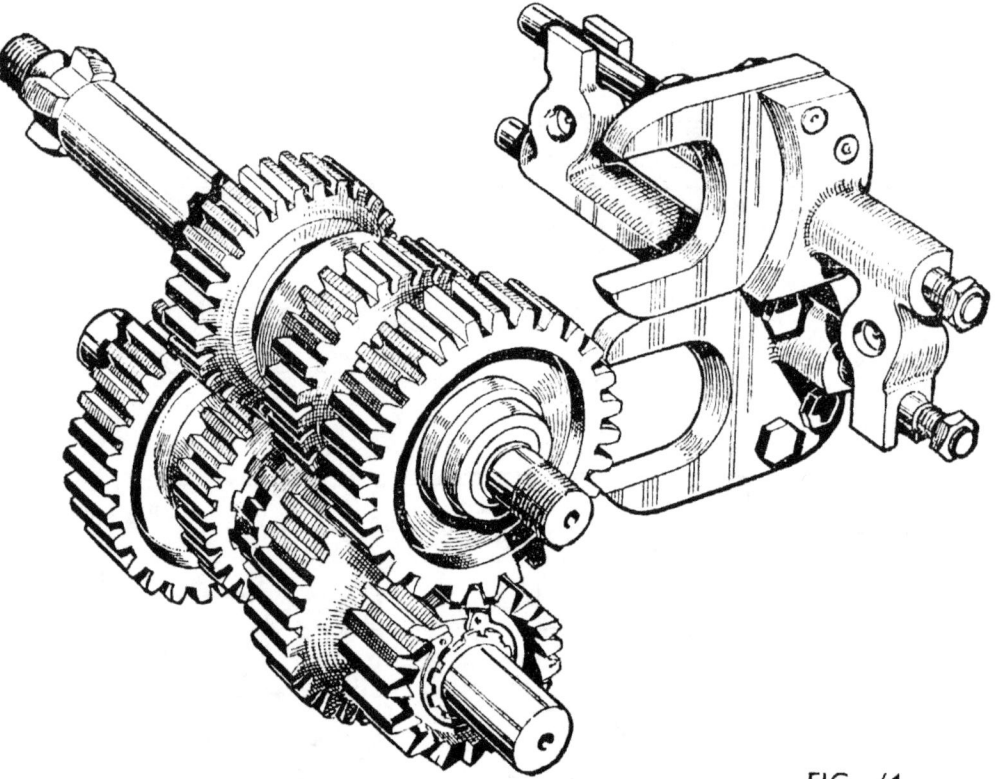

FIG. 41

THE GEARS AND SELECTOR FORKS (MOV and MAC)
(IN CORRECT POSITIONS FOR RE-ASSEMBLING)

(The position of the forks is inverted and to the rear of the gears on the MSS)

The Footstarter.

A swivelling foot-piece pivots in the top of a crank attached to the ratchet, on some Models the whole crank swivels in a lug attached to the ratchet.

Notes on using the Footstarter. It is very important not to kick sharply and the ratchet must be allowed to engage properly before putting heavy pressure on the footpiece. It will be noticed that as the footpiece moves down, the ratchet is allowed to slide into the ratchet housing on the end cover due to the swivel lug running off the disengaging cam formed at the end of the housing. It must be allowed to slide in properly, otherwise the ratchet will not engage properly, and damage may be caused to the teeth on the ratchet and on the ratchet gear. Do not hurry the operation—by being careful and deliberate time will be saved in the long run. Always release the footpiece as soon as the engine starts.

In the unlikely event of the Footstarter failing to return correctly on NO ACCOUNT must the machine be run unless the Foot piece is returned by hand to the disengaged (upright) position and secured there if necessary.

Unless it is necessary to replace the Ratchet or Return spring do not dismantle the Swivel-lug or F/S crank from the end cover. If the Spring is broken and is to be renewed proceed as follows :—

Fitting a Starter Return Spring.

The Footstarter Ratchet Housing should be removed separately, leaving the end cover in place (see page 38). Turn the F/S crank through 90° and drive out the cotter, pull it off from the end of the Ratchet and pull out the Ratchet and part of spring. When doing so take care not to lose the engaging-spring which fits inside the Return-spring or the three Rollers which operate through holes in the Ratchet against the loose Thrust washer. Take out the Anchor pin (already loosened, see " Dismantling the end cover ") and remove the remainder of the Spring. Should the return spring be unbroken a slightly different procedure is necessary for removing the Ratchet as follows :—

Take off the Nut and Washer from the Cotter, now obtain 2 nails about 2-in. long × $\frac{5}{32}$-in. in diameter (or slightly less) and cut off the heads, drive these into the bench $1\frac{19}{32}$-in. apart leaving them protruding about 1-in. Place the Ratchet Housing face downwards over the nails so that these enter the two breather holes which are drilled through the teeth of the Ratchet. Pull the housing round clockwise 90° against the tension of the spring and drive out the cotter. Release the housing, pull off the crank, and lift the Ratchet off the nails. Push the Ratchet through from the outside sufficiently to enable the loop of the Spring to be prised off the fixing lug on the Ratchet. When the Spring is unhooked push the Ratchet right out. The Return spring can now be withdrawn, after removing the Spring anchor peg.

The Return spring is slightly larger in diameter in its free state than the housing to which it is fitted and to replace a spring the following directions must be followed.

The smaller loop engages the Anchor pin, the larger the Ratchet.† Push the end with the smaller loop into the housing so that when it is fully home it will be directly below the Anchor pin hole to permit the tip of the Anchor pin to fit into it.

With a screwdriver press the Spring into the Housing, working round it spirally coil by coil until only sufficient is left out to be slipped over the lug on the Ratchet. Refit the Anchor pin. Place the engaging spring and rollers (or Thrust pins) in position, sticking the Rollers with some

† *See Fig.* 37.

grease. Note that there are 6 holes in the Ratchet, three of which act as breathers. Place the Rollers in those holes which run right through into the parallel ground bearing surface inside the Ratchet.

Place the Ratchet in position, engage the loop of the Spring over the lug and push the Ratchet right home. Place the housing face downwards again with the Ratchet over the nails. Push the crank into place on the end of the Ratchet and pull the housing round against the tension of the spring SUFFICIENTLY FAR ONLY to allow the cotter to be tapped through its hole across the flat on the Ratchet. The cotter must be fitted with the Threaded end facing the rear of the machine. Fit the Nut and Washer and tighten up. If a new Cotter is required file the flat if necessary so that when the Cotter has been driven fully home the head is flush with the surface of the Swivel-lug.

Re-fitting the End Cover.

The footstarter housing need not be fitted until after the end cover has been replaced.‡ *Note specially that on MOV and MAC Models one of the end cover bolts is slightly shorter than the others, and it must be replaced in the correct position in the hole adjacent to the edge of the cam plate. A longer bolt used in this position will foul the operating pawl and prevent the proper working of the gear operating mechanism.*

Place in position the layshaft thrust washer which fits over the ends of the splines protruding from the ratchet gear. *Note that in the case of ex-Army MAC Models a circlip is used to retain the ratchet gear it is illustrated in Fig. 44.* Place the end cover joint washer in position on the face of the end cover and push the end cover into position, locating the ballrace over the end of the gearshaft. Put in and tighten all fixing bolts except the one at the very bottom. Re-fit the nut to the gearshaft, tighten the nut and then refit the distance piece and cap. Fit and tighten the nuts of the selector fork rods and the gearbox is then ready for the footstarter housing and ratchet, etc., to be fitted. ‡Place the hardened thrust washer into the bearing recess in the ratchet, smear the end of the layshaft with oil and slide the floating bush into place. *On some early machines a caged roller race is used in place of this bush.* It is necessary to see that the roller cage of this bearing is fitted so that the open end of the cage is remote from the ratchet gear. Smear the inside of the ratchet with oil, work the housing and ratchet into position over the bearing and tap it carefully into the end cover, finally securing it with the three fixing bolts. The gearbox is then ready for refitting to the frame.

REMOVAL AND REPLACEMENT OF REAR WHEEL.
Removal.

Free the rear stand from the mudguard and raise the machine on to the stand. Always choose level ground, but if compelled to work on a slope, have the machine facing uphill, it is then unlikely to run forward off the stand when the wheel is out. Disconnect the rear lamp and detach the mudguard extension. Disconnect the speedometer drive.

Loosen and take off the three nuts securing the wheel to the Brake-drum, unscrew and pull out the Spindle from the off-side. As it comes clear of the hub catch the distance piece, which is fitted between the hollow spindle of the hub and the Fork-end of the frame. Remove the wheel by lifting it off the studs and pulling it away to the rear.

Replacement.

Lift the wheel into place and fit the three wheel nuts to the studs on the Brake-drum. Place the distance piece in position inside the Fork-end of the Frame. See that the plain washer is in place under the head

‡ *Do not in any circumstances fit a packing washer between the K/S housing and end cover. This is important.*

of the Spindle, screw in and tighten the Spindle fully.

Tighten the three wheel nuts fully and refit the mudguard extension.

Connect the speedometer drive flex to the reduction gearbox.

Notes on Above.

After running about twenty miles after replacing the Rear wheel, check and if necessary tighten the spindle and wheel nuts, in case any bedding down has occurred. On early MOV and MAC Models also check Brake Anchor Bolt for tightness. (See Fig. 43.)

Never lower the machine off the stand on to the wheel unless the Spindle is in position, and on no account remove this spindle unless the weight is taken off the wheel by placing the machine on the stand.

To change a rear Inner-tube it is not necessary to remove the wheel. The old tube can be removed and a new one fitted after removing the Spindle and distance piece.

Removal of Rear Brake.

Take out the Rear Wheel as previously described and on MOV and MAC Models disconnect the Torque-link from the Brake-plate or the Prop-stand Pivot, whichever is the more convenient. Remove chain.

On early MOV and MAC Models the Brake-plate is secured to the frame fork end lug by an anchor bolt which has to be removed to take out the Brake-plate. (See Fig. 43).

Loosen the large hexagon nut on the Dummy-spindle and slide the whole assembly out of the Fork-end of the frame.

By taking the nut right off the Dummy-spindle the Brake-plate and Brake-shoes will lift right out of the Drum. Be careful not to lose the distance tube which fits on the Dummy Spindle outside the Brake-plate.

BRAKES.

When the adjustment available has all been taken up it is often possible to extend the life of the brake linings by packing the brake shoes from the cam. Suitable packings can be cut comparatively easily from sheet steel and are readily fitted. Cut two strips for each brake. Take off the shoes and fit one packing to each shoe. Before refitting the shoes, see that the rivet heads are well below the surface of the linings. If not—punch them down a little. Should new linings or replacement shoes with new linings be fitted, always smear the surface of the linings with the very slightest film of grease. This reduces the possibility of the drums becoming scored and ridged, and although the efficiency of the brakes will at first be affected, it will rapidly improve and the brakes become perfectly normal.

DISMANTLING THE REAR HUB BEARINGS. (Fig. 44.)

Machines supplied new with telescopic front forks have the speedometer reduction gearbox fitted to the rear hub and **the ballrace retaining ring (JJ—Fig 44) is left-hand threaded.** It unscrews from the hub clockwise. The corresponding part on the previous pattern hub is right hand threaded. Otherwise there is very little difference between the two types and when the reduction gearbox has been taken off the procedure for dismantling and reassembling is the same.

Take out the rear wheel. If a speedometer drive gearbox is fitted draw it off from engagement with the ballrace retaining ring. Remove the clamping sleeve (JK). With a suitable punch inserted into the hollow spindle from the right side of the hub drive it out towards the brake side. (A punch turned from brass or steel is needed and should be about 9-in. long, just under $\frac{7}{16}$-in. diameter, turned down at one end to just under $\frac{5}{8}$-in. for a distance of $\frac{1}{2}$-in.)

REMOVAL AND RE-FITTING OF REAR WHEEL.

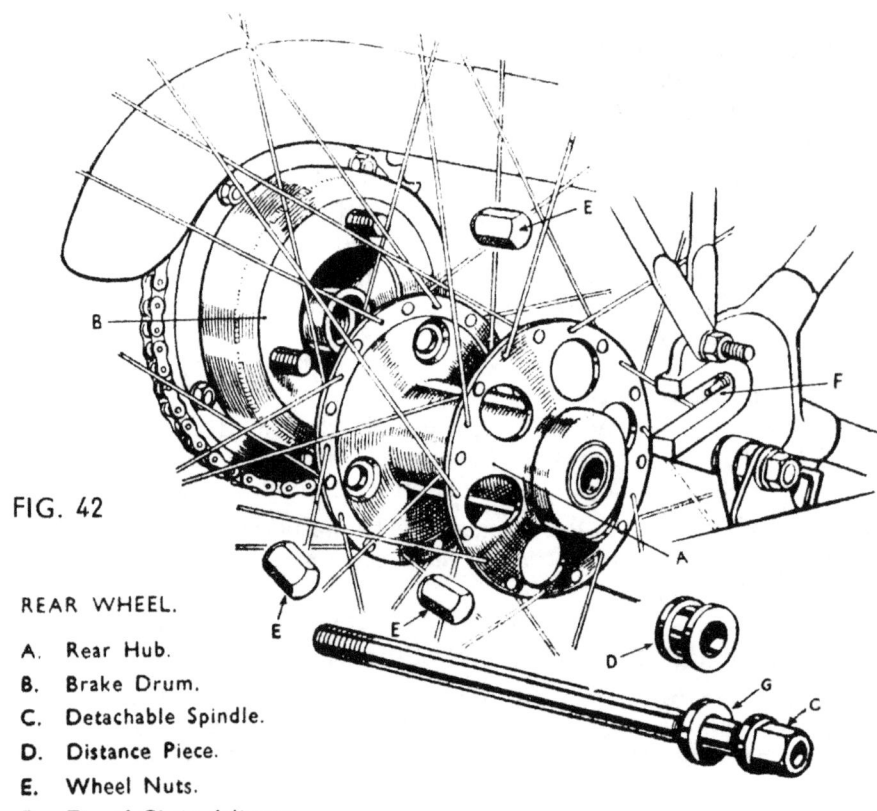

FIG. 42

REAR WHEEL.

A. Rear Hub.
B. Brake Drum.
C. Detachable Spindle.
D. Distance Piece.
E. Wheel Nuts.
F. Tip of Chain Adjuster.
G. Plain Washer.

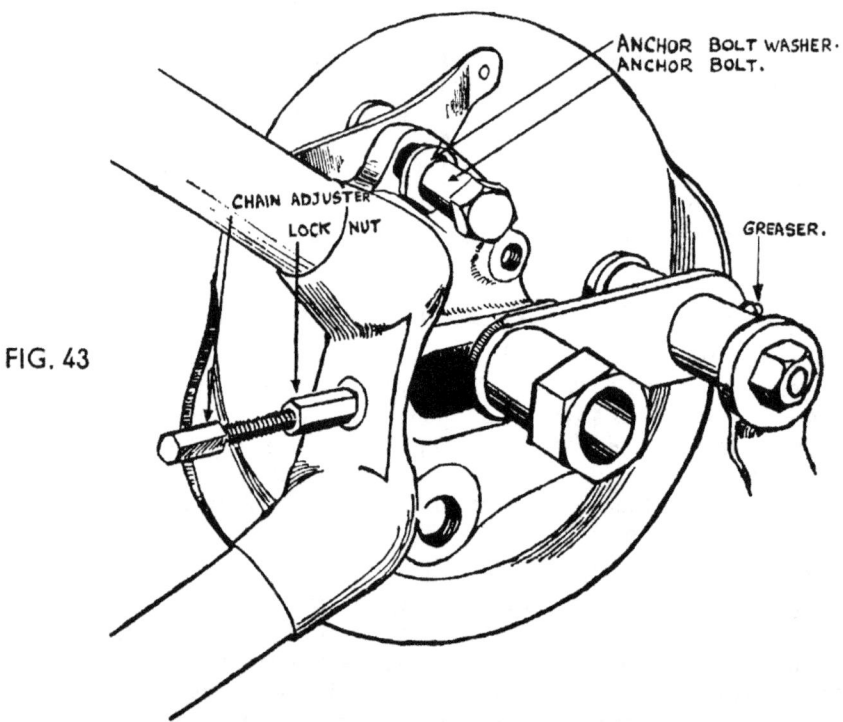

FIG. 43

REAR BRAKE ANCHORAGE (EARLY MOV and MAC Type)

The brake side ballrace will come out with the spindle, taking the dust cap (JE) with it. The grease retainer on this side will be freed for removal.

Next unscrew the ballrace retaining ring. The right-hand thread type is dealt with using the pegged end of the spanner A61/2AS. If the later type a steel bar can be passed across the two wider slots in the ring (JJ) to provide the leverage necessary to unscrew the ring. In this case remember that it unscrews clockwise. Do not damage or burr the edges of the slots or the reduction gearbox will not go back into place. Do not use the narrower slots for unscrewing purposes.

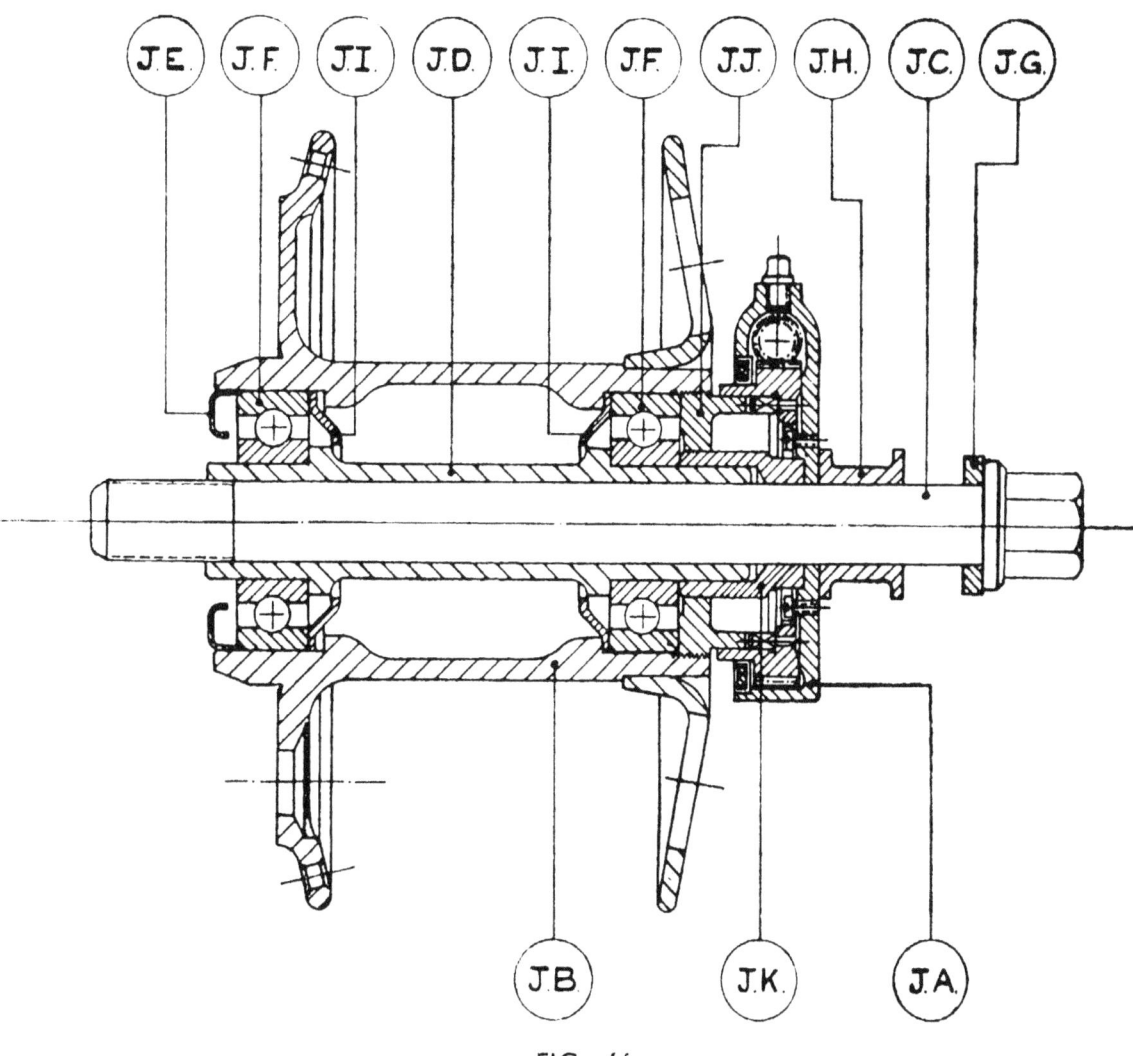

FIG. 44

JA	Reduction Gearbox for Speedometer Drive.	JD.	Hollow Spindle.	JH.	Distance Piece.
JB.	Hub Shell.	JE.	Dust Cap (Brake Side).	JI.	Grease Retainers.
JC.	Detachable Spindle.	JF.	Ballraces.	JJ.	Ballrace Retaining Ring.
		JG.	Spindle Washer.	JK.	Ballrace Clamping Sleeve.

If the purpose of dismantling was to repack the bearings with grease no further stripping is needed as the ballraces can easily be packed and the retaining ring replaced. If the bearings have to be renewed that upon the brake side can be pressed off the hollow spindle and the other one driven out from inside the hub with a suitable punch.

To reassemble the hub first fit the grease retainer into the right-hand bearing housing; convex side inwards (see Fig. 44) and press the bearing into the housing so that it nips the grease retainer. Fit the retaining ring and tighten fully.

Press the other bearing on to the **shorter** of the ground ends of the hollow spindle and fit the other grease retainer; again noting that it fits convex side inwards. Enter the **longer** parallel ground portion of the hollow spindle into the centre of the ballrace that has already been fitted to the hub and the brake side ballrace into its housing and press home. When fully home fit the dust cap (JE). Fit the clamping sleeve (JK) or if an early type hub is being dealt with press the outer dust cap assembly on to the protruding end of the hollow spindle on the right-hand side. Refit the reduction gearbox engaging the internal driving dogs with the narrow slots in the retaining ring.

THE CARBURETTER.
Description and Explanation of Working.

The illustrations provided should be referred to for explanation of the text.

The purpose of the Carburetter is to atomise the correct amount of fuel with the air that is drawn into the engine and thus supply a correctly proportioned mixture at all engine speeds and all throttle settings. This is achieved by the selection of the correct size main jet, and main choke bore, in conjunction with the right adjustment or setting of the jet needle and the Pilot jet.

By means of the Twist grip on the Handlebar the volume of mixture and therefore the power is controlled, and at all positions of the throttle the mixture is correct. The opening of the throttle brings into action first the mixture supply from the Pilot-jet System for idling (*i.e.*, ticking over) at slow speed, then as it progressively opens, via the Pilot By-pass, The mixture is augmented afterwards from the Main-jet, the earlier stages of which action are controlled by the Needle in the Needle-jet. The Main-jet does not directly spray into the Mixing-chamber, but discharges through the Needle-jet into the Primary Air Chamber, and the discharge goes from there as a rich, fuel-air mixture through the Primary Air-choke into the Main Air-Choke. This Primary Air-Choke has a compensating action. A separately operated mixture control is also provided by the Air-valve (operated from the handlebar) for use when starting from cold, and until the engine is warm. This control partially blocks the passage of air through the Main-choke.

The Float-chamber maintains a constant level of fuel at the jets, and cuts off the supply when the engine stops. It is however, always advisable to turn off the fuel at the taps if the machine is stopped for more than a few moments or is not likely to be needed for some time, as this prevents the wastage of fuel which may escape from the Carburetter, particularly if the machine is left leaning towards the right-hand side.

Hints and Tips.

Always see that there is the minimum of backlash or lost motion in the Controls, so that the movement of the Air-lever or Twist grip immediately brings about the movement of the Air and Throttle-valves respectively. The adjustment is made by means of the adjusters on the top of the Mixing-chamber.* Screw the adjusters anti-clockwise to take up slackness. Also see that the control Cables are so arranged on the machine that any movement of the Handlebar does not affect the Carburetter.

Should it be suspected at any time that fuel is not reaching the Carburetter properly, the feed can be verified by detaching the pipe below the float chamber and momentarily turning on each tap in turn. Fuel should gush out if the pipe and taps are clear. A stoppage of the air vent hole in the fuel tank cap can cause an air lock in the tank and stop the flow. See that this hole is kept clear. Flooding may be due to a worn or bent Float-needle, or a leaky Float, but nearly all flooding

---

On pre-war Models throttle cable is adjusted differently (see Page 93).

with new machines is due to impurities (grit, fluff, etc.) from the tank—so clean out the Float-chamber periodically till the trouble ceases. Note that if the Carburetter is flooding with the engine stopped, the overflow from the main jet will not run into the engine but out of the carburetter through the small hole in the side of the Carburetter-body.

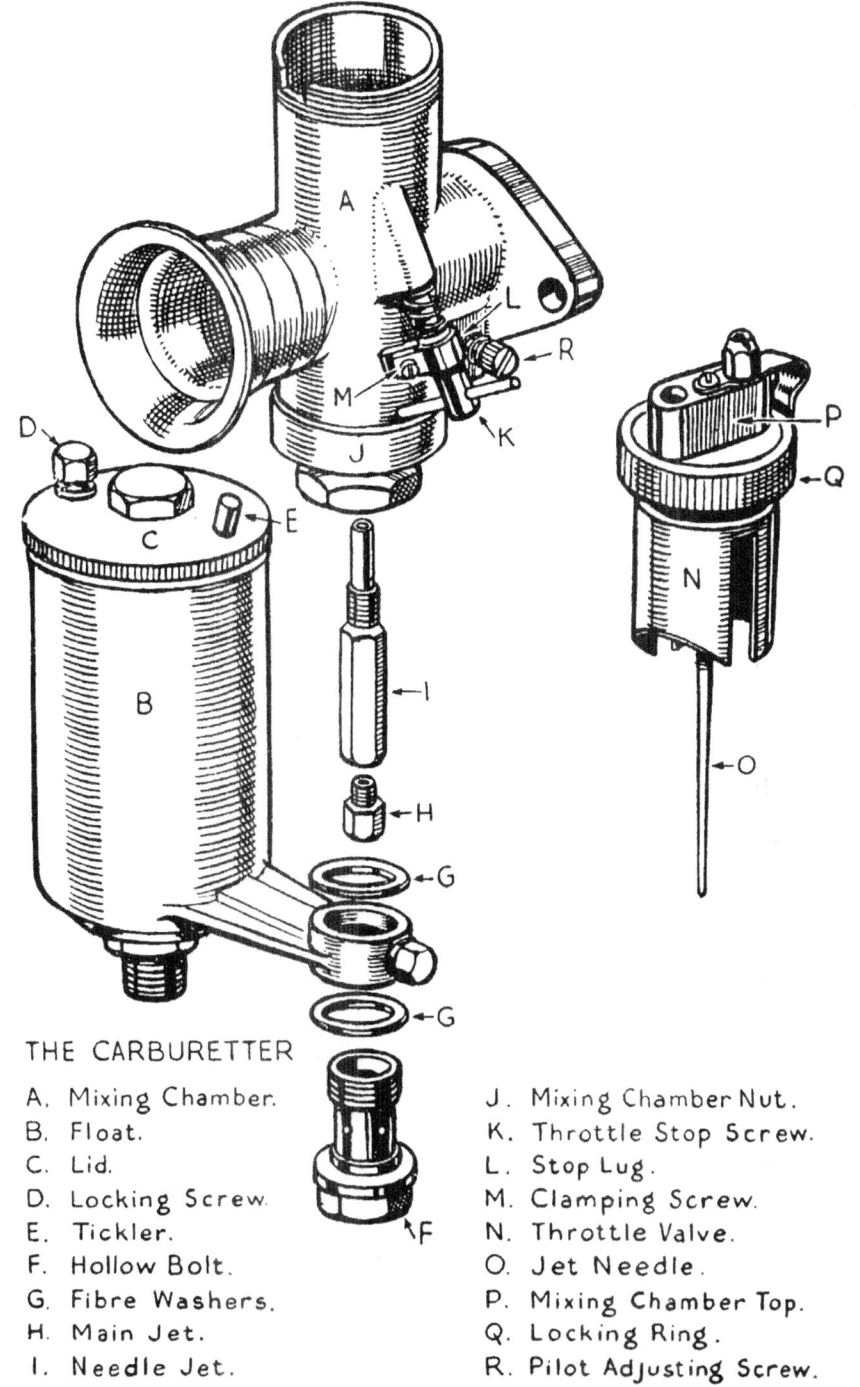

THE CARBURETTER

A. Mixing Chamber.
B. Float.
C. Lid.
D. Locking Screw.
E. Tickler.
F. Hollow Bolt.
G. Fibre Washers.
H. Main Jet.
I. Needle Jet.
J. Mixing Chamber Nut.
K. Throttle Stop Screw.
L. Stop Lug.
M. Clamping Screw.
N. Throttle Valve.
O. Jet Needle.
P. Mixing Chamber Top.
Q. Locking Ring.
R. Pilot Adjusting Screw.

FIG. 45

Erratic slow running is often caused by air leaks, so verify that the joint between the flange of the Carburetter and the Cylinder head is properly made and nuts tight. Check for air leaks by putting a little oil round the edge of the joint packing. On machines which have run a considerable mileage a worn throttle may be responsible.

Banging (*i.e.*, explosions) in the Silencer may be caused by a choked Pilot-jet or to too weak a pilot mixture (through incorrect adjustment) when the throttle is closed or nearly closed—also it may be caused by too rich a pilot mixture or an air leak in the exhaust system. The reason in either case is that the mixture has not fired in the cylinder but has fired in the hot silencer or been ignited there by a incandescent particle of carbon from the exhaust port. If the banging happens when the throttle is fairly wide open it is more likely to be due to ignition. Remove the sparking plug, clean, adjust and refit.

Bad Fuel Consumption may be due to flooding or leaking pipe, and taps—also to a worn Float-needle Valve (if the machine is an old ones) or else to a worn Needle-jet. This can sometimes be remedied or improved by lowering the needle in the Throttle-valve, but if it cannot be—then the only remedy is a new Needle-jet.

Avoid an over rich pilot setting which will make the consumption very heavy if a lot of running is done in conditions of heavy traffic.

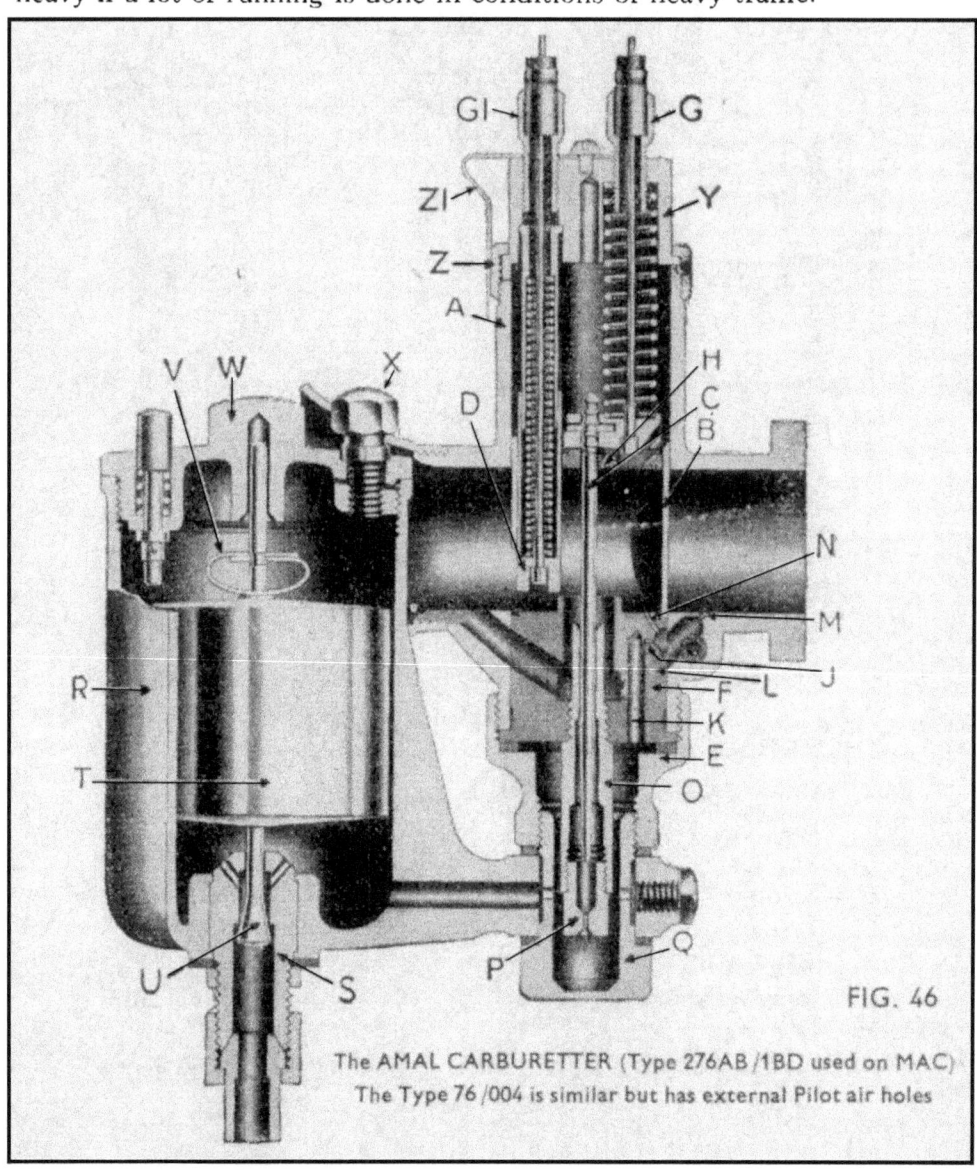

FIG. 46

The AMAL CARBURETTER (Type 276AB/1BD used on MAC)
The Type 76/004 is similar but has external Pilot air holes

Usually when an Air Filter is fitted the main jet is of smaller size than would be used without a Filter, so that if the Air Filter is removed and the machine used without it, care must be taken not to overheat the engine due to too weak a mixture. Testing with the Air Valve will indicate if a larger Main-jet and higher Needle position are required.

88

Faulty running may not be due to Carburation. If the trouble cannot be remedied by making the mixture richer, or weaker with the Air-valve, and it is known that the fuel feed is good and the Carburetter is not flooding, the trouble is elsewhere. When re-assembling the Carburetter after dismantling, always note particularly that the Mixing-chamber Nut (the large hexagon below the Mixing chamber) is tightened up fully on to the red fibre washer below the Jet-block, otherwise fuel will leak up. When replacing the Throttle, see that the Throttle-needle goes into the centre in the Choke-block and once in, note that the Throttle works freely when the Mixing-chamber top Ring is screwed down firmly.

Float Chamber Lid. (Fig. 46).

To remove, first loosen the small hexagon head screw (X) (turn anti-clockwise), and unscrew lid by means of the large hexagon (W) in the centre (unscrew anti-clockwise). To remove the Float (T), pinch the spring bow (V) on top of the Float and pull Float up. When replacing slip the Float over the Needle (U) till the bow clicks into the needle groove' Select the correct groove and pinch the bow to allow the Needle to be engaged in the correct position. Take care always to avoid bending the needle.

The Throttle Stop Screw. (Fig. 45).

This should be set so that when it is turned with the stop lug facing back the throttle is held open sufficiently to keep the engine running slowly when the twist grip is shut off. On Velocette machines an adjustable stop lug is fitted in place of the lock nut illustrated below, and the screw

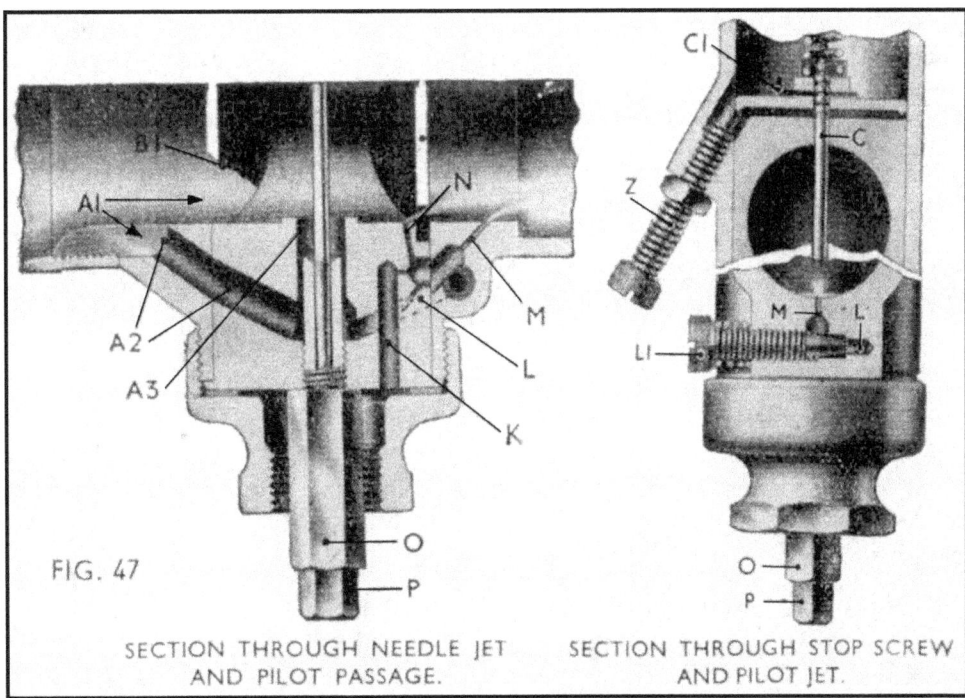

FIG. 47

SECTION THROUGH NEEDLE JET AND PILOT PASSAGE.

SECTION THROUGH STOP SCREW AND PILOT JET.

has a small cross bar to facilitate operation. The stop lug is held by a small clamping screw to the stop screw, and should be tightened up when the correct setting has been obtained. The stop screw is then available for obtaining the correct setting of the Throttle for starting from cold. This position is given by turning the stop screw until the stop lug is right forward. Keep the Twist-grip shut off when starting.

Pilot Air Screw.

This screw regulates the strength of the mixture for "idling" and for initial opening of the Throttle, by controlling the suction on the Pilot petrol Jet by metering the amount of air that mixes with the fuel. Usually it gives the correct mixture when set from 1½ to 2 turns out (anti-clockwise) from the fully screwed-in position.

Main Jet. (Fig. 46).

The main jet (P) controls the fuel supply when the Throttle is more than three-quarters open, but at smaller openings, although the supply of fuel goes through the Main-Jet, the amouht is diminished by the metering effect of the Needle (C) in the Needle-jet (O). Each jet is calibrated and numbered so that its exact discharge is known and two Jets of the same number are alike. Never ream out a Jet. Get another of the right size if a larger Jet is found to be necessary. This however is unlikely, to be required. The bigger the number on a Jet the bigger the Jet.

To get at the Main-jet, undo the Float chamber holding bolt (Q). The Jet is screwed into the bottom of the Needle-jet. If the jet is tight hold the Needle-jet carefully with a spanner whilst unscrewing the Main-jet.

Needle and Needle Jet. (Fig. 46).

The Needle (C) is attached to the Throttle-valve (B) and being taper, either allows more or less fuel to pass through the Needle-jet as The Throttle is opened or closed throughout the range, except when idling or at nearly full throttle. The Needle-jet is of a defined size and is only changed or altered from standard when using special fuels such as Alcohol.

The taper needle position in relation to the Throttle opening can be set according to the mixture required by fixing it to the Throttle-valve with the needle clip spring in a certain groove, thus either raising or lowering it. Raising the needle enriches the mixture and lowering it weakens the mixture at throttle openings from half to three-quarters open. Normally the clip-spring is set in the third groove from the top.

Throttle-Valve Cut-Away.

The atmospheric side of the Throttle valve is cut away to influence the depression on the main fuel supply and thus gives a means of control between the Pilot and Needle-jet range of Throttle opening. The amount of cut-away is recorded by a number stamped on the top of the Throttle valve, viz. 6/4 means type 6 Throttle valve with No. 4 cut-away. A larger cut-away, say 5 gives a weaker mixture and 3 and 2 richer mixtures.

Air Valve.

(D). This is used only for starting and running when the engine is cold, and for experimenting with, when setting the Carburetter. Otherwise it is always set full open.

Tickler.

A small plunger (spring loaded) in the Float-chamber Lid. When pressed down on to the float, the needle valve is pushed off its seat and allows fuel to flow through and " flooding " is thus achieved. Flooding temporarily enriches the mixture until the level of the fuel subsides to normal.

HOW TO SET AND ADJUST THE CARBURETTER.

Proceed in the following order only. By so doing you will not upset good results obtained. See Illustrations of various phases of Throttle opening.

Note.—The Carburetter is automatic throughout the Throttle range—the Air Valve should always be wide open except when used for starting or until the engine has warmed up.

1st. Main Jet with Throttle in Position 1.

Test engine for full throttle. It may be found at full throttle that the power seems better with the Air-valve slightly closed. This indicates too small a main jet.

2nd Pilot Jet with Throttle in Positions 2 and 5.

With engine idling too fast with Twist grip shut off and the Throttle shut down on to the stop screw : (1) Loosen stop lug and turn the stop screw down until the engine runs slower and begins to falter, then screw the pilot air screw in or out to make the engine run regularly and faster ; (2) Now gently lower the Throttle stop screw until the engine runs slower and just begins to falter, then lock the stop lug by means of the small clamping screw so that the lug is in contact with the side of the mixing chamber to the rear of the stop screw. Now begin again to adjust the pilot air screw to get the best slow running. If this second adjustment makes the engine run too fast, go over the job a third time. Finally, lock up the lug tightly without disturbing the correct setting of the screw. Considerable time will be saved if a start is made with the pilot air screw set between $1\frac{1}{2}$ to 2 turns unscrewed from its fully closed position.

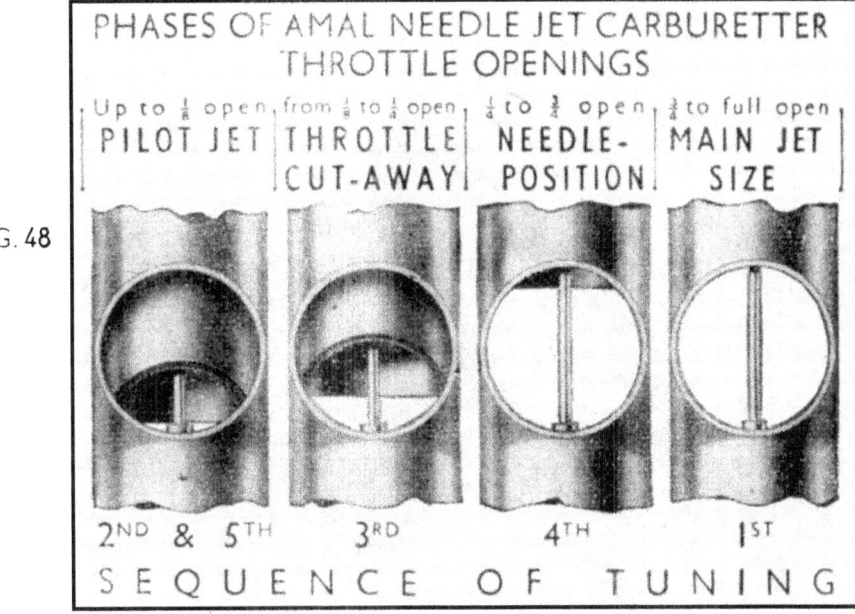

FIG. 48

3rd. Throttle Cut-away with the Throttle in Position 3.

If as the Throttle is opened from the idling position, there is objectionable spitting from the Carburetter, slightly enrich the pilot mixture by screwing the air screw in about half a turn, but if this is not effective, screw it back again and fit a Throttle valve with a smaller cut-away. If the engine jerks under load at this throttle position and there is no spitting, either the throttle needle is much too high or a larger throttle cut-way is required to cure richness.

4th. Needle, with Throttle in Position 4.

The needle controls a wide range of Throttle opening and also the acceleration. Try the needle in as low a position as possible, viz., with the clip in a groove as near the top of the needle as possible, if acceleration is poor and with air valve partially closed the results are better, raise the needle by two grooves, if very much better, try lowering the needle by one groove and leave it where it is best. **Note.**—If the mixture is still too rich with the clip in the top groove—the needle jet probably requires replacement because of wear. The needle itself seldom wears out.

5th. Finally.

Go over the idling again for final touches.

Carburetter Settings.

Model MOV. Main Jet 120
Needle Jet 4/061
Needle No. 5/065
Throttle valve No. 5/3
Throttle needle clip setting—third groove

Model MAC. Main Jet 130
Needle Jet 4/061
Needle No. 6/065
Throttle valve No. 6/4*
Throttle needle clip setting—third groove.

Model MSS. Main Jet 180
Needle Jet 4/061
Needle No. 6/065
Throttle valve No. 6/4
Throttle needle clip setting—third groove

*Type 6/3 is standard for engines with iron heads.

THROTTLE AND AIR CONTROL CABLES.

These should operate freely without lost movement, and normally need no attention except for periodical lubrication. The adjusters for

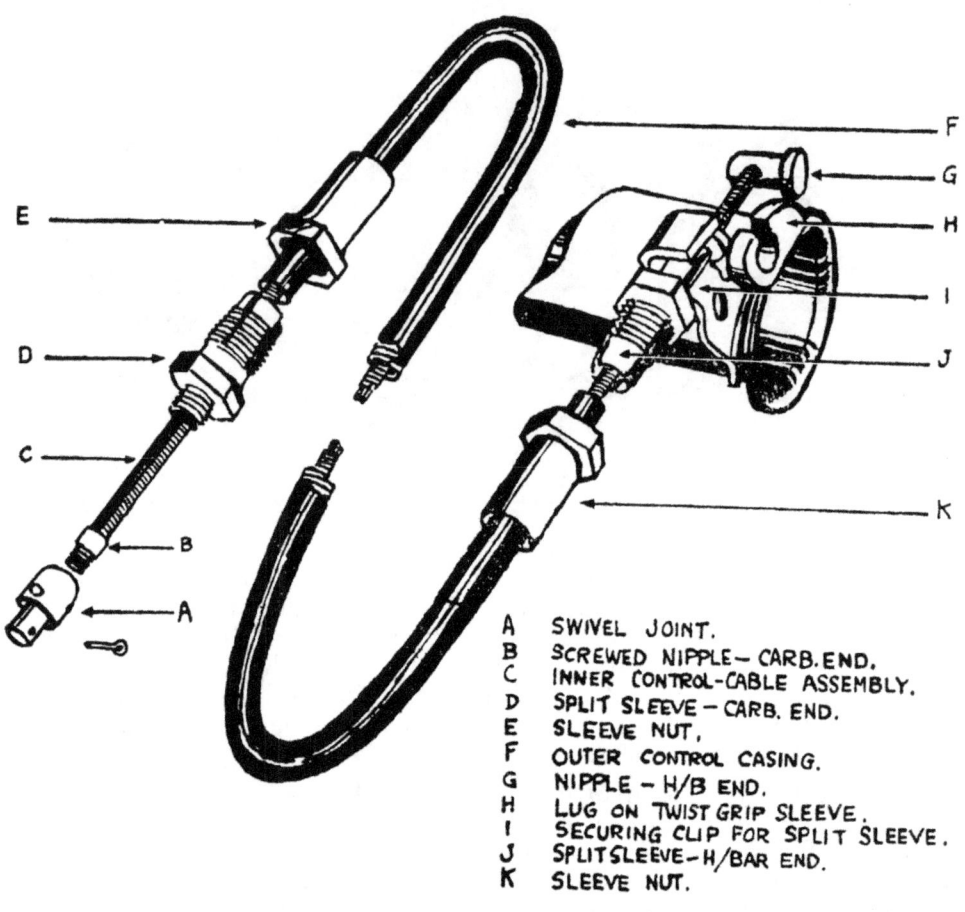

A SWIVEL JOINT.
B SCREWED NIPPLE—CARB. END.
C INNER CONTROL-CABLE ASSEMBLY.
D SPLIT SLEEVE—CARB. END.
E SLEEVE NUT.
F OUTER CONTROL CASING.
G NIPPLE—H/B END.
H LUG ON TWIST GRIP SLEEVE.
I SECURING CLIP FOR SPLIT SLEEVE.
J SPLIT SLEEVE—H/BAR END.
K SLEEVE NUT.

FIG. 49

the Air Control Cable and the Throttle Cable are situated in the mixing chamber top. They are indicated as G1 and G respectively on Fig. 46. Turn anti-clockwise to take up lost movement.

To oil the cables remove them from the handlebar lever and twist grip, and, from thick brown paper make small funnels the small ends of which should then be tied round the ends of the casings. Support the ends as high as possible and fill the paper funnels with thin oil and allow the cables to remain in this way over night, when the oil will penetrate down the inside of the casing.

THROTTLE CABLE AND TWIST GRIP (PRE-WAR TYPE ONLY). Fig. 49.

The Throttle Valve is operated by a push-pull cable from the Twist Grip and no spring is used above the throttle valve. To adjust the cable, first see that with the Twist Grip in the closed position the Throttle Valve is down as far as it will go in the mixing chamber—set the throttle stop screw back. See Page 91. Slacken off the sleeve nut E (Fig. 49), using a second spanner to hold the hexagon of sleeve D to prevent this turning. Slide the outer casing up or down in the sleeve until correct adjustment is obtained, and tighten sleeve nut E. Be careful to hold the sleeve D with a second spanner, otherwise it may be twisted off.

The cable may be lubricated as described previously, or may be completely removed from the casing and smeared with oil.

To remove cable take off the clip I, securing sleeve I to the lug on the handlebar, and slip the cable nipple out of the " ear " on the Twist-Grip Sleeve. Unscrew the ring Q (Fig. 45) from carburetter and draw out both throttle and air valves. Pull out the small pin securing the Swivel Joint A (Fig. 49) to the valve. Unscrew the Swivel Joint from the nipple B and pull out the cable.

The Twist-Grip can be pulled off the end of the handlebar when the clip is free and cable nipple removed. Do not lose the small rectangular friction pad which lies in a slot in the handlebar and which will be freed when the Twist-Grip is taken off. Should the Twist-Grip have been stiff clean the handlebar and smear with grease. When replacing slide up as far as the friction pad, depress the pad into the slot, and slide the Twist-Grip over it into place. Finally replace the clip and cable nipple.

THE SPARKING PLUG.

Sparking plugs which are " detachable," i.e., those that can be taken apart for cleaning such as the K.L.G. FE70, which is standard equipment on the MAC are easily dealt with when they become dirty.

It will be seen from the illustrations that the gland nut (2) can be unscrewed from the body (5) allowing the insulator and electrode assembly to be taken right out. If a K.L.G. Patent plug detacher is not available hold the gland nut in a vice or in a tubular spanner and screw the body off the gland nut. If a vice is used be most careful only to hold the nut firmly enough to stop it turning. Do not grip it tightly or it will be distorted out of round. Do not lose the gland washer (4).

Scrape all carbon deposits out of the plug body, and from the internal insulating surface. The insulation can be cleaned by wire brushing or rubbing with emery cloth.

To put it together again first see that the gland washer is in place, and smear it **very lightly** with a little thin lubricating oil. Put the insulator and electrode assembly into the body and start the gland nut into the thread. Again hold the gland nut and tighten the body on to it.

Adjusting the Firing Points.

After some use and always after cleaning, the firing points will need resetting to the correct gap. The adjustment is made by setting the side electrode (or electrodes) and never by bending the centre electrode. Any attempt to bend the centre electrode will almost certainly crack the insulator and cause plug failure sooner or later.

KLG TYPE F70 SPARKING PLUG (Short Reach)
Used in Iron Heads only

KLG TYPE FE 70 SPARKING PLUG (Extra Long Reach)
Used in Alloy Heads only

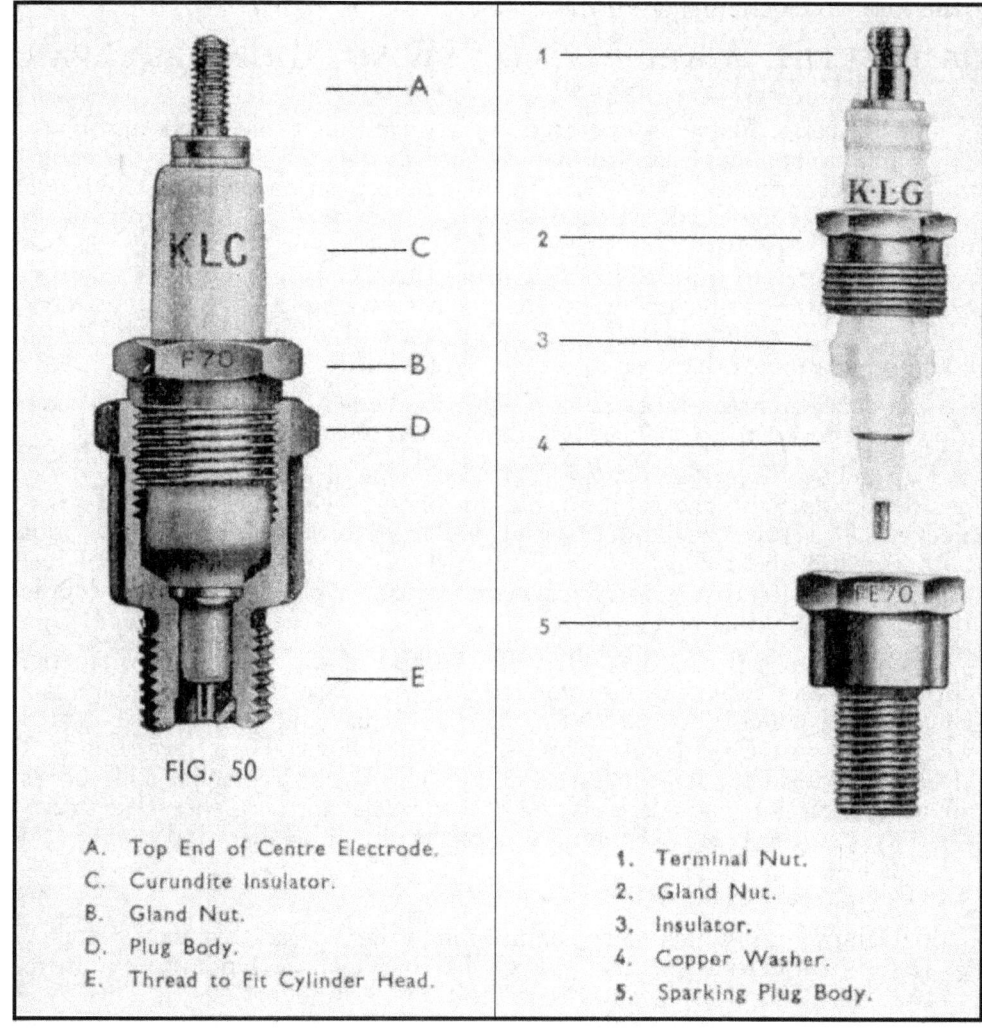

FIG. 50

A. Top End of Centre Electrode.
C. Curundite Insulator.
B. Gland Nut.
D. Plug Body.
E. Thread to Fit Cylinder Head.

1. Terminal Nut.
2. Gland Nut.
3. Insulator.
4. Copper Washer.
5. Sparking Plug Body.

Carefully bend the side electrodes to give a gap of .018-in. to .023-in. Check gap with a feeler gauge.

Before fitting the plug to the cylinder head clean the thread and smear it lightly with graphite grease. After fitting give the external insulation a wipe over with a clean dry cloth.

SPARKING PLUG. Recommended Types.

Sparking plugs are produced in a wide variety of sizes, which includes different diameter threads and threaded portions of different length, i.e., different " reach." Each maker of plugs also lists plugs of widely different characteristics suitable for the many different types of internal combustion engines.

It does not follow therefore, that if a new plug is obtained that will screw into the sparking plug hole it is suitable for the engine. In fact if it is of incorrect reach or the wrong heat resistance grading for the engine it may cause a lot of harm.

The owner of the motor cycle should therefore not accept without question any plug offered for sale, but should insist upon getting the correct type of plug that we specify for the engine of his machine.

In order to give a choice we list below plugs of three makes which we know are suitable for the engines of the models covered by this Service Manual. The MOV and MSS (Rigid frame) models all have cast iron cylinder heads bored to take 14 m.m. Short reach plugs, and this also applies to MAC models up to and including Engine number MAC16459. These engines also have cast iron heads. For the MAC engines following, the 14 m.m. Extra long reach type plug is used.

The plugs recommended by us are :—

Model MAC (Aluminium head)	Champion	NA 8.
	Lodge	HLN.
	K.L.G.	FE 70.
Models MOV and MAC (Cast iron heads)	Champion	L 10S.
	K.L.G.	F 70.
	Lodge	H 14.
Model MSS (Rigid frame)	Champion	L 11S.
	Lodge	HH 14.
	K.L.G.	F 80.

Maintenance of Sparking Plugs.

The instructions above do not apply to the cleaning of plugs with mica insulation. Plugs of this type must in no circumstances be cleaned by sand blasting on the usual type of Service Station cleaning equipment nor must the mica be cleaned by scraping or rubbing with emery cloth or similar abrasive. Clean such plugs only with rag and petrol.

The plugs fitted nowadays have ceramic insulators of an exceedingly hard nature and these can be cleaned by the sand blast method if necessary and if the plug is of the " non-detachable " type.

As there is always a risk of some of the sand remaining up inside the body of the plug after sandblasting however, we consider that it is better to clean out accumulations of oily carbon by brushing with a small wire brush and then to wash out the gas space with petrol. In any case never refit immediately any plug which has been cleaned on a sand-blast apparatus without making sure that the interior is cleared of all sand. A really thorough washing in petrol and scouring out with a jet of compressed air is really essential.

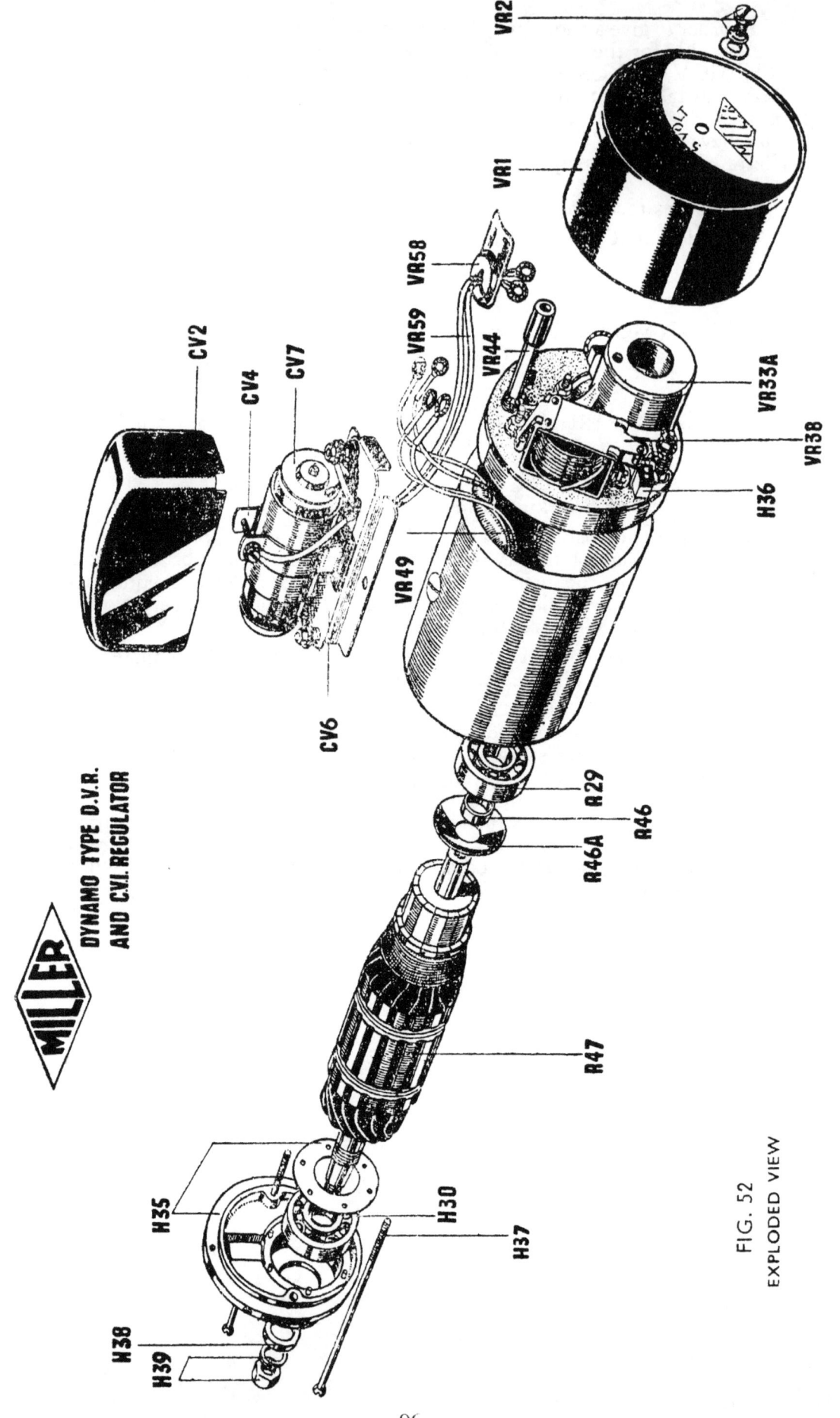

FIG. 52
EXPLODED VIEW

MILLER LIGHTING SET

MAINTENANCE.

The following instructions apply to all Models, except that the wiring in the headlamp differs slightly. Reference to the respective wiring diagrams will explain fully.

CHARGING.

(i) **Dynamo. Type,** Miller DVR. (6 volt)

(ii) **Dynamo—Testing.**

Remove the cover securing screw, then remove cover, this exposes commutator end bracket as Fig. 53. Disconnect the three outside leads (Regulator and Head Lamp) from terminals D.B.S. Clip the negative lead of a good quality moving coil voltmeter, reading from 0-10 volts to a clean earthing point on the dynamo, and clip the positive lead to terminal " B."

Start engine and slowly increase its speed. If no reading is shown on the voltmeter then clip positive lead of voltmeter to terminal " D." If a reading is then shown the cut-out is at fault (try adjusting as instructions). If no reading, the fault is in the dynamo itself. On no account must the engine speed be increased during testing to such an extent that a reading of 8 volts is exceeded. If dynamo and cut-out are in order, re-connect the three leads to terminal D, B and S, and test regulator, para (viii).

(iii) **Dynamo—Removal.**

Electrical breakdown of the dynamo is most unusual, and the unit should be tested as described above, Para. B (ii) before assuming that removal is necessary. Take off belt cover by removing bolt from centre of cover and nut securing cover to primary chain case. Unscrew the dynamo clamping strap bolt about $\frac{5}{16}$-in. (do not completely remove bolt). Turn the dynamo in its mounting until the belt is loose, and remove the belt. Disconnect the three dynamo wires as described in Para. B (ii), and remove dynamo complete.

(iv) **Dynamo—Dismantling.**

Remove belt drive pulley from Armature shaft by taking off the nut and washer and drawing the pulley off the tapered end of the Armature shaft with a " Claw " extractor. Be careful when using the extractor not to damage the thin flanges of the pulley.

Remove brushes "A" and " X " (fig. 53) from their holders. Unscrew and remove the two long bolts securing both end castings of the dynamo yoke. The countersunk heads of these screws can be seen at the driving end.

With the aid of a $\frac{3}{8}$-in. diameter metal punch and hammer, tap the armature spindle at the commutator end. As soon as the ball race at the commutator end is clear of the casting, the armature complete with driving end casting, can be withdrawn.

If it is necessary to remove the driving end casting from the armature spindle, first remove the pulley key from the spindle, then unscrew and remove the bearing lock ring, located on the armature shaft just behind the tapered portion. No attempt should be made to slacken this ring by

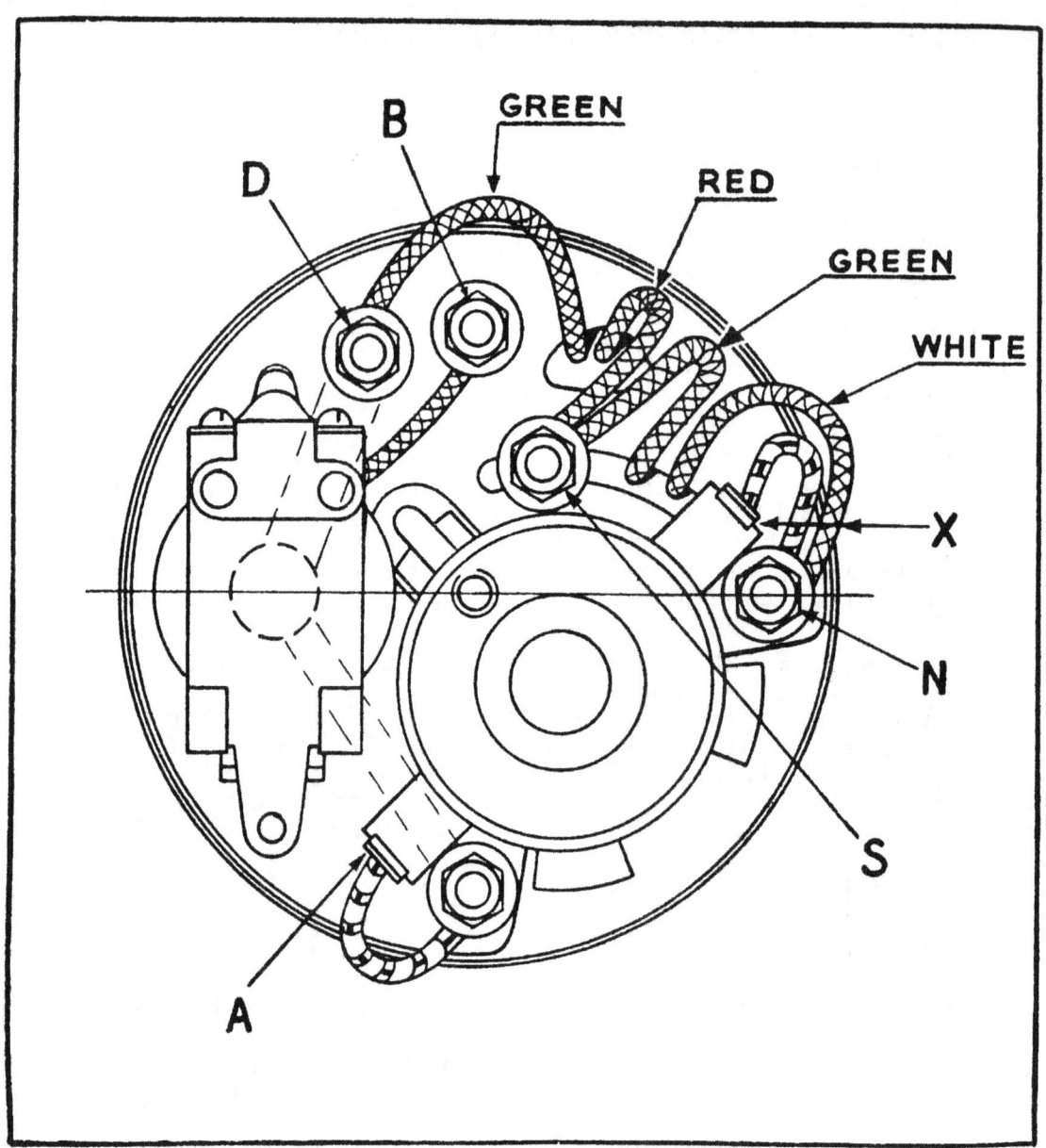

FIG. 53

knocking round with a punch. A special pin spanner should be used as shown in Fig. 54. If this spanner cannot be obtained, it can easily be made. The hardened pins are $\frac{3}{32}$ inches in diameter, with their centres $\frac{23}{32}$ inches apart. The inside diameter of the spanner where it fits around the armature shaft is $\frac{17}{32}$ inches.

By rigidly supporting the bearing retaining plate which will be seen inside the driving end casting, the armature spindle can then be pressed out. Care should be taken not to damage the screwed portion of the shaft during this operation, nor should the centre hole be damaged or the shaft distorted in any way.

To remove the commutator end casting from the yoke, first disconnect at D, N and S, the four insulated leads, as seen in Fig. 53 (one each white and red and two green) which pass through the end casting to the field coil. The end casing can then be pulled away from the yoke, care being necessary to ensure that the four leads are not damaged in passing them through the accommodation slots in the end casting.

(v) **Dynamo Commutator and Brushes.**

Test and Repair. Check that the brushes are clean and move freely

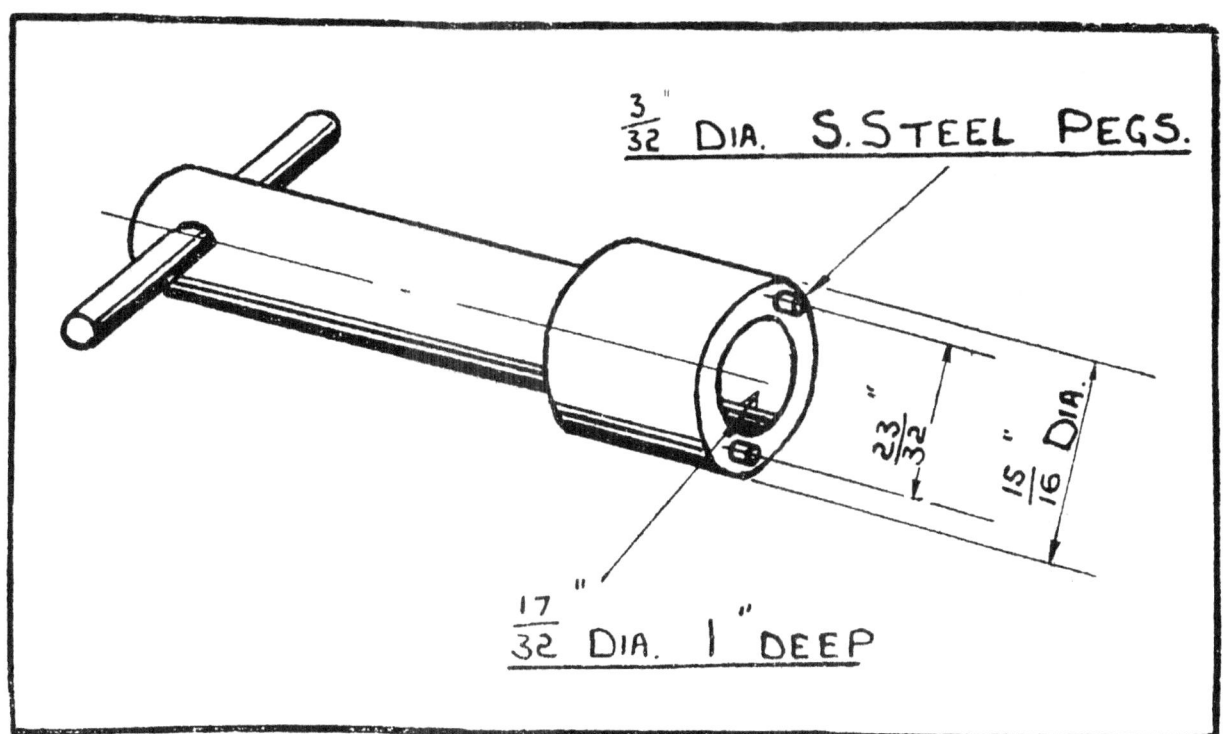

FIG. 54

in their holders. If there is any stickiness, remove the brush and clean the sides with a cloth moistened with petrol, or by lightly polishing with fine glass paper. Always replace brushes in their original positions. Brushes which have been worn so that they do not bear firmly on the commutator, or which expose the embedded end of the flexible on the running face must be replaced. The commutator must be clean and free from traces of oil and dirt. When the dynamo has not been removed a dirty or blackened commutator can be cleaned by pressing a fine duster against it while the engine is slowly turned over. If the commutator is very dirty the duster should be moistened with petrol. (If required, the commutator micas should be undercut to a depth of approximately .025-in., but this operation can only be done after the Armature has been removed).

After fitting new brushes, they must be correctly bedded to ensure that they will make good contact with the commutator. To bed the brushes pass a thin strip of very fine glass paper between the commutator and each of the brushes, making sure that the smooth side of the paper rubs on the commutator, then pull the paper backwards and forwards for a few strokes, and then remove the paper. Wipe away any carbon or glass paper dust after the operation.

Dynamo Field Coil.—Test and Repair.

The resistance of the field winding (red and white leads) should be 4 ohms. +or —.25 ohms., and of the resistance winding (green leads) 7 ohms.+or .25 ohms. Megger test to earth and megger test between field and resistance windings should be not less than 100,000 ohms. When fitting new field coil, force yoke and pole on to a mandrill about 8-in. long, the diameter tapering from 1.773 inches to 1.767 inches. Grip the exposed end of the mandrill in a vice, and by using a robust screwdriver, the countersunk screw securing the pole shoe to the yoke can be screwed up dead tight. It is important that there should be no air gap between the pole shoe and inner face of the yoke.

Dynamo Armature.—Test and Repair.

The resistance of the Armature Coils measured between two adjacent commutator bars should be .2 ohms. +or —.01 ohms. Megger test to earth should be not less than 100,000 ohms.

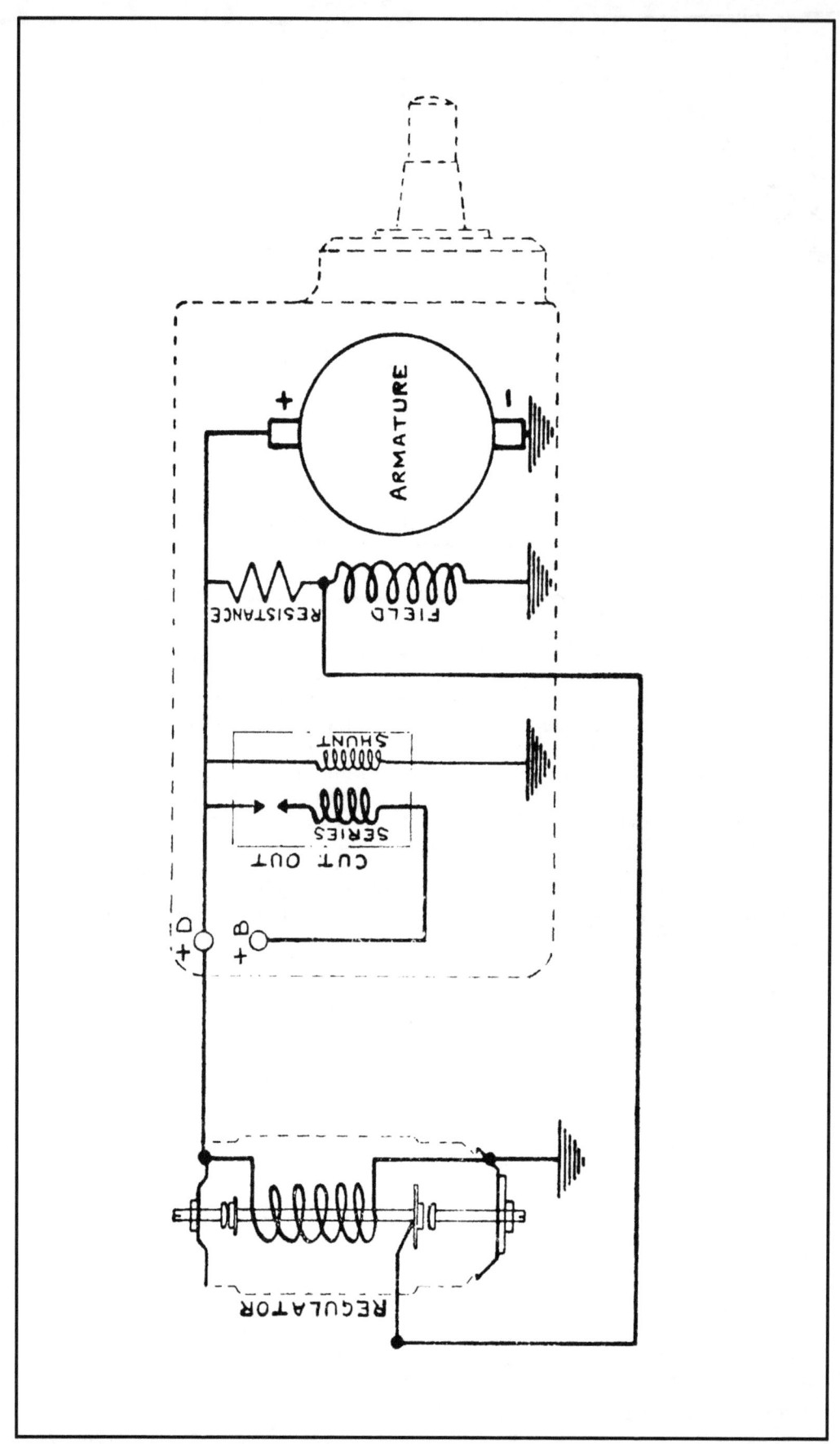

FIG. 55

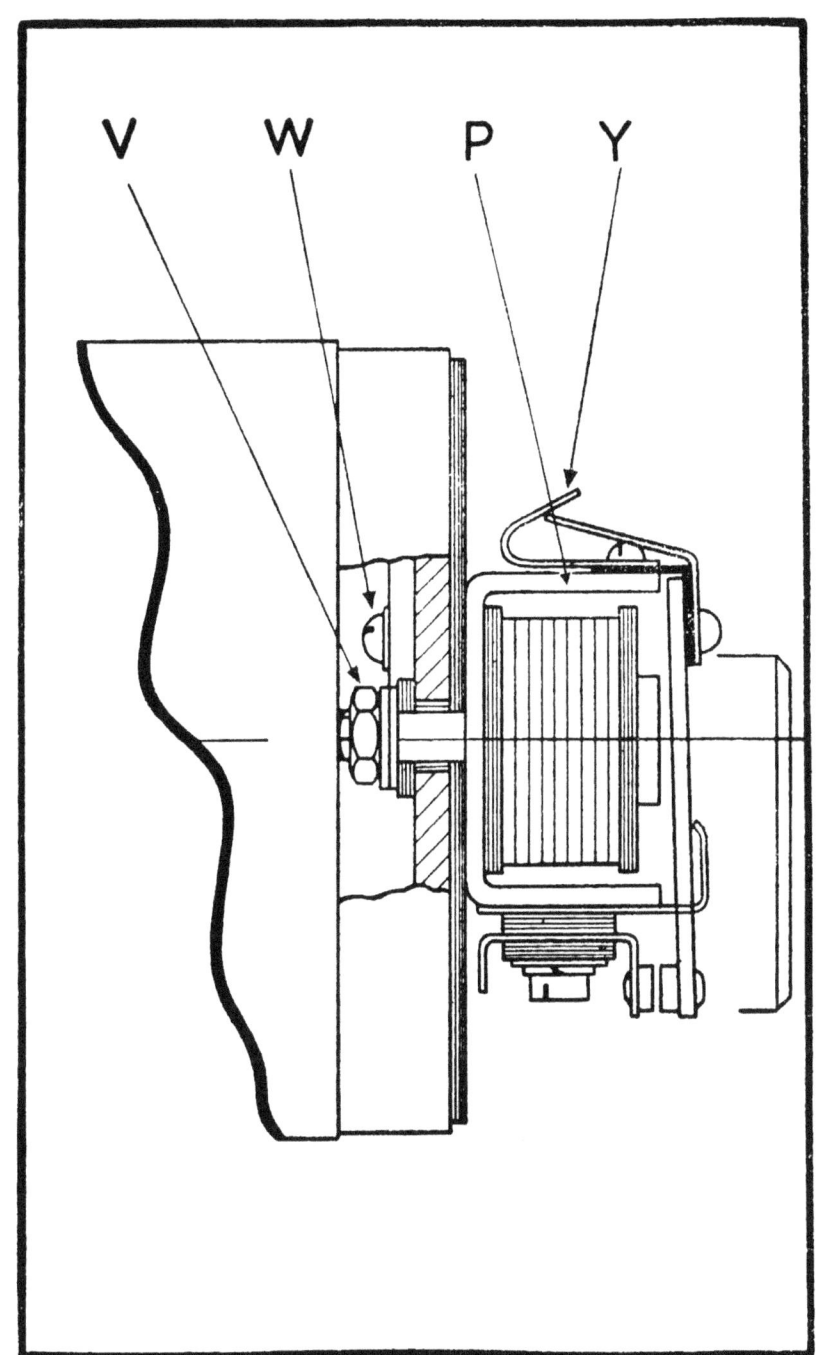

FIG. 56
The Cut Out.

Dynamo Bearings.—Replacement and Lubrication.

The drive end bearing can be removed from the drive end casting by unscrewing the two small screws securing the bearing retaining plate also the small grub screw on the outside boss. The bearing can then be tapped out. The commutator end bearing can be removed from the armature shaft by using a suitable extractor (it is not a very tight fit on the shaft).

Ball bearings must be carefully packed on assembly with High Melting Point Grease. Soft Grease should not be used. Subsequent lubrication in service is by removing the round-headed screw retaining the commutator end cover plate and inserting oil in the screw hole, and to the driving end bearing by removing the grub screw on top of the bearing housing and inserting oil in the screw hole.

(vi) **Regulator Type**—Miller CVI.

The makers advise that in no circumstances is it advisable to tamper with the Regulator and it is in fact very seldom that it gives any trouble at all. In cases investigated we have found that trouble attributed to the Regulator was in fact due to nothing more serious than the driving belt slipping due to requiring re-adjustment. Steps are taken before delivery of machines to see that the belts are properly tensioned but particularly with a new belt there is a certain amount of initial stretch and it is advisable to watch on a new machine to see that re-adjustment is made when it is necessary. A slipping belt will give all the symptoms of a defective regulator. For instance, at tick over speeds the normal 2 amp. charge indicated when the battery is fully charged will be shewn on the Ammeter, but on the engine speed being increased the charge rate will usually drop to nil. The result of this is that the battery, although it may require a compensating charge, does not get it and gradually becomes discharged.

Cut-Out.—Test and Adjust. Fig. 56.

The cut-out "P" is attached to the commutator end casting by one nut "V" and may be removed after disconnecting the lead to the earth retained to the end casting by round headed screw and washer "W," and the lead to the middle of the three terminals "B," Fig. 53.

Resistance of series winding .09 to .1 ohms. Resistance of shunt winding 55 to 56 ohms. Contact clearance $\frac{1}{32}$-inches. Contacts should close at approximately 6 volts, when a current from zero to $\frac{1}{4}$ amp. is being generated, and open when current falls from zero to $\frac{1}{2}$ amp. discharge. The "off" and "on" tension can be adjusted by bending the brass tensioning bracket (Y).

(vii) **Dynamo**—Re-assembly.

Reverse the procedure in Para. B (iv) bearing in mind the following points:—

(a) Fit the commutator end casting to the yoke first.
(b) Pass the red lead and the adjacent lead through the triangular slot in the end casting.
(c) Pass the white lead and the adjacent green lead through the long curved slot in the end casting.
(d) Fit the drive end ball bearing to the end casting, fit the assembly over the tapered end of the armature shaft. Replace the drive side bearing lock ring, tighten fully on armature shaft, then **gently press** the commutator end ball race already on the armature shaft into its housing.
(e) Replace and tighten fully the two long screws securing the end castings to the yoke.
(f) Replace belt pulley.
(g) Fit the rubber bush protecting the leads in position in commutator cover band.
(h) **Connect** wires (interior).
  Green (through triangular slot) to top terminal "D" (Fig. 53).
  Red to bottom terminal "S."
  Green (through long curved slot) to bottom terminal "S."
  White negative right-hand brush terminal "N."
(i) **Connect wires** (outside).
  Black 5 m/m with Red band from regulator to "D" terminal.
  Black 5 m/m plain from regulator clip to "S" terminal.
  Black 5 m/m with Blue band from Head lamp (ammeter) to "B" terminal.
  Replace brushes and fit dynamo to machine, afterwards fitting commutator end cover.

The regulator provides complete automatic control, so that the dynamo output varies according to the load on the battery, or its state of charge. Normally during daytime running, when the battery is in good condition, the dynamo gives only a trickle charge, so that ammeter readings will seldom exceed 1 or 2 amperes.

(viii) **Regulator**—Testing.

If, under normal running conditions, it is found that the battery is continually in a low stage of charge, or is being overcharged, and the test described in para. (ii) has established that the dynamo and cut-out are in order, the regulator may be tested by substitution if a replacement is available. It should be noted that it is quite safe to run the "Miller" dynamo without the regulator cartridge being fitted. When removed, and the dynamo leads left in place, that is, the one with the red identification sleeve connected to the base plate, and the other with the green identification sleeve, to the clip bolt, the dynamo gives a reduced output, with a maximum of approx. $3\frac{1}{2}$ amps. It is therefore advisable to fit a replacement regulator as soon as possible.

To test whether the regulator is at fault, disconnect the battery positive lead, and connect a moving-coil voltmeter to the two regulator base terminals (positive and negative) start the engine and run at an equivalent speed of not less than 20 m.p.h. (approx. 1,000 r.p.m.) If the regulator is in correct adjustment the voltmeter reading should be from 7.5 to 7.9 volts.

Regulator—To adjust.

If the voltmeter reading is below 7.5 volts over regulation is taking place, causing the battery to be continually in a low state of charge. If a spare regulator is not available, a **temporary** adjustment can be made by screwing out the negative contact screw (which is visible at the conical end of the regulator cartridge), two complete turns. Should the voltmeter reading be over 7.9 volts, which would cause overcharging, a temporary adjustment can be made by screwing out the positive contact screw at the other end not more than $\frac{1}{4}$ turn.

Note.—These adjustments will not give the correct voltage readings, but will enable the machine to be run with improved results until it is convenient to fit a replacement regulator.

Regulator—Remove and Replace.

The regulator is fitted to the strap which retains the dynamo in position —the cartridge being easily removed after removal of the cover. The pressed steel base and cartridge clip need not be removed unless broken.

(vix) **Ammeter.** Type—Miller /75V.

The Ammeter is retained to the headlamp shell by a metal bridge and two knurled nuts.

Ammeter. To Test

With engine stationary, switch on the lights, the ammeter should indicate the equivalent lamp load. Upon switching off, the needle should swing back freely to zero. If at fault replace as soon as possible.

Battery.—It is essential to give the battery regular attention, as upon its condition depends the efficiency of the lighting. At least once a month remove the vent plugs from the top of the battery and examine the level of the electrolyte. If necessary, add distilled water to bring the level above the tops of the plates, but well short of the bottom of the vent plugs. This operation is best carried out just before commencing a journey when the agitation due to running and the gassing caused by charging will thoroughly mix the solution.

Should the machine be laid up for several months give the battery a small charge from a separate source of electrical energy about once a fortnight in order to obviate any permanent sulphation of the plates. Do not remove the electrolyte from the battery and allow the plates to dry as certain chemical changes take place which result in loss of capacity. It is best to check the specific gravity of the electrolyte by means of a hydrometer as this gives a good indication of the state of charge of the battery.

Specific gravity figures are :—1.285 to 1.300 fully charged, 1.210 half discharged, and 1.150 fully discharged. Never leave the battery in a discharged condition, and unless some long daylight runs are to be made, during which the battery can be charged, remove the battery from the machine and have it charged from an independent supply.

Always see that the connections are clean and tight and to prevent corrosion smear them with vaseline. Loose or dirty battery connections may cause burned out bulbs.

DIAGRAM OF WIRING (Non-Automatic).

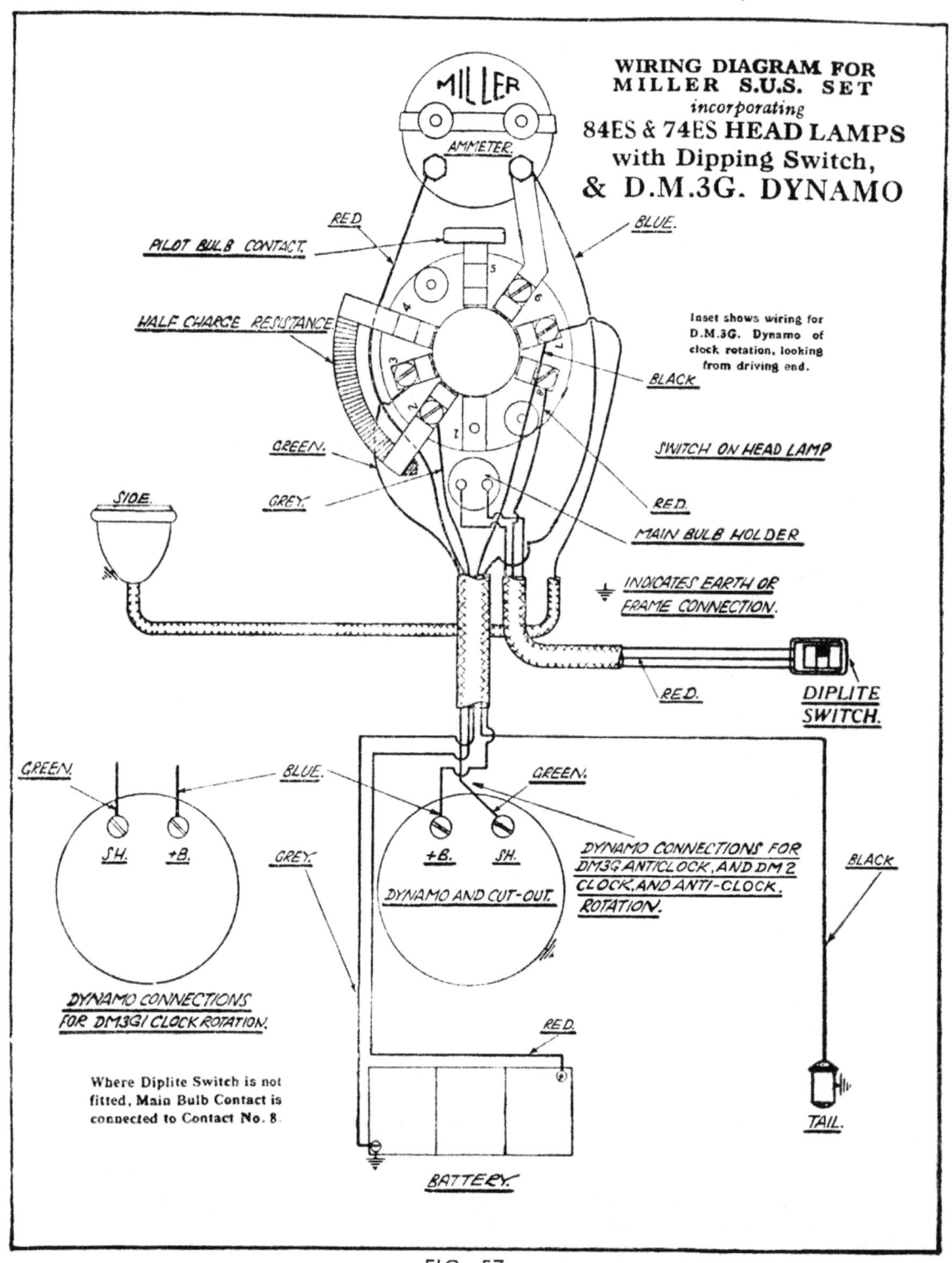

FIG. 57

DIAGRAM OF WIRING (Auto-Voltage Regulated).

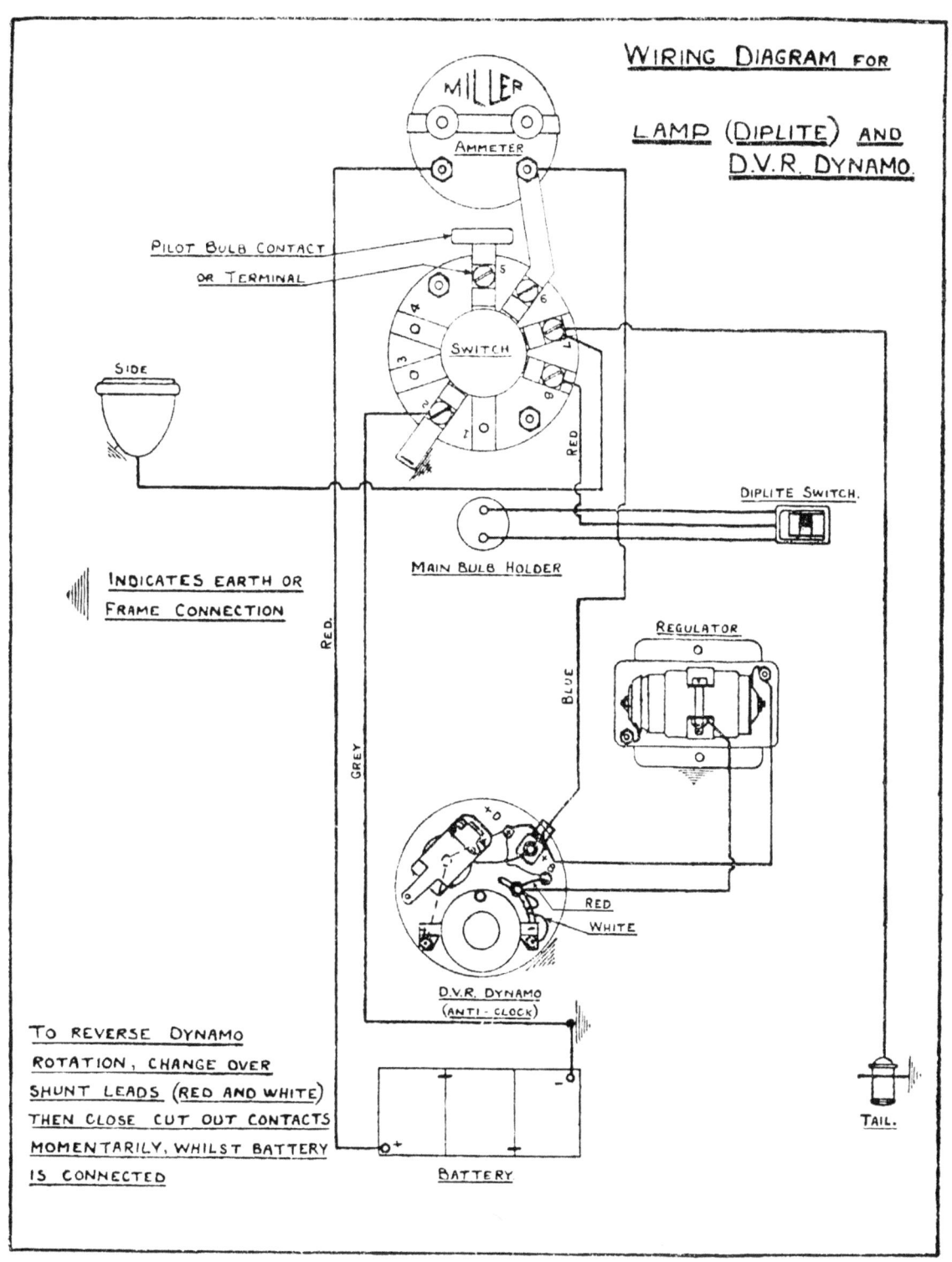

FIG. 58

CLEANING THE MACHINE.
Enemelled and Bare Metal Parts.

Aluminium parts, such as the engine and gearbox, can be cleaned with paraffin and a stiff brush, and afterwards with petrol. These parts are best cleaned before the enamel is tackled.

Accumulated road dirt and mud must never be rubbed or brushed off dry from enamelled parts as the abrasive nature of the dirt will scratch and dull the surface of the enamel.

Always wash off dirt by means of liberal supplies of water, if possible from a hose pipe, but do not employ a high pressure jet.

The water should be set to run at a slow rate so that it does not penetrate where it can do harm, such as into the brakes or items of the electrical equipment and carburetter.

Use a soft cloth or sponge to mop off the dirt when it is properly loosened by the water.

If water is used from a bucket a little household detergent washing powder (such as " Tide ") may be mixed with the water and will help to remove oil or grease.

Dry off with a leather and polish with one of the many polishes now on the market. Chemico " 49 " (Makers : The County Chemical Co., Ltd., 561, Stratford Road, Shirley, Birmingham) will give a high finish which remains waterproof for quite a good time. Proprietary polishes, however, are not a substitute for cleaning and will not give a proper finish unless the surface is properly cleaned first.

Chromium-plated Parts.

Ordinary metal polishes intended for brass, etc., are harmful to chromium plating, which must be cleaned with special chrome cleaner such as "F.L.P." (Maker: G. H. White, 102, Lowestoft Road, Gorleston, Norfolk.)

In some conditions of climate a deposit resembling rust may be seen on the chromium plated ferrous parts. This is not ordinary rust, but is a salt deposit which if treated at once can be removed readily. It must not, however, be neglected, as this will cause deterioration which will progress rapidly.

Remove any deposit with light application of chrome cleaner.

During damp and rainy weather protect the plated parts by lightly smearing with " Tekall " (Makers : 20th Century Finishes, Ltd., 175-177, Kirkgate, Wakefield.)

FIXING TRANSFERS.

The transfers are printed on duplex paper, i.e., one sheet as a guide to place the transfer in position, and the other as a support to the transfer. These two sheets must be separated before transferring. They can be divided by rubbing a corner of the transfer.

Before complete separation is made apply a very thin and even coat of adhesive varnish to the face of the transfer. Keep as closely as possible to the lines of the design so as not to overlap. Allow this varnish to set until it becomes very tacky and then place the transfer in the required position on the article.

Press the transfer down evenly and firmly, and drive out all air bubbles, by rubbing with a soft cloth rolled into a ball, commencing from the centre and working towards the edges. Then with a damp (not wet) sponge or wash leather press down again, taking care not to shift the transfer. It is absolutely essential that the transfer should be in **direct contact with the surface in every part.** When this is certain apply water freely by means of a wet sponge, and when the paper support is well soaked, lift it up by one corner and peel or slide it off. Then press the transfer down again to make sure it is fully in contact.

After doing this, sponge with clean water in order to remove the composition remaining on the surface of the transfer. This is an extremely important detail, as unless it is properly done the transfer will crack.

To remove traces of superfluous adhesive varnish around the transfer, use a wet sponge to which has been added a little paraffin. Then quickly wipe it off with a damp washleather, **away from the centre.**

When the transfer is perfectly dry on the article (usually about 24 hours) it can be varnished to add to its lustre. **It must NOT be varnished directly it is transferred.**

THE MAGNETO.

B.T.H. Type KC1 form N.4 L.H. Rotation, fitted with Form Y5 or YE5 Automatic Timing Device.

Breaker Mechanism.
Lubrication.

FIG. 59

The cam is lubricated by a felt wick in the bottom of the cam ring, which should be given one or two drops of light machine oil. The cam track should also be smeared with oil, but take care to wipe off all surplus oil, leaving only a light oil film on the cam track.

The contact lever bearing is more easily lubricated when the contact breaker is removed for cleaning as described below.

The contact breaker can be removed for cleaning by unscrewing the central hexagon-headed screw (1), and withdrawing the breaker. The contact lever (2) can then be lifted from its bearing bush by first raising and then moving to one side the check spring (3) which is located in the end of the bearing bush.

Care should be taken not to distort in any way the contact lever control spring (4). The points (5 and 6) can be cleaned with a **very fine** emery cloth, but under no circumstances should they be filed. Wipe away any dirt or metal dust with a petrol moistened cloth.

Before replacing the contact lever smear the bearing bush lightly with thin lubricating oil, wiping off any surplus. Also apply one drop to the wick (6) in the bearing bush.

It is of the Utmost Importance that the Points be kept Absolutely Free from Oil.

Adjustment.

To check the contact setting turn the engine until the contacts are fully opened, and insert the 0.012-in. feeler gauge provided between the contact; the gauge should be a sliding fit. If there is any appreciable variation from the gauge, slacken the lock nut (7) and turn the contact screw (5) by its hexagon head until the gap is set to the gauge. Finally, tighten the lock nut.

H.T. Cable.

Should be 7 m/m in diameter. Other sizes such as 5 m/m and 9 m/m will not fit in the High-Tension Brush Holder. The cable must be replaced if the rubber insulation has perished or cracked.

Pick-up.

Periodically remove the pick-up or brush holder and wipe it with a cloth moistened with petrol, also see that the carbon brush moves freely in its holder. Before replacing the brush holder, insert the corner of a clean cloth in the aperture in the housing so that it bears against the slip-ring track and the flanges, at the same time turning the engine slowly.

Dismantling.

Total dismantling of the magneto should be rarely necessary, but instructions are given below in case this should be required.

(1). First remove contact breaker cover and contact breaker.

(2). The collector brush holder or pick-up should next be removed before any attempt is made to withdraw the armature from the housing.

(3). The contact end plate can now be removed by unscrewing the fixing screws and the contact breaker cover spring pillar.

(4). The armature can then be withdrawn from the housing.

NOTE.—**If the armature is actually withdrawn from the housing it will be necessary to re-magnetise the magnet after replacing the armature; unless a soft iron 'U' shaped and good fitting keeper is placed over the magnet poles before the armature is withdrawn.**

Test and Repair.

If the armature has been removed it should be examined for actual structural faults, such as bent or damaged shaft, cracked or broken slip-ring. Special equipment is required to check the winding and condenser and whilst a new condenser can be fitted, in the event of faults of this nature it is desirable to replace with a complete service armature.

Before re-assembling the magneto, carefully examine the bearings, which should be replaced if not in good condition. Special Extractors are required to remove the inner and outer races, and no attempt should be made to remove them by other means. If these extractors are not available, the complete magneto should be returned to the Makers for re-conditioning and a replacement fitted to the machine. When fitting new bearings the following points must be carefully watched :—

(a) The inner race must be square with the shaft, and pressed fully home.

(b) When fitting the inner race at the slip ring end, make sure the washers between the inner race and the slip ring are fitted concentrically, so that the flat washer does not ride on the spindle shoulder.

(c) The outer races are insulated from the housing and contact endplate, with serrated fibre washers. It is important that this fibre washer is centrally located before being pressed home.

The bearings should be packed with a suitable High-Melting Point Grease before re-assembly.

Re-assembling.

When re-assembling, the armature should be set up with an end play of 0.002-in. This end play is adjusted by means of shims which are fitted between the magneto body and the contact breaker endplate.

When re-fitting the contact breaker great care should be taken to ensure that the key on the contact breaker base engages with the slot in the armature endplate.

THE AUTOMATIC TIMING UNIT. (B.T.H.)

Refer to Figs. 25 and 26.

This unit is now superseded by the B.T.H. unit type YE5. They are interchangeable.

Later type units which do not have the limiting stop peg in the gear do not require the use of a sprag when being removed—see Page 57.

The device is incorporated with the magneto driving gear and does not require any attention or adjustment.

Should it be necessary to remove the magneto, the automatic timing device can be removed by undoing the self-extracting nut on the end of the magneto spindle. (*Before removal refer to Pages* 57 *and* 58). After the nut loosens, it will almost immediately tighten again, and it is then that it commences to withdraw the gear and timing device from the tapered magneto spindle.

B.T.H. MAGNETO.

1. CONTACT BREAKER COVER.
2. CONTACT BREAKER.
3. CONTACT BREAKER CAM.
4. CONTACT ENDPLATE and TIMING STOP.
5. PACKING SHIMS.
6. FIBRE INSULATOR FOR BALLRACE.
7. ARMATURE.
8. MAGNET SHIELD.

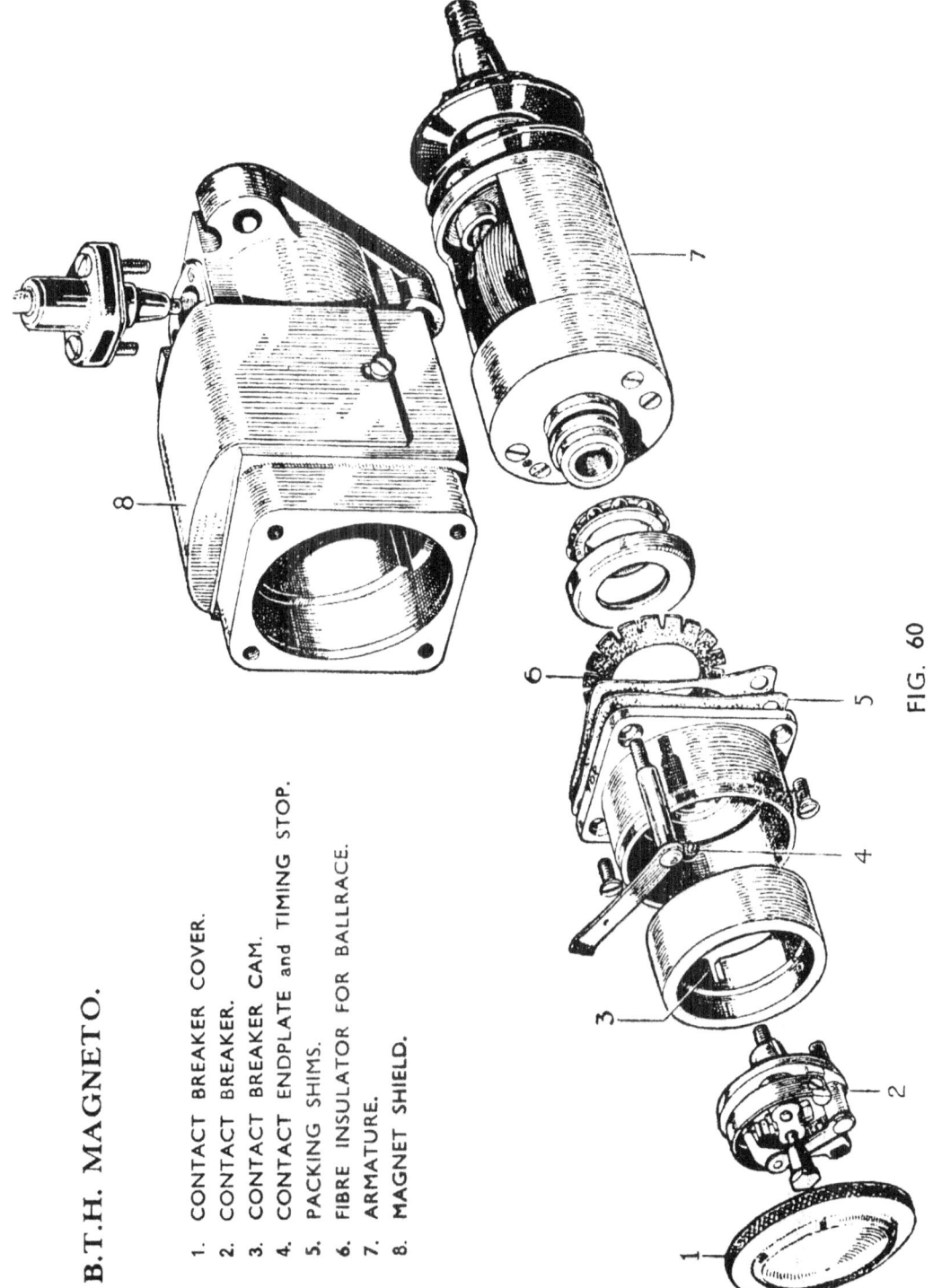

FIG. 60

Should for any reason the gearwheel be damaged it will be necessary to replace the A.T.D. plate, gearwheel and bearing sleeve assembly complete. To effect this replacement the following procedure must be carried out —

To Dismantle the A.T.D.

Remove control spring, being careful not to distort the spring in any way.

Remove circlip.

NOTE.—Special pliers will be required for this operation.

The hub and front plate assembly can now be withdrawn from the gearwheel assembly; also the five roller weights.

To Re-assemble the A.T.D.

Before commencing assembly, smear all surfaces with light machine oil.

Place the five roller weights in position.

Fit the hub and front plate assembly so that the hole in the hub for anchoring the control spring is in the correct relationship with respect to the anchor pin.

Fit circlip, making sure that there are no burrs on the face that rubs against the bearing sleeve. See that the circlip locates correctly in the groove in the hub.

With the circlip fitted, the following conditions must be checked:

(a) Endplay of sleeve on hub must be between 0.008-in. and 0.002-in.

(b) Total clearance between any roller and the front plate must be between 0.012-in. and 0.004-in.

Fit control spring so that the looped end has to be wound up approximately 45° before fitting round anchor pin.

Finally check advance movement of the A.T.D., making sure that the control spring returns the front plate to the closed position when holding the gearwheel. The movement must be smooth in action.

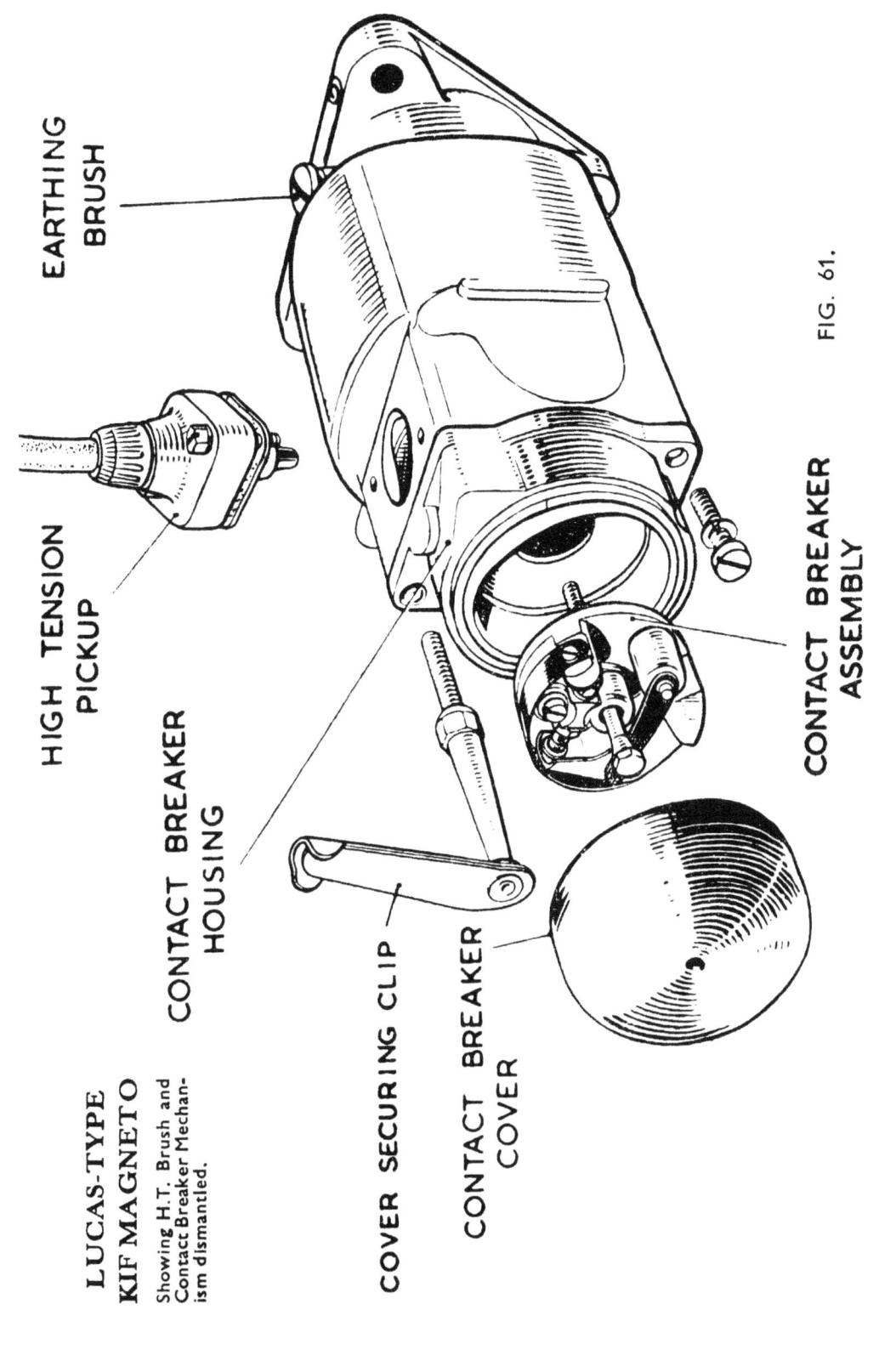

FIG. 61.

LUCAS-TYPE KIF MAGNETO
Showing H.T. Brush and Contact Breaker Mechanism dismantled.

THE MAGNETO. LUCAS TYPE KIF AND AUTOMATIC TIMING UNIT.

Routine Maintenance. Lubrication. Every 3,000 miles remove the contact breaker and after pushing aside the rocker arm retaining spring prise the rocker arm off its bearing and lightly smear the bearing with clean engine oil. At the same time take out the felt pad from the pocket in the contact breaker housing and soak it in thin machine oil (SAE 10). Remove any surplus oil and refit. (This felt lubricates the cam surface via a hole in the cam.) DO NOT ALLOW ANY OIL TO REACH THE CONTACTS. If any gets on them accidentally clean off thoroughly with a clean petrol soaked rag.

Adjustment. At 3,000 miles check the contact point gap and if necessary reset to '012" clearance at maximum opening. Adjustment is made by slacking off the lock-nut on the adjustable point, and turning the hexagon head of the point screw in the direction required. Tighten the lock-nut after adjustment and recheck the clearance in case it has been altered in tightening.

Cleaning. Every 6,000 miles examine the contact breaker points and if burned or blackened clean them with a fine carborundum stone or superfine emery cloth. Cleaning is easier if the contact breaker is removed first. It is held to the armature by a central pin (see Fig. 61).

Remove the high tension pick-up—held to the magneto by two screws and wipe the moulding clean and polish with a fine dry cloth. Check the pick-up brush for freedom—it must work easily in the holder. Clean the magneto slip ring against which the brush bears and the inner flanges by holding a soft cloth against the slip ring and flanges by means of a suitably tapered piece of wood; whilst the engine is rotated slowly. If the brush is worn to with $\frac{1}{8}$" of the shoulder it must be renewed.

Replacement of High Tension Cable. If the cable shows signs of deterioration through perishing or cracking of the insulation it must be replaced by a suitable length of 7 mm. rubber-covered cable. To renew bare the wire at one end by removing the insulation for about $\frac{1}{4}$" and thread the moulded nut over the cable. Thread the bare wire through the washer removed from the old cable and bend back the strands over the washer. Screw the moulded nut back firmly holding the cable in place.

Servicing.

(a) **Testing Magneto in position on engine to locate cause of misfiring or ignition failure.**

   (i) Disconnect the suppressor from the sparking plug. Take the suppressor off the cable and hold the cable by the insulation so that the bare wire is about $\frac{1}{8}$-in. from some part of the cylinder whilst the crankshaft is rotated smartly by means of the kickstarter.

   (ii) If the spark that jumps from the wire is strong and regular, the fault is in the sparking plug. Remove the plug for examination, cleaning, adjustment, or renewal.

   (iii) Next examine the high tension cable for security of fixing to the pick-up and check the insulation for signs of deterioration which could cause short circuiting to some metal part of the machine.

   (iv) Should the magneto have been replaced, check the ignition timing (see below).

(v) If the performance of the magneto is still unsatisfactory the contact breaker may need cleaning and adjusting. See above. Badly burned contacts should be renewed by a Lucas replacement contact set. If the contact breaker is in good order there may be an internal fault in the magneto. If this is suspected the advice of a qualified Service Agent should be sought.

The Automatic Timing Unit (JY16A). This is removable by loosening the hexagon headed centre screw as described on page 57. When refitting note that the timing is set with the unit fully advanced—i.e., with weights fully extended.

Warning.—The Lucas automatic timing unit is unsuitable for use with B.T.H. Magneto and vice versa.

ABRIDGED SPECIFICATION.

Engines.	Model MOV	Model MAC	Model MSS
Type	One Cylinder OHV—4 stroke	One Cylinder OHV—4 stroke	One Cylinder OHV—4 stroke
Bore and Stroke	68 mm. × 68.25 mm.	68 mm. × 96 mm.	81 mm. × 96 mm.
Cubic Capacity (Swept Volume)	248 c.c.	349 c.c.	495 c.c.
Rated Horse-Power (A.C.U. Rating)	2.5 H.P.	3.5 H.P.	5 H.P.
Tappet Clearances (For Running)	Inlet .003-in. Exhaust .006-in.	See Page 66.	Inlet .005-in. Exhaust .010-in.
,, ,, (For Timing)	Inlet .010-in. Exhaust .015-in.		Inlet .025-in. Exhaust .025-in.
	Clearances to be set when Engine is cold.		
Position of Engine Serial Number ..	Stamped (following the serial Letters) on near side of Crankcase below Cylinder. See page 43, Fig. 20.		
Gearboxes	4 speeds. Operated by Right-hand Pedal on all three Models. Downward movement of Pedal engages higher gear. Pre-war Models and some war-time machines operate the opposite way.		
Ratios : With Standard Sprocket ..	Top: 6.35 to 1 Third: 8.45 to 1 Second: 11.1 to 1 **First:** 16.1 to 1	Top: 5.5 to 1 Third: 7.3 to 1 Second: 9.6 to 1 First: 14 to 1†	Top: Solo: 4.9 to 1 Third: 5.91 to 1 Second: 7.76 to 1 First: 11.25 to 1
Position of Gearbox Serial No... ..	Stamped on rear of housing. † 16.8 on WD/MAC., 18.17 on MAF.		

ABRIDGED SPECIFICATION—*Continued.*

Tanks. Fuel Capacity	2.5 gallons 11.35 litres	2.5 gallons 11.35 litres	3.5 gallons 15.9 litres
Oil	½ gall. 2.27 litres	½ gall. 2.27 litres	½ gall. 2.27 litres
Transmission.			
Primary Drive —driver	19 teeth	22 teeth	23 teeth
,, ,, —driven	44 ,,	44 ,,	44 ,,
Final ,, —driver	19 ,,	19 ,,	Solo 18T. S/C 16T.
,, ,, —driven	52 ,,	52 ,,	46 teeth
Chains, Primary Pitch & Width	.5-in. × .305-in.	.5-in. × .305-in.	.5-in. × .305-in.
,, ,, —Roller Diameter	.335-in.	.335-in.	.335-in.
,, ,, —No. of Pitches	74	75	68
,, Rear —Pitch & Width	.5-in. × .305-in.	.5-in. × .305-in.	.625-in. × .380-in.
,, ,, —Roller Diameter	.335-in.	.335-in.	.4-in.
,, ,, —No. of Pitches	108	108	99
Principal Dimensions:—			
Height to Top of Saddle	27.5-in.	27.5-in.	28-in.
Wheel Base	52.25-in.	52.25-in.	55-in.
Width over Handlebars	27.5-in.	27.5-in.	29-in.
Wheels: Rims	WM2×19	WM2×19	WM3×19
Tyres: Front	26-in. × 3.25-in.	26-in. × 3.25-in.	26-in. × 3.5-in.
,, Rear	26-in. × 3.25-in.	26-in. × 3.25-in.	27-in. × 4-in.

CORRESPONDENCE WITH THE WORKS.

At the head of every letter written to us on the subject of a machine we advise that the engine number with serial letters should be quoted. The number and letters will be found stamped on the driving side of the crankcase just below the bottom flange of the cylinder. Registration Numbers are of no help since these are invariably allocated after delivery of the Motor Cycle from the Works. In all communications a really legible signature and the full address are necessary and important.

If a letter addressed to us is in reply to a letter received from us the letter reference, which will be found in the letter heading on the left-hand side, should be quoted so that the letter may be passed immediately to the individual dealing with the matter. Letters asking for advice and technical information should not contain orders for Spares or refer to other subjects. Owners should always order Spares from the nearest Velocette agent.

HOURS OF BUSINESS :

9 a.m. to 12-15 p.m. and 2-0 p.m. to 5-0 p.m. Mondays to Fridays. Closed Saturdays.

Bank Holidays and Special Occasions excepted.

CLAIMS UNDER GUARANTEE.

Terms of the guarantee will be found in our catalogues.

Should it be necessary to claim for an alleged defective **part it is** essential that the original part is returned for examination in accordance with terms and conditions laid down and before any such claim **can be** considered. This does not mean that the machine must be laid up whilst the old part is being returned for examination and a new part may be ordered either through one of our appointed Agents or direct from us, and will in the latter case be sent per C.O.D. unless cash is received with order. The original part should then be returned to us suitably labelled with owner's name and address and the engine number, date of purchase and a brief statement of the circumstances of the case. If the claim is admitted a refund will be made of the cost of the parts if purchased direct from us or credit will be issued to the Agent if replacements were purchased in that way. In the latter circumstances the name and address of the Agent should be given when returning the parts.

Usually it is convenient to send either the original Invoice or Advice Note, which accompanies the purchase of the replacement part. Should a claim be disallowed reasons will be given in detail for our decision. It should be borne in mind, however, that a claim is in no way prejudiced by the acceptance of an Invoice in the first place and every claim is **treated** individually and judged entirely upon merit and the result of the inspection **of the original part.**

DOWTY OLEOMATIC MOTOR CYCLE FORKS

SERVICE AND MAINTENANCE MANUAL

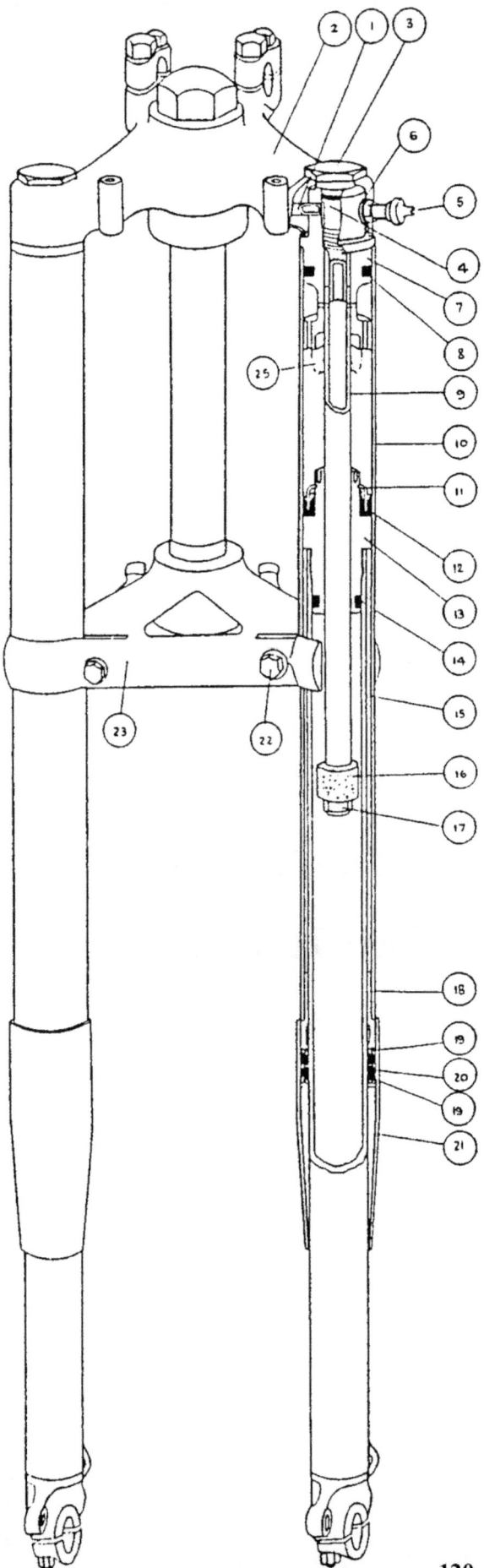

KEY

1. PIPE, PRESSURE BALANCE.
2. CLIP, HANDLE BAR LUG.
3. PLUG FILLER.
4. STATIC SEAL, FILLER PLUG.
5. VALVE, INFLATION.
6. SEAL, INFLATION VALVE.
7. INTERNAL FITTING TOP.
8. STATIC SEAL, INTERNAL FITTING TOP.
9. TUBE, CARRYING BUFFER.
10. TUBE, OUTER.
11. RING, RETAINING PISTON SEAL.
12. SEAL, PISTON.
13. PISTON.
14. STATIC SEAL, PISTON.
15. TUBE, INNER SLIDING.
16. CUSHION, RUBBER.
17. LOCKNUT, CUSHION.
18. BEARING LOWER.
19. RING, LOCATING SCRAPER.
20. RING, SCRAPER.
21. SHROUD TAPER.
22. BOLT, PINCH.
23. CROWN, FORK FITTING.
24. BOLT, STEERING TUBE PINCH.
25. CUSHION, DASHPOT.
    (Not Required on Models 60/70.)

DESCRIPTION

The main members consist of two outer tubes (10), clamped by pinch bolts (22) to the fork crown fitting (23) and attached to the handlebar clip lug (2) by spigots on the top internal fittings (7). A steering tube is brazed into the fork crown fitting and passes through a hole in the handlebar clip lug where it is located by means of a lock nut. A substantial high tensile steel pad bolt prevents rotation of the steering tube relative to the handlebar clip lug.

The axle attachment fittings are brazed into the lower sliding tubes. These vary in design on different machines depending on whether the wheel spindle is fixed or of the 'knock-out' type. The tubes carry light alloy pistons, which are glanded to retain pressure. On Mod. 60/70 forks the piston (13) itself is the upper bearing, its point of application being immediately below the sealing gland. On all Mod. 100 forks the upper bearing is made of 'Mintex' (impregnated asbestos anti-friction material). This bearing is split in two halves so that it may be assembled into a groove in the piston above the gland ring. Synthetic rubber sealing rings (14) below the threaded portion of the piston prevent leakage into the cavity between the inner and outer tubes.

The lower bearings (18) are brazed into the outer tubes and ingress of foreign matter is prevented by double-lipped scraper rings (20) located by tapered shrouds.

Small diameter tubes (9), brazed to the top internal fittings, pass through the piston centres and carry synthetic rubber cushions (16) at their lower ends.

Mod. 100 forks are provided with synthetic rubber dashpot cushions beneath the top internal fittings, whilst in 60/70 models the dashpot is a recess machined into the top internal fitting.

Synthetic rubber seals (8) prevent air leakage from the top internal fittings which are connected by a pressure balance pipe (1).

The inflation valve (5) is fitted to the near-side top internal fitting. It is threaded to fit the normal motor cycle pump connection.

FUNCTION.

The forks are air sprung and oil damped. Air springing has the advantage of allowing considerable deflection for normal surface irregularities whilst maintaining the ability to absorb considerable shocks without excess fork movement.

The movement of the synthetic rubber cushions in oil provides approximately equal and constant damping in both directions without the contact and resultant wear of working parts. These cushions also absorb the shock should the forks extend fully, whilst the oil cushion between the pistons and internal top fittings prevents too rapid closing on compression.

INFLATION AND ADJUSTMENT TO LOAD.

A red dot is positioned on the front of each lower sliding tube. When correctly inflated to the load, the bottom edges of the shrouds should coincide with the red dots with rider or riders in position.

To obtain the correct adjustment, over-inflate the fork slightly by removing the inflation valve dust cap and coupling an ordinary tyre pump to the valve. The rider should then sit on the machine, keeping his feet on the footrests and maintaining balance from some convenient support. Air should then be released in small quantities by depressing the stem of the inflation valve until the bottom of the shrouds line up with the red dots. Replace the dust cap on the inflation valve.

It will be seen from the above that the forks can, without fear of error, be correctly adjusted for solo, sidecar, or pillion riding.

INFLATION VALVE.

The inflation valve is fitted with a special core designed to open at low pressure and fitted with oil resisting rubber seatings. *Under no circumstances* should a normal tyre valve insert be used as the action of the oil would rapidly destroy the natural rubber seatings. Dowty Valve Cores can be obtained from your Dealer or direct from the manufacturers.

TOPPING UP.

Topping up becomes necessary only if 'bottoming' occurs in spite of correct inflation. Scrupulous cleanliness is essential.

Remove inflation valve dust cap, depress valve stem and allow all air to escape. The forks will close.

Rest the crank case on a block so that the forks are 1in. from the fully closed position. Unscrew the filler plugs and fill each leg with one of the recommended oils (See 'FILLING'). Replace and tighten filler plugs.

Remove the block from beneath the crank case and depress the inflation valve, thus allowing surplus oil to drain off and the forks to close completely.

Carry out air inflation procedure, adjust to the load, and replace valve dust cap.

FILLING.

Forks are supplied correctly filled and inflated. When filling, it is important that the recommended grade of oil be used as its viscosity does not change appreciably over a wide range of temperatures. Consequently there is little or no alteration in its damping characteristics.

The recommended oils are :—

Mobiloil Arctic   Essolube 30
Castrolite   Motorine D
Single Shell

The procedure for filling is exactly the same as described under "TOPPING-UP," except that more oil will be required.

Unless dirt has been allowed to enter with the oil during filling or topping up, the oil need never be changed during the life of the machine.

GREASING.

The bottom bearings in each leg should be greased weekly. Six shots with the grease gun should be given to each greaser, situated at the back of the outer tubes, at the lower bearings. Only clean high grade grease should be used. Vent holes are provided in the sides of the outer tubes below the fork crown; these allow surplus grease to escape.

NUTS AND SCREWS.

Periodically check the tightness of all nuts and screws to ensure completely efficient working. It is particularly important that the steering tube pad bolt is really tight, otherwise the fork may become malaligned.

ADJUSTING STEERING HEAD RACE.

Slacken both the clamp bolts on the fork crown fitting and the pad bolt on the handlebar clip plug. Adjust steering head nut as required. Retighten pad bolt hard and clamp bolts on completion of adjustment.

REMOVING AND REPLACING FRONT WHEEL (Fixed Spindle Type).

Place a suitable block under the crank case so that the forks are fully extended and the wheel is clear of the ground. Disconnect the brake cable at the brake drum. Slacken the nuts locating the axle cap on the brake drum side. Screw back the axle nut about two complete turns. Remove both axle caps, supporting the wheel with one hand as it comes clear of the forks.

To replace the wheel, screw up the nuts locating the axle caps to finger tightness only. Tighten the axle nut on the brake drum side so that the wheel is held tightly against the side of the axle fitting. Now tighten axle cap on this side only. Lift the machine off the block and bounce the fork a few times on the ground. Tighten near side axle cap, replace brake cable and adjust.

The object of the procedure explained in the preceding paragraph is to ensure that the lower tubes of the forks slide freely in the outer tubes. It will be noticed that a small clearance for this purpose is allowed between the shoulder on the nearside axle ferrule and the axle fitting. With knock-out spindle wheels, the fork should also be bounced before tightening axle nut and clamp bolt to ensure correct alignment.

DISMANTLING FORKS AND TOOLS REQUIRED

1. Pliers.   2. Screwdriver.   4. Peg Spanner (for dismantling piston).
3. Adjustable Spanner.   5. Circlip Pliers (Mods. 60/70 only).

In the unlikely event of dismantling or major fork repairs being required, the owner is advised to employ his Dealer to carry out the work, as the changing of sealing rings calls for great care. However, if this course is impracticable and the fork is rapidly losing air pressure, proceed as follows:—

First check the inflation valve for leakage. If there is no evidence of air escaping, the forks will have to be dismantled. An air escape from either piston sealing ring will be indicated first by oil leakage, which will appear at the vent in the outer tube. This will be easily distinguishable from surplus grease.

Place a block under the crank case to allow the forks to extend fully. Remove front wheel as previously described. Remove mudguard stay bolts and detach mudguards. Depress inflation valve stem, allowing all air to escape.

Slacken pinch bolts on the fork crown fitting. Grasp the outer tube firmly with both hands at a point below the fork crown fitting and rotate gently, backwards and forwards, at the same time pulling downwards until the brass ring on the tube is clear of the fitting. The top internal fittings will then be fully exposed. Still holding the outer tube in one hand, push the inner tube upwards until the edge of the shroud is resting on the axle fitting, exposing the piston.

Grasp the axle fitting firmly and engage a peg spanner in the holes in the top of the piston. (The spanner for this purpose may be obtained from your Dealer.) Unscrew the piston and gently withdraw the inner and outer tubes together, leaving the piston on the central stop tube. Slide the outer tube off the inner tube and remove screws and greaser from the shroud. Withdraw the shroud, together with the rubber locating and scraper rings. Empty the oil from the tube.

Remove the lock nut and washer at the end of the stop tube, at the same time taking care not to bend the tube. The complete piston may now be removed. On Mod. 100 forks the two halves of the 'Mintex' bearing are now detached, allowing the gland ring and metal spacer to be withdrawn. On 60/70 models the steel circlip at the top of the piston must be removed before the gland ring and spacer may be withdrawn.

Exactly the same procedure is repeated with the other leg of the forks.

Wash all parts in clean paraffin. Do not dry the parts with a cloth as however clean it may appear there is always the probability of small particles of grit adhering to it.

Examine carefully the lips of the piston sealing rings and if they are chipped, however slightly, they must be replaced. If there is evidence of extensive or deep scoring in either outer tube, it should be replaced. Such scoring is caused invariably by dirt being introduced into the fork during filling or topping up, so the importance of cleanliness will be realised. Scoring cannot occur in normal usage and even after many thousands of miles have been covered the tubes will retain their original polished appearance.

It will be noted that the working portion of the forks may be dismantled without removing the fork crown or handlebar clip lug from the machine. Thus it is not necessary to disturb the steering head race adjustment or the balance pipe unit.

REASSEMBLING FORKS.

Insert the rubber scraper ring into the top of the shroud with the longer lip of the ring downwards towards the axle fitting. Place the soft rubber locating ring over the scraper ring, sliding the shroud over the inner sliding tube. Introduce the outer tube over the inner tube and slide the shroud into position, locating it by replacing the screws and greaser. Place new gland ring and spacer in position on the piston and locate with 'Mintex' bearing or circlip according to type of fork. Smear the diameter of the ring with good quality lubricating grease. The static rubber sealing rings at the threaded end of the piston should be similarly treated. Replace the piston in position on the centre tube and attach the rubber out-stop, washer, and locknut. Smear a little grease around the static sealing ring on the top internal fitting.

Fill the inner tube with one of the recommended brands of oil. Hold the outer and inner tubes by the axle fitting, pass them up through hole in fork crown fitting, and screw in the piston with the peg spanner. Take care, during this operation, that the lip of the piston sealing ring is not damaged on the edge of the hole in the fork crown fitting.

Gently force the outer tube upwards until the top edge butts on the flange of the top internal fitting. Rotate the tube so that the vent hole faces outwards. Proceed in the same manner with the alternate leg, finally tightening pinch bolts and replacing mudguard and wheel. Topping up and inflation to load completes the operation.

NOTES

SPARE PARTS LIST

FOR

MAC (RIGID FRAME) MODEL
350 c.c.
(INCLUDING PARTS FOR MOV)

VELOCE LIMITED
: HALL GREEN WORKS :
YORK RD., HALL GREEN
BIRMINGHAM, 28

TELEphone : SPRingfield 1145/6/7
TELEgrams : "Veloce, Birmingham."

INTRODUCTION

HOW TO ORDER SPARE PARTS.

As the prompt despatch of spare parts depends to a great extent upon the orders for them being accurately and clearly made out, we ask for the co-operation of customers in the following requirements:

(1) The printing in block letters of the name and address of the consignee. (We receive quite a number of orders which cannot be executed because forwarding addresses are omitted or are unreadable).

(2) The inclusion of the engine and frame numbers of the machine for which the parts are required. (These should be taken from the engine and frame. Do not rely on the Registration Book.)

(3) The accurate quoting of part numbers—not illustration references —and brief descriptions of the parts. As we work to part numbers these are the more important.

(4) The use of separate sheets for orders, which should be written on one side of the paper only. If technical or other information is needed at the time of ordering please ask for this in a separate letter which may be posted with the order.

(5) Clear directions for despatch, which should state whether parts shall be posted C.O.D., or whether against a remittance with order. If the latter please state amount enclosed, and please do not send coin unless the envelope is registered. Postal Orders, Money Orders, or Cheques, crossed " & Co.," and made payable to Veloce Ltd., are advised.

If the spares are to be sent to an address other than that from which the order is sent, this must be clearly stated. In such cases unless the person ordering is sure that a C.O.D. parcel will be paid for on presentation, remittances must always be sent.

ILLUSTRATIONS. These are not necessarily exact reproductions of the parts they represent and in the case of gears and sprockets do not always show the correct number of teeth. It has not been possible to show all parts so that reference must always be made to the list to identify the parts needed.

EXAMPLE OF ORDER. The following is an example of an order correctly set out:

Please despatch per C.O.D. (or) Please despatch against remittance enclosed value.... to:

NAME AND ADDRESS (In block letters).

FOR MAC MODEL. ENGINE No. MAC/15982

1	M220.	Cylinder head gasket.
1	K180/3	Carburetter gasket.
1	M256	Rocker cover gasket.

(Signed)

TELEGRAPHED ORDERS. The code on page 3 should be used when ordering by telegram. If orders are not to be sent C.O.D. remittances may be sent by Telegraphed Money Order. It is essential, however, to instruct the telegraph clerk to include the sender's name and addres in the message space, otherwise this will not be transmitted.

EXAMPLE OF TELEGRAPHED ORDER.

VELOCE, BIRMINGHAM.
VELOD ONE M 220, ONE K 180/3, ONE M 256.
NAME AND ADDRESS.

TERMS. Strictly nett cash before despatch (Agents and Spares Stockists excepted).

All Spares Invoices will be surcharged a percentage of the total to cover postage, or packing and carriage charges—subject to a minimum surcharge of 6d. C.O.D. fees are charged extra.

Cases and Crates, etc., are charged for on despatch, the charge being recoverable from us upon receipt by us of the returned empty container in good condition if returned within 21 days from the date of Invoice.

The return of empties must be advised and Invoice numbers quoted.

C.O.D. ORDERS. These can be executed by parcels post only. The maximum weight acceptable by the Post Office is 15-lbs., and there are certain limitations as to size. The minimum parcel post charge and C.O.D. fee makes it uneconomical to send orders less than 5/- value by this means. Remittances should, therefore, be sent with any very small or very large orders.

PATTERNS. Old parts may be sent as patterns, but must be cleaned thoroughly before packing, and must be labelled clearly with sender's name and address in block letters, and marked "Pattern(s) to order herewith (or under separate cover)." Do not include coin, Notes, Cheques, or Money Orders with patterns. Patterns will not be returned unless asked for.

REPAIRS. We are usually able to test customers' machines without previous arrangements being made, but it is seldom possible to start repairs and complete them within a specified time, unless an appointment has been made beforehand for the motorcycle to be taken in. Appointments will be arranged on request.

Whilst all reasonable care is taken, customers' motorcycles and property are received, stored, and driven at owners' sole risk. We do not accept responsibility for loss or damage arising from accident, fire, theft, or other causes.

Customers' wishes as to delivery will be met as far as is practicable, but no responsibility can be accepted for delays in the carrying out of any repairs, or for the quality of, or delays in procuring any replacements that are not of our manufacture.

Parts removed and replaced during repairs will be disposed of at once, unless we are instructed before beginning the work that they are to be retained for return to the customer.

ORDERS FOR REPAIRS. The term "overhaul" is capable of different meanings to different people. Customers should, therefore, state exactly and in detail the work required. Otherwise work may have to be stopped for us to obtain sanction to supply and fit parts found to be necessary.

It is particularly important to be specific in the case of engine and transmission units which on being stripped and examined may be found to need more than the owner has authorized.

ESTIMATES. We can prepare Estimates if desired for repairs needed to machines, or component assemblies sent us. In such cases we do not begin repairs until the Estimate is accepted. Estimates are prepared as accurately as possible, but are subject to slight revision if, when repairs are progressing, additional work or parts are required.

In the event of the non-acceptance of an Estimate a charge will be made for stripping, cleaning and assembling. Parts detailed for renewal will be kept available for inspection until the Estimate is accepted, but will be disposed of immediately on acceptance unless instructions are received for their return.

No guarantee is given with any repair if the Estimate is not accepted in full.

NOTIFICATION OF COMPLETION. Customers will be advised by post unless we are instructed otherwise. This notification will normally take the form of an Invoice for the work done and parts fitted.

PAYMENT FOR REPAIRS. Payment is required before despatch, or on collection at the works.

HOURS OF BUSINESS. Mondays to Fridays inclusive : 9 a.m. to 12-15 p.m. and 2 p.m. to 5 p.m. Closed Saturdays. Bank Holidays and special occasions excepted.

VELOCE LTD.,
SERVICE DEPARTMENT.

F132/11R/2M/58.

CODE

For the convenience of customers, to ensure accuracy, and to save cost of telegraphing, we draw attention to the following Code Words and their meanings :—

VEL	Despatch immediately per passenger train to address below.
VELAIR	Despatch immediately per Air.
VELO	Despatch immediately per passenger train to station to be called for.
VELOD	Despatch C.O.D.
VELOR	Despatch immediately per parcels post.
VELOX 1715	Expedite delivery of our Order No. 1715.
VELOC	Send immediately by goods train to address below.
VELORIS	Send immediately by goods train to station to be called for.
VELORUM	Send immediately by registered post.

We strongly advise the use of above Code Words when telegraphing.

When remittance is sent by Telegraphic Money Order, unless NAME and ADDRESS are given in the space provided for a Private Message, the Post Office will not give this information in the Telegram.

PROPRIETARY ARTICLES

Customers are requested to deal direct with the manufacturers of Proprietary Articles for any technical information or claims under guarantee. Overseas owners should obtain the above information either from the Velocette Agent or the Proprietary Manufacturer's Representative in their Territory.

For our Customers' convenience we give the addresses of our suppliers below :—

CARBURETTER EQUIPMENT :—
    Amal Ltd., Holford Road, Witton, Birmingham, 6.

LIGHTING AND IGNITION EQUIPMENT :—
    Jos. Lucas Ltd., Great King Street, Birmingham, 19.
    B.T.H. Co., Ltd., Alma Street, Coventry.
    H. Miller & Co., Ltd., Aston Brook Street, Birmingham, 6.

CHAINS :—
    Renold and Coventry Chain Co., Ltd., Didsbury, Manchester.

SPARKING PLUGS :—
    K.L.G. Sparking Plugs, Ltd., Robinhood Eng. Works, Putney Vale, London, S.W.15.
    Lodge Plugs Ltd., Rugby.
    Champion Sparking Plugs, Feltham, Middlesex.

ELECTRIC HORNS :—
    Clear Hooters Ltd., Hampton Street, Birmingham, 19.

TYRES :—
    Dunlop Rubber Co. Ltd., Fort Dunlop, Birmingham.
    Goodyear Tyre Co., Bushbury, Wolverhampton.

BATTERIES :—
    Chloride Electrical Storage Co., Dale End, Birmingham.
    Varley Dry Accumulators Ltd., By-Pass Road, Barking, Essex.
    J. Lucas Ltd., Gt. King Street, Birmingham, 19.

SPEEDOMETERS :—
    S. Smith & Sons (M.A.) Ltd., Cricklewood Works, Cricklewood, London, N.W.12.

SADDLES AND PILLION SEATS :—
    H. Terry & Sons, Ltd., Redditch.
    J. B. Brooks & Co., Ltd., Great Charles Street, Birmingham, 3.
    Latex Cushion Co., 830, Kingsbury Road, Erdington, Birmingham.

ILLUSTRATION A

ORDER BY PART NUMBERS—DO NOT QUOTE ILLUSTRATION REFERENCES.
FOR PART NUMBERS AND DESCRIPTIONS OF ITEMS SEE PAGES 6 TO 8.

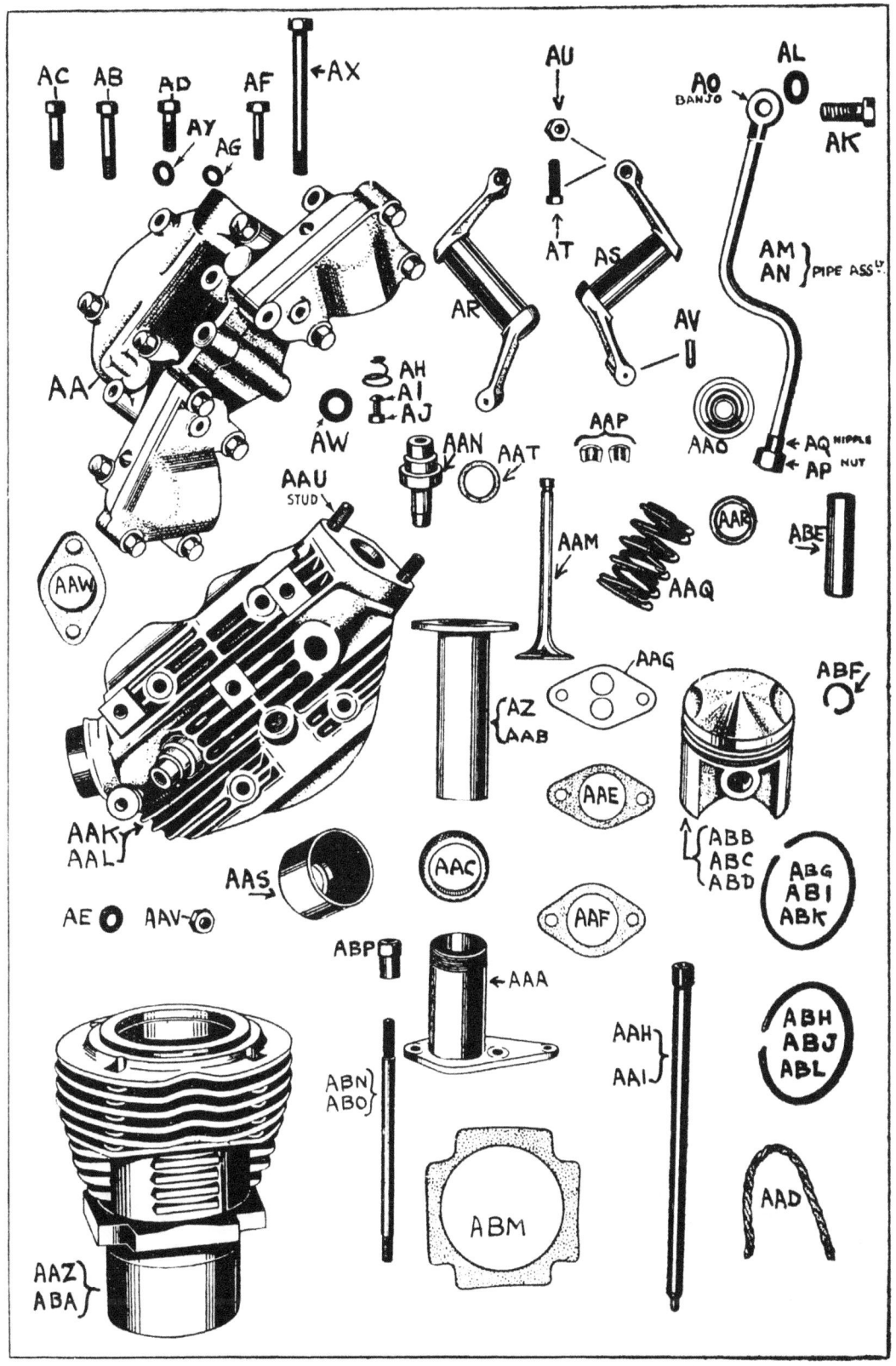

HAVE YOU QUOTED THE ENGINE NUMBER ON YOUR ORDER?

ENGINE SECTION (TO No. MAC15981 ONLY).—ROCKER BOX, ROCKERS, BOLTS, &c. GROUP.

Illustration Ref.	Part No.	Description.	
Not shown	M92AS	Rocker box assembly. Old type, used to Engine M2637 and MAC2993. Obsolete. Replace by using M92/3AS, 1 off, M214, 1 off, A37, 2 off, M215, 1 off, M9/4, 1 off.	
AA	M92/3AS	Rocker box assembly.—Top and bottom halves, tappet covers and bolts.	
AB	SL9/10	Bolts—Rocker box cover to bottom half—$\frac{5}{16}$" 18T. × $1\frac{1}{2}$"	2 off.
AC	SL9/11	Bolts—Rocker box cover to bottom half—$\frac{5}{16}$" 18T. × $1\frac{5}{16}$"	2 off.
AD	SL9/12	Bolts—Rocker box cover to bottom half—$\frac{5}{16}$" 18T. × $\frac{7}{8}$"	2 off.
AE	SL6/41	Plain washers for rocker box bolts.	6 off.
AF	SL8/16	Bolts—Tappet covers to rocker box.	8 off.
BAA	SL30/21	Studs—Push rod tube flange to rocker box.	2 off.
AG	SL6/32	Plain washers for SL8/16 and SL30/21	10 off.
BAB	SL56/4	Nuts for SL30/21.	2 off.
AH	M222	Thrust springs for rockers.	2 off.
AI	SL80/23	Screw (Thrust spring to tappet cover)	2 off.
AJ	SL56/2	Nut for SL80/23.	2 off.
AK	M214	Hollow bolt (Oil-pipe banjo union to rocker box cover).	
AL	A37	Fibre washer for M214.	2 off.
Not shown	A9AS	Oil pipe (timing case to rocker box). To Engine M2637 only with M92AS.	
Not shown	A9/5AS	Oil pipe (timing case to rocker box). To Engine MAC2993 only with M92AS.	
AM	A9/8AS	Oil pipe (timing case to rocker box). From Engine M2638 with M92/3AS.	
AN	A9/9AS	Oil pipe (timing case to rocker box). From Engine MAC2994 with M92/3AS.	
Not shown	M9	Inlet rocker—used with M92AS only to Engine M2637 and MAC2993.	
AR	M9/2	Exhaust rocker.	
AS	M9/4	Inlet rocker, used with M92/3AS only. From Engines M2638 and MAC2994.	
AT	M39	Adjustable tappets.	2 off.
AU	SL56/33	Lock nut for tappet.	2 off.
AV	M41	Rocker tip.	2 off.
AW	BK103	Oil control washer for rockers. (To Eng. No. MAC15443).	2 off.
	M258	Oil control disc—from Eng. No. MAC15444.	2 off.
AX	SL9/5	Bolt. Rocker box assembly to cylinder head.	3 off.
AY	SL6/40	Plain washers for SL9/5.	3 off.

ENGINE SECTION—continued.
PUSH ROD AND PUSH ROD COVER GROUP.

AZ	M50AS	Push rod tube and flange. Top. MOV model.	
AAA	M50/2AS	Push rod tube and flange. Bottom.	
AAB	M50/3AS	Push rod tube and flange. Top. MAC model.	
AAC	M52	Gland nut for push rod tube.	1 off.
AAD	K53	Abestos string packing for M52.	1 off.

Illustration Ref.	Part No.	Description.	
		Engine Section—continued.	
AAE	M120	Joint washer for top flange.	2 off.
AAF	M120/2	Joint washer for bottom flange.	1 off.
AAG	M234	Guide plate for push rods.	1 off.
AAH	M196AS	Push rod with ends. MOV model	2 off.
AAI	M196/5AS	Push rod with ends. MAC model	2 off.

ENGINE SECTION—continued.
CYLINDER HEAD, VALVE AND SPRING GROUP.

AAK	M1/2	Cylinder Head. Model MOV.	
AAL	M1/3	Cylinder head. Model MAC	
A2—8	M220	Gasket for cylinder head. Used only on engines up to M3473 and MAC 5080, but not required if replacement cylinders M22/7 or M22/9 are used as replacements on early engines.	
AAM	M2/2	Valve. Inlet or exhaust.	2 off.
AAN	M3	Valve guide. Inlet or exhaust.	2 off.
Not shown	K4	Top collar for valve spring. Used up to Engines M2769 and MAC3228.	2 off.
AAO	K4/5	Top collar for valve spring. Used from Engines M2770 and MAC3229.	2 off.
AAP	K5/4	Valve cotter. (Two halves.)	2 off.
Not shown	K6/2	Valve spring, outer. Used with K4 only, to Engines M2769 and MAC3228	2 off.
Not shown	K7/3	Valve spring, inner. Used with K4 only, to Engines M2769 and MAC3228	2 off.
AAQ	K6/7/7/6	Valve springs, inner and outer. Not supplied apart. From M2770 and MAC3229.	2 off.
AAR	M38/2	Bottom washer for springs—inside covers.	2 off.
AAS	M197/2	Valve spring covers.	2 off.
AAT	M224/2	Joint washer (between valve spring cover and valve guide).	4 off.
AAU	SL31/4	Stud—carburetter to head.	2 off.
AAV	SL56/6	Nut for carburetter stud.	2 off.
AAW	K180	Joint washer (between carburetter and head).	1 off.

ENGINE SECTION—continued.
CYLINDER AND PISTON GROUP.

AAZ	†M22/7	Cylinder. MOV model.	
ABA	†M22/9	Cylinder. MAC model.	
ABB	M27	Piston. Standard diameter.	
ABC	M27/0	Piston. Plus .020-in. on diameter.	
ABD	M27/1	Piston. Plus .040-in. on diameter.	
ABE	M31	Gudgeon pin.	
ABF	K149	Circlip. For retaining gudgeon pin.	
ABG	SL3/18	Compression piston rings. Standard diameter.	2 off.

† Needs no cylinder head gasket. See Service Manual.

Illustration Ref.	Part No.	Description.	
Engine Section—continued.			
ABH	SL3/19	Slotted oil control ring. Standard diameter.	1 off.
ABI	SL3/20	Compression piston rings. Plus ·020 in. on diameter.	2 off.
ABJ	SL3/21	Slotted oil control ring. Plus ·020 in. on diameter.	1 off.
ABK	SL3/33	Compression piston rings. Plus ·040 in. on diameter.	2 off.
ABL	SL3/34	Slotted oil control ring. Plus ·040 in. on diameter.	1 off.
A2—17	M203	Compression plate.	As required.
ABM	M70	Joint washer for cylinder base.	
ABN	SL31/7	Cylinder studs (securing cylinder and head). MOV models only.	4 off.
ABO	SL31/9	Cylinder studs (securing cylinder and head). MAC models only.	4 off.
ABP	M208	Nuts for cylinder head.	4 off.

ILLUSTRATION B.

ORDER BY PART NUMBERS—DO NOT QUOTE ILLUSTRATION REFERENCES.
FOR PART NUMBERS AND DESCRIPTIONS OF ITEMS SEE PAGES 10 TO 14.

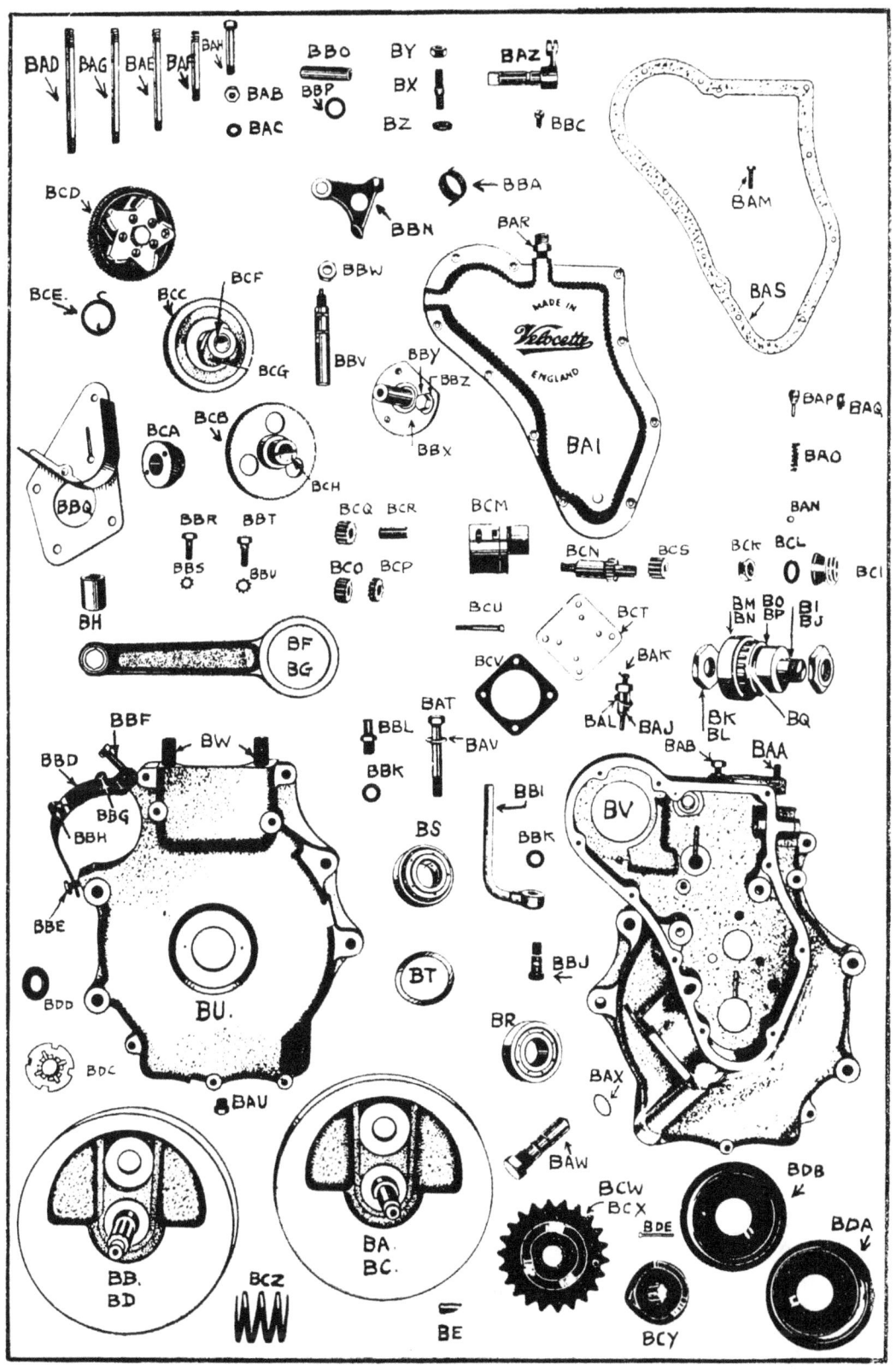

THE LETTERS PREFIXING THE ENGINE NUMBER ARE ESSENTIAL TO IDENTIFY
THE TYPE OF MACHINE.

ENGINE SECTION—continued. See Illustration "B" Page 9.
FLYWHEEL ASSEMBLY GROUP.

Illustration Ref.	Part No.	Description.
BA	M23AS	Flywheel with mainshaft, timing side. MOV model.
BB	M25AS	Flywheel with mainshaft, driving side. MOV model.
BC	M23/4AS	Flywheel with mainshaft, timing side. MAC model.
BD	M25/4AS	Flywheel with mainshaft, driving side. MAC model.
BE	K36/2	Key for crankshaft pinion—in timing side mainshaft.
BF	M28AS	Connecting rod with small end bush. MOV model.
BG	M28/2ASM	Connecting rod with small end bush. MAC model.
BH	M29	Small end bush.
BI	M192AS	Crankpin with nuts. MOV model.
BJ	K192AS	Crankpin with nuts. MAC model.
BK	M62	Crankpin nuts. MOV model.
BL	K62/4	Crankpin nuts. MAC model.
BM	M190	Outer ring for big end—in connecting rod. MOV model.
BN	K190	Outer ring for big end—in connecting rod. MAC model.
BO	M193	Roller cage. MOV model.
BP	K193	Roller cage. MAC model.
BQ	K191	Big end rollers. Standard diameter. 16 off on MAC. 14 off on MOV.
BQ	K191/3	Big end rollers. .0004-in. oversize on dia.
BQ	K191/4	Big end rollers. .0002-in. oversize on dia.
BR	K87	Mainshaft ballrace, timing side.
BS	K87/2	Mainshaft roller race, driving side.
BT	K174	Mainshaft bearing, packing shim, .005-in. thick.
BT	K174/2	Mainshaft bearing, packing shim, .003-in. thick.
BT	K174/3	Mainshaft bearing, packing shim, .012-in. thick.

ENGINE SECTION—continued.
CRANKCASE AND TIMING COVER GROUP.

BU	M43/5	Crankcase—driving side half. Obsolete, see Note *	
BV	M44/5	Crankcase—timing side half. Obsolete, see Note *	

* For replacement crankcases for engines numbered MAC15523 to MAC15791, refer to page 17. Owing to M43/5 and M44/5 no longer being available the crankcase M43/44/8 must also be used for MAC models before MAC15523 and MOV models, but in such circumstances the parts shown * on page 61 will be needed in addition.

BW	M56/2	Cylinder holding studs—in crankcase	4 off.
BX	SL31/3	Magneto fixing stud.	3 off.
BY	SL56/13	Nut for magneto stud.	3 off.
BZ	SL6/40	Plain washer for magneto stud nut.	3 off.
BAA	SL30/21	Stud, push rod tube flange to crankcase.	2 off.
BAB	SL56/4	Nut, for SL30/21 and for crankcase studs.	12 off.

Illustration Ref.	Part No.	Description.	
BAC	SL6/32	Plain washers for SL56/4.	24 off.
BAD	SL30/1	Crankcase stud, 4¼-in. long	1 off.
BAE	SL30/2	Crankcase stud, 3½-in. long.	1 off.
BAF	SL30/14	Crankcase stud, 1¾-in. long.	1 off.
BAG	SL30/24	Crankcase stud, 4-in. long.	1 off.
BAH	SL8/24	Crankcase bolt, ¼" 20T × 2"	2 off.
Not shown	M45/2	Timing cover (for engines before M1724 and MAC1611 only).	
Not shown	M45/2D	Timing cover for engines between M1725 to M3472, and MAC1612 to MAC5079 with direct oil feed to camspindle but no supplementary cylinder feed.	
BAI	M45/4	Timing cover for engines from M3473 and MAC5080.	
	M45/6	Timing cover used on engines Nos. MAC15791 to MAC15981.	
BAJ	M212	Crankshaft oil jet.	
BAK	SL80/22	Screw for crankshaft oil jet.	
BAL	A37/2	Fibre washer for oil jet.	
BAM	K55	Timing cover screw. 10 off.	
BAN	K100	Ball for check valve. ¼-in. diameter.	
BAO	RT115	Spring for check valve.	
BAP	M69	Check valve screwed plug—from 1941 only.	
BAQ	M225	Check valve spring plate—before 1941 only.	
BAR	K119	Timing cover oil pipe union.	
BAS	M68	Timing cover joint washer.	
BAU	B38	Crankcase drain plug.	
BAT	M237	Oil feed bolt.	
BAV	A37/3	Fibre washer for oil feed bolt.	
BAW	K246/3	Suction filter plug.	
BAX	KA115/2	Suction filter plug fibre washer.	
BAZ	M11	Exhaust lifter lever.	
BBA	M155/2	Exhaust lifter lever spring.	
BBC	K76	Exhaust lifter lever screw.	
BBD	MAS44/2	Dynamo strap. Replaces E6/4AS.	
BBE	SL8/2	Bolt ¼-in. strap to crankcase.	
BBF	SL9/21	Bolt 5/16-in. to clamp dynamo strap.	
BBG	SL80/21	Screws. Voltage regulator to dynamo strap.	
BBH	LE336	Lock-washer for SL80/21.	
BBI	{ A9/12AS	Oil feed pipe, engine end, .375" o/d.	
	†A9/4AS	Oil feed pipe, engine end, .312" o/d.	
BBJ	M214	Hollow bolt—oil feed pipe to crankcase.	
BBK	{ A37	Washer for oil pipe banjo union and return hose union.	3 off.
	A37/4	Washer between A9/12AS and Crankcase	
BBL	K119/4	Oil return union—in crankcase.	

†Beginning on Engines Nos. MOV6253 and MAC10149 the oil feed pipe is increased on outside diameter from .312" to .375". See also Page 61.

ENGINE SECTION—continued.
TIMING GEAR AND CAM FOLLOWER GROUP.

BBN	M9/3	Cam follower.	2 off.
BBO	M10	Pivot pin for cam follower.	
BBP	M216	Belleville thrust washer between cam follower and crankcase.	

Illustration Ref.	Part No.	Description.
BBQ	M199/2AS	Steady plate and oil trough, for timing gear spindles.
BBR	M210	Bolt, steady plate to intermediate gear and cam follower pivot pin. 2 off.
BBS	LE367	Lock-washer for M210. 2 off.
BBT	M211	Bolt, steady plate to crankcase. 2 off.
BBU	LE368	Lock-washer for M211. 2 off.
Not shown	M15	Camwheel spindle. Only used up to Engine M1724 and MAC 1611. Obsolete, replace with M15/2, 1 off and M244 1 off.
BBV	M15/2	Camwheel spindle.
BBW	M244	Nut—cam spindle to steady plate.
Not shown	M200	Intermediate gear spindle and flange. Obsolete—replace with M200/2AS and rebush gear with M202/2 bush.
BBX	M200/2AS	Intermediate gear spindle. To Eng. No. MAC15522 only.
BBX	M200/4	Intermediate gear spindle—from Eng. No. MAC15523.
BBY	SL8/5	Bolt—intermediate gear spindle flange to crankcase. 3 off.
BBZ	SL6/32	Plain washer for SL8/5. 3 off.
Not shown	†M32	Crankshaft pinion. 24 teeth. Straight cut. (Pre-war models only).
Not shown	†M32/2	Crankshaft pinion. 47 teeth. 15° helix angle. (Pre-war models only).
Not shown	†M32/3	Crankshaft pinion. 47 teeth. 11° helix angle. (Pre-war models only).
BCA	†M32/4	Crankshaft pinion. 46 teeth. 16° helix angle.
Not shown	†M33AS	Intermediate gear and bush. 49 teeth, straight cut. (Pre-war models only).
Not shown	†M33/2AS	Intermediate gear and bush. 95 teeth. 15° helix angle. (Pre-war models only).
Not shown	†M33/3AS	Intermediate gear and bush. 95 teeth. 11° helix angle. (Pre-war models only).
BCB	†M33/4AS	Intermediate gear and bush. 93 teeth. 16° helix angle. To Eng. MAC15522 only.
BCB	MASI	Intermediate gear and bush—from Eng. No. MAC15523.
Not shown	†M18AS	Cam wheel, cam and bush assembly. 48 teeth. Straight cut. (Pre-war models only).
Not shown	†M18/2ASM	Cam wheel, cam and bush assembly. 94 teeth. 15° helix angle. (Pre-war models only).
Not shown	†M18/3ASM	Cam wheel, cam and bush assembly. 94 teeth. 11° helix angle. (Pre-war models only).
BCC	†M18/4AS2	Cam wheel, cam and bush assembly. 92 teeth. 16° helix angle.
Not shown	†M72	"Tuffnol" magneto gear. 48 teeth. Straight cut. (Pre-war models only).
Not shown	†M72/4	"Tuffnol" magneto gear. 94 teeth. 15° helix angle. (Pre-war models only).
Not shown	†M72/5	"Tuffnol" magneto gear. 94 teeth. 11° helix angle. (Pre-war models only).
Not shown	†M72/6	"Tuffnol" magneto gear. 92 teeth. 16° helix angle. (Pre-war models only).

† See Note Page 13.

Illustration Ref.	Part No.	Description.

†**IMPORTANT.**—Before the introduction of the 16° helical timing gears at MOV model engine M1876 and MAC model Engine No. MAC 1841 before the war, there were three other types of gears used which are **interchangeable only in sets**. These are all listed above. All post-war models have 16° helical timing gears. When only one gear is needed for any engine previous to the two mentioned above the correct type should be found by reference to the list of Engine Numbers below, and as old engines may have had the whole set of gears changed it is often advisable to submit the original gear as a pattern. The different types were fitted as follows :—

Straight cut to M877 and MAC413.

15° helical from M878 to M1671 and from MAC414 to MAC1569 inclusive.

11° helical from M1672 to M1875 and from MAC 1570 to MAC1840 inclusive.

16° helical from M1876 and MAC1841 onwards, including all engines carrying serial letters MDD or MAF (Army types).

BCD	††M72 7AS	Automatic Timing Unit. (B.T.H.)

††**Note.**—The "Tuffnol" gear for the timing unit is not supplied separately. In the event of a gear only being needed return the Unit to the B.T.H. Co., Ltd., Alma Street, Coventry.

Not shown	M72/2	Magneto gear centre—for models with hand controlled ignition only.
Not shown	M221	Extractor plate for magneto gear—for M72/2.
Not shown	M223	Bolt—for M72/2. 3 off.
Not shown	M218	Extractor nut—for M72/2.
BCE	M241	Return spring for Auto Timing unit. (B.T.H.)
BCF	M12/2	Cam wheel bush.
BCG	M17	Cam.
Not shown	*M202	Bush for intermediate gear M33 or M33/2.

*In the event of an early type gear with this bush requiring a new bush it is advisable to fit bush M202/2 and replace the old intermediate gear spindle with the later type M200/2AS, discarding the distance piece M201.

Not shown	M202/2	Bush for intermediate gear. Used up to Engines M1724 and MAC1611 only.
BCH	M202 3	Intermediate gear bush. From Engines M1725 and MAC1612 to MAC15522, and on all Engines with serial letters MDD or MAF.
	M202 4	Intermediate gear bush—from Eng. No. MAC 15523.
—	M201	Distance piece for intermediate gear spindle. Used with M200 only.
BCI	M206	Oil pump—worm, single start. To Eng. MAC 15443.
	M206 2	Oil pump—worm, two start. From Eng. MAC15444.
BCK	SL56 32	Nut for mainshaft—left-hand thread. Securing M206.
BCL	K127	Tongued washer for mainshaft.

ENGINE SECTION—continued.

OIL PUMP ASSEMBLY GROUP †

†A modified oil pump (which is interchangeable as an assembly) was fitted first on MOV Model Eng. No. MOV 6251 and on MAC Model MAC 10149. The modification consists of the reduction of the spindle diameter to .436″ and the corresponding reduction of the bore diameter in the pump cover to suit. In addition the width of the two feed gears is increased from .249″ to .311″ The later pump body and cover M78/2AS may therefore be used for early machines if the spindle M80/2 and gear M82 are also fitted.

Illustration Ref.	Part No.	Description.
Not shown	MAS 47	Oil pump assembly.
Not shown	M78/AS	Oil pump body and cover.
Not shown	M80	Oil pump spindle. .561″ dia. spindle.
BCM	M78/2AS	Oil pump body and cover.
BCN	M80/2	Oil pump spindle. .436″ dia. spindle.
BCO	K81	Oil pump gear (Return—loose—wide).
BCP	M82	Oil pump gear (Feed—loose—narrow). .311″ wide.
Not shown	K82	Oil pump gear (Feed—loose—wide). .249″ wide.
BCQ	K83	Oil pump gear (Return—fixed—wide).
BCR	K98	Fixed spindle.
BCS	M217	Oil pump driven gear, to Eng. No. MAC15443.
	M217/2	Oil pump driven gear. From Eng. No. MAC15444.
BCT	M207	Oil pump base plate.
BCU	M97	Screw. Pump body and cover to base plate.
BAM	K55	Screw. Base plate to crankcase.
BCV	M226	Joint washer for pump base plate.

ENGINE SECTION—continued.

SHOCK ABSORBER AND SPROCKET GROUP.

Not shown	M89	Engine sprocket. 5 lobe type. MOV model. Obsolete, use M89/4 with M91/3.
Not shown	M89/3	Engine sprocket. 5 lobe type. MAC model. Obsolete, use M89/5 with M91/3.
BCW	M89/4	Engine sprocket. 3 lobe type. MOV model.
BCX	M89/5	Engine sprocket. 3 lobe type. MAC model.
Not shown	M91	Shock absorber clutch. 5 lobe type. Obsolete. Replace with M91/3 and M89/4 or M89/5.
BCY	M91/3	Shock absorber clutch. 3 lobe type.
BCZ	M90	Spring for shock absorber.
BDA	E19/4	Pulley for dynamo drive.
BDB	E19/5	Flange for pulley.
BDC	M93	Nut for shock absorber.
BDD	SL6/67	Plain washer—between shock absorber nut and mainshaft.
BDE	SL71/1	Split pin for shock absorber nut.

ILLUSTRATION A2

ORDER BY PART NUMBERS—DO NOT QUOTE ILLUSTRATION REFERENCES.

FOR PART NUMBERS AND DESCRIPTIONS OF ITEMS
{ 1 to 40 see page 16
41 to 73 ,, ,, 17
74 to 93 ,, ,, 18 }

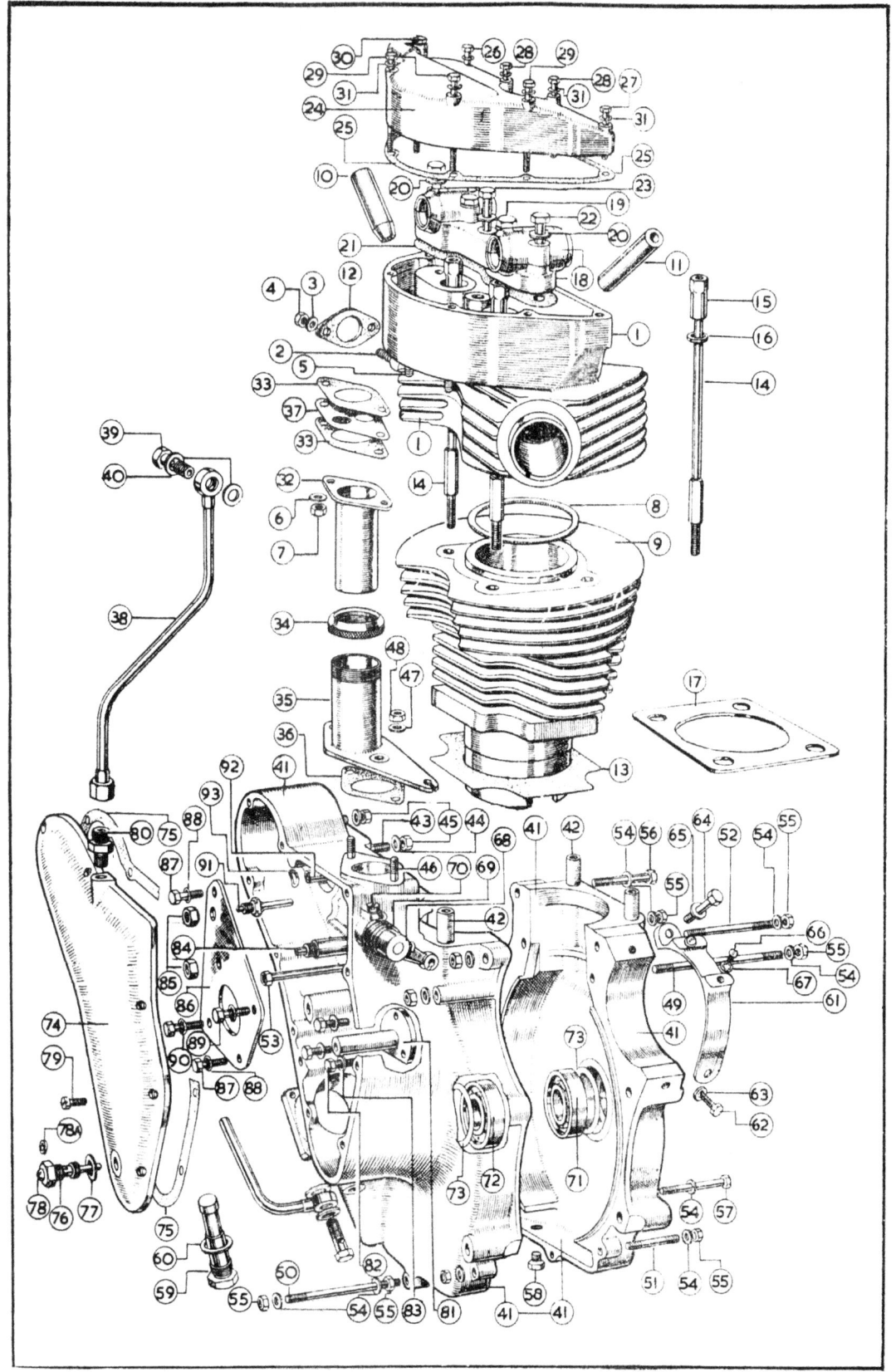

DO NOT OMIT THE ENGINE NUMBER—AND PREFIX LETTERS—FROM ORDER.

15

ENGINE SECTION—ALUMINIUM ALLOY HEAD TYPE (STARTING AT No. MAC 15982).
Cylinder Head and Cylinder Group—Illustrated on page 15.

Note.—Quote Part Numbers when ordering—NOT Illustration References.

Illustration Ref.	Part No.	Description.	
1	MAS32	Cylinder head assembly. Includes items marked thus §	1
2	§SL103/2	Cylinder head stud. Carburetter fixing. $\frac{5}{16}$" B.S.F. × $1\frac{3}{16}$"	2
3	SL6/40	Cylinder head stud washer. Carburetter fixing $\frac{5}{16}$"	2
4	SL56/38	Cylinder head stud nut. Carburetter fixing. $\frac{5}{16}$" B.S.F.	2
5	§SL102/11	Cylinder head stud. Push rod cover fixing. $\frac{1}{4}$" B.S.F. × $\frac{7}{8}$"	2
6	SL6/32	Cylinder head stud washer. Push rod cover fixing. $\frac{1}{4}$"	2
7	SL56/4	Cylinder head stud nut. Push rod cover fixing. $\frac{1}{4}$" B.S.F.	2
8	M220	Cylinder head gasket	1
9	M22/10	Cylinder barrel. Cast iron type	1
	M22/11	Cylinder barrel. Alum. Alloy jacketed type	1
10	§M3/6	Cylinder head inlet valve guide	1
11	§M3/4	Cylinder head exhaust valve guide	1
		§ Items included in Assembly MAS32.	
12	K180/3	Carburetter gasket—heat insulating	1
13	M70	Cylinder base gasket	1
14	M249	Cylinder holding down stud	4
15	M208	Cylinder stud nut	4
16	M251	Cylinder stud washer	4
17	M203	Compression plate .031" thick	As reqd
	M203/4	Compression plate .010" thick	As reqd
18	MAS17	Rocker bearing bracket assembly. Includes items marked thus *	1
19	*SL109/4	Rocker bearing cap bolt. $\frac{5}{16}$" B.S.F. × 1"	2
20	*SL6/40	Rocker bearing cap and bracket bolt washer	5
		* Included in Assembly MAS17 (2 off SL6/40)	
21	M250	Rocker bearing bracket gasket	1
22	SL109/7	Rocker bearing bracket bolt, $\frac{5}{16}$" B.S.F. × $2\frac{1}{16}$"	2
23	SL109/8	Rocker bearing bracket bolt, $\frac{5}{16}$" B.S.F. × $1\frac{7}{16}$"	1
24	M247/2	Rocker cover	1
25	M256	Rocker cover gasket	1
26	SL107/3	Rocker cover bolt. 2BA × $1\frac{1}{8}$"	1
27	SL107/6	Rocker cover bolt. 2BA × $1\frac{5}{8}$"	1
28	SL107/7	Rocker cover bolt. 2BA × $1\frac{15}{16}$"	2
29	SL107/8	Rocker cover bolt. 2BA × $2\frac{1}{4}$"	3
30	SL107/9	Rocker cover bolt. 2BA × $2\frac{11}{16}$"	1
31	LE366	Rocker cover bolt lockwasher, $\frac{3}{16}$"	8

ENGINE SECTION—Continued.
PUSH ROD COVER AND ROCKER OIL PIPE GROUP.
Illustrated on page 15.

32	M50AS	Push rod cover assembly—Top	1
33	M120	Push rod cover flange gasket—Top	2
34	M52	Push rod cover gland nut	1
35	M50/2AS	Push rod cover assembly—Bottom	1
36	M120/2	Push rod cover flange gasket—Bottom	1
37	M234	Push rod guide plate	1
38	MAS18	Rocker oil pipe assembly	1
39	M214	Rocker oil-pipe hollow bolt	1
40	A37	Oil-pipe hollow bolt gasket	2

ENGINE SECTION—Continued.
CRANKCASE GROUP. Illustrated on page 15.

Illustration Ref.	Part No.	Description.	
41	M43/44/8	Crankcase assembly. Two halves with items marked thus †	1
42	†M56/2	Crankcase stud. Cylinder base	4
43	†SL31/3	Crankcase stud. Magneto fixing. $\frac{5}{16}''$ 18 × 18T × $1\frac{11}{16}''$	3
44	SL6/40	Crankcase stud washer. Magneto fixing, $\frac{5}{16}''$	3
45	SL56/13	Crankcase stud nut. Magneto fixing. $\frac{5}{16}''$ 18T	3
46	†SL30/21	Crankcase stud. Push rod cover fixing. $\frac{1}{4}''$ B.S.F. × $\frac{13}{16}''$	2
47	SL6/32	Crankcase stud washer. Push rod cover fixing, $\frac{1}{4}''$	2
48	SL56/4	Crankcase stud nut. Push rod cover fixing, $\frac{1}{4}''$	2
49	†SL30/1	Crankcase stud. Through crankcase. $\frac{1}{4}''$ B.S.F. × $4\frac{1}{4}''$	1
50	†SL30/2	Crankcase stud. Through crankcase. $\frac{1}{4}''$ B.S.F. × $3\frac{1}{2}''$	1
51	SL30/14	Crankcase stud. Through crankcase. $\frac{1}{4}''$ B.S.F. × $1\frac{3}{4}''$	1
52	†SL30/23	Crankcase stud. Through crankcase. $\frac{1}{4}''$ B.S.F. × $2\frac{5}{8}''$	1
53	SL30/24	Crankcase stud. Through crankcase. $\frac{1}{4}''$ B.S.F. × $4\frac{1}{16}''$	1
54	SL6/32	Crankcase stud and bolt washer	11
55	†SL56/4	Crankcase stud nut	10
		† Included in assembly M43/44/8. (8 off SL56/4, 7 off SL6/32).	
56	SL8/11	Crankcase bolt, $\frac{1}{4}''$ 20T × $1\frac{1}{2}''$	1
57	SL8/24	Crankcase bolt, $\frac{1}{4}''$ 20T × $2''$	1
58	B38	Crankcase drain-plug, $\frac{1}{8}''$ B.S.P.	1
59	K246/5	Crankcase filter plug	1
60	KA115	Crankcase filter plug gasket	1
61	MAS44/2	Dynamo strap assembly	1
62	SL8/2	Dynamo strap bolt, $\frac{1}{4}''$ 20T × $\frac{9}{16}''$	1
63	SL6/32	Dynamo strap bolt washer, $\frac{1}{4}''$	1
64	SL9/21	Dynamo strap clamp bolt, $\frac{5}{16}''$ B.S.F. × $1\frac{1}{8}''$	1
65	SL6/40	Dynamo strap clamp bolt washer, $\frac{5}{16}''$	1
66	SL80/21	Voltage control box screw, 2BA × $\frac{1}{4}''$	2
67	LE366	Voltage control box lockwasher, $\frac{3}{16}''$	2
68	M11	Exhaust valve lifter lever	1
69	M155/2	Exhaust valve lifter lever spring	1
70	K76	Exhaust valve lifter lever screw	1
—	M261	Exhaust valve lifter lever oil seal	1

ENGINE SECTION—Continued.
CRANKCASE BEARING GROUP. Illustrated on page 15.

Illustration Ref.	Part No.	Description.	
71	K87/2	Driving shaft roller bearing	1
72	K87	Timing shaft ball bearing	1
73	K174	Timing or driving side bearing shim. .005" thick	As reqd.
	K1174/2	Timing or driving side bearing shim. .002" thick	As reqd.
	K174/3	Timing or driving side bearing shim. .010" thick	As reqd.

ENGINE SECTION—Continued.

TIMING COVER, TIMING SPINDLE, AND STEADY PLATE GROUP. Illustrated on page 15.

Illustration Ref.	Part No.	Description.	
74	M45/7	Timing cover	1
75	M68	Timing cover gasket	1
76	M212	Timing cover oil jet	1
77	A37/2	Timing cover oil jet gasket	1
78	SL80/22	Timing cover oil jet screw—2BA $\times \frac{3}{8}''$	1
78a	A37/6	Timing cover oil jet screw gasket	1
79	K55	Timing cover fixing screw	10
80	K119	Timing cover oil union, $\frac{1}{8}'' \times \frac{1}{4}''$ B.S.P.	1
81	M200/4	Intermediate gear spindle	1
82	SL8/5	Intermediate gear spindle bolt, $\frac{1}{4}''$ B.S.F. $\times \frac{3}{4}''$	3
83	SL6/32	Intermediate gear spindle washer, $\frac{1}{4}''$	3
84	M15/2	Cam wheel spindle	1
85	M244	Camwheel spindle and steady plate oil jet nut	2
86	M199/2	Timing gear steady plate	1
87	M210	Steady plate bolt, $\frac{1}{4}''$	2
88	LE367	Steady plate lockwasher, $\frac{1}{4}''$	2
89	M211	Steady plate bolt, $\frac{5}{16}''$	2
90	LE368	Steady plate lockwasher, $\frac{5}{16}''$	2
91	M259	Steady plate oil jet. Cam feed	1
92	M10	Bottom rocker spindle	1
93	M216	Bottom rocker thrust washer	1

ILLUSTRATION B2

ORDER BY PART NUMBERS—**DO NOT** QUOTE ILLUSTRATION REFERENCES.

FOR PART NUMBERS AND DESCRIPTIONS OF ITEMS { 1 to 21 see page 20 / 22 to 57 ,, ,, 21 / 58 to 67 ,, ,, 22

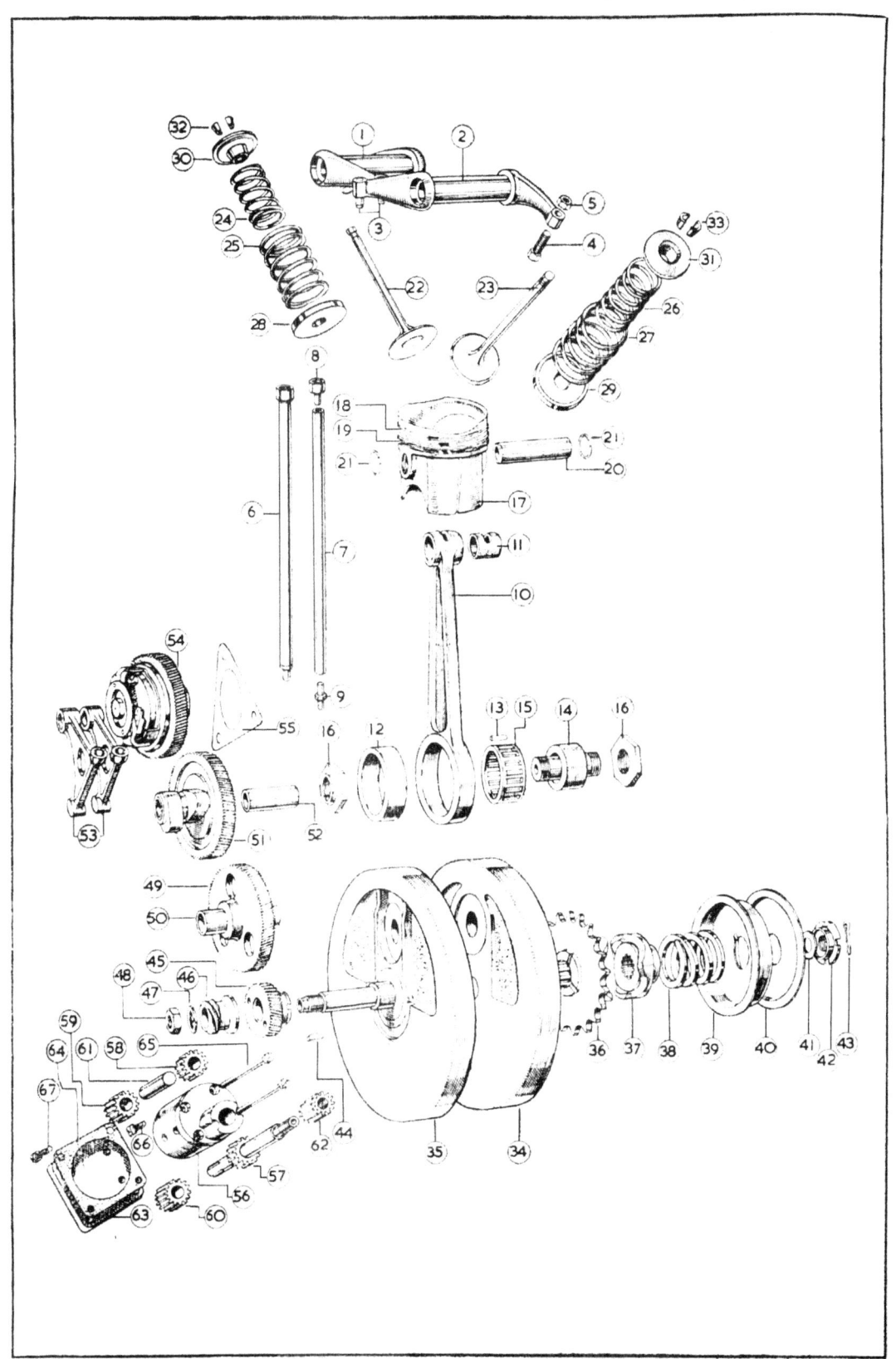

PLEASE SEE THAT THE FORWARDING ADDRESS ON ORDER IS CLEAR.

ENGINE SECTION—Continued.

ROCKER ASSEMBLY AND PUSH ROD GROUP. Illustrated on page 19.

Note.—Quote Part Numbers when ordering—NOT Illustration References.

Illustration Ref.	Part No.	Description.	
1	M9/4AS	Rocker assembly—Inlet. Includes item marked thus §	1
2	M9/2AS	Rocker assembly—Exhaust. Includes item marked thus §	1
3	§M41	Rocker end	2
4	M39	Rocker tappet	2
5	SL56/33	Rocker tappet locknut. $\frac{5}{16}$" 26T. .447" hexagon	2
6	M196/6AS	Push rod assembly. Assembly of items marked thus *	2
7	*M196/6	Push rod	2
8	*M194	Push rod end—Top	2
9	*M195	Push rod end—Bottom	2

ENGINE SECTION—Continued.

CONNECTING ROD, BIG END BEARING, AND PISTON GROUP.

10	M28/2ASM	Connecting rod assembly. Includes small end bush	1
11	M29	Connecting rod small end bush	1
12	K190	Connecting rod outer race	1
13	K191	Connecting rod roller. Standard diameter	16
	K191/3	Connecting rod roller, .0004" oversize	As reqd.
	K191/4	Connecting rod roller, .0002" oversize	As reqd.
14	K192AS	Crankpin assembly. Includes nuts	1
15	K193	Connecting rod roller cage	1
16	K62/4	Crankpin nut. Included in assembly K192AS	2
17 ‡	M27/4	Piston. Standard diameter	1
	M27/5	Piston. +.020" diameter	As reqd.
	M27/6	Piston. +.040" diameter	As reqd.
	M27/7	Piston. +.060" diameter	As reqd.
18	SL3/18	Piston ring—compression. Standard diameter	2
	SL3/20	Piston ring—compression. +.020" diam.	As reqd.
	SL3/33	Piston ring—compression. +.040" diam.	As reqd.
	SL3/51	Piston ring—compression. +.060" diam.	As reqd.
19	SL3/53	Piston ring—scraper. Standard diameter	1
	SL3/54	Piston ring—scraper. +.020" diameter	As reqd.
	SL3/55	Piston ring—scraper. +.040" diameter	As reqd.
	SL3/56	Piston ring—scraper. +.060" diameter	As reqd.
20	M31	Gudgeon pin. Standard diameter	1
	M31/2	Gudgeon pin. +.001" diameter	As reqd.
21	K149	Gudgeon pin circlip	2

‡ Pistons with rings, gudgeon pin and circlips may be ordered assembled as follows:—

M27/4AS	Piston assembly. Standard diameter	As reqd.
M27/5AS	Piston assembly. +.020" diameter	As reqd.
M27/6AS	Piston assembly. +.040" diameter	As reqd.
M27/7AS	Piston assembly. +.060" diameter	As reqd.

ENGINE SECTION—Continued.
VALVE, VALVE SPRING, COLLAR AND COTTER GROUP.

Illustration Ref.	Part No.	Description.	
22	M2/8	Valve—inlet	1
23	M2/8	Valve—exhaust	1
24	K7/6	Valve spring. Inner, inlet ⎫ Supplied together	1
25	K6/7	Valve spring. Outer inlet ⎭	1
26	K7/6	Valve spring. Inner, exhaust ⎫ Supplied together	1
27	K6/7	Valve spring. Outer, exhaust ⎭	1
28	M38/3	Valve spring washer—bottom. Inlet	1
29	M38/3	Valve spring washer—bottom. Exhaust	1
30	K4/5	Valve spring collar—Inlet	1
31	K4/5	Valve spring collar—Exhaust	1
32	K5/4	Valve spring cotter—Inlet	1
33	K5/4	Valve spring cotter—Exhaust	1

ENGINE SECTION—Continued.
FLYWHEEL, PUMP DRIVE, AND SHOCK ABSORBER GROUP.

34	M25/4AS	Flywheel and shaft assembly. Driving side	1
35	M23/4AS	Flywheel and shaft assembly. Timing side	1
36	M89/5	Engine sprocket. 22T.	1
37	M91/3	Shock absorber clutch	1
38	M90	Shock absorber spring	1
39	E19/4	Dynamo driving pulley	1
40	E19/5	Dynamo driving pulley flange	1
41	SL6/67	Mainshaft plain washer	1
42	M93	Shock absorber spring collar	1
43	SL71/7	Split cotter. $\frac{3}{32}'' \times 1''$	1
44	K36/2	Timing shaft key	1
45	M32/4	Timing pinion	1
46	M206/2	Oil pump driving worm	1
47	K127	Timing shaft washer	1
48	SL56/32	Timing shaft nut. $\frac{1}{2}''$ 20 L.H.T.	1

ENGINE SECTION—Continued.
TIMING GEAR, TIMING GEAR BUSH, AND OIL PUMP GROUP.

49	MAS1	Intermediate gear assembly. Includes bush M202/4	1
50	M202/4	Intermediate gear bush. Included in assembly MAS1	1
51	MAS19/2	Camwheel assembly. Includes bush M12/2	1
52	M12/2	Camwheel bush. Included in assembly MAS19/2	1
53	M9/3	Bottom rocker	2
54	⎰ M72/7AS	Automatic timing unit. B.T.U. Type YE5	1
	⎱ MAS40	Automatic timing unit. Lucas	1
55	M260	Magneto flange gasket	1
56 ‡	⎰ M78/2AS	Oil pump body and cover assembly. For .316" wide feed gears	1
	⎱ MAS98/2	Oil pump body and cover assembly. For .186" wide feed gears	1
57 ‡	⎰ M80/2	Oil pump spindle. For .311" wide feed gear	1
	⎱ M80/4	Oil pump spindle. For .186" wide feed gear	1

Illustration Ref.	Part No.	Description	

Engine Section—continued.

58	‡ ⎰ M82	Oil pump feed gear. .311″ wide	1
	⎱ M82 2	Oil pump feed gear. .186″ wide	1
59	‡K81	Oil pump return gear—loose	1
60	‡K83	Oil pump return gear—fixed	1
61	K98	Oil pump fixed spindle	1
62	‡M217 2	Oil pump driven gear	1
63	‡M207	Oil pump base plate	1
64	M226	Oil pump base plate gasket	1
65	‡M97	Oil pump fixing screw	4
		‡Oil pump assemblies are available including parts marked ‡ as :	
	MAS47	Oil pump assembly. (With .311″ width feed gears)	
	MAS47 3	Oil pump assembly. (With .186″ width feed gears) As assemblies these are interchangeable.	
66	K55	Oil pump fixing screw. Short	3
67	K95	Oil pump fixing screw. Long. Inner front corner	1

ILLUSTRATION C.

ORDER BY PART NUMBERS—DO NOT QUOTE ILLUSTRATION REFERENCES.
FOR PART NUMBERS AND DESCRIPTION OF ITEMS SEE PAGES 25 TO 28.

THE LETTERS PREFIXING THE ENGINE NUMBER ARE ESSENTIAL TO IDENTIFY
THE TYPE OF MACHINE.

ILLUSTRATION D.

ORDER BY PART NUMBERS—DO NOT QUOTE ILLUSTRATION REFERENCES.
FOR PART NUMBERS AND DESCRIPTIONS OF ITEMS SEE PAGES 25 TO 28.

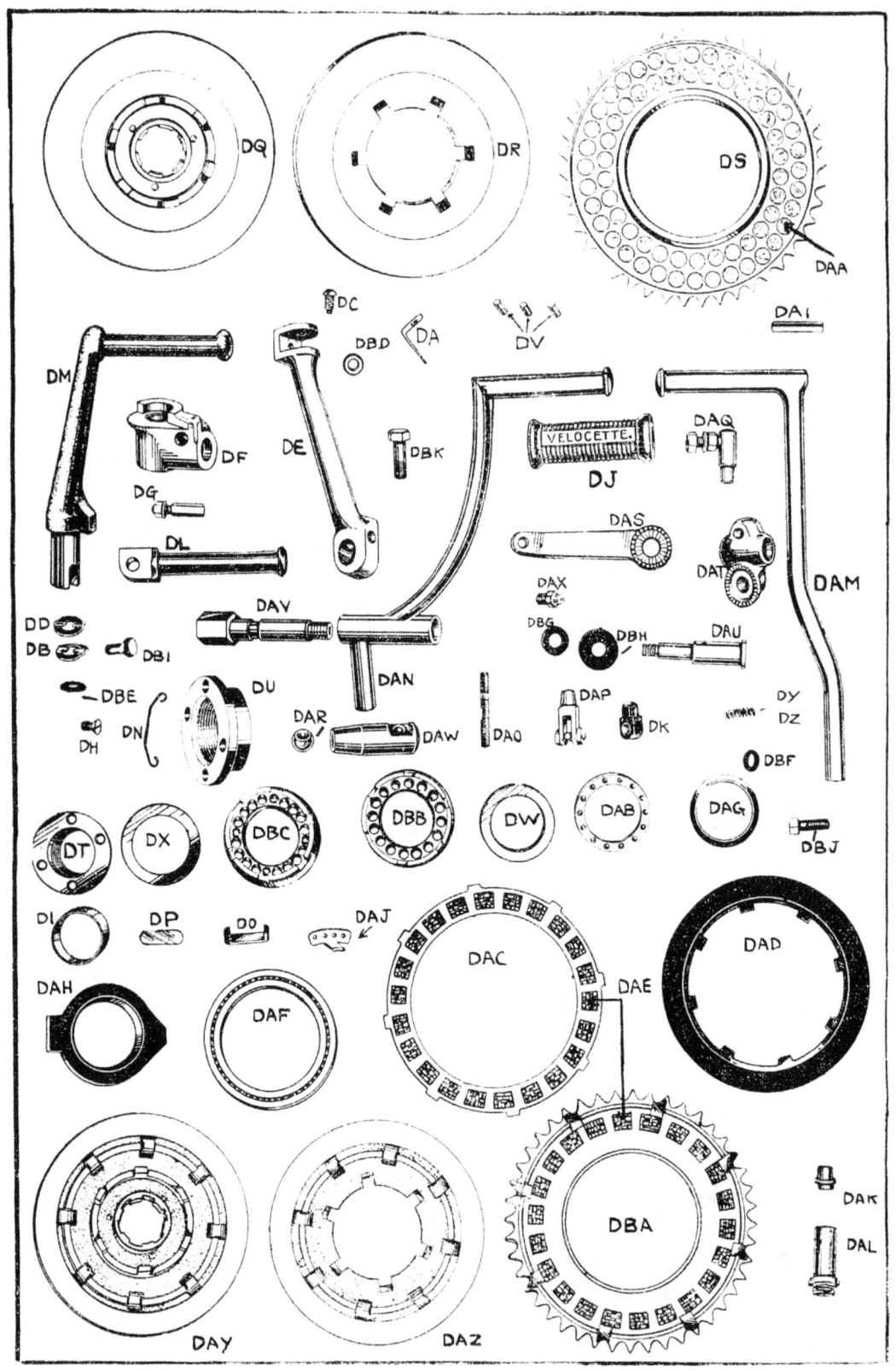

PLEASE WRITE YOUR ORDER CLEARLY—PARTICULARLY YOUR NAME AND ADDRESS.

GEARBOX AND CLUTCH SECTION.
See Illustrations " C " and " D."

Illustration Ref.	Part No.	Description.
DA	A254	Spring for footstarter swivelling footpiece Pre 1946 models only.
DB	A254/2	Spring washer for swivelling footstarter crank. From 1946.
DC	A257	Hammer drive screw for A254.
DD	A278	Clickwasher for swivelling footstarter crank. From 1946.
CA	B1/8	Gearbox housing.
CB	B2/4	End cover. To Eng. No. MAC15791 only.
	B2/9	End cover. From Eng. No. MAC15792.
CC	B3	Cap for gearshaft ballrace in end cover.
CD	B5/4	Gearshaft.
CE	B6/2AS	Sleeve gear, bushed. 16 teeth.
CF	B7/4	Bush for sleeve gear.
CG	B9/4AS	First gear, driven, and bush, on gearshaft. 26 teeth.
CH	B10/6	Layshaft.
DE	B12/2	Crank for footstarter. Pre-1946 models only.
DF	B12/3	Lug for swivelling footstarter crank. From 1946.
DG	LE242	Cotter.
CI	B22	Ballrace for sleeve-gear.
CJ	B22/3	Ballrace for layshaft.
CK	B23	Ballrace for gearshaft.
CL	B31/2	Oil retaining shim for B22. 2 off.
DH	B34	Screw for sleeve gear nut locking plate and wire clip. 3 off.
DI	B35/2	Distance piece for sleeve gear.
CM	B38	Oil drain plug.
CN	B38/2	Oil level plug. To Eng. No. MAC15791.
	B38/4	Oil level plug. From Eng. No. MAC15792.
CO	B39/26	Retaining ring for sleeve gear ballrace.
CP	B54/4	Half clip. Gearbox to frame tube. 2 off.
DJ	B60/5	Rubber for footstarter and gear control pedal. 2 off.
DK	B69	Knuckle joint for gear control rod—pre-1946 models only.
CQ	B75	Bush for first gear.
CR	B78	Double sliding gear, driven, on gearshaft. 22 and 19 teeth.
CS	B86	Layshaft gear, driven. 28 teeth.
CT	B87	Ratchet gear, driver on layshaft. 18 teeth.
CU	B88AS	Second gear, bushed. Driver, on layshaft. 22 teeth.
CV	B89AS	Third gear, bushed. Driver, on layshaft. 25 teeth.
CW	B90	Rod for selector fork. To MAC15791 2 off.
	B90/2	Selector fork rod. From Eng. No. MAC15792.
CX	B91	Bush for second or third speed layshaft gear. 2 off.
	B96	Gearbox end cap sleeve. From MAC15792.
CY	BK4	Housing for footstarter ratchet.
CZ	BK14	Ratchet for footstarter.
DL	BK18	Swivelling footpiece. Pre-1946.
DM	BK18/2	Swivelling footstarter crank. From 1946.
CAA	BK19	Return spring for footstarter.

Illustration Ref.	Part No.	Description.	

Gearbox and Clutch Section—continued.

Illustration Ref.	Part No.	Description.	
CAB	BK19/2	Engaging spring for footstarter.	
CAC	MAS43	Selector fork. Includes BK32.	2 off.
CAE	BK32	Pin for selector fork.	2 off.
CAD	BK33	Oil thrower for sleeve gear.	
CAF	BK36/2	Bush for striking lever spindle in housing.	
CAG	BK40	Oil filler plug.	
CAH	BK43/2	Joint washer for end cover.	
CAI	BK50	Slotted nut. Sprocket to gearshaft.	
DN	BK52	Wire clip for thrust cup.	
CAJ	BK64/2	Pivot for camplate.	
CAK	BK65/3	Outside striking lever, with threaded end. Pre-1946 models.	
CAL	BK65/4	Outside striking lever, plain end. From 1946.	
CAM	BK66	Indexing pawl.	
CAN	BK68	Spring for indexing pawl.	
DO	BK70	Bearing for clutch thrust cup.	
CAO	BK73/2	Anchor pin for footstarter return spring.	
CAP	BK77	Sliding dog on layshaft.	
CAQ	BK80/2	Camplate.	
CAR	BK81/2	Gear striker.	
CAS	BK82	Thrust disc for layshaft in footstarter ratchet.	
CAT	BK83	Pivot for indexing pawl.	
CAU	BK84	Cap for layshaft ballrace in housing.	
CAV	BK85/2	Floating bush for layshaft.	
CAW	BK96	Shim for camplate pivot.	As required.
DP	BK97	Shim for thrust cup bearing.	As required.
CAX	BK98	Gear operating ratchet in camplate.	
CAY	BK99	Centralising lever.	
CAZ	BK100/2	Pivot for centralising lever.	
CBA	BK101	Spring for centralising lever.	
CBB	BK102	Sleeve for centralising lever pivot.	
CBC	BK103	Shim for centralising lever pivot. As required.	
DQ	C1/3	Back plate for clutch. Used on MAC to 1940 only and on all MOV models.	
DR	C2/2	Front plate for clutch. Used on MAC to 1940 only and on all MOV models.	
DS	C3/3AS	Chain wheel with cork inserts. Used on MAC to 1940 only and on all MOV models.	
DT	C5	Sleeve gear nut. Used on MAC to 1940 only and on all MOV models.	
DU	C5/25	Sleeve gear nut. Used on all MAC models after 1940.	
DV	C6/2	Thrust pin for back plate.	3 off.
DW	C7/26	Plain thrust ring.	
DX	C8	Shim for sleeve gear nut—between flange of nut and springs.	1 off.
DY	C12	Clutch spring. Used on MAC to 1941 only, and on all MOV models.	16 off.
DZ	C12/3	Clutch spring. Used on all MAC models after 1940.	16 off.
DAA	C13	Cork insert for chain wheel. Used on MAC to 1940 only, and on all MOV models.	16 off.
DAB	MAS57	Thrust bearing.	
DAC	C23AS	Clutch plate with ferodo inserts. Used on all MAC models after 1940.	2 off.
DAD	C24	Steel clutch plate. Used on all models after 1940.	2 off.

Illustration Ref.	Part No.	Description.

Gearbox and Clutch Section—continued.

Illustration Ref.	Part No.	Description.
DAE	C25	Ferodo clutch insert. Used on all MAC models after 1940. 66 off.
DAF	C26AS	Ballrace for clutch chain wheel.
DAG	C28	Spherical thrust washer.
DAH	C29/26	Thrust Cup.
DAI	C30	Thrust pin, long, in housing. 1 off.
CBD	C31/3	Clutch operating lever, in gearbox.
DAJ	C32	Locking plate for C5/25.
DAK	CK14/2	Stop for clutch control cable casing.
DAL	CK21/2	Holder for cable stop.
CBE	CK34/3	Connecting piece—cable to operating lever.
CBF	F18/3	Chain adjuster draw bolt.
CBG	F218	Bolt for F18/3.
DAM	GC4/14AS	Gear control pedal. Pre-war type.
DAN	GC4/18AS	Gear control pedal. 1946 onwards.
DAO	GC8/13	Gear control rod. Pre-war type.
DAP	GC9/2	Jaw joint with pin and nut.
CBH	GC23/2	Gear operating pawl.
CBI	GC24/2	Spring for GC23/2.
DAQ	GC35	Ball joint for gear control rod. Pre-war type.
DAR	GC35/2	Swivel ball for outside striking lever. 1946 onwards.
DAS	GC41/5AS	Gear operating lever. Pre-war type.
CBJ	GC42/2	Bush for gear lever pivot. Pre-war type.
DAT	GC44	Clamp for gear control pedal. Pre-war type.
DAU	GC45	Pivot for gear lever. Pre-war type.
DAV	GC45/2	Pivot for gear control pedal. 1946 onwards.
DAW	GC48	Sleeve for gear control pedal. 1946 onwards.
CBK	K191	Thrust pin for layshaft—in footstarter ratchet. 3 off.
DAX	KA46	Grease nipple for B12/3 and GC45/2. 2 off.
DAY	KC1/25	Back plate for clutch. Only on MAC from 1941.
DAZ	KC2/25	Front plate for clutch. Only on MAC from 1941.
DBA	KC3/25AS	Clutch chain wheel with inserts. Only on MAC from 1941.
DBB	KC40AS	Clutch spring holder and spacer. Used on MAC to 1941 only and on all MOV models.
DBC	KC40/3AS	Clutch spring holder and spacer. Only on MAC model from 1941.
BBS	LE367	Shakeproof washers $\frac{1}{4}''$ for end cover bolts. 6 off.
CBL	S32	Pin. Cable connecting piece to clutch operating lever.
CBM	SL6/32	Plain washer $\frac{1}{4}''$ for SL8/13.
DBD	SL6/32	Plain washer $\frac{1}{4}''$ for hammer drive screw A257.
DBE	SL6/39	Plain washer $\frac{5}{16}''$ for bottom of swivelling footstarter crank BK18/2.
DBF	SL6/41	Plain washer $\frac{5}{16}''$, for SL9/6.
DBG	SL6/50	Plain washer $\frac{3}{8}''$, for GC45 or GC45/2.
DBH	SL6/60	Plain washer for backing gear operating lever.
CBO	SL6/65	Plain washer, $\frac{1}{2}''$ between sprocket and sprocket nut on gearshaft.
CBP	SL8/13	Pivot bolt for C31/3.
	SL8/6	End cover bolt, $\frac{1}{4}''$ 20T. $\times 1\frac{3}{32}''$. For B29. 5 off.

Illustration Ref.	Part No.	Description

Gearbox and Clutch Section—continued.

	SL8/16	End cover bolt, $\frac{1}{4}''$ 20T. $\times 1''$. For B2/9 1 off.
CBQ	SL8/17	Bolt $\frac{1}{4}'' \times \frac{19}{32}''$. Top of end cover.
CBR	SL8/20	Bolt $\frac{1}{4}''$. End cover to gearbox. 4 off.
CBS	SL8/21	Bolt $\frac{1}{4}'' \times 1\frac{3}{4}''$. Bottom of end cover.
CBT	SL8/22	Bolt $\frac{1}{4}''$. Footstarter ratchet housing to end cover, and end cover to gearbox. 3 off.
DBI	SL9/3	Bolt $\frac{5}{16}''$. Bottom of swivelling footstarter crank BK18/2.
DBJ	SL9/6	Bolt $\frac{5}{16}''$. For gear lever clamp GC44.
DBK	SL11/15	Bolt $\frac{3}{8}''$. Swivelling footpiece BK18 to B12/2.
CBU	SL31/8	Stud $\frac{5}{16}''$. Gearbox housing to frame. 4 off.
CBV	SL56/4	Nut $\frac{1}{4}''$, for SL8/13, BK65/3, BK83. 2 off on 1946 models, 3 off to 1941.
CBW	SL56/6	Nut $\frac{5}{16}''$, for stud SL31/8. 4 off.
CBX	SL56/7	Nut $\frac{5}{16}''$, for outside striking lever.
CBY	SL56/8	Nut $\frac{3}{8}''$, for GC45/2 and BK100/2. 2 off.
CBZ	SL56/9	Nut $\frac{7}{16}''$, for F18/3. 2 off.
CCA	SL56/21	Nut, for gearshaft to secure gearshaft ballrace.
CCB	SL56/33	Nut $\frac{5}{16}''$, for B90. 2 off.
CCC	SL71/1	Split pin for BK50.
CCD	SL71/2	Split pin for S32.
CCE	SL71/3	Split pin for F218.
CCF	SL80/15	Screw for bottom of end cover. Superseded on 1946 models by SL8/21.
CCG	SL91/4	Gearbox sprocket, on mainshaft, 19 teeth, MOV and MAC models.
CCH	SL91/7	Gearbox sprocket, on mainshaft, 22 teeth. Used up to Engine MAC 973 only.

ILLUSTRATION E.

ORDER BY PART NUMBERS—DO NOT QUOTE ILLUSTRATION REFERENCES.
FOR PART NUMBERS AND DESCRIPTIONS OF ITEMS ON THIS PAGE SEE PAGE 30.

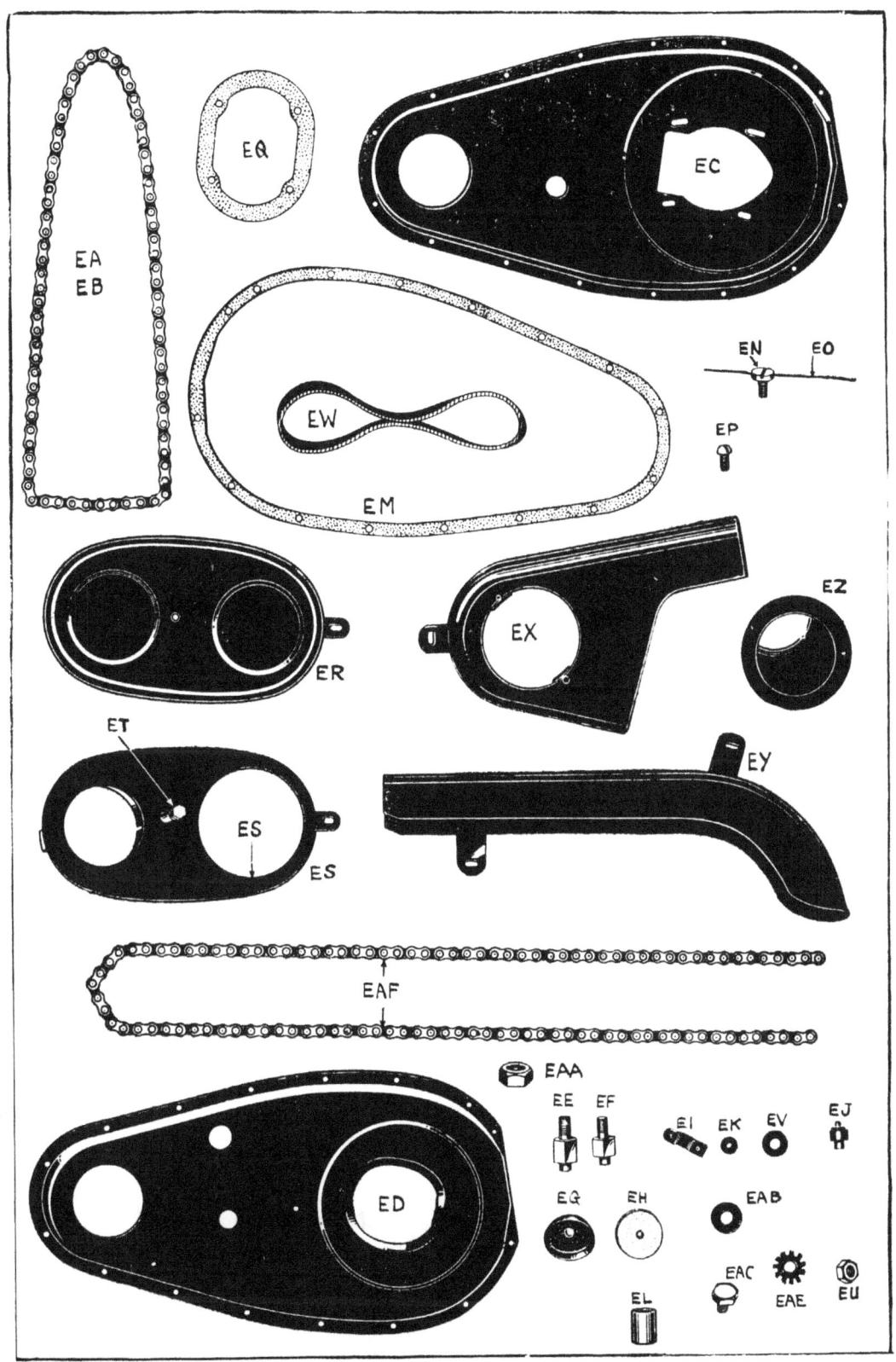

HAVE YOU QUOTED THE ENGINE NUMBER ON YOUR ORDER?

TRANSMISSION SECTION—CHAINS AND COVERS GROUP.
See Illustration "E" Page 29.

Illustration Ref.	Part No.	Description.
EA	A27/6	Primary chain. MAC model except early models to Engine MAC973. 75 Pitches
EB	KA27	Primary chain. MOV model and on MAC up to Engine MAC973 only. 74 Pitches
EC	F45/2AS	Cover for primary chain, inner half. To Eng. No. MAC15627.
ED	F46/2AS	Cover for primary chain, outer half. To Eng. No. MAC15627.
	F46/4AS	*Primary chain cover assembly (outer)
	F45/4	*Primary chain cover (inner).
	MAS16	*Primary chain cover strap assembly. Retaining joint moulding.
	SL107/4	*Primary chain cover strap fixing pin 2BA × 1"
	F284	*Primary chain cover joint moulding. *Used from Engine No. MAC. 15628.
EE	FK206	Stud. Rear chain guard to primary cover.
EF	FK207	Stud. Dynamo belt cover to primary cover.
EG	T71/19K	Inspection cap.
EH	KA244	Washer for inspection cap.
EI	T72/19	Clip for inspection cap.
EJ	T95/2	Stud for clip T72/19.
EK	SL6/8	Plain washer for T95/2.
EL	FK205/2	Distance tube—inside and between halves of primary cover.
EM	KA179	Joint washer for primary cover.
EN	F201	Screws. Inner half primary cover to gearbox. 4 off.
EO	FK210	Locking wire for F201. 2 off.
EP	SL80/22	Screws for primary cover joint, 16 off, and for cover KA261. 2 off.
EQ	A179/3	Joint washer, primary cover (inner) to gearbox.

BELT DRIVE AND COVER GROUP.

ER	KA93/3AS	Belt cover, outer.
ES	KA93/6AS	Belt cover, inner.
ET	SL8/26	Bolt. Belt cover outer to inner cover.
EU	SL56/4	Nut. Belt covers to primary cover, and for SL8/26. 2 off.
EV	SL6/32	Plain washer for SL8/26 and FK207. 3 off.
EW	E16/2	Driving belt for dynamo.

Note.—The driven pulley on the dynamo is made by H. Miller & Co., Ltd., Aston Brook Street, Birmingham 6.

REAR CHAIN COVER GROUP.

EX	F60/7A	Cover for rear chain—front end.
EY	F60/7B	Cover for rear chain—rear end.
EZ	KA261	Cover for clutch adjustment opening.
EAA	SL56/6	Nut $\frac{5}{16}$", rear chain cover to primary cover.
EAB	SL6/40	Plain washer $\frac{5}{16}$", for FK206.
EAC	SL8/28	Bolt—rear chain cover to mudguard valance.
EAE	LE367	Shakeproof washer.
EAF	A28/4	Rear chain. 108 Pitches

ILLUSTRATION F.

ORDER BY PART NUMBERS—DO NOT QUOTE ILLUSTRATION REFERENCES.
FOR PART NUMBERS AND DESCRIPTIONS OF ITEMS ON THIS PAGE SEE PAGE 32.

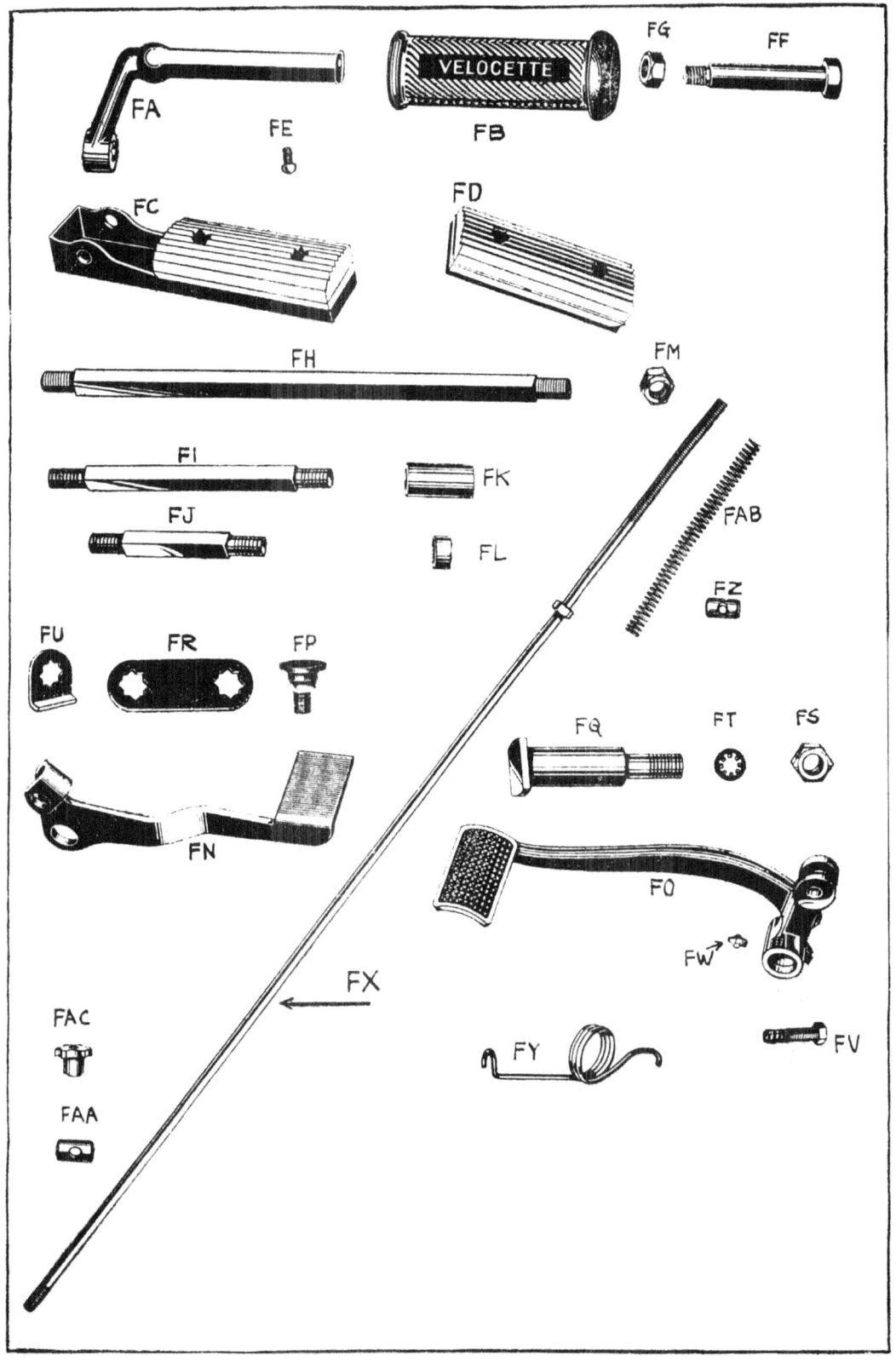

THE LETTERS PREFIXING THE ENGINE NUMBER ARE ESSENTIAL TO IDENTIFY
THE TYPE OF MACHINE.

FOOTREST AND REAR BRAKE CONTROL SECTION.
See Illustration " F " Page 31.

Illustration Ref.	Part No.	Description.
FA	F126/2	Footrest.
FB	KA76/2	Rubber for footrest.
FC	KA168	Pillion footrest. **Less rubber.**
FD	KA169/2	Rubber for pillion footrest.
FE	SL80/22	Screw. Pillion footrest rubber to footrest. 4 off.
FF	KA170	Pivot pin. Pillion footrest to frame.
FG	SL56/4	Nut for pivot pin.
EAE	LE367	Shakeproof washer for pivot pin nut. 2 off.
FH	FK23/2	Footrest square bar. For tubular base frames, to 1941 and from MAC15326.
FI	FK23/10	Footrest square bar. Right-hand side (long), with cradle lug frame, to Eng. No. MAC15325.
FJ	FK23/11	Footrest square bar. Left-hand side (short) with cradle lug frame, to Eng. No. MAC15325.
FK	SL60/4	Distance tube. Right-hand side. For use with FK23/2 or FK23/10.
FL	SL60/18	Distance tube. To 1941 only.
—	SL60/11	Dist. tube, left-hand, from Eng. No. MAC15326.
FM	SL56/9	Nut for square bar. 2 off per bar.
FN	F39/4	Brake pedal, for pre-1946 models. With tubular base frames only.
FO	F39/9	Brake pedal. From 1946.
—	F39/10	Brake pedal. From Eng. No. MAC15326.
FP	F130/7	Pivot for brake pedal. Pre-1946 models only with F39/4 pedal.
FQ	F130/10	Pivot for brake pedal. From 1946 with F39/9 pedal. To Eng. No. MAC15325.
FR	F195	Support for brake pedal pivot. Pre-1946 models only with F39/4 pedal.
FS	SL56/8	Nut 3/8", for pedal pivots F130/7 or F130/10.
FT	LE369	Shakeproof washer for SL56/8.
FU	F196	Brake pedal stop. Pre-1946 models only with F39/4 pedal. To Eng. No. MAC15325.
FV	SL8/13	Adjustable pedal stop bolt, for F39/9 only.
FG	SL56/4	Nut 1/4", for locking SL8/13.
	F196/3	Brake pedal stop. From Eng. No. MAC15326.
	SL109/5	Brake pedal stop bolt. From Eng. No. MAC15326.
	LE369	Brake pedal stop lockwasher. From Eng. No. MAC 15326.
FW	KA46	Grease nipple for brake pedal.
FX	SL30/37AS	Brake control rod.
FY	F233	Return spring for brake pedal for F39/9 only.
—	F233/4	Brake pedal spring. From Eng. No. MAC15326.
FZ	FK43	Trunnion, threaded. For brake pedal end of control rod.
FAA	FK43/2	Trunnion, plain hole. For remote end of control rod.
FAB	KS43/2	Spring for brake rod.
FAC	KS44	Adjusting nut for brake rod.

ILLUSTRATION G.

ORDER BY PART NUMBERS—DO NOT QUOTE ILLUSTRATION REFERENCES.
FOR PART NUMBERS AND DESCRIPTIONS OF ITEMS ON THIS PAGE SEE PAGES 34 AND 35.

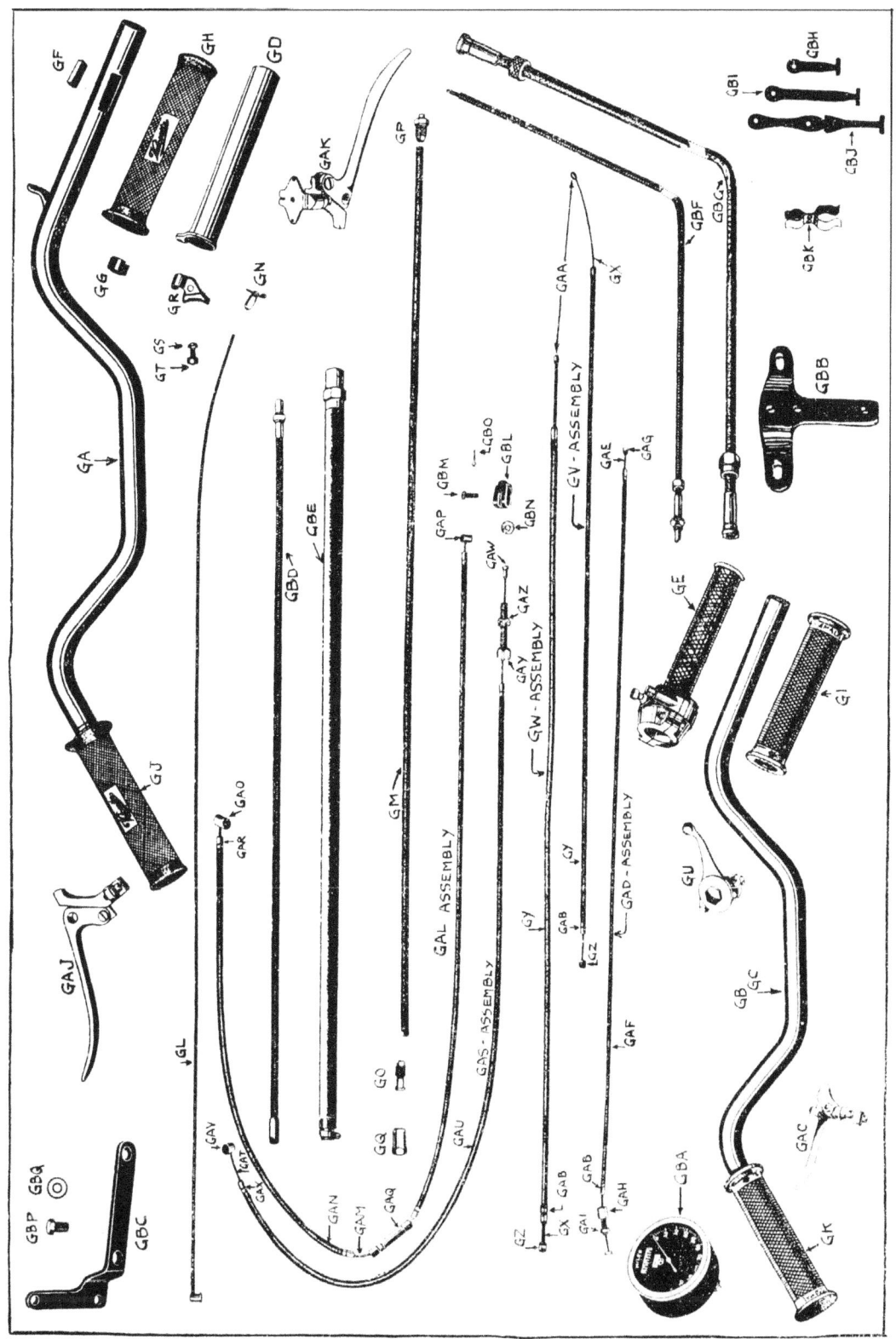

PLEASE SEE THAT THE FORWARDING ADDRESS ON ORDER IS CLEAR.

HANDLEBAR, CONTROL LEVER AND CONTROL CABLE SECTION. See Illustration "G" Page 33.

Illustration Ref.	Part No.	Description.
GA	FK61/4AS	Handlebar. To 1941 only. For machines with Velocette "push pull" throttle cable.
GB	F61/3	Handlebar. 1946/7 models. With Webb fork.
GC	FK61/8	Handlebar. For machines with telescopic forks.
GD	A211AS	Sleeve for Velocette twist grip. To 1941 only.
GE	A211/2	Amal twist grip assembly. Amal No. 16/117.
GF	A216	Friction pad, in handlebar, for Velocette twist grip. To 1941 only.
GG	A219	Spring for friction pad.
GH	A220	Twist grip rubber, for A211AS.
GI	A220/2	Twist grip rubber, for Amal twist grip.
GJ	A225	Dummy grip rubber, for FK61/4AS only.
GK	A225/2	Dummy grip rubber, for F61/3 and FK61/8 only.
GL	A234/9AS	Throttle cable, inner assembly. Velocette "push-pull" type.
GM	A235/6	Outer casing for A234/9AS.
GN	A255	(Amal No. 4-250/1) swivel joint for A234/9AS. Carburetter end.
GO	A222	Holding sleeve for A235/6—twist grip end.
GP	A223	Holding sleeve for A235/6—remote end.
GQ	A224	Contraction nuts for A222 and A223. 2 off.
GR	A213	Clip. A222 to handlebar.
GS	SL80/22	Screw. A213 to handlebar.
GT	SL56/2	Nut for SL80/22.
Not shown	A36/2	Control lever for ignition. Used only on early models.
GU	A36/3	Air control lever.
GV	A237/3AS	Air control cable and casing assembly. (Amal).
GW	A234/10AS	Throttle control cable and casing assembly. (Amal).
GAC	A72/3	Exhaust lifter trigger lever.
GAD	A125/4AS	Exhaust lifter control cable and casing assembly
GAH	C14	Adjuster for exhaust lifter cable.
GAI	SL56/3	Lock nut for C14.
GAJ	KC16/3	Clutch control lever, with plain clip.
GAK	KC16/4	Brake or clutch control lever, with platform clip for horn button.
GAL	KC17/7AS	Clutch control cable, casing, and adjuster assembly.
GAQ	KC39	Adjuster for clutch control cable.
GAS	W33/5AS	Brake cable casing, and adjuster assembly (for girder fork only).
GAS	W33/6AS	Brake cable, casing, and adjuster assembly (for telescopic fork).
Not shown	W50/2	Brake cable adjuster—on fork girder—for pre-1939 models only.
Not shown	W51/2	Lock nut for W50/2—for pre-1939 models only.
Not shown	W30/2	Adjuster body and nut, on fork girder—for pre-1939 models only.
Not shown	W53	Stop for A241 in W30/2 on fork girder—for pre-1939 models only.

Illustration Ref.	Part No.	Description.

Handlebar Section—continued.

GAY	W50/3	Brake cable adjuster on brake plate, from 1939.
GAZ	W51/3	Lock nut for W50/3, from 1939.
GBA	KA268/5	Speedometer (registering in miles per hour). If required to register in kilometres this must be stated when ordering.
GBB	KA269/3	Bracket for telescopic fork.
GBC	KA269/2	Bracket for girder fork.
GBD	KA270	Flexible inner driving cable for speedometer (up to 1941 only).
GBE	KA271	Flexible outer casing for KA270 (up to 1941 only).
GBF	KA270/2	Flexible inner driving cable for speedometer. For front wheel drive.
GBG	KA271/2	Flexible outer casing for KA270/2. For front wheel drive.
GBF	KA270/3	Flexible inner driving cable for speedometer. For rear wheel drive.
GBG	KA271/3	Flexible outer casing for KA270/3. For rear wheel drive.
Not shown	KA276	Bulb for speedometer.
Not shown	KA277	Bulb holder.
Not shown	KA278	Retaining ring for bulb holder.
GBH	A256/2	Cable clip (small).
GBI	A256/3	Cable clip (medium).
GBJ	A256/4	Cable clip (large).
GBK	KA288/2	Clip. Speedometer drive flex to fork girder.
GBL	FB54	Front brake cable shackle.
GBM	S32	Plain pin for FB54.
GBN	FB61	Felt washer for S32.
GBO	SL71/2	Split pin for S32.
GBP	SL9/3	Bolt. Speedometer bracket to fork.
GBQ	SL6/40	Washer for SL9/3

ILLUSTRATION H.

ORDER BY PART NUMBERS—DO NOT QUOTE ILLUSTRATION REFERENCES.
FOR PART NUMBERS AND DESCRIPTIONS OF ITEMS ON THIS PAGE SEE PAGES 37 TO 40.

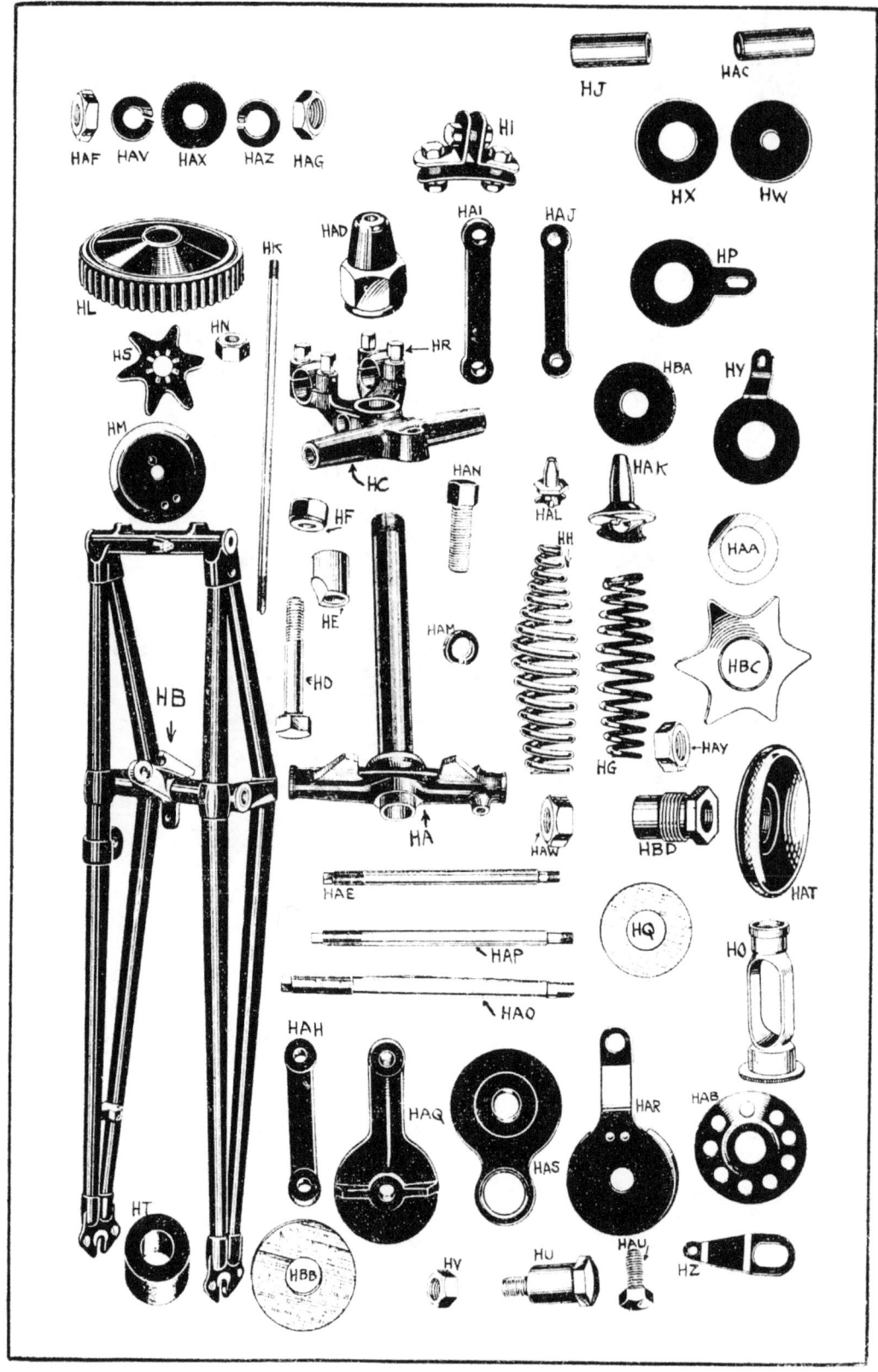

REFER TO NOTE ON PAGE 37 BEFORE ORDERING WEBB FORK PARTS.

FORK SECTION. "WEBB" LINK TYPE
See Illustration "H" Page 36.

Note.—Various modifications have been made to the "Webb" fork as fitted to MOV and MAC models from time to time, and attention is called to the following :—

During 1933 a few machines had forks with girders bushed with steel bushes, and the change over from steel to bronze bushes involved increasing the diameter of the bosses carrying the shock absorber adjuster sleeves on the girder. The original girder (2M) has been obsolete for some time, so that when replacing a steel bushed girder with a bronze bush one (2/2M) it will be essential also to order 78/2P (2 off) and 80/2P (2 off).

During 1937 the "single-side" type fork was introduced, having, as the term implies, a shock absorber on one side only, instead of on both sides as on the "double-side" type. The two types are referred to as "S/S" and "D/S" respectively.

For the 1939 season the fork girder was modified by the omission of the small lug previously fitted to carry the brake cable adjuster, and the cable adjuster transferred to the brake plate. Girders with the adjuster can be used as replacements for any S/S type fork, with $\frac{3}{8}''$ dia. top spindle bushes. The steering damper knob and rod were also altered, and the early type knob 14M is now obsolete. When replacing 14M use 14/2M knob with one each 13/2M and 16/2M.

Late in 1939 (for the un-completed 1940 season) a heavier type fork was used on MAC models only. This fork has a girder built from stouter tubes and the top spindle diameter increased to $\frac{7}{16}''$ in the bushes, and on both MOV and MAC machines the column was modified to use a different type of steering damper. The original type column was provided with a friction plate welded on.

On the resumption of the manufacture of civilian models the "heavy" type fork was used on both MOV and MAC models, but a limited number of 1946 machines have forks with links of equal length top and bottom ($3\frac{7}{8}''$ centres) and a fork spring differing in shape from previous types. The spring 8/2M is interchangeable with 8M if used with its appropriate top fixing lug 66/2P.

During 1946 the pre-war type linkage was reverted to namely, $3\frac{3}{8}''$ centre top links and $3\frac{11}{16}''$ centre bottom links. All post war Webb forks on MOV and MAC machines have $\frac{7}{16}''$ spindles top and bottom.

Illustration Ref.	Part No.	Description.
Not shown	1M	Steering column. D/S type fork. 1934/36.
Not shown	1/2M	Steering column. S/S type fork. 1937/38.
HA	1/3M	Steering column. S/S type fork. 1939 on.
Not shown	2/2M	Fork girder. D/S type. 1934/36.
Not shown	2/3M	Fork girder. S/S. MOV 1937/40, MAC 1937/8.
HB	2/5M	Fork girder. S/S. MAC 1939 on, MOV 1946 on.
Not shown	3M	Top clip, with half clips and bolts. MOV 1934/39. MAC 1934/38. Bushed for $\frac{3}{8}''$ dia. spindle.
HC	3/2M	Top clip, with half clips and bolts. MOV 1946. MAC 1939 on. Bushed for $\frac{7}{16}''$ dia. spindle.
HD	4/2M	Clamping bolt for top clip.
HE	5/2M	Sleeve for clamping bolt.
HF	6/2M	Nut for clamping bolt.
HG	8M	Spring.
HH	8/2M	Spring.

Illustration Ref.	Part No.	Description.

Fork Section—continued.

Illustration Ref.	Part No.	Description.
HI	9M	Clip with bolts and nuts—front mudguard to girder.
HJ	11/2M	Bush, $\frac{3}{8}''$ bore, for top spindle.
HK	13/2M	Steering damper rod.
HL	14/2M	Steering damper knob.
HM	15/2M	Locating plate.
HN	16/2M	Lock nut for steering damper knob.
Not shown	18M	Bottom friction plate and screwed sleeve for steering damper. 1934/8.
HO	18/2M	Screwed sleeve for steering damper.
Not shown	19M	Anchor plate for steering damper—to engage lug on frame.
Not shown	19/2M	Anchor plate for steering damper—to fix to threaded stud on frame, with $\frac{3}{4}''$ dia. central hole. 1938 only.
HP	19/3M.	Anchor plate, $\frac{31}{32}''$ dia. central hole. 1940/46 type.
Not shown	20M	Friction disc for steering damper. 1934/38.
HQ	20/2M	Friction disc. 1939/46.
HR	21M	Bolt, for handlebar clips. 4 off.
HS	22M	Star spring.
Not shown	23M	Rubber buffer for shock absorber centre plate. 1936/38.
HT	23/2M	Rubber buffer for shock absorber centre plate. 1939 on.
Not shown	24M	Bolt for shock absorber buffer, $\frac{1}{4}''$ thread. 1936/38.
HU	24/2M	Bolt for shock absorber buffer, $\frac{5}{16}''$ thread. 1939 on.
Not shown	SL56/4	Nut for 24M.
HV	SL56/6	Nut for 24/2M.
HW	26M	Outer washer for shock absorber buffer. $1\frac{3}{8}'' \times \frac{5}{8}''$.
Not shown	27M	Inner washer for shock absorber buffer. $1\frac{3}{8}'' \times \frac{5}{16}''$. 1936/38.
HX	27/2M	Inner washer for shock absorber buffer. $1\frac{3}{8}'' \times \frac{7}{16}''$. 1939 on.
HY	28M	Bottom plate.
HZ	29M	Fixing plate for 18/2M.
HAA	30M	Brass washer for 18/2M.
HAB	31M	Perforated plate.
HAC	11MS	Bush for $\frac{7}{16}''$ dia. spindles.
HAD	53P	Steering column lock-nut.
Not shown	55P	Top spindle, $\frac{3}{8}''$ dia. See introductory note to Section.
HAE	55/2P	Top spindle, $\frac{7}{16}''$ dia. See introductory note to Section.
Not shown	56P	Spring washer, $\frac{3}{8}''$, for R/H end of 55P.
Not shown	57P	Nut, $\frac{3}{8}''$, for R/H end of 55P.
HAF	57/2P	Nut, $\frac{7}{16}''$, for R/H end of 55/2P.
Not shown	58P	Knurled washer, $\frac{3}{8}''$, for 55P.
Not shown	59P	Nut, $\frac{5}{16}''$, for L/H end of 55P.
HAG	59/2P	Nut, $\frac{3}{8}''$, for L/H end of 55/2P.
Not shown	60P	Spring washer, $\frac{5}{16}''$, for L/H end of 55P.
Not shown	61P	Bottom link, L/H, $\frac{3}{8}''$ plain holes at $3\frac{9}{16}''$ centres. D/S type only.
Not shown	61/2P	Bottom link, L/H, $\frac{3}{8}''$ in plain holes at $3\frac{11}{16}''$ centre. S/S type, 1937/38.

Illustration Ref.	Part No.	Description.

Fork Section—continued.

Illustration Ref.	Part No.	Description.
HAH	61/3P	Bottom link, L/H, $\frac{3}{8}''$ plain holes at $3\frac{11}{16}''$ centre. S/S type, 1939 on.
Not shown	61/4P	Bottom link, L/H, $\frac{3}{8}''$ in plain holes at $3\frac{7}{8}''$ centre. S/S type. Part 1946 only.
Not shown	62P	Friction disc for shock absorber. D/S only, 1934/36.
Not shown	63P	Top link, L/H, $\frac{5}{16}''$ plain holes at $3\frac{1}{4}''$ centres. D/S type.
Not shown	63/2P	Top link, L/H, $\frac{5}{16}''$ plain holes at $3\frac{3}{8}''$ centres. S/S, 1937/8.
HAI	63/3P	Top link, L/H, $\frac{3}{8}''$ plain holes at $3\frac{3}{8}''$ centres. S/S, 1939 on.
Not shown	63/4P	Top link, L/H, $\frac{3}{8}''$ plain holes at $3\frac{7}{8}''$ centres. S/S. Part 1946 only.
Not shown	64P	Top link, R/H, $\frac{3}{8}''$ threaded holes at $3\frac{1}{4}''$ centres. D/S type only.
Not shown	64/2P	Top link, R/H, $\frac{3}{8}''$ threaded holes at $3\frac{3}{8}''$ centres. S/S type, 1937/38.
HAJ	64/3P	Top link, R/H, $\frac{7}{16}''$ threaded holes at $3\frac{3}{8}''$ centres. S/S, 1939 on.
Not shown	64/4P	Top link, R/H, $\frac{7}{16}''$ threaded holes at $3\frac{7}{8}''$ centres. S/S. Part 1946 only.
HAK	66P	Lug for fork spring, used with 8M only.
HAL	66/2P	Lug for fork spring, used with 8/2M only.
HAM	67P	Spring washer for spring lug bolt.
HAN	68P	Bolt for spring lug.
Not shown	72P	Knurled washer, $\frac{7}{16}''$, for bottom spindles.
HBD	73/3P	Nut, for bottom front spindle. S/S type.
Not shown	75P	Bottom spindle, $\frac{7}{16}''$. D/S type, 1934/36.
Not shown	75/2P	Bottom spindle (front), $\frac{7}{16}'' \times 9\frac{7}{16}''$. S/S type, 1937/38.
Not shown	75/3P	Bottom spindle (rear), $\frac{7}{16}'' \times 8\frac{1}{4}''$. S/S type, 1937/38.
HAO	75/4P	Bottom spindle, front, $\frac{7}{16}'' \times 9\frac{1}{2}''$. S/S type. 1939 on.
HAP	75/5P	Bottom spindle, rear, $\frac{7}{16}'' \times 8\frac{3}{8}''$. S/S type, 1939 on.
Not shown	76P	Bottom link, R/H, $\frac{7}{16}''$ threaded holes at $3\frac{9}{16}''$ centres. D/S type.
Not shown	76/2P	Bottom link, R/H, $\frac{7}{16}''$ threaded holes at $3\frac{11}{16}''$ centres. S/S, 1937/38.
HAQ	76/3P	Bottom link, R/H, $\frac{7}{16}''$ threaded holes at $3\frac{11}{16}''$ centres. S/S, 1939 on.
Not shown	76/4P	Bottom link, R/H, $\frac{7}{16}''$ threaded holes at $3\frac{7}{8}''$ centres. S/S. Part 1946 only.
Not shown	77/2P	Inner steel friction plate for shock absorber. D/S.
Not shown	77/3P	Inner steel friction plate. S/S type, 1937/38.
HAR	77/4P	Outer steel friction plate—holes at $3\frac{11}{16}''$ centres. S/S, 1939 on.
HAS	77/5P	Inner steel friction plate—double plunged type, 1939 on.
Not shown	77/6P	Outer steel friction plate—holes at $3\frac{7}{8}''$ centres. S/S. Part 1946.
Not shown	78/2P	Adjuster for shock absorber. D/S type.
HAT	78/4P	Adjuster for shock absorber. S/S type. Replaces wing nut type when used with 73/3P nut.

Illustration Ref.	Part No.	Description.

Fork Section—continued.

Illustration Ref.	Part No.	Description.
Not shown	79P	Star spring for shock absorber. D/S type only.
Not shown	80/2P	Screwed sleeve for shock absorber adjuster. D/S type only.
HAU	SL8/3	Bolt to secure 29M to steering column.
HAV	19F	Spring washer, $\frac{3}{8}''$, for spindle nut.
HAW	20F	Nut, $\frac{3}{8}''$, for bottom spindle, L/H ends.
HAX	22F	Knurled washer, $\frac{7}{16}''$, for top or bottom spindles.
HAY	28F	Nut, $\frac{7}{16}''$.
HAZ	31F	Spring washer, $\frac{7}{16}''$.
HBA	32F	Knurled washer, $\frac{7}{16}''$, for bottom spindle.
Not shown	33F	Friction disc for shock absorber. S/S type. MOV 1937/1940, MAC 1939 on.
HBB	33/2F	Friction disc for shock absorber. S/S type. MAC 1940, MOV and MAC 1946 on.
HBC	35F	Star spring for shock absorber. S/S type.

ILLUSTRATION OF FORK. H 2

ORDER BY PART NUMBERS—DO NOT QUOTE ILLUSTRATION REFERENCES.
FOR PART NUMBERS AND DESCRIPTIONS OF ITEMS SEE PAGE 42.

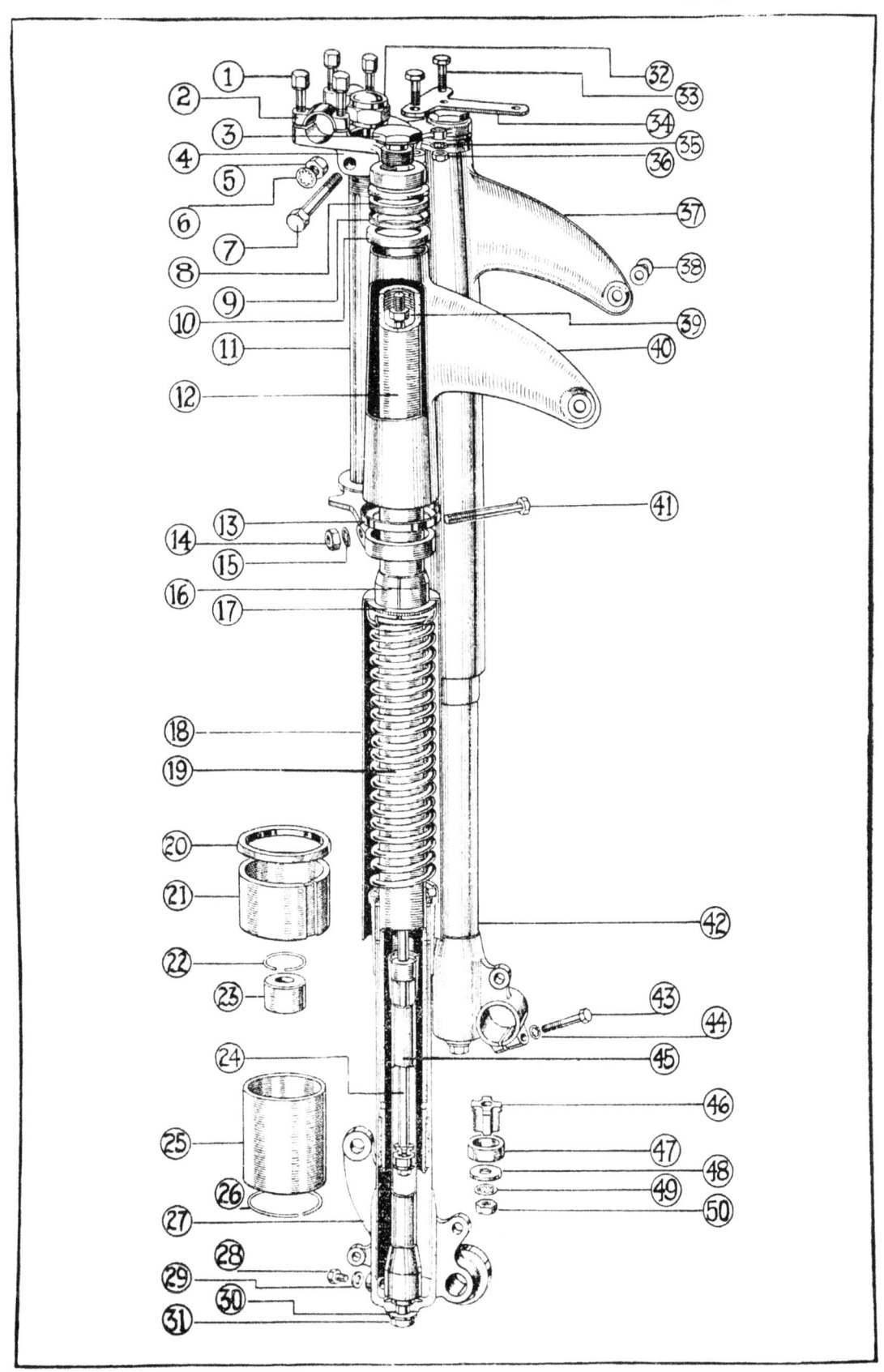

PLEASE WRITE ORDERS CLEARLY—BLOCK LETTERS PLEASE.

FRONT FORK SECTION. VELOCETTE TELESCOPIC TYPE.

See Illustration " H2 " Page 41.

When ordering quote Part Numbers—NOT Illustration Numbers.

Illustration Ref.	Part No.	Description.	
	MAS10	Front fork assembly	1
1	F269	Handlebar clip bolt	4
2	F268	Handlebar clip	2
3	F253	Fork damper piston rod adapter	2
4	F249	Fork cross member (top)	1
5	SL56/7	Fork cross member nut, $\tfrac{3}{8}$" BSF	1
6	LE369	Fork cross member lockwasher $\tfrac{3}{8}$"	1
7	SL110/4	Fork cross member clamp bolt $\tfrac{3}{8}$" BSF $\times 1\tfrac{29}{32}$"	1
8	F272	Headlamp bracket rubber sleeve	2
9	F278	Rubber sleeve housing	4
10	F271	Head lamp bracket locating cup. Top	2
11	MAS7	Steering column assembly—and bottom cross member	1
12	F246	Front fork tube	2
13	F257	Headlamp bracket cup. Bottom	2
14	SL56/38	Fork cross member nut $\tfrac{5}{16}$" BSF. For bottom cross member	2
15	LE368	Fork cross member lockwasher $\tfrac{5}{16}$". For bottom cross member	2
16	F262	Fork tube sleeve (split)	2
17	F282	Front fork dust cover washer (Rubber)	2
18	F245	Fork spring dust cover	2
19	F252	Fork spring	2
20	LE335/2	Fork slider oil seal	2
21	F256	Fork slider tube bush	2
22	F267	Fork damper bush circlip	2
23	F260	Fork damper bush	2
24	F259	Fork damper piston rod	2
25	LE216	Fork tube bush	2
26	LE191	Fork tube circlip	2
27	MAS4	Fork slider tube assembly. Right hand	1
28	SL8/1	Fork oil drain bolt, $\tfrac{1}{4}$" BSF $\times \tfrac{3}{8}$"	2
29	A37/5	Fork oil drain bolt gasket	2
30	SL6/50	Fork damper tube adapter washer	2
31	SL56/7	Fork damper tube adapter nut, $\tfrac{3}{8}$" BSF	2
32	MAS6	Steering head lock nut assembly	1
33	SL109/2	Speedometer bracket bolt. $\tfrac{5}{16}$" BSF $\times \tfrac{7}{8}$"	2
34	KA269/3	Speedometer bracket	1
35	LE368	Speedometer bracket bolt lockwasher	2
36	SL56/38	Speedometer bracket bolt nut, $\tfrac{5}{16}$" BSF	2
37	MAS8	Head lamp bracket assembly. Left hand	1
38	F274	Headlamp washer. Nearside (Left-hand side)	2
39	SL56/38	Fork damper piston rod locknut, $\tfrac{5}{16}$" BSF	2
40	MAS9	Headlamp bracket assembly. Right hand	1
41	SL109/6	Fork cross member clamp bolt, $\tfrac{5}{16}$" BSF $\times 1\tfrac{31}{32}$"	2
42	MAS3	Fork slider tube assembly. Left hand	1
43	SL109/3	Wheel spindle clamp bolt, $\tfrac{5}{16}$" BSF $\times 1\tfrac{3}{32}$"	1
44	LE368	Wheel spindle clamp bolt lockwasher	1
45	MAS5	Fork damper tube assembly	2
46	F251	Fork damper valve	2
47	F265	Fork damper piston	2
48	F266	Fork damper piston rod washer	2
49	LE366	Fork damper piston rod lockwasher, $\tfrac{3}{16}$"	2
50	SL56/2	Fork damper piston road nut, 2BA	2

ORDER BY PART NUMBERS—DO NOT QUOTE ILLUSTRATION REFERENCES.
FOR PART NUMBERS AND DESCRIPTIONS OF ITEMS ON THIS PAGE SEE PAGE 44.

ILLUSTRATION I.

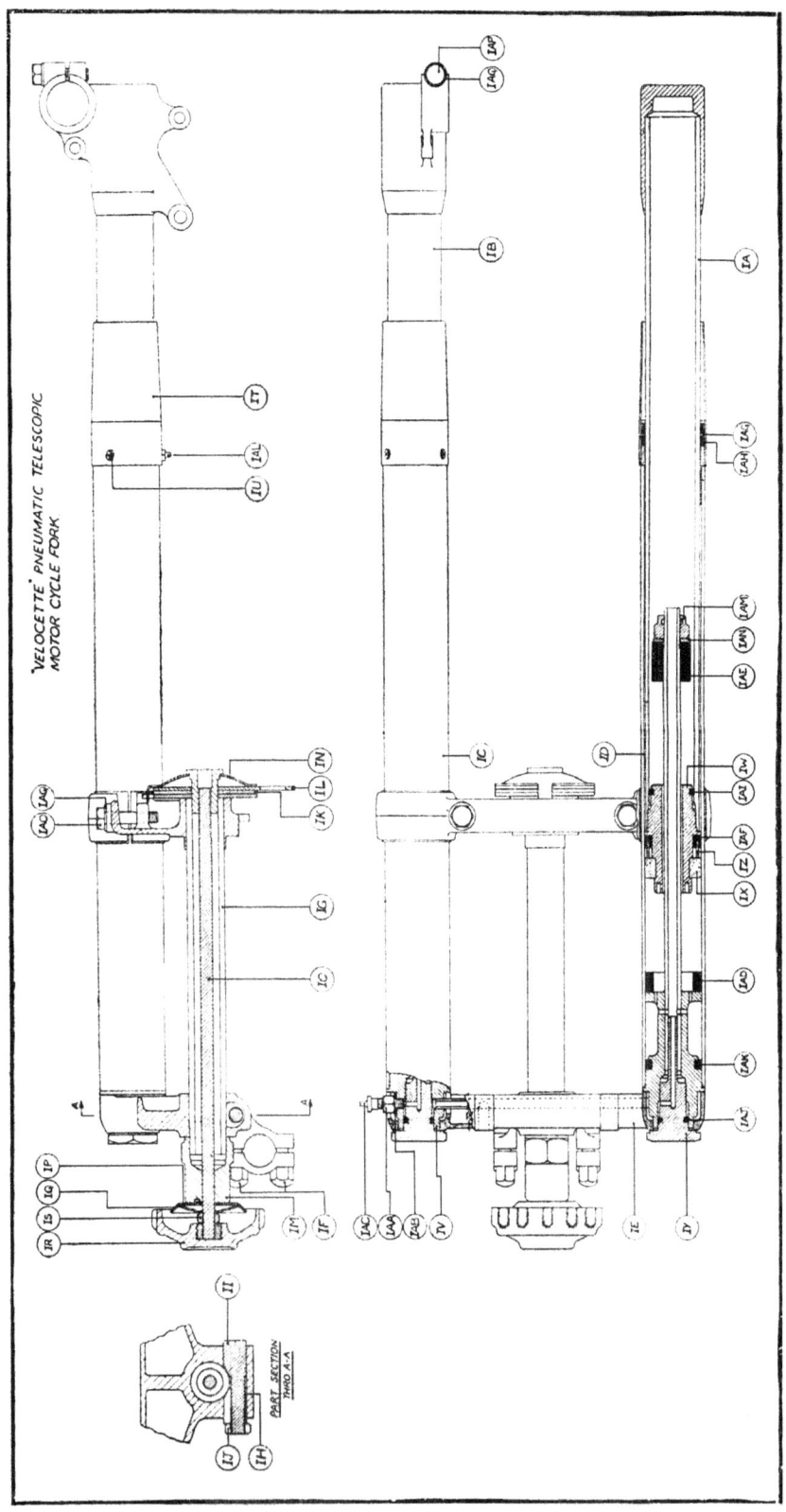

FORK SECTION—DOWTY-OLEOMATIC TYPE.
See Illustration "I" Page 43.

When ordering Quote Veloce Part Numbers—NOT Illustration References

Illustration Key	Veloce No.	Dowty No.	Description	
IA	50F	PC1701-2	Axle fitting and inner tube (right hand).	
IB	51F	PC1701-3	Axle fitting and inner tube (left hand).	
IC	52F	PD1701-4A	Outer tube (left hand).	
ID	53F	PD1701-4B	Outer tube (right hand).	
IE	54F	PC1701-5	Top clip lug with caps and handlebar bolts.	
IF	55F	PD1561-41	Handlebar bolt for top clip lug, 4 off.	
IG	56F	PD1701-19	Steering column.	
IH	57F	PD1701-22	Sleeve for top clip clamping bolt.	
II	58F	PD1701-23	Clamping bolt for top clip.	
IJ	SL56/8	N.D.	Nut for clamping bolt 58F.	
IK	59F	PD1701-27	Friction disc for steering damper.	
IL	60F	PD1701-28	Bottom friction plate for steering damper.	
IM	61F	PD1701-26	Nut for steering column.	
IN	62F	PD1701-31	Bottom nut and plate for steering damper.	
IO	63F	PD1502/6B	Screwed rod for steering damper.	
IP	64F	PD1502/7	Locating plate for steering damper star spring.	
IQ	65F	PD1502/8	Star spring for steering damper.	
IR	66F	PD1502/10	Knob for steering damper.	
IS	67F	PD1454/34	Locknut for steering damper knob.	
IT	68F	PD1682	Shroud for bottom of 52F and 53F.	2 off.
IU	69F	PD1811	Screw—shroud to outer tube.	4 off.
IV	70F	PD1701-9	Balance pipe and top fitting unit assembly.	
IW	71F	PD1676	Piston.	2 off.
IX	72F	PD1677	Upper bearing (each bearing is in two halves).	2 off.
IY	73F	PD1678	Filler plug.	2 off.
IZ	74F	PD1685	Spacer for piston gland ring.	2 off.
IAA	75F	PD1651	Inflation valve body.	
Not shown	76F	D9351	Inflation valve core (Kilner).	
IAB	77F	PD1561-43	Bonded seal for inflation valve.	
IAC	78F	ND	Inflation valve cap (Schrader).	
IAD	79F	PD1701-16	Dashpot buffer.	2 off.
IAE	80F	PD1701-30	Lower buffer.	2 off.
IAF	81F	PP12-23	Gland ring.	2 off.
IAG	82F	PP16-14	Scraper ring.	2 off.
IAH	83F	PP16-15	Packing seal—for scraper ring.	2 off.
IAI	84F	PP17-1	Static seal—for piston.	2 off.
IAJ	85F	PP17-17	Static seal—for filler plug.	2 off.
IAK	86F	PP17-22	Static seal—for top fitting.	2 off.
IAL	87F	P6B	Greaser (Tecalemit).	2 off.
IAM	88F	PL1	Simmonds nut for lower buffer.	2 off.
IAN	89F	N.D.	Washer for 88F.	2 off.
IAO	90F	N.D.	Clamping bolt—steering column to outer tubes.	2 off.
IAP	91F	N.D.	Clamping bolt for axle in axle fitting.	
IAQ	SL57/2	N.D.	Spring washer $\frac{5}{16}$ in 90F. and 91F.	
Not shown	SL9/2	—	Bolt speedometer bracket to top clip lug.	2 off.
Not shown	SL6/40	—	Plain washer for SL9/2.	2 off.

ILLUSTRATION J.

ORDER BY PART NUMBERS—DO NOT QUOTE ILLUSTRATION REFERENCES.
FOR PART NUMBERS AND DESCRIPTIONS OF ITEMS ON THIS PAGE SEE PAGES 47 TO 49.

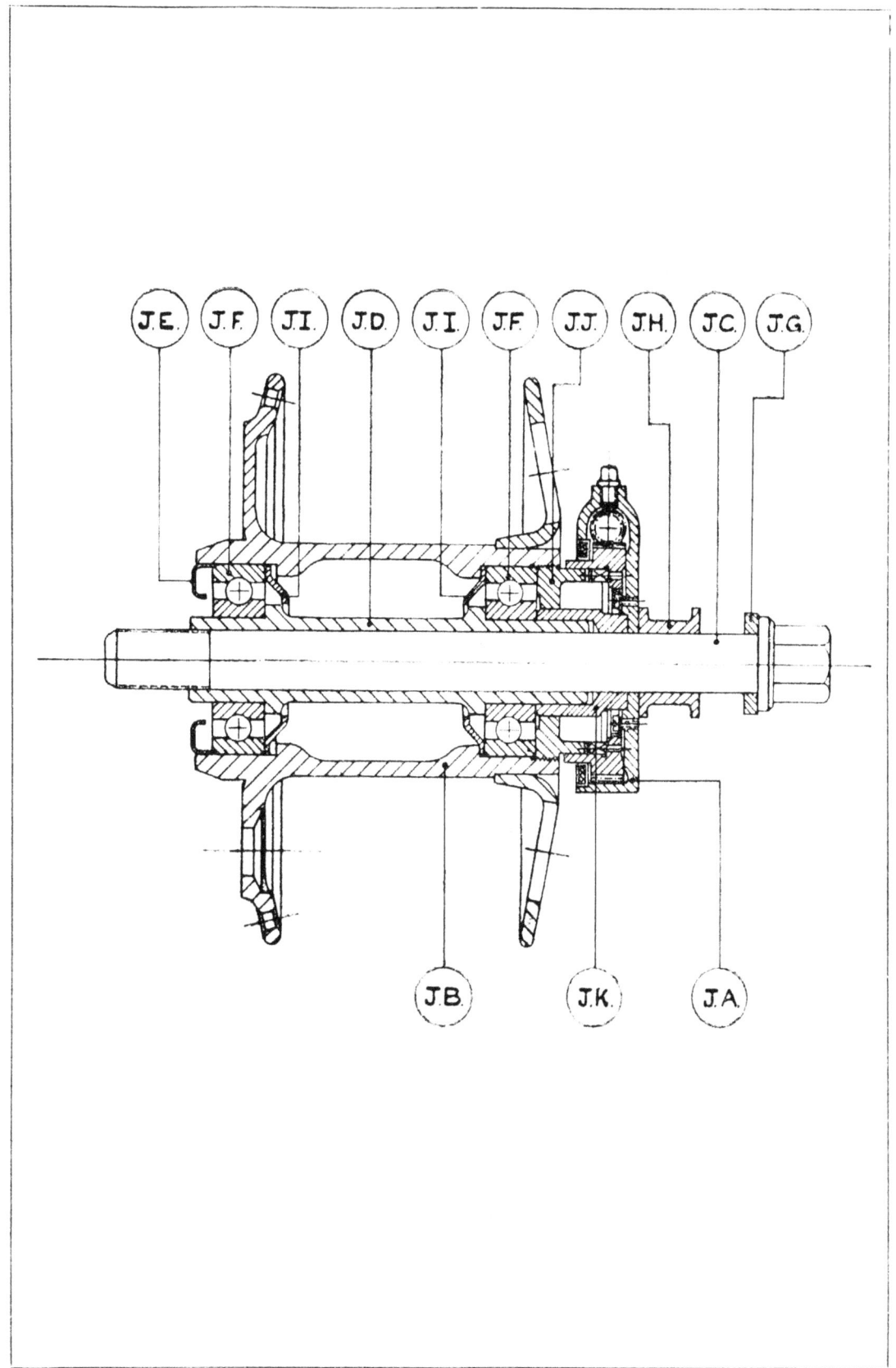

RIMS ARE NOT ILLUSTRATED. FOR DETAILS SEE PAGE 47.

ILLUSTRATION K.

ORDER BY PART NUMBERS—DO NOT QUOTE ILLUSTRATION REFERENCES.

FOR PART NUMBERS AND DESCRIPTIONS OF ITEMS ON THIS PAGE SEE PAGES 47 TO 49.

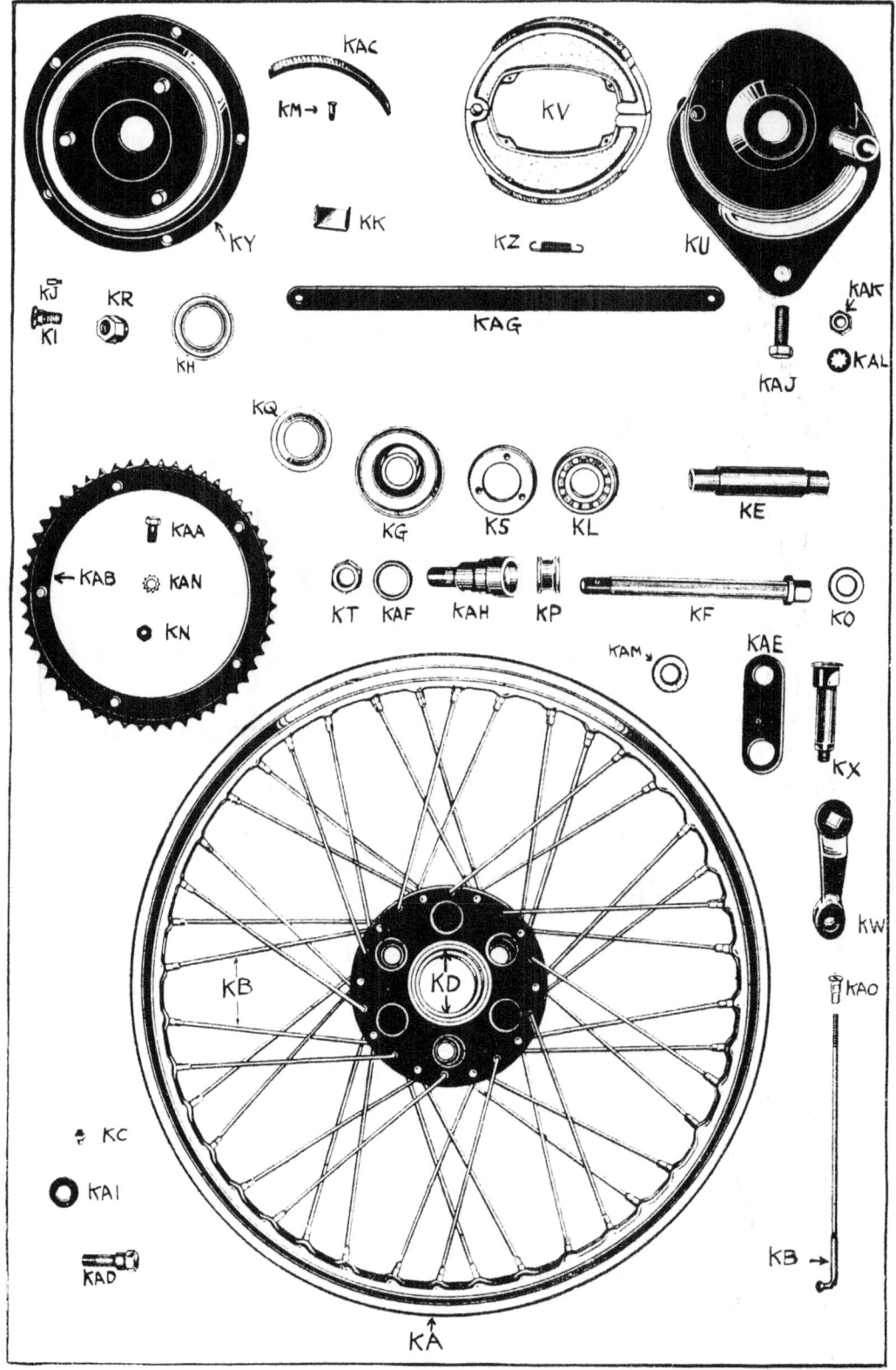

THIS ILLUSTRATION DOES NOT SHOW ALL PARTS.   REFER TO PAGE 47.

REAR WHEEL AND BRAKE SECTION.
See Illustrations "K" and "J" Pages 45 and 46.

Note.—As a result of the change from "Webb" to Telescopic type forks the speedometer drive has been moved from the front to the rear hub, and there have accordingly been certain modifications to the rear hub assembly. Many of the components are, however, interchangeable between both types, and this is indicated by the part numbers being similar.

Illustration Ref.	Part No.	Description.
Not shown	A17/6	Rear wheel rim—WM2×19 punched 40 holes. For non-detachable hub, to 1937.
KA	A17/7	Rear wheel rim—WM2×19 punched 40 holes. For all models from 1937.
KB	A18/4	Spoke, brake side, for A17/6 only. 20 off.
	KA18/10	Spoke, right side, for A17/6 only. 20 off.
	KA18/25	Spoke, for A17/7. 40 off.
JA	KA272/2	Reduction gearbox for rear wheel speedometer drive.
KC	KA46	Greaser for cam spindle bearing.
KD	KS7/7	Rear hub, for machines with **front** wheel driven speedo. only.
JB	KS7/10AS	Rear hub, for machines with **rear** wheel driven speedo. only.
KE	KS8/5	Hollow spindle for machines with **front** wheel driven speedo. only.
JC and KF	KS8/6	Detachable wheel spindle.
JD	KS8/9	Hollow spindle for machines with **rear** wheel driven speedo. only.
KG	MAS73	Outer dust cap and sleeve, for machines with **front** wheel driven speedo. only.
JE and KH	KS11/4	Inner dust cover. 2 off.
KI	KS12/2	Rear wheel stud (For S6/2 only). 3 off.
KJ	KS12/3	Dowel for KS12/2. 3 off.
	KS12/4	Rear wheel stud for S6/3 only. 3 off.
	KS73	Rear wheel stud dowel for S6/3 only. 3 off.
KK	KS16	Slipper between brake shoe and cam. 2 off.
LW	KS18/2	Taper roller bearing, for non-detachable pre-1937 hub.
JF and KL	KS18/3	Ballrace for hub. From 1937. 2 off.
KM	KS31	Rivet for brake lining. 12 off per pair of shoes.
KN	KS35	Nut for chain wheel bolt. 5 off.
JG and KO	KS51/2	Washer for detachable spindle KS8/6.
JH and KP	KS52/2	Distance piece for detachable spindle.
KQ	KS57/2	Grease retaining washer between bearing and centre of hub **KS7/7** only. 2 off.
JI	KS57/3	Grease retaining washer between bearing and centre of hub **KS7/10AS** only. 2 off.
KR	KS60	Rear wheel nuts. 3 off.
KS	KS61	Retaining ring for ballrace. Right-hand thread for KS7/7 hub only.
JJ	KS61/2	Retaining ring for ballrace. Left-hand thread for KS7/10AS hub only.
JK	KS62/3	Clamping sleeve for ballrace, for KS7/10AS hub only.
KT	KS67	Nut for dummy spindle.
Not shown	S1/3	Rear brake plate, for $\frac{7}{16}''$ non-detachable type spindle. Pre-1937.

Illustration Ref.	Part No.	Description.

Rear Wheel and Brake Section—continued.

KU	‡S1/6	Rear brake plate. See Note below.

‡**Note.**—On pre-war machines with detachable type wheels there were two earlier types of brake plates fitted, the one with a $\frac{1}{2}''$ diameter cam spindle bearing, and both were secured to the frame with an anchor bolt, through the left-hand rear frame fork end. These are both now obsolete and must be replaced by S1/6 with the later type rear brake torque arm. The parts needed in such a case would be : S1/6—1 off, S55—1 off, SL11/11—1 off, SL56/8—1 off, LE369—1 off, F4/8—1 off, F241—1 off. In addition to these the following will be needed if the brake plate to be replaced is the earlier pattern with $\frac{1}{2}''$ dia. cam : S4/3—1 off, W12/3—1 off, S41/4—1 off, S3/4—1 off, SL56/8—1 off, LE369—1 off.

KV	S2/4, S2/5	Brake shoes, with liners. Supplied in pairs only.
Not shown	S3/3	Cam lever for $\frac{1}{2}''$ dia. brake cam only. Pre-1939.
KW	S3/4	Cam lever for $\frac{5}{8}''$ dia. brake cam only. Current type.
Not shown	S4/2	Brake cam, with $\frac{1}{2}''$ dia. spindle. Pre 1939.
KX	S4/3	Brake cam, with $\frac{5}{8}''$ dia. spindle. Current type.
KY	†S6/2	Rear brake drum with studs.
	†S6/3	Rear brake drum with integral chain wheel, with studs. 1 off.
Not shown	S10	Outer dust cap, for non-detachable type hub.
Not shown	S12/4	Rear hub, non-detachable type.
Not shown	S13/4	Spindle for non-detachable type hub.
Not shown	S18/3	Inner dust caps for non-detachable type hub. 2 off.
KZ	S27/2	Springs for brake shoes. 2 of.
KAA	S28/3	Bolts—chain wheel to brake drum. 5 off.
KAB	†S29/4	Chain wheel, 52 teeth. Not made in different sizes.
KAC	S30/3	Brake liners. 2 off.
KAD	S36/23AC	Anchor bolt for rear brake plate. Pre-war type only.
KAE	S41/2	Steady for cam spindle bearing. For brake plates with $\frac{1}{2}''$ dia. cam bearing only.
	S41/4	Steady for cam spindle bearing. Current type.
Not shown	S48/2	Felt washer for hub. Non-detachable type only.
KAF	S52	Distance piece between brake plate and frame. For $\frac{7}{16}''$ spindle only.
	S52/4	Distance piece between brake plate and frame.
	†S52/5	Distance piece for brake plate locking bolt. Between plate and fork end. 1 off.
KAG	S55	Torque arm, brake plate to prop stand pin.
	*S55/2	Rear brake torque arm. For use with MAS 2/3 frame only. 1 off.
KAH	S66	Dummy spindle—supporting brake plate.
	†S66/2	Rear brake plate locking bolt. For S6/3 only. 1 off.
KAI	SL6/48	Plain washer for S36/23AC.
Not shown	SL6/57	Plain washer, $\frac{7}{16}''$, for spindle nuts. Non-detachable type.
KAJ	SL11/11	Bolt, $\frac{3}{8}''$. Torque stay to brake plate.

Illustration Ref.	Part No.	Description.

Rear Wheel and Brake Section—continued.

Illustration Ref.	Part No.	Description.	
	SL11/20	Rear brake torque stay bolt, $\frac{3}{8}"$ 26 T.P.I. $\times 1\frac{7}{16}"$. Stay to frame lug of MAS 2/3.	1 off.
KAK {	SL56/6	Nut, $\frac{5}{16}"$, for $\frac{1}{2}"$ dia. cam spindle.	
	SL56/8	Nut, $\frac{3}{8}"$, for $\frac{5}{8}"$ dia. cam spindle and rear torque stay bolt.	2 off.
Not shown	SL56/9	Nut, $\frac{7}{16}"$, for S13/4 spindle.	2 off.
Not shown	SL56/24	Nut, $\frac{1}{2}"$, for locking wheel bearing adjuster nut. Non-detachable type.	
Not shown	SL56/34	Nut, $\frac{1}{2}"$, for wheel bearing adjustment. Non-detachable type.	
KAN	LE368	Shakeproof washer, $\frac{5}{16}"$, 5 off for chain wheel bolt. 1 off for cam spindle.	
KAL	LE369	Shakeproof washer, $\frac{3}{8}"$, 1 off for torque stay bolt, 1 off for cam spindle.	
SW & LAN	W12/2	Felt for $\frac{1}{2}"$ dia. cam spindle.	
KAM	W12/3	Felt for $\frac{5}{8}"$ dia. cam spindle.	
Not shown	W60	Grease retainer between taper roller bearing and centre of hub S12/4 only.	

*S55/2 is only used with MAS2/3 frame, which has separate torque arm and prop stand lugs. S55 is used on all previous types.

†S6/3 may be used to replace S6/2, and S29/4, but requires in addition S52/5, 1 off, and S66/2, 1 off.

ILLUSTRATION L.

ORDER BY PART NUMBER—DO NOT QUOTE ILLUSTRATION REFERENCES.
FOR PART NUMBERS AND DESCRIPTIONS OF ITEMS ON THIS PAGE SEE PAGE 51 AND 52.

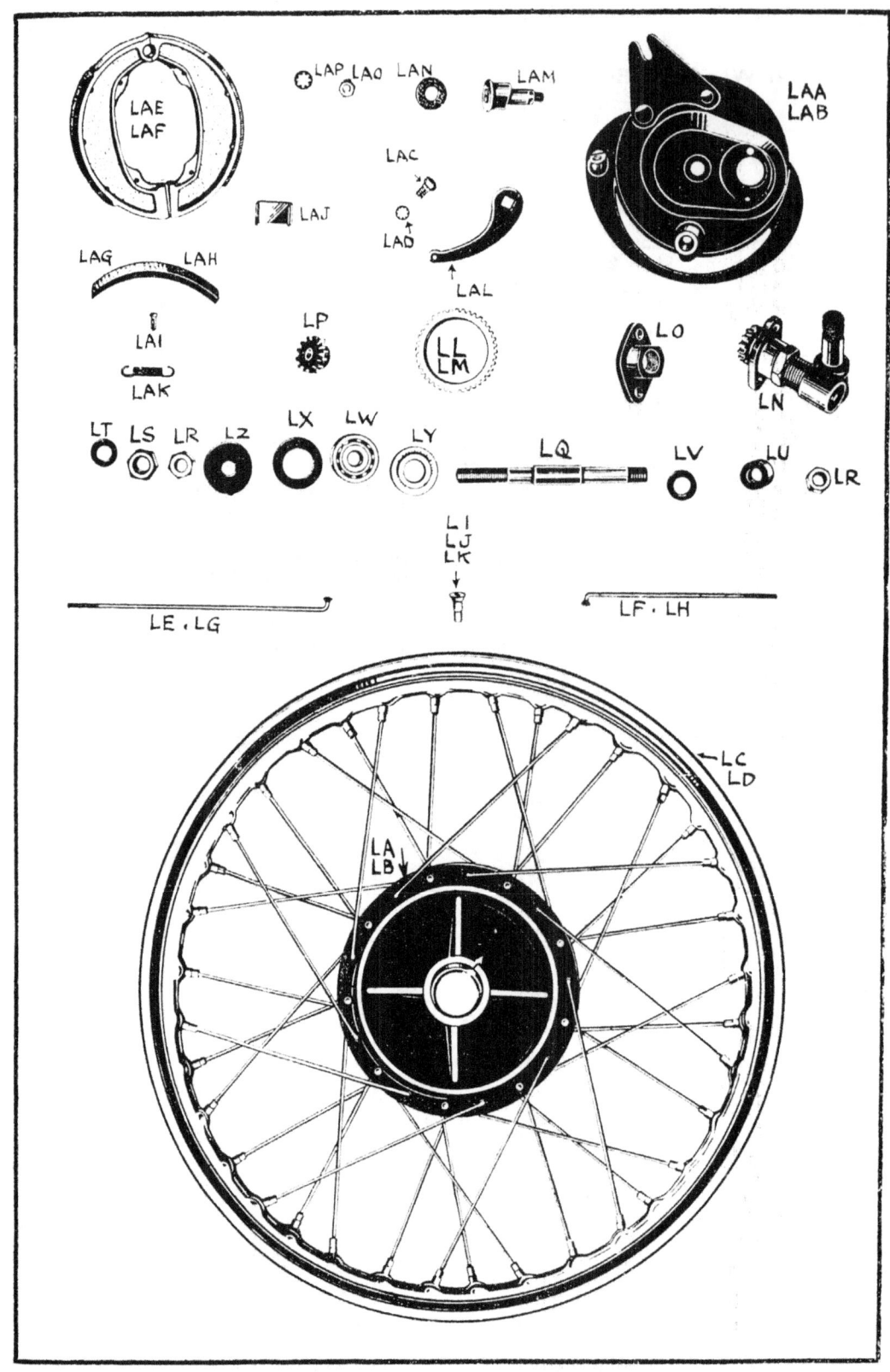

DO NOT OMIT ENGINE NUMBER AND PREFIX LETTERS FROM ORDER.

FRONT WHEEL, FRONT BRAKE AND SPEEDOMETER DRIVE SECTION—WITH "WEBB" FORK. See Illustration "L."

Illustration Ref.	Part No.	Description.
LA	FB2/3	Front hub—pressed steel type. To 1940 only.
LB	FB2/4	Front hub—cast iron drum type. From 1941.
LC	A17/2	Front wheel rim WM2×19″. Punched 36 holes for 12 gauge nipples.

Note.—This rim is now obsolete and must be replaced with A17/8 rim and spoke nipples A19/2. Alternatively enlarge spoke holes and use A18/7 (18 off). KA18/24 (18 off) and KA19 (36 off).

Illustration Ref.	Part No.	Description.
LD	A17/8	Front wheel rim—WM 2×19. Punched 36 holes for 10 gauge nipples.
LE	A18/2	Spoke, 8⅝″—12 gauge, left-hand side. Pre-war only. 18 off.
LF	A18/3	Spoke, 8⅛″, 12 gauge, brake side. Pre-war only. 18 off.
LG	KA18/24	Spoke, 10 gauge, left-hand side. 1946/47 type. 18 off.
LH	A18/7	Spoke, 10 gauge, brake side. 1946/47 type. 18 off.
LI	A19	Nipple for 12 gauge spoke. Used with A17/2 rim only. 36 off.
LJ	A19/2	Nipple, 10 gauge outside but tapped for 12 gauge spoke. See Note above. 36 off.
LK	KA19	Nipple for 10 gauge spoke. 1946/47. 36 off.
LL	A166	Driving gear for speedometer. Used with FB2/3 only.
LM	A166/2	Driving gear for speedometer. Used with FB2/4 only. This gear has same number of teeth and is the same pitch as A166, but is larger in internal diameter to fit larger boss on hub.
LN	A272/2	Reduction gearbox for speedometer drive, with flange and pinion.
LP	A273/2	Pinion for reduction gearbox. 13 teeth.
LO	A274	Flange for reduction gearbox.
LQ	FB21/3	Spindle for front hub.
LR	SL56/34	Nut for spindle and bearing adjustment. 3 off.
LS	SL56/24	Lock-nut for wheel bearing adjustment.
LT	S19/2	Plain washer for spindle nut, in fork end. 2 off.
LU	FB52	Distance piece for spindle, between brake plate and fork end.
LV	FB52/2	Plain washer, between brake plate and wheel bearing.
LW	KS18/2	Taper roller wheel bearing. 2 off.
LX	S18/3	Dust caps—inner. 2 off.
LY	W60	Grease retainer—between bearing and centre of hub. 2 off.
LZ	W6/3	Outer dust cap.
LAA	FB6/5	Brake plate, with plain lug for cable stop. To 1939 only.
LAB	FB6/6	Brake plate, with threaded lug for brake cable adjuster. From 1939.
LAC	SL8/28	Bolt, reduction bearbox to brake plate. 2 off.

Illustration Ref.	Part No.	Description

Front Wheel Section—continued.

LAD	LE367	Shakeproof washer, $\frac{1}{4}''$, for SL8/28. 2 off.
LAE	†S2/2/S2/3	Brake shoes, lined. $\frac{3}{4}''$ wide, for FB2/3 hub only.
LAF	†S2/4/S2/5	Brake shoes, lined. $\frac{7}{8}''$ wide, for FB2/4 hub only.
		† Separate brake shoes cannot be supplied. Shoes are sold in pairs only.
LAG	S30/2	Brake lining, $\frac{3}{4}''$. 2 off.
LAH	S30/3	Brake lining, $\frac{7}{8}''$. 2 off.
LAI	KS31	Rivet for brake lining. 12 off per pair shoes.
LAJ	KS16	Slipper, between brake shoes and cam 2 off.
LAK	S27/2	Spring for brake shoe. 2 off.
LAL	FB11/4	Lever for cam. 1 off.
LAM	FB9/2	Brake cam. 1 off.
LAN	W12/2	Felt washer for cam spindle, between cam lever and bearing in brake plate. 1 off.
LAO	SL56/6	Nut, $\frac{5}{16}''$. Cam lever to cam.
LAP	LE368	Shakeproof washer, $\frac{5}{16}''$, for cam spindle nut. 1 off.
SU	FB60	Square hole washer for cam. 1 off.

ILLUSTRATION L2

ORDER BY PART NUMBERS—DO NOT QUOTE ILLUSTRATION REFERENCES

FOR PART NUMBERS AND DESCRIPTIONS OF ITEMS ON THIS PAGE see page 54

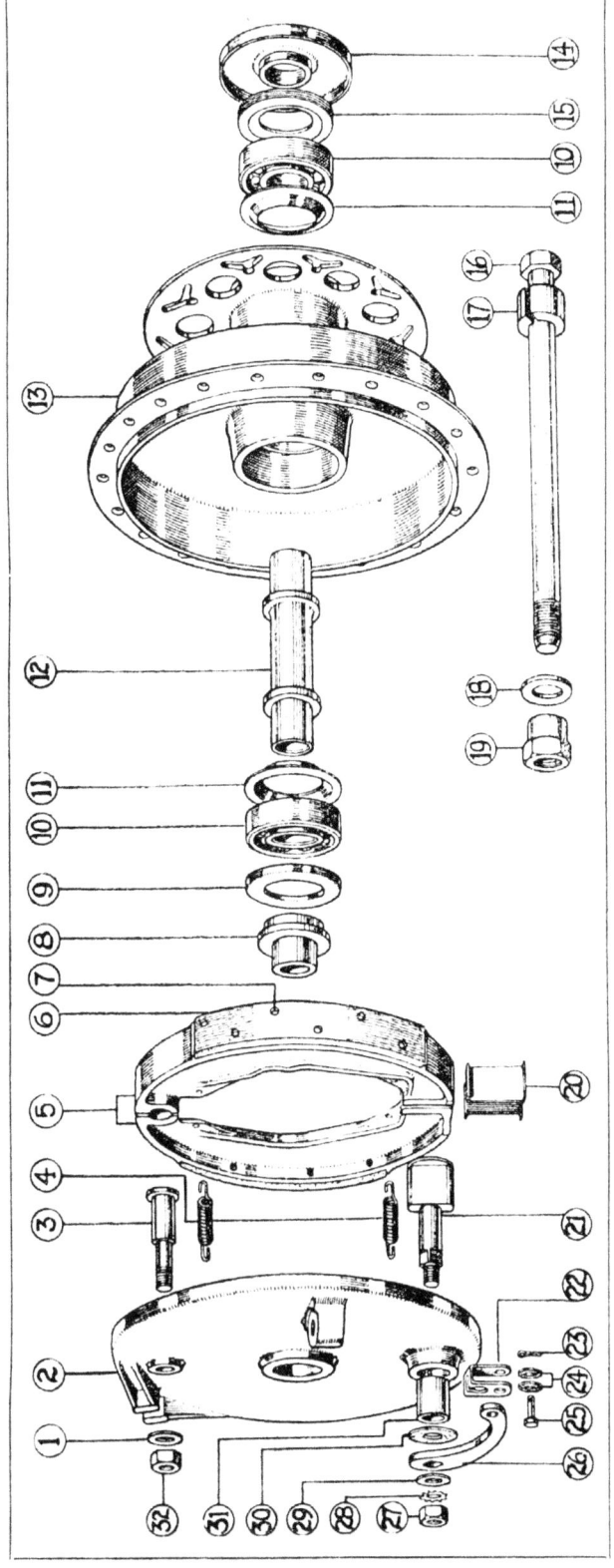

FOR DETAILS OE RIM AND SPOKES SEE PAGE 54.

FRONT WHEEL AND BRAKE SECTION. TELESCOPIC FORKS. See Illustration "L2," page 53.

Note.—Quote Part Numbers when ordering. NOT Illustration Reference Numbers.

Illustration Ref.	Part No.	Description.	
1	SL6/50	‡Front brake shoe fulcrum pin washer, $\frac{3}{8}$"	1
2	MAS72	‡Front brake plate assembly. Includes W71 bush	1
3	W10/4	‡Front brake shoe fulcrum pin	1
4	S27/2	‡Brake shoe spring	2
5	MAS74/75	‡Brake shoe assembly. Left and right-hand Includes lining and rivets ... pair	1
6	KS19/2	Brake shoe lining. Included in assemblies MAS74 and MAS75	2
7	KS31	Brake shoe lining rivet. Included in assemblies MAS74 and MAS75	12
8	W52/3	‡Front brake plate distance-piece	1
9	KS11/4	*Front hub inner dust cap	1
10	KS18/3	*Front hub ball bearing	2
11	KS57/3	*Front hub grease retainer	2
12	W62/2	*Front hub hollow spindle	1
13	MAS70	*Front hub shell assembly	1
14	MAS73	*Front hub outer dust cover assembly	1
15	KS61	*Front hub lockring	1
16	W21/6	Front wheel spindle	1
17	W64/2	Front wheel spindle distance piece	1
18	KS51/2	Front wheel spindle washer	1
19	W65/2	Front wheel spindle nut	1
20	KS16/2	Brake shoe slipper. Included in assemblies MAS74 and MAS75	2
21	MAS76	‡Front brake cam assembly	1
22	FB54	‡Front brake cable shackle	1
23	SL71/2	‡Clevis pin split cotter, $\frac{1}{16}$" × $\frac{1}{2}$"	1
24	FB61	‡Cable shackle felt washer	2
25	S32	‡Cable shackle clevis pin	1
26	FB11/5	‡Front brake cam lever	1
27	SL56/6	‡Front brake cam nut, $\frac{5}{16}$" 26 T.P.I.	1
28	LE368	‡Front brake cam lock washer, $\frac{5}{16}$"	1
29	FB60	‡Front brake cam lever washer	1
30	W12/2	‡Front brake cam felt washer	1
31	W71	Front brake cam bush. Included in assembly MAS72	1
32	SL56/8	Brake shoe fulcrum pin nut, $\frac{3}{8}$" 26 T.P.I.	1
Parts not illustrated—			
	A17/8	†Front wheel rim, WM2 × 19" (36 holes)	1
	KA18/5	†Front wheel spoke, 10 S.W.G. × $6\frac{5}{8}$" long. Brake side	18
	KA18/26	†Front wheel spoke, 10 S.W.G. × $7\frac{1}{4}$" long. Left side	18
	KA19	†Front wheel spoke nipple, 10 S.W.G.	36
		*These items may be ordered assembled as :	
	MAS69	Front hub assembly.	
		†These items plus MAS69 may be ordered assembled as :	
	MAS67	Front wheel assembly.	
		‡These items may be ordered assembled as :	
	MAS71	Brake plate and shoe assembly.	

ILLUSTRATION M.

ORDER BY PART NUMBERS—DO NOT QUOTE ILLUSTRATION REFERENCES.
FOR PART NUMBERS AND DESCRIPTIONS OF ITEMS ON THIS PAGE SEE PAGES 56 TO 58.

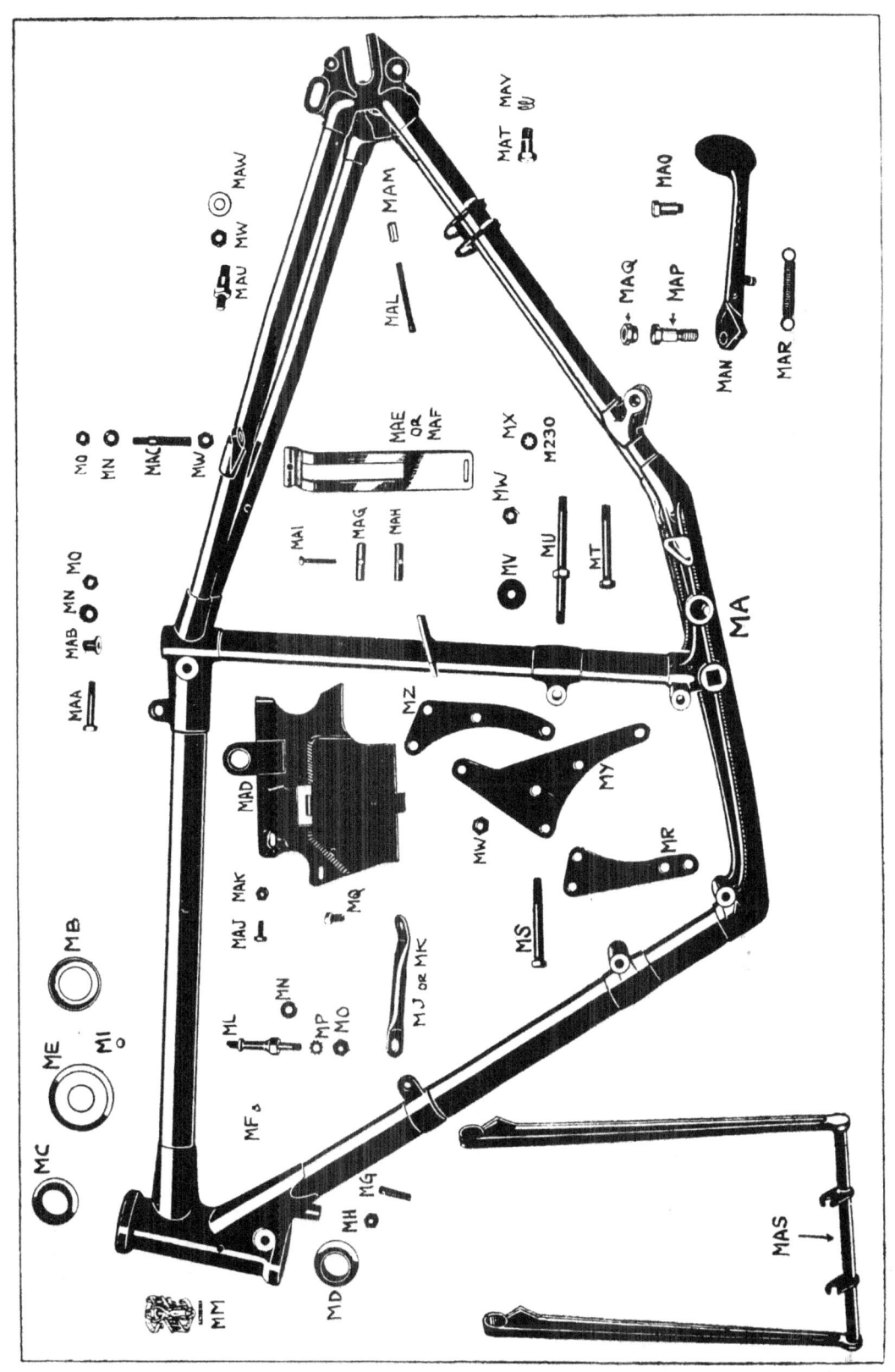

HAVE YOU QUOTED THE ENGINE NUMBER ON YOUR ORDER?

FRAME, ENGINE MOUNTING AND REAR STAND SECTION.
See Illustration "M," page 55.

Illustration Ref.	Part No.	Description.
Not shown	†F200/2	Frame 1934/36 only. For non-detachable type rear wheel only.
Not shown	†F200/4	Frame 1937. For detachable rear wheel.
Not shown	†F200/4B	Frame. Used from Serial No. MD7391. As F200/4 but with lug for cylinder head steady.
Not shown	†F200/6	Frame. As F200/4B but with stud fixing for steering damper. To 1941 only.
MA	†F200/9AS	Frame. Cradle lug type. To Eng. No. MAC15325.
		† All these frames are now obsolete. If replacement is required use MAS2/3 with additional parts to convert. Details on application.
	MAS2*	Frame, 1951. From Eng. No. MAC15326. Tubular base type with lug for rear attachment of cylinder head steady, but no steady and horn lug on front down tube. 1 off.
		* When this frame is used with engines fitted with cast-iron cylinder heads the cylinder head steady and horn are attached to the down tube, using clips A43/3, 2 off, and A43/4, 1 off.
	MAS2/2	Frame 1951 type. As MAS2 but has lug for horn and head steady on down tube.
	MAS2/3	Frame, 1951/1952 type. As MAS2/2, but has separate lugs for prop stand and torque stay.
MB	F31/3	Cups for steering head bearing. 2 off.
MC	F32/3	Cone for steering column—top.
MD	F32/4	Cone for steering column—bottom.
ME	F165	Dust cover for steering head bearing.
MF	KA46	Greaser for steering head.
MG	†FK239	Stud, steering damper plate to head lug. See also note above†.
MH	†SL56/6	Nut, $\frac{5}{16}$", for FK239—2 off. See also note above†.
MI	K100	Bearing ball $\frac{1}{4}$", for steering head. 38 off.
MJ	FK75/4	Cylinder head steady. MOV model
MK	FK75/12	Cylinder head steady. MAC model To Eng. No. MAC15981.
ML	FK185/3	Stud. Electric horn and cylinder head steady to frame.
	FK75/14	Cylinder head steady. For rear mounted head steady on aluminium alloy head. From Eng. No. MAC15982.
	SL109/4	Cylinder head steady bolt, $\frac{5}{16}$" B.S.F. ×1" to Alloy head and frame. 2 off.
	SL56/38	Cylinder head steady nut $\frac{5}{16}$" B.S.F. 2 off.
	LE368	Cylinder head steady lockwasher. 2 off.
MM	A133	Transfer for steering head.
MN	SL6/40	Plain washer for FK185/3 and SL9/3.
MO	SL56/6	Nut, $\frac{5}{16}$", for FK185/3. 2 off.
MP	LE368	Lock-washer, $\frac{5}{16}$", for FK185/3.
MQ	SL9/3	Bolt. Cylinder head steady to cylinder head.
Not shown	A43/3	Quarter clip. Cylinder head steady to frame F200/2 or F200/4 only. 2 off.

Illustration Ref.	Part No.	Description.	Quantity Off

Frame Section—continued.

Illustration Ref.	Part No.	Description.	Quantity Off
Not shown	A43/4	Half clip. A43/3 to frame.	
Not shown	SL9/2	Bolt for A43/3 and A43/4.	2 off.
MO	SL56/6	Nut for SL9/2.	
MN	SL6/40	Washer for SL56/6	2 off.
MR	F174/3	Engine plate—front.	2 off.
MS	SL11/2	Bolt. Front engine plate to frame and crank case.	4 off.
MT	SL11/1	Bolt. Rear engine plate to frame and crank case.	3 off.
MU	F49/2	Stud. Chain cover and gear lever pivot to rear engine plates.	
MV	SL6/49	Plain washer, $\frac{3}{8}''$, for F49/2.	
MW	SL56/8	Nut, $\frac{3}{8}''$. For engine bolts and F49/2.	8 off.
MX	LE369	Lock-washer, $\frac{3}{8}''$, for engine bolt nuts.	8 off.
MY	F110/7	Engine plate, rear, left-hand. To Eng. No. MAC15522.	
MZ	F110/8	Engine plate, rear, right-hand. To Eng. No. MAC15522.	
	F110/15	Rear engine plate—left-hand. Used with crankcase M43/44/8. From. Eng. MAC15523.	1 off.
	F110/16	Rear engine plate, right-hand. Used with crankcase M43/44/8. From Eng. No. MAC15523.	1 off.
	SL11/1	Rear engine bolt, $\frac{3}{8}''$ 26 T.P.I. $\times 2\frac{3}{4}''$. Additional for use with M43/44/8.	4 off.
MAA	SL9/17	Bolt. Front of saddle to frame.	
MAB	A209	Bush for front saddle bolt.	2 off.
MO	SL56/6	Nut for SL9/17.	
MP	LE368	Shakeproof washer for SL9/17.	
MAC	FK166	Stud. Saddle spring to frame.	2 off.
MO	SL56/6	Nut, $\frac{5}{16}''$. Saddle spring to stud.	2 off.
MN	SL6/40	Plain washer, $\frac{5}{16}''$, for saddle stud.	2 off.
MW	SL56/8	Nut, $\frac{3}{8}''$. Saddle stud to frame.	4 off.
MAD	E8/5AS	Battery platform.	
MAE	E9/4	Strap for battery, front, chromium plated finish	
MAF	E9/5	Strap for battery, rear, black finish.	
MAG	E51	Trunnion for front battery strap, plain hole.	
MAH	E51/2	Trunnion for rear battery strap, threaded hole.	
MAI	E53	Bolt for battery strap.	
MAJ	SL8/3	Bolt—battery platform to frame.	2 off.
MAK	SL56/4	Nut, for battery platform bolt.	2 off.
Not shown	M288	Lock-washer, $\frac{1}{4}''$, for battery platform bolt	2 off.
MAL	F14	Rear chain adjuster.	2 off.
MAM	SL56/20	Lock nut for F14.	2 off.
MAN	FK29/10	Prop stand.	
MAO	F4/25	Pivot pin for prop stand—up to 1941 models only.	
MAP	F4/8	Pivot pin for prop stand—with extended thread for brake torque arm nut. Post-war.	
MAQ	F241	Spigot nut for F4/8—securing torque arm to frame.	
MAR	F69/4	Spring for prop stand.	
	FK29/11	Prop stand. For use with MAS2/3 frame	1 off.

Illustration Ref.	Part No.	Description	
		Frame Section—continued.	
	F69/5	Prop stand spring. For use with MAS 2/3 frame.	1 off.
	F4/10	Prop stand pivot bolt. For use with MAS 2/3 frame.	
MAS	FK171/7AS	Rear stand.	
Not shown	F4/3	Pivot pin for rear stand. For early type frames with plain hole in frame.	2 off.
MAT	F4/5	Pivot pin for rear stand. For threaded frame fork end. Left side.	
MAU	F4/6	Pivot pin for rear stand and silencer support. Right hand side.	
MAV	SL57/24	Thackray washer for stand pivot pin	2 off.
Not shown	SL56/14	Nut for F4/3.	
MW	SL56/8	Nut, $\frac{3}{8}''$. Silencer to stand pin.	
MAW	SL6/48	Plain washer for SL56/8.	

ILLUSTRATION N.

ORDER BY PART NUMBER—DO NOT QUOTE ILLUSTRATION REFERENCES.

FOR PART NUMBERS AND DESCRIPTIONS OF ITEMS ON THIS PAGE SEE PAGES 60 AND 61

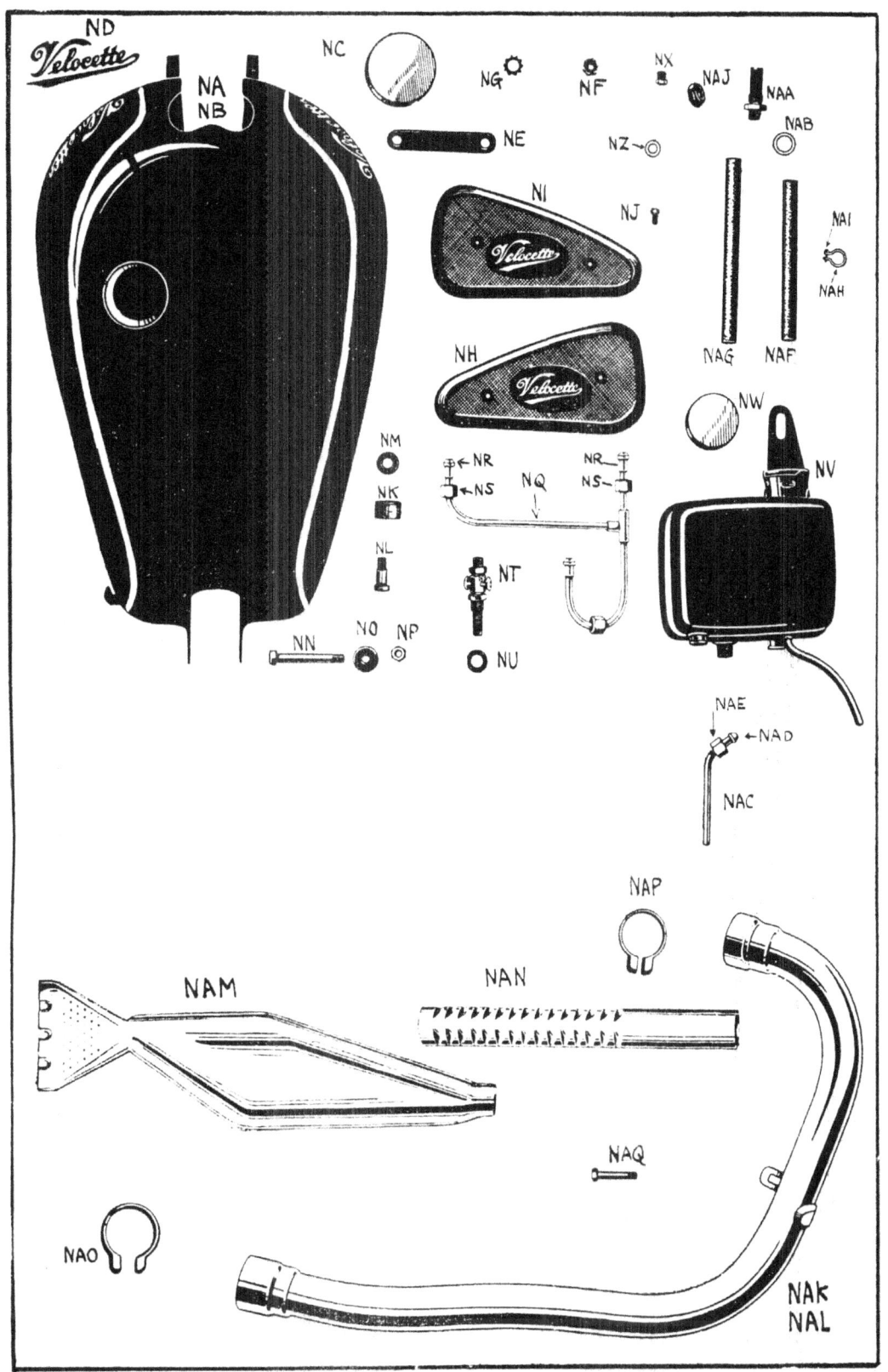

IF YOU HAVE A TECHNICAL ENQUIRY FOR US PLEASE DO NOT INCLUDE IT ON THE SAME SHEET AS YOUR ORDER.

PETROL TANK, PIPE AND KNEE GRIP SECTION.
See Illustration " N " Page 59.

Illustration Ref.	Part No.	Description.	
Not shown	A1/19	Petrol tank, to 1939. With studs to hold knee grip plates.	
NA	A1/20	Petrol tank, 1940/46/47 type. With threaded holes to take knee grip screws.	
NB	A1/24	Petrol tank—as A1/20, but shaped at front to clear Telescopic fork.	
NC	KA4/9	Filler cap.	
ND	A132	Name transfer for tank.	
Note.—The gold lines are applied by hand brushwork—transfers not supplied.			
NE	A276	Strengthening strap—across front of tank underneath.	
NF	SL56/4	Nut, $\frac{1}{4}''$, for A276.	
NG	LE367	Lock-washer, $\frac{1}{4}''$, for A276.	
Not shown	KA70/4R	Knee grip, right hand. Up to 1940 only.	
Not shown	KA70/4L	Knee grip, left hand. Up to 1940 only.	
Not shown	KA80/4R	Plate for right hand knee grip. Up to 1940 only.	
Not shown	KA80/4L	Plate for left hand knee grip. Up to 1940 only.	
Not shown	SL56/5	Nut, $\frac{1}{4}''$, 20T., for securing knee grip plate to tank.	
NH	KA70/5AS	Knee grip, right hand. 1940 onwards.	
NI	KA70/6AS	Knee grip, left hand. 1940 onwards.	
NJ	KA287	Screw. Knee grip KA70/5AS and KA70/6AS to tank.	
NK	FK151/2	Buffer for front tank mounting.	2 off.
NL	FK152/2	Bolt for front tank mounting.	2 off.
NM	SL6/57	Washer for FK152/2.	2 off.
NN	SL9/18	Bolt, rear tank mounting to frame.	
NO	SL6/39	Plain washer, for rear tank bot.	2 off.
NP	SL56/6	Nut, $\frac{5}{16}''$, for rear tank bolt.	
NQ	A31/5AS	Petrol pipe assembly.	
NR	K138	Nipple for petrol pipe, tank end.	2 off.
NS	K139	Union nut for petrol pipe, tank end.	2 off.
NT	A2/5	Petrol tap.	2 off.
NU	KA115	Fibre washer for petrol tap.	2 off.

OIL TANK AND PIPE SECTION. †
†See Footnote, Page 11.

NV	A201AS	Oil Tank. To Eng. No. MAC15791.	
	MAS13	Oil tank assembly. With chamber for fabric oil filter. From Eng. No. MAC15792.	1 off.
	A134/4	Oil tank transfer.	
	LE343	Oil tank filter cap. Bottom.	1 off.
	LE570	Oil tank filter cap. Top.	1 off.
	A287	Oil tank filter cap gasket (bottom).	1 off.
	LE572	Oil tank filter cap gasket (top).	1 off.
	MAS94	Oil tank filter tube and adaptor assembly. Embodies oil return union.	1 off.
	SL102/12	Oil tank filter tube stud $\frac{1}{4}''$ B.S.F. $\times 5\frac{3}{8}''$	1 off.
	A291	Oil tank filter tube stud nut. Retains top cap on tank.	1 off.

Illustration Ref.	Part No.	Description	

Oil Tank and Pipe Section—continued.

	A37/5	Fibre washer for stud nut.	1 off.
	A288	Oil tank filter element.	1 off.
	KA115	Fibre washer. Between filter tube adapter and bottom filter cap.	1 off.
	*MAS14	Oil tank check valve union assembly for feed.	1 off.
	*M253	Oil tank check valve body.	1 off.
	*KA115/3	Fibre washer between check valve body and ball valve union.	1 off.
	*M255	Check valve spring.	1 off.
	*W15/2	Check valve ball.	1 off.
		*See Crankcase Group, page 10.	
NW	KA6/6	Filler cap.	
NX	B38	Drain plug.	
NZ	A37	Fibre washer for drain plug.	
NAA	A8/2	Oil feed union and strainer gauze.	
NAB	KA115/2	Washer for A8/2.	
NAC	MAS15	Oil feed pipe, .375″ o/d, with nipple. Tank end. From Eng. No. MAC10149.	
NAC	†A9/11AS	Oil feed pipe, .312″ o/d, with nipple. Tank end.	
NAF	KA221	Oil return hose. 6″ long. May be ordered by the foot as KA102. For A201AS tank.	
NAF	KA221/14	Oil return hose, $\frac{5}{16}$″ bore, 12″ long, for MAS13 tank.	
NAG	KA221/2	Oil feed hose. 7″ long. May be ordered by the foot as KA102.	
NAH	KA100	Clip for oil hose.	4 off.
NAI	KA101	Screw for KA100.	4 off.
NAJ	CK20/2	Nut, securing bottom of oil tank to battery platform.	

EXHAUST PIPE AND SILENCER SECTION.

NAK	A39/6AS	Exhaust pipe. MOV model only.	
NAL	{ A39/7AS	Exhaust pipe. MAC model to No. MAC15981 only.	
	A39/8AS	Exhaust pipe. For aluminium alloy cylinder head. From Eng. No. MAC15982.	1 off.
NAM	MAS30/3	Silencer with integral fishtail.	
NAN	KA142/2	Baffle tube.	
NAO	A141/2	Clip. Silencer to exhaust pipe.	
NAP	A141/3	Clip. Exhaust pipe to cylinder head.	
NAQ	SL8/8	Bolt for exhaust pipe clip.	2 off.
NF	SL56/4	Nut for clip bolt.	2 off.

ILLUSTRATION O.

ORDER BY PART NUMBER—DO NOT QUOTE ILLUSTRATION REFERENCES.
FOR PART NUMBERS AND DESCRIPTIONS OF ITEMS ON THIS PAGE SEE PAGE 63.

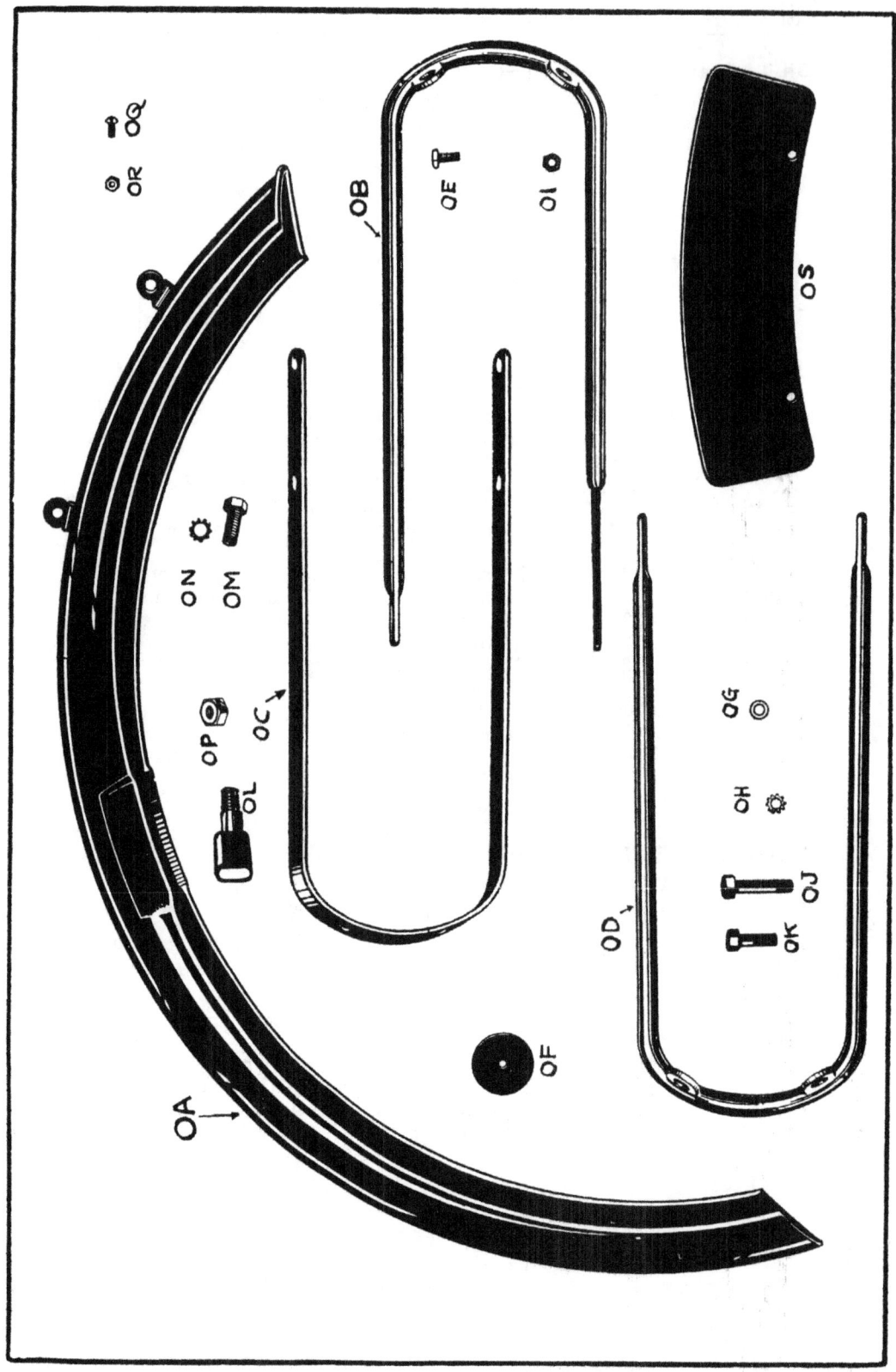

HAVE YOU QUOTED THE ENGINE NUMBER ON YOUR ORDER?

FRONT MUDGUARD AND STAY SECTION—WITH TELESCOPIC FORK. See Illustration "O" Page 62.

Illustration Ref.	Part No.	Description	
OA	KA16/9	Front mudguard.	
OB	FK157/14AS	Front mudguard stay, front.	
OC	FK157/15	Front mudguard stay, centre.	
OD	FK157/16AS	Front mudguard stay, bottom.	
OE	SL8/3	Bolt, $\frac{1}{4}''$. Stays to mudguard.	6 off.
OF	KA145/2	Strengthening washer for mudguard bolts.	4 off.
OG	SL6/32	Plain washers, $\frac{1}{4}''$.	2 off.
OH	LE367	Lock-washer, $\frac{1}{4}''$.	10 off.
OI	SL56/4	Nut, $\frac{1}{4}''$.	10 off.
OJ	SL8/14	Bolt, $\frac{1}{4}'' \times 1''$—bottom and centre stays to fork.	2 off.
OK	SL8/29	Bolt, $\frac{1}{4}'' \times \frac{3}{8}''$—front stay to fork.	2 off.
OL	FK50/2	Brake plate anchor bolt.	
OM	SL9/6	Bolt, $\frac{5}{16}''$—centre stay to fork.	
ON	LE368	Lock-washer, —", for SL9/6 and and FK50/2.	2 off.
OP	SL56/6	Nut, $\frac{5}{16}''$, for SL9/6 and FK50/2.	
OQ	SL80/22	Screw, 2BA—number plate to guard	2 off.
OR	SL56/2	Nut, 2BA, for SL80/22.	2 off.
OS	A23	Front number plate.	

ILLUSTRATION P.

ORDER BY PART NUMBERS—DO NOT QUOTE ILLUSTRATION REFERENCES.

FOR PART NUMBERS AND DESCRIPTIONS OF ITEMS ON THIS PAGE SEE PAGES 65 AND 66.

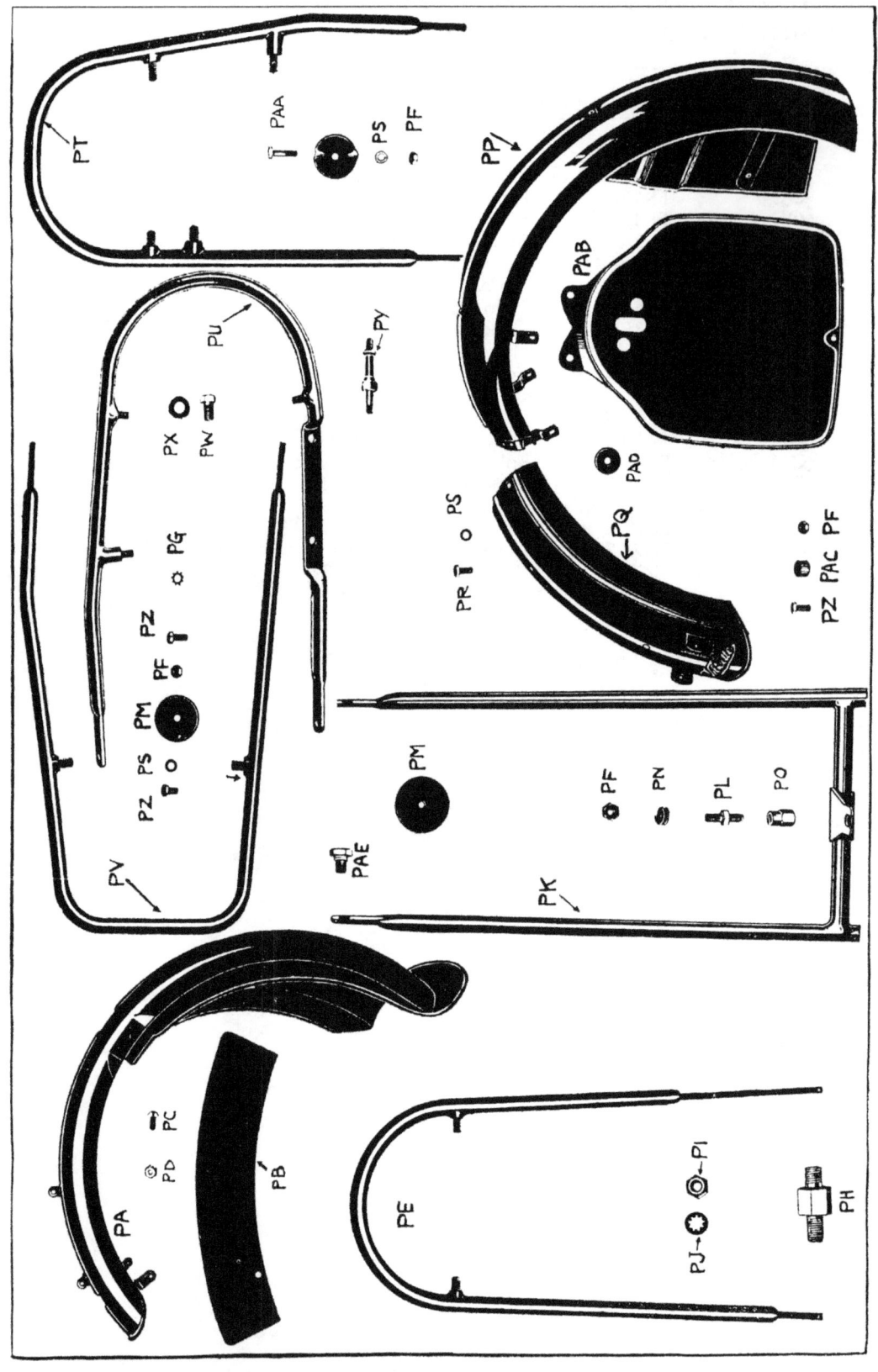

THE LETTERS PREFIXING THE ENGINE NUMBER ARE ESSENTIAL TO IDENTIFY THE TYPE OF MACHINE.

FRONT MUDGUARD SECTION—WITH "WEBB" FORK.
See Illustration "P" Page 64.

Illustration Ref.	Part No.	Description.	
PA	KA16/5	Front mudguard.	
PB	A23	Front number plate.	
PC	SL80/22	Screw—number plate to guard.	
PD	SL56/2	Nut, 2BA, for SL80/22.	
PE	FK157/11AS	Frong mudguard stay.	
PF	SL56/4	Nut, ¼". Front stay to bridge on guard.	2 off.
PG	LE367	Lock-washer, ¼", for SL56/4.	2 off.
PH	FS8/4	Stud. Front stay to fork end.	2 off.
PI	SL56/6	Nut, 5/16". Front stay to FS8/4.	2 off.
PJ	LE368	Lock-washer, 5/16", for SL56/6.	2 off.
PK	FS1/2KAS	Front stand.	
PL	FS4/2	Stud—front stand to guard.	
PM	KA145/2	Strengthening washer, inside guard, for FS4/2	
PF	SL56/4	Nut, ¼". FS4/2 to guard.	
PN	SL57/21	Thackray washer, for FS4/2, inside guard.	
PO	T66	Nut. Front stand to guard.	
PAE	FS8/2K	Stud. Front stand to fork end.	2 off.

REAR MUDGUARD AND STAY SECTION.
See Illustration "P" Page 64.

PP	A15/5	Rear mudguard. All types to 1951 except 1940.	
Not shown	A15/8	Rear mudguard with hinged extension. 1940 **only.**	
	A15/11	Rear mudguard from 1952.	
PQ	A172/2	Extension for rear guard A15/5.	
Not shown	A131	Name transfer for rear extension.	
PR	KA303	Bolt. A172/2 to rear guard.	2 off.
PS	SL6/32	Plain washer for KA303.	2 off.
PT	FK58/25AS	Vertical stay for mudguard. For machines up to 1937 only.	
PU	FK58/42AS	Vertical stay for mudguard. For machines 1938/39, and 1946 to 1951.	
Not shown	FK58/43AS	Vertical stay for mudguard, A15/8 only. 1940 models only.	
PV	FK58/26AS	Rear lifting handle stay.	
	MAS11	Lifting handle stay. Use with A15/11.	
	MAS12	Vertical stay, L/H. Use with A15/11.	
	FK58/59	Vertical stay, R/H. Use with A15/11.	
PF	SL56/4	Nut, ¼". Securing stays to guard.	
PG	LE367	Lock-washer, ¼", for SL56/4.	
PW	SL9/2	Bolt, 5/16", vertical stay and lifting handle to frame.	
PX	SL6/40	Plain washer, 5/16", for SL9/2.	
PY	FK185/5	Stud. Stays and silencer to frame. Used with early type silencer only. Not needed with replacement silencers as now supplied.	
PI	SL56/6	Nut, 5/16", for FK185/5.	1 off.
PX	SL6/40	Plain washer, 5/16", for FK185/5.	1 off.
PZ	SL8/3	Bolt, ¼". Mudguard to bottom frame bridge and battery platform.	3 off.
PF	SL56/4	Nut, ¼", for SL8/3.	3 off.
PG	LE367	Lock-washer, ¼", for SL8/3.	3 off.
PAA	SL8/14	Bolt, ¼". Rear guard to seat stay bridge.	

Illustration Ref.	Part No.	Description.

Rear Mudguard Section—continued.

PF	SL56/4	Nut, $\frac{1}{4}''$, for SL8/14.
PG	LE367	Lock-proof washer, $\frac{1}{4}''$, for SL8/14.
PM	KA145/2	Strengthening washer inside guard, for mudguard bolts.
Not shown	A22/19	Rear number plate. 1940 type only.
Not shown	E29/4AS	Support bracket—A22/19 to rear guard.
PAB	A22/20	Rear number plate.
PZ	SL8/3	Bolt, $\frac{1}{4}''$. Number plate to guard. Top. 2 off.
PF	SL56/4	Nut, $\frac{1}{4}''$, for SL8/3. 2 off.
PS	SL6/32	Plain washer, $\frac{1}{4}''$, for SL8/3. 2 off.
PG	LE367	Lock-washer, $\frac{1}{4}''$, for SL8/3.
PAC	A181	Rubber buffer for bottom of number plate.
PAD	A20	Rubber bush for tail lamp cable through number plate.

ILLUSTRATION R.

ORDER BY PART NUMBER——DO NOT QUOTE ILLUSTRATION REFERENCES.
FOR PART NUMBERS AND DESCRIPTIONS OF ITEMS ON THIS PAGE SEE PAGE 68.

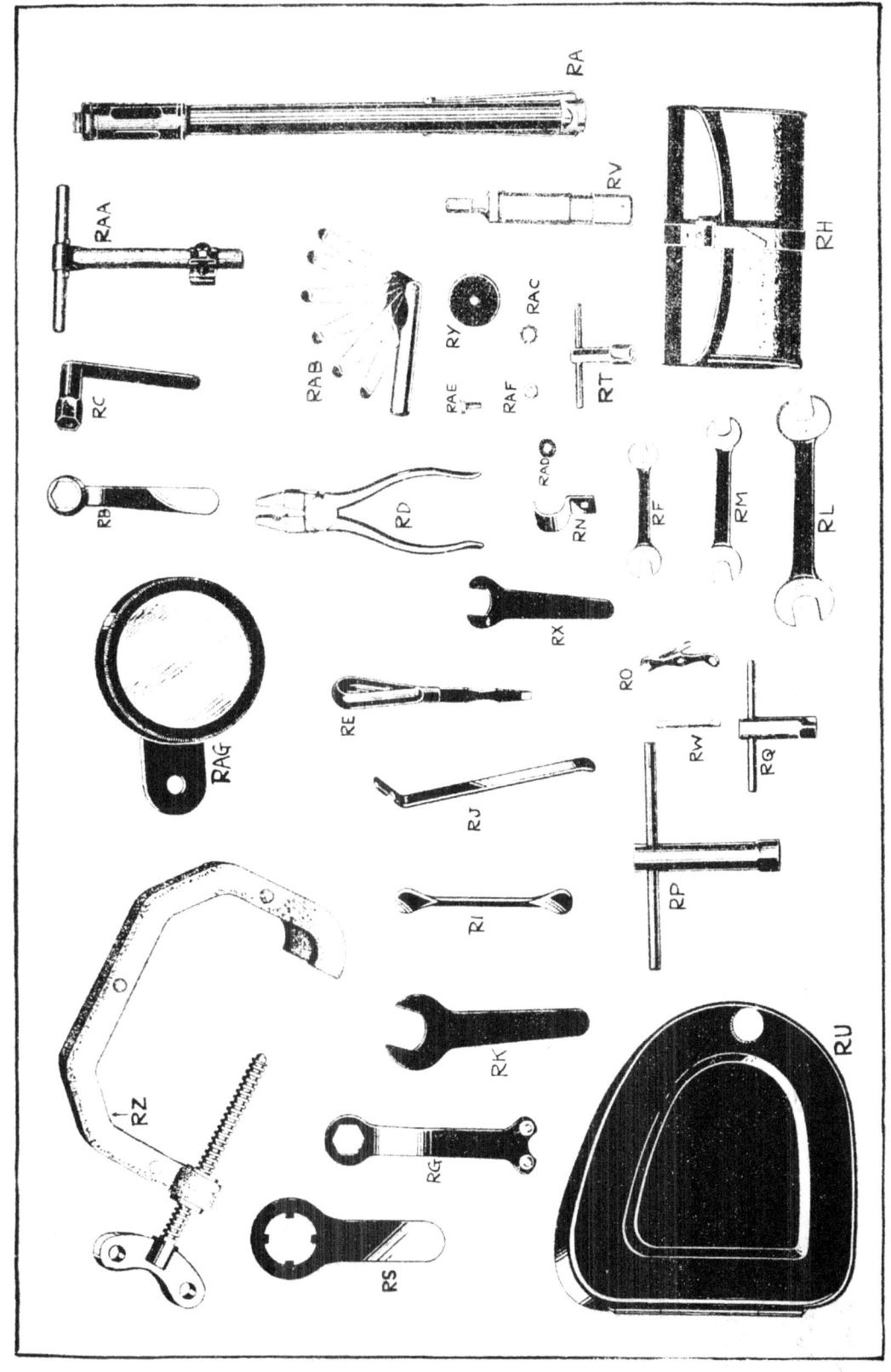

THE ENGINE NUMBER AND PREFIX LETTERS ARE STAMPED ON THE DRIVE SIDE CRANKCASE BELOW THE CYLINDER BASE.

TOOL BOX AND TOOL SECTION. Illustration "R" Page 67.

NOTE.—Items indicated thus † are not included in the Tool equipment issued with the Motorcycle at the time of delivery but may be purchased extra.

Illustration Ref.	Part No.	Description.
RA	A25	Tyre inflater with connection.
RB	†A55/3	Spanner for sparking plug. Issued as standard with pre-war models.
RC	A55/4	Spanner for sparking plug and oil filter. From 1946.
RD	†A56	Pliers.
RE	A57	Screwdriver.
RF	A58	Open—double ended spanner. $\frac{3}{16}'' \times \frac{1}{8}''$.
RG	A61/2AS	Spanner for sleeve gear nut and dummy spindle nut.
RH	A63	Tool wrap.
RI	A64	Tyre lever—spoon type.
RJ	†A64/2	Tyre lever—spoke fitting.
RK	A65/2	Spanner for column lock nut.
RL	A101	Open double ended spanner, $\frac{3}{8}'' \times \frac{5}{16}''$.
RM	A102	Open double ended spanner, $\frac{1}{4}'' \times \frac{5}{16}''$.
RN	A153/2	Toolbox clip.
RO	A154/2	Magneto spanner.
RP	A227	Tubular spanner with bar, $\frac{7}{16}''$.
RQ	A228	Tubular spanner with bar, $\frac{5}{16}''$.
RS	A229	Ring spanner for shock absorber nut on engine shaft.
RT	†A248	Tubular spanner and bar, $\frac{1}{4}''$.
RU	KA12/10AS	Toolbox.
RV	KA51	Grease gun.
RW	KA62/2	Clutch adjustment peg.
RX	KA119	Spanner for front wheel bearing adjustment (for machines with "Webb" fork).
RY	KA145/2	Strengthening washer for toolbox fixing bolts.
RZ	†KA163/2	"Terry" valve spring compresser.
RAA	†KA164/2	"Terry" valve grinding tool.
RAB	†KA231	"Terry" clearance gauges.
Not shown	KA251	Knob for toolbox lid.
Not shown	KA253	Stud for toolbox knob.
RAC	LE367	Lock-washer, $\frac{1}{4}''$, for toolbox bolt.
RAD	SL6/36	Plain washer, $\frac{1}{4}''$.
RAE	SL8/3	Bolt, $\frac{1}{4}''$, for fixing toolbox.
RAF	SL56/4	Nut, $\frac{1}{4}''$, for SL8/3.
Not shown	SL57/21	Thackray washer for toolbox lid stud.
RAG	A157	License holder with glass.

PILLION SEAT SECTION.

	KA198/2	Pillion seat (Pad type).	1 off.
	KA198/4	Pillion seat (saddle type).	1 off.
	SL8/3	Pillion seat bolt, $\frac{1}{4}''$ B.S.F. —"	4 off.
	SL56/4	Pillion seat bolt nuts, $\frac{1}{4}''$ B.S.F	4 off.
	KA145/2	Strengthening washer for bolt.	4 off.
	LE367	Lockwasher for nut, $\frac{1}{4}''$.	4 off.

VELOCEPRESS MANUALS – MOTORCYCLE BY MAKE

AJS 1932-1948 SINGLES & TWINS 250cc THRU 1000cc (BOOK OF)
AJS 1945-1960 SINGLES 350cc & 500cc MODELS 16 & 18 (BOOK OF)
AJS 1955-1965 SINGLES 350cc & 500cc (BOOK OF)
AJS 1957-1966 FACTORY WSM - ALL SINGLES & TWINS
ARIEL UP TO 1932 (BOOK OF)
ARIEL 1932-1939 PREWAR MODELS (BOOK OF)
ARIEL 1933-1951 (WORKSHOP MANUAL)
ARIEL 1939-1960 4 STROKE SINGLES (BOOK OF)
ARIEL 1958-1964 LEADER & ARROW (BOOK OF)
BMW R26 R27 (1956-1967) FACTORY WORKSHOP MANUAL
BMW R50 R50S R60 R69S (1955-1969) FACTORY WORKSHOP MANUAL
BRIDGESTONE 90 SERIES FACTORY WSM & PARTS CATALOGUE
BRIDGESTONE 175 SERIES FACTORY WSM & PARTS CATALOGUE
BRIDGESTONE 350 SERIES FACTORY WSM & PARTS CATALOGUES
BSA SERVICE SHEETS MASTER CATALOGUE ALL MODELS 1945-1967
BSA BANTAM D1 TO D7 1948-1966 FACTORY SERVICE SHEETS MANUAL
BSA BANTAM ALL MODELS FROM 1948 ONWARDS (BOOK OF)
BSA DANDY FACTORY WORKSHOP MANUAL (COMPILATION)
BSA SINGLES & V-TWINS UP TO 1927 (BOOK OF)
BSA SINGLES & V-TWINS UP TO 1930 (BOOK OF)
BSA SINGLES & V-TWINS UP TO 1935 (BOOK OF)
BSA SINGLES & V-TWINS 1936-1939 (BOOK OF)
BSA C10, C11 & C12 1945-1958 FACTORY SERVICE SHEETS MANUAL
BSA OHV & SV SINGLES 250-600cc 1945-1959 (BOOK OF)
BSA C15 & B40 1958-1967 FACTORY SERVICE SHEETS MANUAL
BSA OHV & SV SINGLES 250cc (ONLY) 1954-1970 (BOOK OF)
BSA B31, B32, B33 & B34 1945-60 FACTORY SERVICE SHEETS MANUAL
BSA OHV SINGLES 350 & 500cc 1955-1967 (BOOK OF)
BSA M20, M21 & M33 1945-1963 FACTORY SERVICE SHEETS MANUAL
BSA TWINS A7 & A10 1948-1962 FACTORY SERVICE SHEETS MANUAL
BSA TWINS A7 & A10 1948-1962 (BOOK OF)
BSA TWINS A50 & A65 1962-1965 FACTORY WORKSHOP MANUAL
BSA TWINS A50 & A65 1962-1969 (SECOND BOOK OF)
DOUGLAS 1929-1939 PREWAR ALL MODELS (BOOK OF)
DOUGLAS 1948-1957 POSTWAR ALL MODELS FACTORY SHOP MANUAL
DUCATI 160cc, 250cc & 350cc OHC MODELS FACTORY SHOP MANUAL
HONDA 50cc ALL MODELS UP TO 1970 INC MONKEY & TRAIL (BOOK OF)
HONDA 90cc ALL MODELS UP TO 1966 (BOOK OF)
HONDA 50-65-70-90cc OHC SINGLES 1959-1983 FACTORY WSM
HONDA 100-125cc SINGLES CB/CD/CL/SL/TL 1970-1984 FACTORY WSM
HONDA 125-150cc TWINS C/CS/CB/CA FACTORY WORKSHOP MANUAL
HONDA 125-160-175-200cc TWINS 1965-1978 WORKSHOP MANUAL
HONDA 250-305cc TWINS C/CS/CB 1959-1967 FACTORY WSM
HOHDA 250-350cc TWINS CB/CL/SL 1968-1973 FACTORY WSM
HONDA 450cc CB/CL 1965-1974 K0 TO K7 WORKSHOP MANUAL
HONDA 750cc SHOC 4 CYL 1969-1978 K0~K8 WORKSHOP MANUAL
HONDA C100 SUPER CUB FACTORY WORKSHOP MANUAL
HONDA C110 SPORT CUB 1962-1969 FACTORY WORKSHOP MANUAL
HONDA TWINS & SINGLES 50cc THRU 305cc 1960-1966 (BOOK OF)
HONDA TWINS ALL MODELS 125cc THRU 450cc UP TO 1968 (BOOK OF)
INDIAN PONYBIKE, BOY RACER & PAPOOSE ILL PARTS LIST & SALES LIT
J.A.P. ENGINES 1927-1952 & MOTORCYCLES 1934-1952 (BOOK OF)
MATCHLESS 1931-1939 ALL MODELS 250cc THRU 990cc (BOOK OF)
MATCHLESS 1945-1956 350 & 500cc SINGLES (BOOK OF)
MATCHLESS 1955-1966 350 & 500cc SINGLES (BOOK OF)
MATCHLESS 1957-1966 FACTORY WSM - ALL SINGLES & TWINS
NEW IMPERIAL ALL SV & OHV FROM 1935 ONWARDS (BOOK OF)
NORTON 1932-1939 PREWAR MODELS (BOOK OF)
NORTON 1932-1947 (BOOK OF)
NORTON 1938-1956 (BOOK OF)
NORTON 1955-1963 MODELS 19, 50 & ES2 (BOOK OF)
NORTON 1955-1965 DOMINATOR TWINS (BOOK OF)
NORTON 1960-1970 TWIN CYLINDER FACTORY WORKSHOP MANUAL
NORTON 1970-1975 COMMANDO 850 & 750cc FACTORY WSM
NORTON 1975-1978 MK 3 COMMANDO 850 cc FACTORY WSM
PANTHER 1932-1958 LIGHTWEIGHT MODELS 250 & 350cc (BOOK OF)
PANTHER 1938-1966 HEAVYWEIGHT MODELS 600 & 650cc (BOOK OF)
RALEIGH MOTORCYCLES 1919-1933 (BOOK OF)
ROYAL ENFIELD 1934-1946 SINGLES & V TWINS (BOOK OF)
ROYAL ENFIELD 1937-1953 SINGLES & V TWINS (BOOK OF)
ROYAL ENFIELD 1946-1962 SINGLES (BOOK OF)
ROYAL ENFIELD 1958-1966 250cc & 350cc SINGLES (SECOND BOOK OF)
ROYAL ENFIELD 1962-1970 INTERCEPTOR WSM'S & PARTS (Compilation)
RUDGE 1933-1939 (BOOK OF)
SUNBEAM 1928-1939 (BOOK OF)
SUNBEAM 1946-1957 S7 & S8 (BOOK OF)
SUZUKI 50cc & 80cc UP TO 1966 (BOOK OF)
SUZUKI T10 1963-1967 FACTORY WORKSHOP MANUAL
SUZUKI T20 & T200 1965-1969 FACTORY WORKSHOP MANUAL
SUZUKI TWINS 1962 ONWARDS 125-500cc WORKSHOP MANUAL
TRIUMPH 1935-1949 SINGLES & TWINS (BOOK OF)
TRIUMPH 1937-1951 (WORKSHOP MANUAL)
TRIUMPH 1945-1955 FACTORY WORKSHOP MANUAL
TRIUMPH 1945-1959 TWINS (BOOK OF)
TRIUMPH 1956-1969 TWINS (BOOK OF)
TRIUMPH 1963-1970 UNIT CONSTRUCTION 650cc FACTORY WSM
TRIUMPH 1963-1974 UNIT CONSTRUCTION 350-500cc FACTORY WSM
TRIUMPH 1968-1974 TRIDENT T150 & T150V FACTORY WSM
VELOCETTE 1925-1970 ALL SINGLES & TWINS (BOOK OF)
VELOCETTE 1933-1952 MOV-MAC-MSS RIGID FRAME FACTORY WSM
VELOCETTE 1954-1971 MSS-VENOM-THRUXTON-VIPER FACTORY WSM
VILLIERS ENGINE UP TO 1959 INC. 3 WHEELERS (BOOK OF)
VILLIERS ENGINE UP TO 1969 (BOOK OF)
VINCENT 1935-1955 (WORKSHOP MANUAL)
YAMAHA 1961-1967 YA5 & YA6 (WORKSHOP MANUAL & ILL PARTS LIST)
YAMAHA 1971-1972 JT1 & JT2 (WORKSHOP MANUAL & ILL PARTS LIST)

VELOCEPRESS TECHNICAL BOOKS – MOTORCYCLE

1930'S BRITISH MOTORCYCLE CARBS & ELEC COMPONENTS (BOOK OF)
1930'S BRITISH MOTORCYCLE ENGINES (OVERHAUL & MAINTENANCE)
1930'S BRITISH MOTORCYCLE GEARBOXES & CLUTCHES (BOOK OF)
CATALOG OF BRITISH MOTORCYCLES (1951 MODELS)
LUCAS ELECTRONICS BRITISH M/CYCLES REPAIR & PARTS (1950-1977)
MOTORCYCLE ENGINEERING (P.E. Irving)
MOTORCYCLE ROAD TESTS 1949-1953 (Motor Cycle Magazine UK)
SPEED AND HOW TO OBTAIN IT (Motor Cycle Magazine UK)
TUNING FOR SPEED (P.E. Irving)
WIPAC (COMBO) MANUAL NUMBER 3 + M/CYCLE & SCOOTER MANUAL

VELOCEPRESS MANUALS – SCOOTERS BY MAKE

BSA SUNBEAM SCOOTER WORKSHOP MANUAL 1959-1965
BSA SUNBEAM SCOOTER 1959-1965 (BOOK OF)
LAMBRETTA 1947-1957 ALL 125 & 150cc MODELS (BOOK OF)
LAMBRETTA 1957-1970 LI & TV MODELS (SECOND BOOK OF)
NSU PRIMA 1956-1964 ALL MODELS (BOOK OF)
TRIUMPH TIGRESS SCOOTER WORKSHOP MANUAL 1959-1965
TRIUMPH TIGRESS SCOOTER (BOOK OF)
VESPA 1951-1961 (BOOK OF)
VESPA 1955-1963 125 & 150cc & GS MODELS (SECOND BOOK OF)
VESPA 1955-1968 GS & SS (BOOK OF)
VESPA 1963-1972 90, 125 & 150cc (THIRD BOOK OF)

VELOCEPRESS MANUALS – MOPEDS & MOTORIZED BICYCLES

CYCLEMOTOR (BOOK OF)
NSU QUICKLY 1953-1963 ALL MODELS (BOOK OF)
PUCH MAXI N & S MAINTENANCE & REPAIR (3 MANUAL COMPILATION)
RALEIGH MOPEDS 1960-1969 (BOOK OF)

VELOCEPRESS MANUALS - THREE WHEELER'S

BOND MINICAR THREE WHEELER 1948-1967 (BOOK OF)
BMW ISETTA FACTORY WORKSHOP MANUAL
BSA THREE WHEELER (BOOK OF)
RELIANT REGAL THREE WHEELER 1952-1973 (BOOK OF)
VINTAGE MORGAN THREE WHEELER (BOOK OF)

VELOCEPRESS MANUALS – AUTOMOBILE BY MAKE

ALFA ROMEO GIULIA WORKSHOP MANUAL 1300 TO 2000cc 1962-1975
ALFA ROMEO GIULIA TECH MANUAL CARBURETED CARS FROM 1962
ALFA ROMEO GIULIA TECH MANUAL FUEL INJECTED CARS FROM 1969
ALFA ROMEO GIULIETTA & GIULIA 750 & 101 SERIES 1955-1965 WSM
AUSTIN-HEALEY SPRITE & MG MIDGET WORKSHOP MANUAL 1958-1971
BMW 600 LIMOUSINE FACTORY WORKSHOP MANUAL
BMW 600 LIMOUSINE OWNERS HAND BOOK & SERVICE MANUAL
BMW 2000 & 2002 1966-1976 WORKSHOP MANUAL
CORVAIR 1960-1969 WORKSHOP MANUAL
CORVETTE V8 1955-1962 WORKSHOP MANUAL
FERRARI HANDBOOK ROAD & RACE CARS (SERVICE/SPECS) 1948-1958
FERRARI 250/GT SERVICE & MAINTENANCE MANUAL 1956-1965
FIAT 500 FACTORY WORKSHOP MANUAL 1957-1973
FIAT 600, 600D & MULTIPLA FACTORY WORKSHOP MANUAL 1955-1969
JAGUAR E-TYPE 3.8 & 4.2 SERIES 1 & 2 WORKSHOP MANUAL
JAGUAR MK 7, 8, 9 & XK120, 140, 150 WORKSHOP MANUAL 1948-1961
METROPOLITAN FACTORY WORKSHOP MANUAL
MGA & MGB OWNERS HANDBOOK & WORKSHOP MANUAL
MG MIDGET TC, TD, TF & TF1500 WORKSHOP MANUAL
PORSCHE 356 1948-1965 WORKSHOP MANUAL
PORSCHE 911 2.0, 2.2, 2.4 LITRE 1964-1973 WORKSHOP MANUAL
PORSCHE 911 2.7, 3.0, 3.2 LITRE 1973-1989 WORKSHOP MANUAL
PORSCHE 912 WORKSHOP MANUAL
TRIUMPH TR2, TR3, TR4 1953-1965 WORKSHOP MANUAL
VOLKSWAGEN TRANSPORTER, TRUCKS & WAGONS 1950-1979 WSM
VOLVO 1944-1968 ALL MODELS WORKSHOP MANUAL

VELOCEPRESS TECHNICAL BOOKS - AUTOMOBILE

HOW TO BUILD A FIBERGLASS CAR
HOW TO BUILD A RACING CAR
HOW TO RESTORE THE MODEL 'A' FORD
MASERATI OWNER'S HANDBOOK
PERFORMANCE TUNING THE SUNBEAM TIGER
SOUPING THE VOLKSWAGEN
SOLEX CARBURETORS (EMPHASIS ON UK & EU AUTOMOBILES)
SU CARBURETORS (EMPHASIS ON UK AUTOMOBILES)
WEBER CARBURETORS (EMPHASIS ON ALFA & FIAT)

VELOCEPRESS BOOKS & GUIDES - AUTOMOBILE

COMPLETE CATALOG OF JAPANESE MOTOR VEHICLES
FERRARI 308 SERIES BUYER'S AND OWNER'S GUIDE
FERRARI BROCHURES AND SALES LITERATURE 1968-1989
FERRARI SERIAL NUMBERS PART I - ODD NUMBERS TO 21399
FERRARI SERIAL NUMBERS PART II - EVEN NUMBERS TO 1050
HENRY'S FABULOUS MODEL "A" FORD
MASERATI BROCHURES AND SALES LITERATURE

VELOCEPRESS BOOKS – RACING

CARRERA PANAMERICANA - MEXICAN ROAD RACE (BOOK OF)
DIALED IN - THE JAN OPPERMAN STORY
VEDA ORR'S NEW REVISED HOT ROD PICTORIAL

Please check our website:

www.VelocePress.com

for a complete
up-to-date list of
available titles

www.ingramcontent.com/pod-product-compliance
Lightning Source LLC
Chambersburg PA
CBHW060251240426
43673CB00047B/1909